GOOD HOUSEKEEPING
ALL COLOUR
COOK BOOK

GOOD HOUSEKEEPING

ALL COLOUR
COOK BOOK

OVER 300 RECIPES STEP BY STEP

EBURY PRESS LONDON

Published by Ebury Press
an imprint of the Random Century Group
Random Century House
20 Vauxhall Bridge Road
London SW1V 2SA

First impression 1989
This edition first published 1991
Text copyright © 1989 by The National Magazine Company Ltd
Illustrations copyright © 1989 by The National Magazine Company Ltd

The Good Housekeeping Institute is the food and consumer research centre of
Good Housekeeping magazine.

ISBN 0 09 175261 2

Photography by Jan Baldwin, Martin Brigdale, Laurie Evans, John Heseltine,
James Jackson, David Johnson, Paul Kemp

Drawings by Kate Simunek, John Woodcock, Bill le Fever

Printed and bound in Italy by New Interlitho S.p.a., Milan

Contents

COOKERY NOTES

Follow either metric or imperial measures for the recipes in this book as they are not inter-changeable. Sets of spoon measures are available in both metric and imperial size to give accurate measurement of small quantities. All spoon measures are level unless otherwise stated. When measuring milk we have used the exact conversion of 568 ml (1 pint).

* Size 4 eggs should be used except when otherwise stated.

† Granulated sugar is used unless otherwise stated.

● Plain flour is used unless otherwise stated.

OVEN TEMPERATURE CHART

°C	°F	Gas mark
110	225	$\frac{1}{4}$
130	250	$\frac{1}{2}$
140	275	1
150	300	2
170	325	3
180	350	4
190	375	5
200	400	6
220	425	7
230	450	8
240	475	9

KEY TO SYMBOLS

$\boxed{1.00*}$ Indicates minimum preparation and cooking times in hours and minutes. They do not include prepared items in the list of ingredients; calculated times apply only to the method. An asterisk * indicates extra time should be allowed, so check the note below symbols.

⊟ Chef's hats indicate degree of difficulty of a recipe: no hat means it is straightforward; one hat slightly more complicated; two hats indicates that it is for more advanced cooks.

✳ Indicates that a recipe will freeze. If there is no symbol, the recipe is unsuitable for freezing. An asterisk * indicates special freezer instructions so check the note immediately below the symbols.

$\boxed{309\ cals}$ Indicates calories per serving, including any suggestions (e.g. cream, to serve) given in the ingredients.

METRIC CONVERSION SCALE

LIQUID				SOLID		
Imperial	*Exact conversion*	*Recommended ml*		*Imperial*	*Exact conversion*	*Recommended g*
$\frac{1}{4}$ pint	142 ml	150 ml		1 oz	28.35 g	25 g
$\frac{1}{2}$ pint	284 ml	300 ml		2 oz	56.7 g	50 g
1 pint	568 ml	600 ml		4 oz	113.4 g	100 g
$1\frac{1}{2}$ pints	851 ml	900 ml		8 oz	226.8 g	225 g
$1\frac{3}{4}$ pints	992 ml	1 litre		12 oz	340.2 g	350 g

For quantities of $1\frac{3}{4}$ pints and over, litres and fractions of a litre have been used.

14 oz	397.0 g	400 g
16 oz (1 lb)	453.6 g	450 g

1 kilogram (kg) equals 2.2 lb.

INTRODUCTION

This bumper cookbook is packed with imaginative dishes that all the family will enjoy. In addition to recipes for everyday meals there are recipes for all those special family occasions. Every possible mealtime is covered—from snacks and suppers to main courses, desserts and barbecues.

Every one of the 327 recipes in the main section of the book is illustrated with a colour photograph so that you can see at a glance the finished dishes. There are also helpful step-by-step illustrations to guide you smoothly through the method, ensuring that all the recipes are simple to follow. Special symbols indicate how long each recipe takes to make, the degree of difficulty involved, whether it will freeze and the calorie count. What's more, all the recipes have been double-tested so you can be absolutely sure of achieving successful results every time.

We hope very much that you enjoy these recipes and feel sure that they will become all-time family favourites.

Soups

*A*VGOLEMONO

| 0.35 | 🍴 | 98 cals |

Serves 4

1.5 litres (2½ pints) homemade
   chicken stock

50 g (2 oz) long grain rice

2 egg yolks

100 ml (4 fl oz) freshly squeezed
   lemon juice

salt and freshly ground pepper

lemon slices and coriander sprigs,
   to garnish

1 Bring the stock to the boil in a
large saucepan. Add the rice
and simmer uncovered for 20
minutes until the rice is cooked.

2 Put the egg yolks and lemon
juice in a bowl and whisk in a
few tablespoonfuls of the hot
chicken stock.

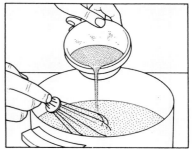

3 Pour the mixture gradually
into the pan of stock, whisking
all the time. Simmer gently without boiling for a few minutes, then
add salt and pepper to taste.

4 Pour into warmed individual
bowls and garnish each one
with a lemon slice and a sprig of
coriander. Serve hot.

Menu Suggestion
Serve this tangy, lemon-flavoured
soup with hot pitta bread before a
main course of chicken or lamb.

CHINESE-STYLE HOT AND SOUR SOUP

0.30	🍶	✳ 136 cals

Serves 4

225 g (8 oz) button mushrooms

100 ml (4 fl oz) medium dry sherry

75 ml (5 tbsp) soy sauce

30 ml (2 tbsp) chopped fresh
  coriander

225 g (8 oz) cooked chicken or pork

125 g (4 oz) spring onions

125 g (4.4 oz) jar whole baby
  sweetcorn

75 ml (5 tbsp) white wine vinegar

freshly ground pepper

1 Slice the mushrooms thinly. Place in a large saucepan with the sherry, soy sauce, coriander and 1.1 litres (2 pints) water. Bring to the boil. Simmer, uncovered, for 15 minutes.

2 Thinly shred the chicken (or finely dice the pork) and spring onions. Thinly slice the sweetcorn.

3 Stir the prepared meat and vegetables into the mushroom mixture, with the wine vinegar and season to taste with pepper. Simmer for a further 5 minutes. Serve hot.

Menu Suggestion
Serve with prawn crackers for a Chinese-style meal. Follow with spareribs or a stir-fried dish of meat and vegetables.

11

GOULASH SOUP WITH CARAWAY DUMPLINGS

| 2.45 | 🍴 | ✳* | 515–772 cals |

* freeze without dumplings

Serves 4–6

700 g (1½ lb) silverside or lean chuck steak

salt and freshly ground pepper

25 g (1 oz) butter

2 onions, skinned and chopped

1 small green pepper, seeded and chopped

4 tomatoes, skinned and quartered

141-g (5-oz) can tomato paste

600 ml (1 pint) rich beef stock

15 ml (1 tbsp) paprika

450 g (1 lb) potatoes, peeled

100 g (4 oz) self-raising flour

50 g (2 oz) shredded suet

5 ml (1 tsp) caraway seeds

chopped fresh parsley, to garnish

142 ml (5 fl oz) soured cream

1 Remove any excess fat or gristle from the silverside or chuck steak and cut the meat into small pieces. Season well.

2 Melt the butter in a large saucepan, add the onions and green pepper and sauté for 10 minutes until tender.

3 Add the meat pieces, tomatoes, tomato paste, stock and paprika. Stir well and bring to the boil. Reduce the heat, cover and simmer for 2½ hours, stirring occasionally.

4 Half an hour before the end of cooking, cut the potatoes into bite-sized pieces, bring to the boil in salted water and simmer until cooked. Drain well and add to the soup while it is simmering.

5 Make the dumplings. Put the flour, suet, caraway seeds and seasoning in a bowl and add enough cold water to form a firm mixture. Roll into about sixteen small dumplings.

6 Twenty minutes before end of cooking, drop dumplings into the soup, cover and simmer until the dumplings are cooked.

7 Garnish with chopped parsley and serve the soured cream separately, for each person to spoon into their soup.

Menu Suggestion

Serve with fresh French bread and butter and a tossed green salad.

GOULASH

Goulash soup is simply a more liquid version of goulash, with a similar base of meat and potatoes for easy eating. Both are popular in Austria and Hungary—no-one is quite sure in which country the recipe first originated.

Austrian goulash is usually a simple dish made with beef and potatoes, while Hungarian goulash is often made with veal and far more ingredients— usually red and green peppers and mushrooms, sometimes sauerkraut and smoked pork sausage as well. Four ingredients which are common to all goulash recipes are caraway seeds, onions, paprika and tomatoes—the latter giving the dish its characteristic bright red colour. Dumplings and soured cream are optional extras.

WATERCRESS SOUP

| 0.25 | ✳ | 325 cals |

Serves 4

100 g (4 oz) butter or margarine

1 medium onion, skinned and chopped

2 bunches watercress

50 g (2 oz) plain flour

750 ml (1¼ pints) chicken or veal stock

300 ml (½ pint) milk

salt and freshly ground pepper

1 Melt the butter in a saucepan, add the onion and cook gently for 10 minutes until soft but not coloured.

2 Meanwhile, wash and trim the watercress, leaving some of the stem, then chop roughly.

3 Add the chopped watercress to the onion, cover the pan with a lid and cook gently for a further 4 minutes.

4 Add the flour and cook gently, stirring, for 1–2 minutes. Remove from the heat and gradually blend in the stock and milk. Bring to the boil, stirring constantly then, simmer for 3 minutes. Season to taste.

5 Sieve or purée the soup in a blender or food processor. Return to the rinsed-out pan and reheat gently, without boiling. Taste and adjust seasoning, if necessary. Serve hot.

Menu Suggestion
Watercress soup makes a delicious starter for a winter dinner party. Follow it with roast game and end with fruity dessert.

CREAM OF CARROT WITH ORANGE SOUP

| 0.55 | 🍴 | ✳ | 73–110 cals |

Serves 4–6

25 g (1 oz) butter or margarine

700 g (1½ lb) carrots, peeled and sliced

225 g (8 oz) onion, skinned and sliced

1 litre (1¾ pints) chicken or ham stock

salt and freshly ground pepper

1 orange

1 Melt the butter in a saucepan, add the vegetables and cook gently for 10 minutes until softened slightly.

2 Add the stock and bring to the boil. Lower the heat, cover and simmer for about 40 minutes, or until the vegetables are tender.

3 Sieve or purée the vegetables with half of the stock in a blender or food processor. Add this mixture to the stock remaining in the pan.

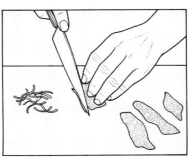

4 Meanwhile, pare half of the orange rind thinly, using a potato peeler, then cut it into shreds. Cook the shreds in gently boiling water until tender.

5 Finely grate the remaining orange rind into the soup. Stir well to combine with the ingredients in the pan.

6 Squeeze the juice of the orange into the pan. Reheat the soup gently, then taste and adjust seasoning. Drain the shreds of orange rind and use to garnish the soup just before serving. Serve hot.

Menu Suggestion
This is an everyday soup made from basic ingredients, but the orange rind and juice give a delicious 'kick' to the flavour. Serve for an informal family meal.

FRENCH ONION SOUP

| 1.15 | 🍴 | ✳ | 388 cals |

Serves 4

50 g (2 oz) butter
15 ml (1 tbsp) vegetable oil
450 g (1 lb) onions, skinned and
    finely sliced
2.5 ml (½ tsp) sugar
salt and freshly ground pepper
15 ml (1 tbsp) plain flour
1 litre (1¾ pints) beef stock
150 ml (¼ pint) dry white wine
75 g (3 oz) Gruyère, grated
4 slices French bread, toasted on
    both sides
45 ml (3 tbsp) brandy

1 Melt the butter with the oil in a large, heavy-based saucepan. Add the onions, stir well, cover and cook gently, stirring occasionally, for 20 minutes.

2 When the onions are completely soft, add the sugar and a pinch of salt and increase the heat to high. Cook for about 2 minutes until the onions caramelise slightly. Stir in the flour and cook for 1 minute until light brown.

3 Stir in the stock and wine, add pepper to taste and bring to the boil. Lower the heat, half cover with a lid and simmer for 40 minutes.

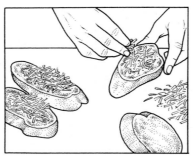

4 Pile a little grated Gruyère onto each round of toasted bread and brown lightly under a preheated grill.

5 Add the brandy to the soup. Stir well, then taste and adjust seasoning. Pour into warmed soup bowls and float the pieces of toasted bread on top. Serve immediately.

Menu Suggestion
French Onion Soup is very filling, so serve before a light French main course such as lamb cutlets grilled with rosemary and herb butter. Alternatively, serve the soup on its own as a supper or lunchtime dish, with crusty fresh French bread.

FRENCH ONION SOUP

Soupe à l'oignon gratinée, as the French call this soup, was made famous in Les Halles, the fruit and vegetable market that used to be in the centre of Paris. In the days when Les Halles was a bustling, lively market, the traders would finish their night's work by calling into one of the numerous cafés or bars and having a bowl of onion soup to revive them. Although onion soup is not exactly the sort of dish you would normally think of eating in the early hours of the morning, it is certainly very sustaining, especially in cold wintry weather. Now that Les Halles no longer exists as a market, Parisian bistros have made the soup their own speciality, and if you visit Paris you will see it on restaurant menus everywhere.

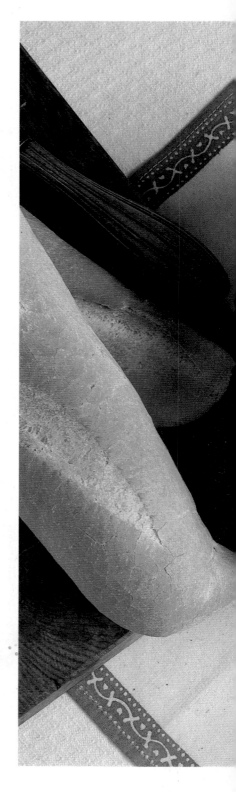

CRÈME DUBARRY

| 0.55 | ✳ | 210 cals |

Serves 4

1 firm cauliflower
40 g (1½ oz) butter or margarine
45 ml (3 tbsp) plain flour
900 ml (1½ pints) chicken or veal
    stock
salt and freshly ground white
    pepper
150 ml (¼ pint) single cream
pinch of grated nutmeg

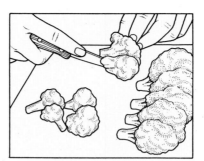

1 Divide the cauliflower into small sprigs, discarding the green leaves. Wash thoroughly.

2 Melt the butter in a saucepan, add the flour and cook gently for 1–2 minutes. Remove from the heat and gradually blend in the stock. Bring to the boil, stirring constantly, then simmer for 3 minutes until thick and smooth.

3 Add the cauliflower to the pan, reserving about 12 well-shaped tiny sprigs. Add salt and pepper to taste, cover and simmer for about 30 minutes.

4 Meanwhile, cook the reserved cauliflower sprigs in boiling salted water for about 10 minutes, until tender but not broken. Drain thoroughly.

5 Sieve or purée the soup in a blender or food processor. Return to the rinsed-out pan, stir in the cream and nutmeg and reheat gently, without boiling. Taste and adjust seasoning. Serve hot, garnished with the cauliflower sprigs.

Menu Suggestion
This creamy cauliflower soup is a French classic. Serve for a party before a main course of lamb.

CURRIED POTATO AND APPLE SOUP

| 0.50 | ✳* | 267 cals |

* freeze at step 3, after puréeing

Serves 4

50 g (2 oz) butter or margarine

4 medium old potatoes, peeled and diced

2 eating apples, peeled, cored and diced

10 ml (2 tsp) curry powder

1.2 litres (2 pints) vegetable stock or water

salt and freshly ground pepper

150 ml ($\frac{1}{4}$ pint) natural yogurt, at room temperature

1 Melt the butter or margarine in a large saucepan. Add the potatoes and apples and fry gently for about 10 minutes until lightly coloured, shaking the pan and stirring frequently.

2 Add the curry powder and fry gently for 1–2 minutes, stirring. Pour in the stock or water and bring to the boil. Add salt and pepper to taste. Lower the heat, cover the pan and simmer for 20–25 minutes or until the potatoes and apples are really soft.

3 Sieve or purée the soup in a blender or food processor, then return to the rinsed-out pan.

4 Stir the yogurt until smooth, then pour half into the soup. Heat through, stirring constantly, then taste and adjust seasoning.

5 Pour the hot soup into warmed individual bowls and swirl in the remaining yogurt. Serve immediately.

Menu Suggestion

This soup is delicately spiced, with a sweet flavour of apples. Serve with crisp poppadoms and chilled lager for an informal supper or lunch.

CURRIED POTATO AND APPLE SOUP

It is important to fry the curry powder in step 2 of the recipe, or the spices will taste raw in the finished soup. Natural yogurt has a tendency to curdle when stirred into very hot liquids. This problem can be overcome if the yogurt is brought to room temperature and stirred well before use.

CHICKEN AND SWEETCORN CHOWDER

1.45	✳*	331 cals

* freeze after step 4

Serves 6

1.6 kg (3½ lb) chicken

1 litre (1¾ pints) water

salt and freshly ground pepper

1 stick of celery, roughly chopped

1 parsley sprig

1 medium onion, skinned and
   roughly chopped

1 bay leaf

10 peppercorns

two 335-g (11.8-oz) cans sweetcorn,
   drained

6 hard-boiled eggs

45 ml (3 tbsp) chopped fresh
   parsley

150 ml (5 fl oz) single cream, to
   serve

1 Place the chicken in a large saucepan with the water, salt, celery, parsley sprig, onion, bay leaf and peppercorns.

2 Bring to the boil and simmer gently for 1–1½ hours until the chicken is completely tender.

3 When cooked, remove the chicken from the pan and cut the meat into large bite-size pieces. Discard skin and bones.

4 Strain the chicken stock, return it to the saucepan and add the chicken flesh and sweetcorn and simmer for about 5 minutes.

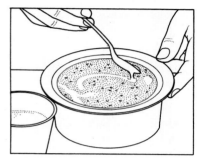

5 Chop the hard-boiled eggs. Add to the soup with the chopped parsley and salt and pepper to taste. Heat through gently, then pour into warmed individual bowls.

6 Swirl cream into each portion and serve the chicken and sweetcorn chowder immediately.

Menu Suggestion
This is a substantial meal-in-itself soup. Serve for a warming supper with garlic bread or French bread and butter, and a sharp, hard cheese such as Farmhouse Cheddar.

CHICKEN AND SWEETCORN CHOWDER

Chowder is a traditional American dish, which originally described thick and chunky fish soups. Nowadays the term is used more loosely and a chowder can be made from a variety of ingredients as long as the finished dish is a cross between a soup and a stew. Juicy, yellow sweetcorn is a common addition to many chowders.

If time is short, you can make a quick chicken chowder by using ready-cooked chicken, skinned, boned and cut into pieces. Simmer them in 900 ml (1½ pints) stock (made from a cube if necessary), with the vegetables and seasonings in the recipe above for 20 minutes. Drain, discarding the vegetables and seasonings and simmer the chicken pieces and stock with the sweetcorn for 5 minutes, then follow the recipe exactly as from step 5.

WINTER VEGETABLE SOUP

1.45	✳	446 cals

Serves 4

10 ml (2 tsp) lemon juice

225 g (8 oz) Jerusalem artichokes

½ small cabbage, washed

450 g (1 lb) carrots, peeled

225 g (8 oz) turnips, peeled

2 onions, skinned, or 2 leeks, trimmed and washed

2–3 celery sticks, trimmed

1 rasher of bacon, rinded and chopped

75 g (3 oz) dripping or butter

100 g (4 oz) haricot beans, soaked in cold water overnight and drained

bouquet garni

brown stock or water

salt and freshly ground pepper

chopped parsley and grated cheese, to serve

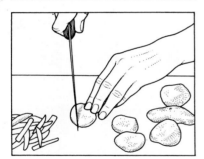

1 Fill a bowl with cold water and pour the lemon juice into it to acidulate it. Peel the artichokes, slice them and then cut them into strips. Drop them into the acidulated water as you work, to prevent them from discoloring.

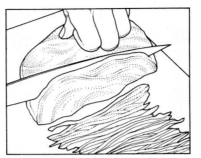

2 Shred the cabbage coarsely, discarding all thick or woody stalks. Cut the remaining vegetables into fairly small pieces.

3 In a large saucepan, dry fry the bacon lightly. Add the dripping and heat gently until melted, then add all the vegetables (except the cabbage and beans) and fry for about 10 minutes, stirring, until soft but not coloured. Add the beans, bouquet garni and enough stock or water to cover. Add plenty of pepper and bring to the boil, then lower the heat, cover with a lid and simmer for 45 minutes to 1 hour.

4 Add the cabbage and salt to taste. Cook for a further 20–30 minutes, adding more liquid as required. When all the ingredients are soft, discard the bouquet garni and taste and adjust seasoning.

5 Serve the soup hot, sprinkled with freshly chopped parsley and grated cheese handed separately.

Menu Suggestion

This is a really substantial soup, best served as a meal in itself, with crusty French bread or crisp bread rolls. If you like, you can serve it with wedges of cheese as well. A sharp farmhouse Cheddar would hold its own against the definite flavours in the soup—so too would Stilton, if you prefer a blue cheese.

Spiced Lentil and Carrot Soup

| 0.35 | ✳ | 171 cals |

Serves 4

50 g (2 oz) butter or margarine

200 g (7 oz) carrots, peeled and grated

1 medium onion, skinned and finely sliced

10 whole green cardamoms

50 g (2 oz) lentils

1.2 litres (2 pints) chicken stock

salt and freshly ground pepper

parsley sprigs, to garnish

1 Melt the butter in a heavy-based saucepan, add the carrots and onion and cook gently for 4–5 minutes.

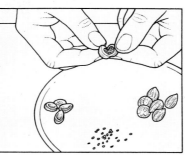

2 Meanwhile, split each cardamom and remove the black seeds. Crush the seeds in a pestle and mortar, or use the end of a rolling pin on a wooden board.

3 Add the crushed cardamom seeds to the vegetables with the lentils. Cook, stirring, for a further 1–2 minutes.

4 Add the chicken stock and bring to the boil. Lower the heat, cover the pan with a lid and simmer gently for about 20 minutes, or until the lentils are just tender. Season to taste with salt and freshly ground pepper. Serve hot garnished with parsley sprigs.

Menu Suggestion
This is a substantial soup for cold, wintry days. Serve for a family supper, with melted cheese on toast.

———— VARIATION ————

Use **ham stock** instead of chicken and add a **ham bone** with the stock, removing it before serving. Scrape the ham off the bone and return to the soup.

Split Pea and Ham Soup

| 2.00 | ✳ | 332 cals |

Serves 4

2 pig's trotters, split (optional)

1 ham bone

225 g (8 oz) dried green split peas, soaked overnight in 900 ml (1½ pints) water

225 g (8 oz) potatoes, peeled and sliced

3 whole leeks, trimmed, sliced and washed

3 celery sticks, sliced, with leaves reserved

salt and freshly ground pepper

30 ml (2 tbsp) chopped fresh parsley

about 175 g (6 oz) cooked ham, diced

1 Place the pig's trotters (if using) and the ham bone in a large saucepan. Cover with 900 ml (1½ pints) water and bring to the boil. Skim off any scum with a slotted spoon, then lower the heat and simmer for 1 hour.

2 Add the peas and their soaking water. Continue to cook for about 20 minutes.

3 Add the sliced potatoes, leeks (including green parts) and celery and continue cooking for another 40 minutes until the peas are soft. Season to taste with salt and freshly ground pepper.

4 Remove the ham bone and trotters from the pan. Scrape the meat from the bones, discarding fat and gristle. Return the meat to the soup.

5 Thin the soup, if necessary, with a little extra liquid. Chop most of the reserved celery leaves and add to the soup with the parsley and diced ham. Heat through, then taste and adjust seasoning. Serve hot garnished with the celery leaves.

Menu Suggestion
An old-fashioned soup, which is both nutritious and warming. Serve it for a winter lunch or early evening supper, with fresh whole-meal or granary bread rolls.

SPLIT PEA AND HAM SOUP

Pig's trotters are an old-fashioned ingredient which are not always easy to come by. Traditional butchers may sell them, but you may have to order in advance. Although not essential to the soup, they do make a wonderfully tasty and gelatinous stock.

CHICKEN AND PASTA BROTH

0.55	131–197 cals

Serves 4–6

two 275 g (10 oz) chicken portions

1–2 small leeks, trimmed, sliced and washed

2 carrots, peeled and thinly sliced

900 ml (1½ pints) chicken stock

1 bouquet garni

salt and freshly ground pepper

50 g (2 oz) small pasta shapes

60 ml (4 tbsp) chopped fresh parsley, to garnish

1 Put the chicken portions in a large pan. Add the leeks and carrots, then pour in the stock and 900 ml (1½ pints) water. Bring to the boil.

2 Add the bouquet garni and salt and pepper to taste, then lower the heat, cover the pan and simmer for 30 minutes until the chicken is tender. Remove the chicken from the liquid and leave until cool enough to handle.

3 Meanwhile, add the pasta to the pan, bring back to the boil and simmer for 15 minutes, stirring occasionally, until tender.

4 Remove the chicken from the bones and cut the flesh into bite-sized pieces, discarding all skin. Return to the pan and heat through. Discard the bouquet garni and taste and adjust seasoning. Serve hot in warmed soup bowls, each one sprinkled with 15 ml (1 tbsp) parsley.

Menu Suggestion
With meat, vegetables and pasta in one dish, this soup makes a hearty first course or even a meal in itself. If serving it as a first course, be sure to follow with something light such as fish.

SMOKED FISH CHOWDER

0.40	✳	261 cals

Serves 4 as a main meal

1 large onion, skinned

225 g (8 oz) potato, peeled

125 g (4 oz) celery, trimmed and finely chopped

450 g (1 lb) smoked haddock fillet, skinned

568 ml (1 pint) milk

salt and freshly ground pepper

15 ml (1 tbsp) lemon juice

paprika, to garnish

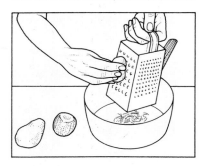

1 Grate the onion and potato into a saucepan. Add the celery and 600 ml (1 pint) water and bring to the boil. Lower the heat, cover the pan with a lid and simmer for 10 minutes.

2 Add the fish and milk and bring back to the boil. Lower the heat, add salt and pepper to taste, then cover the pan with a lid and simmer for 15 minutes until the fish is tender.

3 Using a slotted spoon, lift the fish out of the pan. Discard the fish bones and flake the flesh.

4 Return the flaked fish to the pan. Add the lemon juice, check the seasoning and heat through gently. Serve hot, sprinkled with paprika.

Menu Suggestion
Serve this substantial American-style soup as a supper or lunch dish with crusty French bread. If liked, pour the soup into individual heatproof bowls, grate Cheddar cheese thickly on top and pop under the grill until bubbling and golden.

SMOKED FISH CHOWDER

A chowder is an American soup usually made with fish, potatoes and milk. American cookbooks have many different recipes for chowders, but the most famous of them all is undoubtedly New England Clam Chowder, made with raw shucked (shelled) clams and salt pork, onion, potatoes and milk. If you would like to make clam chowder, simply follow the recipe above, sub-stituting bottled or canned clams for the smoked haddock. To serve 4 people as a main meal you will need two 170 g (6 oz) jars or cans of clams in brine or natural juices. Use the liquid from the jar or can for added flavour, adding it to the onion and potato instead of some of the measured water in step 1. Cook the clams for only 5 minutes in step 2.

CHILLED PEA AND MINT SOUP

1.30*	✳	224 cals

* plus 2–3 hours chilling

Serves 6

900 g (2 lb) fresh peas

50 g (2 oz) butter or margarine

1 onion, skinned and roughly chopped

568 ml (1 pint) milk

600 ml (1 pint) chicken stock

2 large sprigs of fresh mint and mint sprigs to garnish

pinch of caster sugar

salt and freshly ground pepper

150 ml (5 fl oz) single cream

3 Cover and simmer gently for about 30 minutes, until the peas are really tender. Cool slightly, reserving about 45 ml (3 tbsp) peas to garnish and rub the remaining peas through a sieve or place in a blender or food processor and blend to form a smooth purée.

4 Pour into a large bowl. Adjust seasoning, cool. Stir in the fresh cream and chill for 2–3 hours before serving. To serve, garnish with the reserved boiled peas and sprigs of mint.

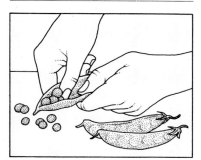

1 Shell the peas. Then melt the butter in a saucepan, add the onion, cover and cook gently for about 15 minutes until it is soft but not brown.

2 Remove from the heat and stir in the milk, stock, peas, the two mint sprigs, sugar and seasoning. Bring to the boil, stirring.

USING FRESH PEAS

This recipe for Chilled Pea and Mint Soup uses fresh peas – perfect for early summer when you can pick fresh peas from the garden or buy them easily at local farms and markets. There is nothing like the sweet, fragrant flavour of freshly picked peas in summer, so it is a good idea to make at least a double quantity of this soup and freeze some to remind you of the summer. If you want to make this soup at other times of year, it can also be made with frozen peas, in which case you will need half the weight specified in the recipe for fresh. There is no need to defrost them – just add them straight from the packet after adding the milk and stock in step 2 and cook as fresh peas.

ICED TOMATO AND HERB SOUP

| 0.20* | ✳ | 133 cals |

* plus 2 hours chilling

Serves 4

450 g (1 lb) ripe tomatoes

1 small onion, skinned and sliced

20 ml (4 tsp) tomato purée

411 g (14½ oz) can chicken consommé

30 ml (2 tbsp) chopped fresh herbs e.g. basil, coriander, parsley

salt and freshly ground pepper

25 g (1 oz) fresh white breadcrumbs

150 ml (¼ pint) soured cream

fresh basil leaves, to garnish

1 Roughly chop the tomatoes and process them with the onion, tomato purée, consommé and herbs until smooth.

2 Rub the tomato mixture through a nylon sieve into a saucepan. Heat gently to remove the frothy texture, then add plenty of salt and pepper.

3 Pour the soup into a large serving bowl and stir in the breadcrumbs. Chill in the refrigerator for at least 2 hours.

4 Stir the soured cream until smooth, then swirl in. Float the fresh basil leaves on top.

Menu Suggestion
Serve this elegant soup for a summer dinner party starter. Follow with barbecued lamb kebabs and a rice pilaf.

COLD CUCUMBER SOUP

0.20*	267 cals

* plus 8 hours chilling

Serves 4

2 medium cucumbers, peeled

100 g (4 oz) walnuts, chopped

30 ml (2 tbsp) olive oil or a mixture of walnut and olive oil

300 ml (½ pint) chicken stock, skimmed

1 garlic clove, skinned and crushed

30 ml (2 tbsp) chopped fresh dill or 10 ml (2 tsp) dried dill

salt and freshly ground pepper

300 ml (½ pint) natural yogurt or soured cream

sprigs of fresh dill, to garnish

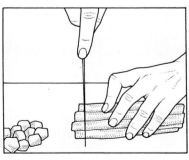

1 Cut the cucumbers into small dice and place in a bowl. Add the walnuts, oil, stock, garlic and chopped dill and season to taste with salt and pepper.

2 Stir the soup well, cover the bowl with cling film and chill in the refrigerator for at least 8 hours, or overnight.

3 To serve, uncover and whisk in the yogurt or soured cream. Ladle into individual soup bowls surrounded by crushed ice and garnish with the sprigs of dill.

Menu Suggestion
Cool, creamy and refreshing, this cucumber soup is best served with crisp Melba toast and chilled dry white wine.

VICHYSOISSE

| 0.50* | ✳ | 296 cals |

* plus 2 hours chilling

Serves 4

50 g (2 oz) butter

4 leeks, trimmed, sliced and
    washed

1 onion, skinned and sliced

1 litre (1¾ pints) chicken stock

2 potatoes, peeled and thinly sliced

salt and freshly ground pepper

200 ml (7 fl oz) single cream

snipped chives, to garnish

1 Melt the butter in a heavy-
based saucepan, add the leeks
and onion and cook gently for
about 10 minutes, until soft but
not coloured. Add the stock and
potatoes and bring to the boil.

2 Lower the heat, add salt and
pepper to taste and cover the
pan with a lid. Simmer for about
30 minutes until the vegetables are
completely soft.

3 Sieve or purée the soup in a
blender or food processor.
Pour into a large serving bowl and
stir in the cream. Taste and adjust
seasoning if necessary. Chill for at
least 4 hours in the refrigerator.
Sprinkle with chives just before
serving.

Menu Suggestion
Nothing could make a more
sophisticated starter to a summer
meal than this chilled leek and
potato soup. Serve with Melba
toast and butter curls, and follow
with a main course of chicken,
veal or duck to continue the
elegant theme of the meal.

ICED AVOCADO AND CHICKEN SOUP

0.10*	293 cals

* plus 2 hours chilling

Serves 6

2 ripe avocados

1 small onion, skinned and chopped

finely grated rind and juice of 1 lemon

142 ml (5 fl oz) natural yogurt

142 ml (5 fl oz) soured cream

600 ml (1 pint) cold chicken stock

175 g (6 oz) cooked chicken, diced

salt and freshly ground pepper

snipped chives, to garnish

1 Halve the avocados and discard the stones. Scoop out the flesh with a teaspoon.

2 Purée together the avocado flesh, onion, lemon rind and juice, yogurt and soured cream in a blender or food processor.

3 Turn out into a large serving bowl or tureen, gradually whisk in the stock, then add the chicken and seasoning to taste. Cover tightly and chill for at least 2 hours.

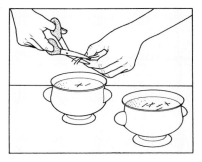

4 As a garnish, snip chives over the surface of the soup just before serving.

Menu Suggestion

The perfect soup for a summer dinner party or barbecue. Rich and creamy, yet icy cool, serve with crispbreads or wholemeal crackers and chilled white wine.

ICED AVOCADO AND CHICKEN SOUP

Avocado pears are often sold when still hard and unripe. To help them ripen, wrap in newspaper and put in a warm place. After 3–4 days they will be ready. To test for ripeness, apply gentle pressure with your thumb to the tapered end—the skin and flesh should yield slightly.

When choosing avocados, look for the roundish, dark green ones with uneven skins. These often seem to have more flavour than the more egg-shaped, paler green kind with smooth skins.

Avocado flesh discolours quickly on contact with the air, so don't cut open the pears until just before you are ready to make the soup.

MEDITERRANEAN SUMMER SOUP

0.45* ✳* 149 cals

* plus at least 1 hour chilling; freeze
after step 4

Serves 4

**2 very large Marmande or
Beefsteak tomatoes**

1 medium Spanish onion, skinned

1 green pepper, cored and seeded

450 g (1 lb) can potatoes, drained

4 garlic cloves, skinned

60 ml (4 tbsp) wine vinegar

1 litre (1¾ pints) water

30 ml (2 tbsp) olive oil

2.5 ml (½ tsp) paprika

salt and freshly ground pepper

**a few ice cubes and fresh mint
sprigs, to serve**

1 Chop all the vegetables and
the garlic roughly and then put
half of them in a blender or food
processor with the vinegar and
about 150 ml (¼ pint) of the
measured water. Work to a
smooth purée.

2 Sieve the purée to remove the
tomato skins, working it into a
large soup tureen or bowl.

3 Repeat the puréeing and
sieving with the remaining
vegetables and another 150 ml
(¼ pint) of the water. Add to the
purée in the tureen or bowl.

4 Pour the remaining water into
the soup and add the oil,
paprika and seasoning to taste.
Stir well to mix, cover and chill in
the refrigerator for at least 1 hour
before serving.

5 To serve, taste and adjust the
seasoning, then stir in the ice
cubes. Float mint sprigs on top.

Menu Suggestion
Serve as a starter for a summer
luncheon or barbecue party, with
bowls of garnish such as tiny
bread croûtons (fried or toasted),
diced red and green pepper, diced
cucumber and finely chopped
hard-boiled eggs.

MEDITERRANEAN SUMMER SOUP

To make croûtons for floating on
top of this soup: remove the
crusts from 3 slices of stale white
bread. Cut the bread into dice,
then deep-fry in hot oil until
golden brown and crisp. Remove
with a slotted spoon and drain on
absorbent kitchen paper. For
toasted croûtons, toast the crust-
less bread first, then cut into
dice. Croûtons can be successfully frozen.

For a professional touch, try
cutting the bread or toast into
different shapes with tiny aspic
jelly cutters, available from
specialist kitchen shops and
catering suppliers.

Starters

ARTICHOKE HEARTS À LA GRÈCQUE

0.30		103 cals

Serves 6

75 ml (5 tbsp) olive oil

15 ml (1 tbsp) white wine vinegar

10 ml (2 tsp) tomato purée

1 large garlic clove, skinned and crushed

7.5 ml (1½ tsp) chopped fresh thyme or basil

salt and freshly ground pepper

175 g (6 oz) button onions, skinned

5 ml (1 tsp) caster sugar

225 g (8 oz) small button mushrooms, wiped

two 400-g (14-oz) cans artichoke hearts

1 Make the dressing. Place 45 ml (3 tbsp) oil, vinegar, tomato purée, garlic, thyme and seasoning in a bowl and whisk together.

2 Blanch onions in boiling water for 5 minutes; drain well. Heat remaining oil; add onions and sugar and cook for 2 minutes.

3 Add mushrooms and toss over a high heat for a few seconds. Tip contents of pan into dressing. Drain artichoke hearts, rinse and dry. Add hearts to dressing and toss together. Cover and chill.

CRUDITÉS WITH AÏOLI

| 0.45 | 464–698 cals |

Serves 4–6

4 garlic cloves, skinned

1 egg yolk

300 ml (½ pint) olive oil

lemon juice, to taste

salt and freshly ground pepper

6 celery sticks, trimmed

4 carrots, peeled

½ cucumber

1 large red pepper, washed, cored,
    seeded and cut into strips

1 large green pepper, washed,
    cored, seeded and cut into strips

175 g (6 oz) button mushrooms,
    wiped

1 small cauliflower, cut into florets

1 bunch radishes, trimmed

6 spring onions, trimmed

1 First make the aïoli. Pound
the garlic in a mortar and
pestle. Stir in the egg yolk. Add
the oil a drop at a time, beating
until the mixture begins to thicken.
This may happen quite suddenly.

2 Continue adding the oil in a
thin, steady stream to make a
smooth, thick mayonnaise. Stir in
lemon juice and salt and pepper to
taste. Turn into a bowl, cover and
keep in a cool place.

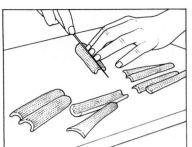

3 Meanwhile, prepare the vegetables. Cut the celery in half
crossways, then cut into sticks
lengthways. Cut the carrot and
cucumber into thin sticks.

4 Lay the mushrooms down with
the stalks uppermost, and,
using a sharp knife, slice downwards into 'T' shapes.

5 To serve, arrange all the vegetables on one large or two
small serving dishes. Serve with
the dip.

CRUDITÉS

Crudités – French for raw vegetables – does not have to include
all the vegetables suggested in
the recipe on this page. The
choice depends simply on
personal taste and seasonal
availability. Make sure, however,
that they are all as crisp and fresh
as possible.

If you want to make this
starter ahead of time, the
aïoli – garlic mayonnaise – will
keep in a covered container for
several days in the refrigerator.
The vegetables can be prepared
1–2 hours ahead of time and kept
in a bowl of iced water in the
refrigerator.

LEEKS À LA VINAIGRETTE

| 0.30* | 467–600 cals |

* plus 30 minutes chilling

Serves 4–6

12 small leeks
salt and freshly ground pepper
150 ml (¼ pint) olive oil
60 ml (4 tbsp) red wine vinegar
15 ml (1 tbsp) tomato purée
**15 ml (1 tbsp) coriander seeds,
    lightly crushed**
2.5 ml (½ tsp) sugar
coriander sprigs, to garnish
hot garlic bread, to serve

1 Trim the root ends of the leeks and cut off the damaged tops. Then slit each leek lengthways in two or three places.

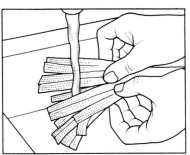

2 Hold under cold running water and wash away any grit caught between the leaves. Cook the leeks in boiling salted water for 6–8 minutes until just tender. Drain, refresh under cold running water, then leave to drain and dry on absorbent kitchen paper.

3 Make the dressing. Put the oil and vinegar in a bowl with the tomato purée, coriander seeds, sugar and salt and pepper to taste. Whisk vigorously with a fork until thick.

4 Arrange the cold leeks in a shallow serving dish and pour the dressing over them. Chill in the refrigerator for at least 30 minutes before serving. Garnish with sprigs of coriander and serve with hot garlic bread.

STUFFED COURGETTES WITH WALNUTS AND SAGE

1.20		422 cals

Serves 4

4 large courgettes, total weight about 700 g (1½ lb)

1 onion, skinned and chopped

90 g (3½ oz) butter or margarine

50 g (2 oz) walnut pieces, chopped

50 g (2 oz) fresh white breadcrumbs

10 ml (2 tsp) chopped fresh sage

15 ml (1 tbsp) tomato purée

1 egg, beaten

salt and freshly ground pepper

30 ml (2 tbsp) plain flour

300 ml (½ pint) chicken stock

30 ml (2 tbsp) chopped parsley

walnut halves and fresh sage sprigs, to garnish

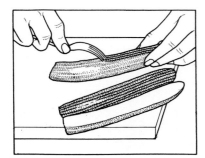

1 Wipe the courgettes. Using a fork, score down skin at 1-cm (½-inch) intervals, then halve each one lengthwise.

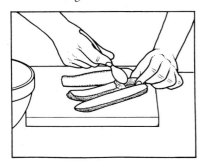

2 Hollow out the centres of the courgettes using a teaspoon. Blanch in boiling water for 4 minutes, drain, then hold under cold tap. Cool for 15–20 minutes.

3 Make the stuffing. Fry the onion in 25 g (1 oz) butter for 5–10 minutes until golden. Remove from heat and stir in half the walnuts, breadcrumbs, half the sage, the tomato purée, beaten egg and plenty of seasoning. Sandwich the courgettes with the stuffing.

4 Place in a buttered ovenproof dish and dot with a little more butter. Cover the courgettes and bake in the oven at 190°C (375°F) mark 5 for about 30 minutes.

5 Meanwhile, make the sauce. Melt 50 g (2 oz) butter in a pan, stir in the flour and cook gently for 1 minute, stirring.

6 Remove from the heat and gradually stir in the stock. Bring to the boil and continue to cook, stirring until the sauce thickens. Stir in the parsley, seasoning and remaining sage and walnuts. Remove from heat and cover the sauce.

7 To serve, reheat the sauce. Pour some over the courgettes and serve the rest separately. Garnish with walnut halves and sage sprigs.

BANG BANG CHICKEN

| 2.00* | 🍴 | 252–378 cals |

* plus cooling and overnight marinating

Serves 4–6

15 ml (1 tbsp) finely chopped fresh root ginger

1.4 kg (3 lb) chicken

salt and freshly ground pepper

60 ml (4 tbsp) soy sauce

3 carrots, peeled and very thinly sliced

75 g (3 oz) beansprouts

60 ml (4 tbsp) vegetable oil

30 ml (2 tbsp) sesame oil

30 ml (2 tbsp) sesame seeds

10 ml (2 tsp) crushed dried red chillies

5 ml (1 tsp) soft brown sugar

45 ml (3 tbsp) dry sherry

lettuce, to serve

spring onion tassels, to garnish

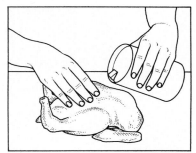

1 Put the ginger inside the cavity of the chicken, then rub the outside of the bird with salt and pepper. Place the bird in a large saucepan and sprinkle over half of the soy sauce. Leave to stand for 30 minutes.

2 Pour enough water into the pan to just cover the chicken. Bring to the boil, then lower the heat, cover and simmer for about 1 hour until the chicken is tender. Leave to cool in the cooking liquid, then remove.

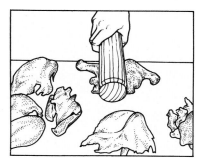

3 Separate the legs and wings from the carcass, then cut the carcass into four. Bang the pieces several times with a rolling pin to loosen the meat from the bones.

4 Cut the meat into neat slices (not too small) or strips. Discard the bones and skin. Combine with carrots and beansprouts.

5 Heat the oils in a heavy-based pan, add the sesame seeds and chillies and fry over brisk heat for a few minutes, stirring until lightly coloured. Remove from the heat and stir in the remaining soy sauce with the sugar and sherry.

6 Pour over the chicken and vegetables, cover and marinate in the refrigerator overnight.

7 To serve, put the chicken and vegetables into a shallow serving dish, lined with lettuce leaves. Pour over any remaining marinade and garnish with spring onion tassels. Serve cold.

Menu Suggestion
A refreshing starter for the first course of a Chinese meal. Serve with a dry white wine.

CRISPY CHICKEN PARCELS

0.45*	🗂 🗂	❄*

803–857 cals

* plus 30 minutes chilling; freeze after step 5

Serves 4

25 g (1 oz) butter or margarine

50 g (2 oz) flour

300 ml (½ pint) milk

225 g (8 oz) cooked chicken, diced

15 ml (1 tbsp) chopped fresh tarragon or 10 ml (2 tsp) dried tarragon

75 g (3 oz) Gruyère cheese, grated

good pinch of ground mace

salt and freshly ground pepper

15 ml (1 tbsp) vegetable oil

8–12 cannelloni tubes

180 ml (12 tbsp) dried breadcrumbs

180 ml (12 tbsp) grated Parmesan cheese

1 egg, beaten

oil, for deep-frying

1 Melt the fat in a heavy-based saucepan, sprinkle in the flour and cook for 2 minutes, stirring.

2 Remove from the heat and gradually stir in the milk, then bring to the boil, stirring all the time until very thick. Add the chicken, tarragon, Gruyère, mace and salt and pepper to taste. Stir to mix.

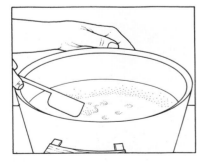

3 Bring a large pan of salted water to the boil, then swirl in the oil. Drop in the cannelloni. Simmer for 5 minutes, drain.

4 Using a teaspoon, or a piping bag fitted with a large plain nozzle, fill each cannelloni tube with the chicken mixture. Pinch the edges to seal.

5 Mix the breadcrumbs and Parmesan in a shallow bowl. Dip the cannelloni tubes first in the beaten egg, then in the bread-crumbs mixed with the Parmesan, making sure they are evenly coated. Chill in the refrigerator for 30 minutes.

6 Heat the oil in a deep-fryer to 180°C (350°F). Deep-fry the parcels a few at a time until golden brown and crisp. Drain on ab-sorbent kitchen paper while frying the remainder. Serve hot.

Menu Suggestion

A substantial, hot starter which needs no accompaniment other than a dry white wine. Can also be served for a tasty lunchtime snack, with a mixed salad.

MARINATED KIPPERS

| 0.20* | 395 cals |

* plus at least 8 hours marinating

Serves 4

4 boneless kipper fillets

150 ml (¼ pint) olive oil

75 ml (5 tbsp) lemon juice

1.25 ml (¼ tsp) mustard powder

1 small onion, skinned and very finely chopped

1–2 garlic cloves, skinned and crushed

freshly ground pepper

a few raw onion rings, parsley sprigs and paprika, to garnish

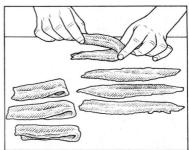

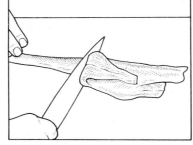

1 Skin the kipper fillets. Place them skin side down on a board, grip each one at the tail end and work the flesh away from the skin with a sharp knife, using a sawing motion.

2 In a jug, whisk together the remaining ingredients, except the garnish, adding pepper to taste.

3 Put the kippers in a shallow dish and pour over the marinade. Cover and chill in the refrigerator for at least 8 hours. Turn the kippers in the marinade occasionally during this time.

4 To serve, remove the kippers from the marinade and cut each one in half lengthways. Fold each half over crossways, then place in a single layer in a dish.

5 Pour the marinade over the kippers and garnish the top with onion rings, parsley sprigs and a sprinkling of paprika.

Menu Suggestion
Serve this chilled starter with granary bread or rolls and butter, and a bottle of dry white wine.

MARINATED KIPPERS

Kippers are herrings which are split and gutted, soaked in brine, then smoked. The best kippers are said to come from Loch Fyne in Scotland, although those from the Isle of Man are also considered to be very good. The choice of kippers is quite confusing—at fishmongers they are sold whole, boned, and as fillets, whereas in supermarkets they are available frozen as fillets and in vacuum 'boil-in-the-bag' packs. For this recipe you can use fresh or frozen fillets. Avoid buying those which are a deep, chestnut-brown colour as they have probably been dyed.

Coarse Liver Pâté

$\boxed{3.20*}$ ✳ $\boxed{454 \text{ cals}}$

* plus cooling and overnight chilling

Serves 8

225 g (8 oz) unsmoked rashers of streaky bacon, rinded

300 ml (½ pint) milk

slices of onion, bay leaf, peppercorns and 1 or 2 cloves, for flavouring

25 g (1 oz) butter or margarine

20 g (¾ oz) plain flour

450 g (1 lb) belly of pork, rinded

450 g (1 lb) pig's liver

1 small onion, skinned and quartered

2 garlic cloves, skinned and crushed

30 ml (2 tbsp) medium dry sherry

salt and freshly ground pepper

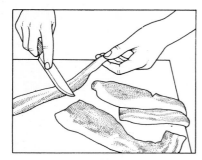

1 Put the bacon rashers on a board and stretch using the back of a knife. Use to line the base and sides of a 1.4 litre (2½ pint) dish or terrine.

2 Pour the milk into a saucepan, add the flavouring ingredients and bring slowly to the boil. Remove from the heat, cover and leave to infuse for 15 minutes.

3 Strain the milk and reserve. Melt the butter in the rinsed-out pan, add the flour and cook gently, stirring, for 1–2 minutes. Remove from the heat and gradually blend in the milk. Bring to the boil, stirring constantly, then simmer for 3 minutes until thick and smooth. Cover and leave to cool slightly.

4 Cut the pork and liver into small pieces. Pass the meats and onion through a mincer, fitted with the coarsest blade. Alternatively, chop in a food processor.

5 Put the minced mixture into a bowl, add the garlic, then stir in the sherry and plenty of salt and pepper. Gradually beat in the cooled sauce and continue beating until well mixed. The mixture may seem a little sloppy, but it will firm up on cooking.

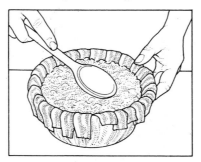

6 Spoon the mixture into the prepared dish and press down with the back of the spoon. Fold over any overlapping bacon. Cover the dish tightly with foil.

7 Place the dish in a roasting tin and half fill with boiling water. Bake in the oven at 180°C (350°F) mark 4 for about 2¼ hours until firm to the touch and the juices run clear when the centre of the pâté is pierced with a fine skewer.

8 Remove the dish from the roasting tin and replace the foil with a fresh piece. Place a plate or dish, small enough just to fit inside the dish, on top of the pâté. Top with heavy weights.

9 Leave the pâté to cool for 1 hour, then chill overnight. To serve, dip the dish into hot water for about 30 seconds then invert the pâté on to a plate.

Menu Suggestion

Coarse Liver Pâté makes a substantial starter for an informal supper party, served with salad, French bread and a full-bodied red wine such as a Côtes du Rhône. Alternatively, cut the pâté into thick slices and use for packed lunches and picnics, with a selection of salads.

CHICKEN LIVER PÂTÉ

| 0.20* | ✳ | 232 cals |

* plus 20 minutes cooling and 2 hours chilling

Serves 8

100 g (4 oz) butter

1 medium onion, skinned and chopped

1 garlic clove, skinned and crushed

450 g (1 lb) chicken livers, cleaned and dried

75 ml (5 tbsp) double cream

15 ml (1 tbsp) tomato purée

15 ml (1 tbsp) brandy

salt and freshly ground pepper

pink peppercorns and fresh bay leaves, to garnish

1 Melt half of the butter in a saucepan, add the onion and garlic and fry gently for 5 minutes. Add the chicken livers and cook for 5 minutes.

2 Cool slightly, then add the cream, tomato purée, brandy and plenty of salt and pepper.

3 Purée the mixture in a blender or food processor, then spoon into a serving dish.

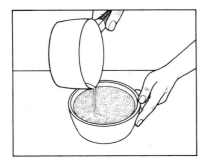

4 Melt the remaining butter gently. Pour the butter over the pâté and leave to cool. Chill for at least 2 hours. Garnish with peppercorns and bay leaves.

Menu Suggestion
Serve this rich, creamy pâté with Melba toast and a dry red wine.

POTTED CHICKEN WITH TARRAGON

| 2.00* | ✳ | 205–274 cals |

* plus at least 4 hours chilling
and 30 minutes to come to room
temperature

Serves 6–8

1.4 kg (3 lb) oven-ready chicken
45 ml (3 tbsp) dry sherry
**15 ml (1 tbsp) fresh chopped
    tarragon or 5 ml (1 tsp) dried**
50 g (2 oz) butter
1 onion, skinned and chopped
1 carrot, peeled and chopped
salt and freshly ground pepper
fresh tarragon sprigs, to garnish

1 Place the chicken in a flameproof casserole with the
sherry, tarragon, butter,
vegetables and salt and pepper.
Cover tightly and cook in the oven
at 180°C (350°F) mark 4 for about
1½ hours.

2 Lift the chicken out of the
casserole, cut off all the flesh,
reserving the skin and bones.
Coarsely mince the chicken meat
in a food processor or mincer.

3 Return the skin and broken up
bones to the casserole. Boil
the contents rapidly until the
liquid has reduced to 225 ml
(8 fl oz). Strain, reserving the
juices.

4 Mix the minced chicken and
juices together, then check the
seasoning. Pack into small dishes,
cover with cling film and chill in
the refrigerator for at least
4 hours.

5 Leave at cool room
temperature for 30 minutes
before serving. Garnish with fresh
tarragon sprigs.

Menu Suggestion
Serve this subtly flavoured starter
with Melba toast and chilled dry
white wine or French dry cider.

SMOKED MACKEREL MOUSSE

0.50* ✳ 220 cals

* plus 20 minutes cooling and 2 hours chilling

Serves 6

300 ml (½ pint) milk

a few slices of onion and carrot

1 bay leaf

25 g (1 oz) butter or margarine

30 ml (2 tbsp) plain flour

10 ml (2 tsp) gelatine

275 g (10 oz) smoked mackerel fillet

50 g (2 oz) onion, skinned and chopped

15 ml (1 tbsp) creamed horseradish

150 ml (¼ pint) natural yogurt

15 ml (1 tbsp) lemon juice

salt and freshly ground pepper

2 egg whites

lamb's lettuce or watercress sprigs and lemon twists, to garnish

1 Pour the milk into a saucepan, add the flavourings and bring slowly to the boil. Remove from the heat, cover and leave to infuse for 30 minutes.

2 Strain the infused milk into a jug. Discard the flavourings. Melt the butter in the rinsed-out pan, add the flour and cook gently, stirring, for 1–2 minutes. Remove from the heat and gradually blend in the infused milk. Bring to the boil, stirring constantly, then simmer for 3 minutes until thick and smooth.

3 Remove the pan from the heat and sprinkle in the gelatine. Stir briskly until dissolved. Pour into a bowl and leave to cool for 20 minutes.

4 Meanwhile, flake the smoked mackerel fillet, discarding the skin and bones.

5 Work the cooled sauce, mackerel, onion and horseradish in a blender or food processor until smooth. Pour into a bowl and stir in the yogurt, lemon juice and salt and pepper to taste.

6 Whisk the egg whites until they stand in soft peaks, then fold gently through the fish mixture.

7 Spoon the mousse into 6 individual ramekins or soufflé dishes and chill in the refrigerator for at least 2 hours until set. Serve chilled, garnished with lamb's lettuce or watercress sprigs and lemon twists.

Menu Suggestion
For an informal supper party or a buffet party, serve with fingers of wholemeal toast and butter. Follow with a meaty main course such as a casserole, and finish the meal with a glazed open fruit tart.

FRESH HADDOCK MOUSSE

| 0.40* | 🗑 | 359 cals |

* plus 30 minutes cooling, 2 hours chilling and 30 minutes to come to room temperature

Serves 6

| 350 g (12 oz) fresh haddock fillet |
| 200 ml (7 fl oz) milk |
| 1 bay leaf |
| 6 peppercorns |
| salt and freshly ground pepper |
| 25 g (1 oz) butter or margarine |
| 30 ml (2 tbsp) plain flour |
| 7.5 ml (1½ tsp) gelatine |
| 15 ml (1 tbsp) Dijon mustard |
| 5 ml (1 tsp) tomato purée |
| 5 ml (1 tsp) Worcestershire sauce |
| 90 ml (6 tbsp) double cream |
| 150 ml (¼ pint) mayonnaise |
| 15 ml (1 tbsp) lemon juice |
| cucumber, to garnish |

1 Place the haddock in a sauté or frying pan. Pour in the milk and add the bay leaf, peppercorns and a good pinch of salt. Bring slowly to the boil, cover and simmer for 5–10 minutes, or until the fish flakes easily when tested with a fork.

2 Strain the cooking liquid from the fish and reserve. Skin and flake the flesh, discarding any bones.

3 Melt the butter in a saucepan, add the flour and cook gently, stirring for 1–2 minutes. Remove from the heat and gradually blend in the strained cooked liquid. Bring to the boil, stirring constantly, then simmer for 3 minutes until thick and smooth. Remove the pan from the heat and sprinkle in the gelatine. Stir briskly until dissolved.

4 Work the sauce in a blender or food processor with the fish, mustard, tomato purée, Worcestershire sauce and salt and pepper to taste. Transfer to a bowl and leave to cool for 30 minutes.

5 Lightly whip the cream and stir it into the fish mixture with the mayonnaise and lemon juice. Check the seasoning.

6 Spoon the mousse into 6 individual ramekins or soufflé dishes and chill in the refrigerator for at least 2 hours until set. Leave at cool room temperature for 30 minutes before serving, garnished with cucumber.

Menu Suggestion
This mousse is light and delicate in flavour. Serve for a dinner party starter with Melba toast; followed by a main course of chicken or veal, then a fresh, fruity dessert.

55

INDONESIAN PORK SATÉ

0.40*	468 cals

* plus 30 minutes marinating

Serves 4

450 g (1 lb) pork fillet
30 ml (2 tbsp) dark soy sauce
45 ml (3 tbsp) lemon juice
7.5 ml (1½ tsp) ground ginger
125 g (4 oz) unsalted peanuts
30 ml (2 tbsp) oil
1 garlic clove, skinned and crushed
2.5 ml (½ tsp) ground coriander
1.25 ml (¼ tsp) chilli powder
1.25 ml (¼ tsp) salt
450 ml (¾ pint) coconut milk
5 ml (1 tsp) soft brown sugar
freshly ground pepper
½ cucumber

1 Cut the pork fillet into small cubes. Thread on to 8 long saté sticks, or metal skewers.

2 Mix together the soy sauce, lemon juice and 5 ml (1 tsp) of the ginger. Pour over the pork skewers and leave to marinate for at least 30 minutes, turning occasionally.

3 Meanwhile, finely chop the peanuts or grind them in a nut mill. Heat the oil in a saucepan. Add the peanuts, garlic, coriander, chilli powder, remaining ginger and salt and fry for about 4–5 minutes until browned, stirring.

4 Stir in the milk and sugar. Bring to the boil and simmer for about 15 minutes or until the sauce thickens. Check the seasoning, adding pepper to taste.

5 Grill the pork skewers for about 6 minutes, or until the meat is tender, turning occasionally.

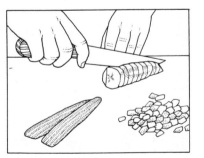

6 Meanwhile, shred the cucumber finely Serve the saté hot, with the shredded cucumber, and the peanut sauce for dipping.

Menu Suggestion

These kebabs come with their own sauce for dipping, and so need no accompaniment. Follow with an Indonesian-style main course of whole steamed or baked fish, or a fish curry.

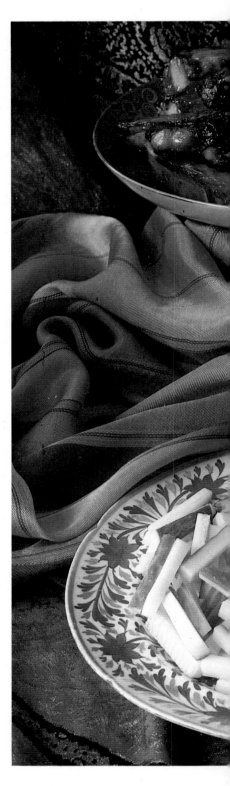

SPICY SPARERIBS

0.20* | 274 cals

* plus 2 hours marinating

Serves 4

1.8 kg (4 lb) pork spareribs
1 onion, skinned and sliced
350 ml (12 fl oz) tomato juice
45 ml (3 tbsp) cider vinegar
30 ml (2 tbsp) clear honey
10 ml (2 tsp) salt
5 ml (1 tsp) paprika
3.75 ml ($\frac{3}{4}$ tsp) chilli powder

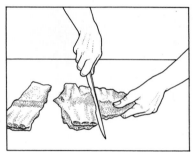

1 Separate the spareribs into sections of 2–3 ribs. Place in a shallow dish. Mix all the remaining ingredients together and pour over the ribs. Cover and marinate in the refrigerator for 2 hours.

2 Place the spareribs on a pre-heated grill. Brush with the marinade. Grill for 20 minutes, brushing occasionally with the marinade and turning. Heat the marinade and serve as a sauce.

Menu Suggestion
Serve as a first course for a Chinese-style supper party.

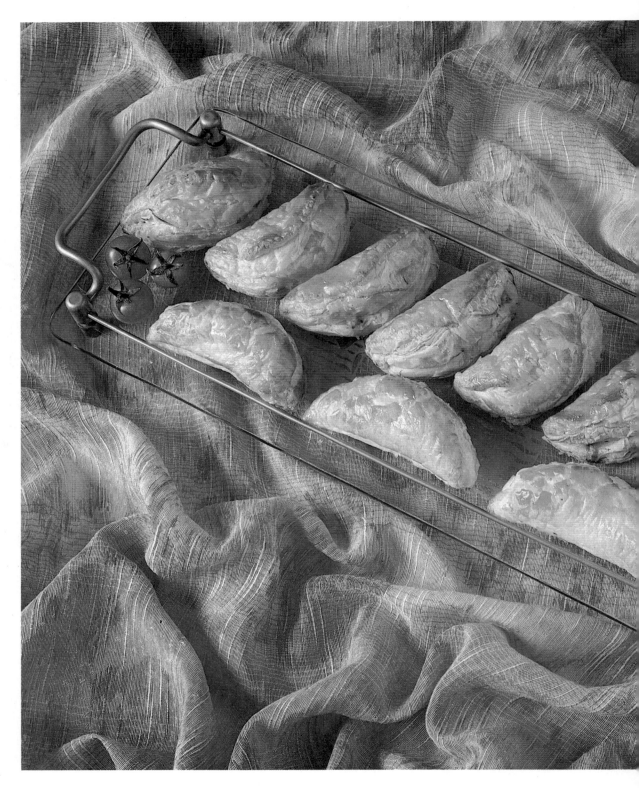

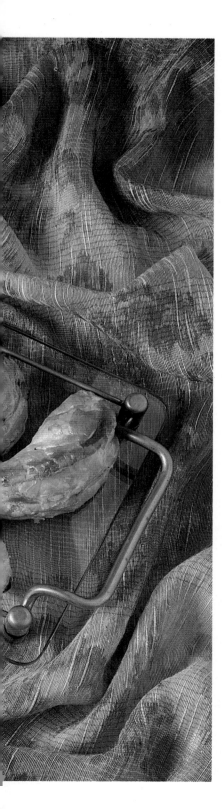

CREAMY HAM AND MUSHROOM PUFFS

1.00* ✳* 430–645 cals

* plus cooling; freeze at the end of step 5

Serves 4–6

75 g (3 oz) button mushrooms

1 small onion, skinned

40 g (1½ oz) butter or margarine

30 ml (2 tbsp) plain flour

100 ml (3½ fl oz) milk

100 ml (3½ fl oz) double cream

75 g (3 oz) boiled ham, finely diced

10 ml (2 tsp) chopped fresh tarragon or 5 ml (1 tsp) dried

salt and freshly ground pepper

350 g (12 oz) packet frozen puff pastry, thawed

1 egg, beaten, to glaze

1 Chop the mushrooms and onion very finely. Melt half of the butter in a pan, add them to it and fry over moderate heat for 2–3 minutes. Remove and drain.

2 Melt the remaining butter in the pan, add the flour and cook gently, stirring, for 1–2 minutes. Remove from the heat and gradually blend in the milk. Bring to the boil, stirring constantly. Add the cream and simmer for 3 minutes until thick. Off the heat, fold in the mushroom mixture, ham and seasonings.

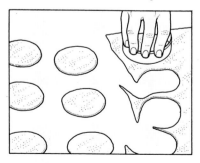

3 Roll out the pastry on a lightly floured surface and cut out 12 rounds using a 10 cm (4 inch) plain round cutter.

4 Put spoonfuls of the ham and mushroom filling on one half of each pastry round.

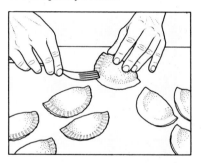

5 Brush the edges of the pastry rounds with beaten egg, then fold the plain half of the pastry over the filling. Seal the edges and crimp with the prongs of a fork.

6 Place the turnovers on a dampened baking sheet. Brush with beaten egg to glaze, then bake in the oven at 220°C (425°F) mark 7 for 15–20 minutes until puffed up and golden. Serve hot.

Menu Suggestion

These puff pastry turnovers are rich and filling. Follow with a light main course such as grilled or barbecued fish kebabs. A tangy lemon or orange soufflé or mousse would make the ideal dessert.

MUSHROOMS IN SOURED CREAM

0.35*	207 cals

* plus cooling and chilling

Serves 4

450 g (1 lb) button mushrooms

1 bunch of spring onions

4 cardamom pods

25 g (1 oz) butter

30 ml (2 tbsp) olive oil

2 garlic cloves, crushed

juice of 1 lemon

150 ml ($\frac{1}{4}$ pint) soured cream

30 ml (2 tbsp) chopped fresh
    coriander

salt and freshly ground pepper

coriander and paprika, to garnish

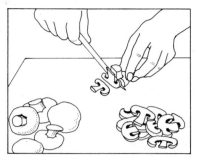

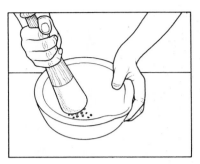

1 Wipe the mushrooms. Slice them thickly and evenly into 'T' shapes. Trim the spring onions and slice finely.

2 Split open the cardamom pods with your fingernails to release the seeds. Crush the seeds with a mortar and pestle or the end of a rolling pin.

3 Melt the butter with the oil in a large frying pan. Add the spring onions and garlic and fry gently for 5 minutes until the onions soften slightly.

4 Add the crushed cardamom seeds to the pan and fry for 1–2 minutes, then increase the heat and add the mushrooms. Cook the mushrooms for a few minutes only until tender, stirring frequently and shaking the pan to ensure even cooking.

5 Transfer the mushrooms and cooking juices to a bowl. Leave to cool then stir in the lemon juice, soured cream and coriander with salt and pepper to taste. Chill in the refrigerator until serving time. Stir well and garnish with coriander and paprika just before serving.

Menu Suggestion
Serve this rich, creamy starter with fresh wholemeal or poppyseed rolls. Any light main course such as chicken or fish would be suitable to follow, with a tangy, fresh fruit dessert to finish.

INDIVIDUAL MUSHROOM SOUFFLÉS

| 0.50 | 330 cals |

Serves 6

75 g (3 oz) butter

100 g (4 oz) flat mushrooms, wiped and roughly chopped

20 ml (4 tsp) anchovy essence

squeeze of lemon juice

40 g (1½ oz) plain flour

225 ml (9 fl oz) milk

salt and freshly ground pepper

4 eggs, size 2, separated

freshly grated Parmesan

1 Brush the insides of 6 150 ml (¼ pint) individual soufflé dishes liberally with 15 g (½ oz) butter and set aside.

2 Melt 25 g (1 oz) butter in a saucepan, add the mushrooms, anchovy essence and lemon juice and stir fry over high heat for 2–3 minutes. Transfer the mushrooms with a slotted spoon to a large bowl.

3 Melt the remaining butter in the pan, add the flour and cook gently, stirring, for 1–2 minutes. Remove from the heat and gradually blend in the milk. Bring to the boil, stirring constantly, then simmer for 3 minutes until thick and smooth.

4 Remove the pan from the heat and add the sauce to the mushrooms. Stir well to mix, adding salt and pepper to taste. Beat in the egg yolks one at a time.

5 Whisk the egg whites until stiff, then fold into the soufflé mixture until evenly incorporated. Divide equally between the 6 prepared dishes and sprinkle with Parmesan. Bake immediately in the oven at 200°C (400°F) mark 6 for 15 minutes or until well risen. Serve immediately.

Menu Suggestion
Individual soufflés make an impressive dinner party dessert. Serve with hot garlic or herb bread and follow with a main course such as the French fish stew *bouillabaisse*. A chilled lemon cheesecake would make a suitably refreshing dessert.

HUMMUS
(MIDDLE EASTERN CHICK PEA AND TAHINI DIP)

| 1.20* | ✳* | 277–416 cals |

* plus overnight soaking and a few hours chilling; freeze without the garnish

Serves 4–6

| 175 g (6 oz) chick peas, soaked in cold water overnight |
| about 150 ml (¼ pint) lemon juice |
| 150 ml (¼ pint) tahini paste |
| 3 garlic cloves, skinned and crushed |
| salt |
| 30 ml (2 tbsp) olive oil |
| 5 ml (1 tsp) paprika |
| crudités, to serve (see box) |

1 Drain the soaked chick peas and rinse well under cold running water. Put the chick peas in a large saucepan and cover with plenty of cold water.

2 Bring slowly to the boil, then skim off any scum with a slotted spoon. Half cover the pan with a lid and simmer gently for about 1 hour, until the chick peas are very tender.

3 Drain the chick peas, reserving 60 ml (4 tbsp) of the cooking liquid. Set a few whole chick peas aside for the garnish, then put the remainder in a blender or food processor. Add the reserved cooking liquid and half of the lemon juice and work to a smooth purée.

4 Add the tahini paste, garlic and 5 ml (1 tsp) salt and work again. Taste and add more lemon juice until the dip is to your liking, then blend in 30 ml (2 tbsp) hot water.

5 Turn into a serving bowl and cover with cling film. Chill in the refrigerator until serving time. Before serving, mix the oil with the paprika and drizzle over the Hummus. Arrange the reserved whole chick peas on top.

PAPA GHANOOYE
(ARABIC AUBERGINE DIP)

| 0.50* | ✳* | 322–483 cals |

* plus a few hours chilling; freeze without the garnish

Serves 4–6

| 2 large aubergines |
| salt |
| 2–3 garlic cloves, skinned and roughly chopped |
| 10 ml (2 tsp) cumin seeds |
| 100 ml (4 fl oz) olive oil |
| 150 ml (¼ pint) tahini paste |
| about 100 ml (4 fl oz) lemon juice |
| thin tomato slices, to garnish |
| crudités, to serve (see box) |

1 Slice the aubergines, then place in a colander, sprinkling each layer with salt. Cover with a plate, put heavy weights on top and leave to dégorge for 30 minutes.

2 Meanwhile, crush the garlic and cumin seeds with a pestle and mortar. Add 5 ml (1 tsp) salt and mix well.

3 Rinse the aubergines under cold running water, then pat dry with absorbent kitchen paper. Heat the oil in a large, heavy-based frying pan until very hot. Add the aubergine slices in batches and fry until golden on both sides, turning once. Remove from the pan with a slotted spoon and drain again on kitchen paper.

4 Put the aubergine slices in a blender or food processor with the garlic mixture, the tahini paste and about two-thirds of the lemon juice. Work to a smooth purée, then taste and add more lemon juice and salt if liked.

5 Turn into a serving bowl, cover with cling film and chill in the refrigerator until serving time. Serve chilled, garnished with tomato slices.

SKORDALIA
(GREEK GARLIC DIP)

| 0.30* | 381–572 cals |

* plus a few hours chilling

Serves 4–6

| 75 g (3 oz) crustless white bread |
| 60 ml (4 tbsp) milk |
| 6 garlic cloves |
| 250 ml (8 fl oz) olive oil |
| about 50 ml (2 fl oz) lemon juice |
| salt and freshly ground pepper |
| black olives and finely chopped parsley, to garnish |
| crudités, to serve (see box) |

1 Tear the bread into small pieces into a bowl. Add the milk, mix and soak for 5 minutes.

2 Skin the cloves of garlic, chop roughly, then crush with a pestle and mortar.

3 Squeeze the bread with your fingers, then mix with the crushed garlic. Add the olive oil a drop at a time to form a paste.

4 When the mixture thickens, add a few drops of lemon juice, then continue with the olive oil. Add more lemon juice and salt and pepper. Turn into a bowl and cover with cling film. Chill in the refrigerator and garnish with olives and parsley before serving.

VEGETABLE DIPS
Dips make good starters for informal supper parties, or to serve at a drinks party. Crudités (raw vegetables) are ideal for dipping and dunking. To serve 4–6 people: 4 carrots, peeled and cut into thin sticks, 1 small cauliflower, divided into florets, 4–6 celery sticks, halved, ½ cucumber, seeds removed and cut into sticks, 1 red and 1 green pepper, cored seeded and sliced, 1 bunch of radishes, trimmed. Fingers of hot pitta bread can also be served.

STUFFED PLAICE FILLETS

0.45		251 cals

Serves 6

3 large double plaice fillets

75 g (3 oz) butter

5 ml (1 tsp) lemon juice

125 g (4 oz) mushrooms, wiped

175 g (6 oz) leeks, trimmed and washed

50 g (2 oz) long grain rice, cooked and drained

30 ml (2 tbsp) chopped fresh tarragon or 10 ml (2 tsp) dried

salt and freshly ground pepper

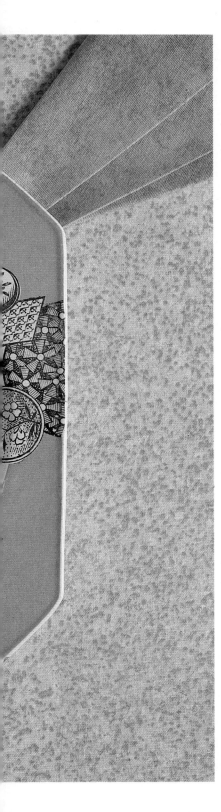

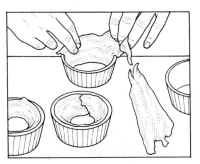

1 Skin the plaice, then cut each into 2 long fillets.

2 Place 1 fillet, skinned side out, round the inside of each of 6 buttered ramekins or individual soufflé dishes.

3 Make the lemon butter. Beat together 50 g (2 oz) of the butter and the lemon juice. Wrap in greaseproof paper and chill in the refrigerator for at least 30 minutes.

4 Meanwhile, finely chop the mushrooms and leeks. Melt remaining butter in a frying pan, add the vegetables and cook gently until softened. Remove from the heat and stir in the rice and tarragon. Season to taste.

5 Spoon the vegetable mixture into the centre of each ramekin, pressing down well.

6 Cover the ramekins with buttered foil, place in a bain marie (page 59) and bake in the oven at 190°C (375°F) mark 5 for about 25 minutes.

7 To serve, invert the ramekins on to serving plates. With the dishes still in place, pour off any excess liquid. Remove the dishes and serve hot, with a knob of lemon butter on top.

Menu Suggestion

Serve for a special dinner party starter with warm bread rolls and butter. Serve lamb chops or steaks en croûte with seasonal vegetables for the main course, and a fresh fruit pavlova for dessert.

65

SALADES RÂPÉES CRUES
(GRATED RAW VEGETABLES WITH GARLIC DRESSING)

0.20	240 cals

Serves 4

175 g (6 oz) carrot, peeled
175 g (6 oz) courgettes
175 g (6 oz) celeriac
15 ml (1 tbsp) lemon juice
175 g (6 oz) raw beetroot
90 ml (6 tbsp) olive or vegetable oil
30 ml (2 tbsp) wine vinegar
2.5 ml (½ tsp) sugar
2.5 ml (½ tsp) mustard
1 garlic clove, skinned and crushed
salt and freshly ground black pepper
chopped fresh parsley, to garnish

1 Grate the carrot avoiding the central core. Grate the courgettes and mix with the carrots.

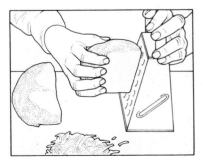

2 Peel and grate the celeriac, toss immediately in the lemon juice and add to the carrot and courgette mixture. Lastly, peel and grate the beetroot and add to the mixture.

3 Put the oil, vinegar, sugar, mustard and garlic in a screw-top jar with salt and pepper to taste. Shake the jar until the dressing is emulsified.

4 Pour the dressing over the vegetables and toss lightly just to coat. Serve immediately, garnished with chopped parsley.

Menu Suggestion
Serve this French starter as part of a bistro-style meal with hot garlic bread. Follow with a casserole such as boeuf bourguignon, and a selection of French cheeses and fresh fruit to finish.

ARABIC AUBERGINE CREAM

1.10*	201–301 cals

* plus 1 hour chilling

Serves 4–6

2 large aubergines
salt and freshly ground pepper
100 ml (4 fl oz) olive oil
10 ml (2 tsp) ground cumin
150 ml (¼ pint) natural yogurt
juice of ½ lemon
2 garlic cloves, crushed
chopped fresh coriander and oil, to garnish

1 Slice the aubergines thinly, then place in a colander, sprinkling each layer lightly with salt. Cover with a plate, place heavy weights on top, then leave to drain for 30 minutes.

2 Rinse the aubergine slices under cold running water, then pat thoroughly dry.

3 Heat some of the oil in a frying pan and fry the aubergines in batches until golden.

4 Blend or process the aubergines until smooth. Add the remaining ingredients, except garnish, and work again. Season.

5 Turn the cream into a bowl, rough up the surface with a fork and sprinkle with chopped coriander and oil. Chill.

Menu Suggestion
Serve with fingers of hot pitta bread and raw vegetables.

IMAM BAYILDI
(COLD STUFFED BAKED AUBERGINE)

1.40*	372 cals

* plus 1 hour cooling and 2 hours chilling

Serves 6

6 long, small aubergines

salt and freshly ground pepper

200 ml (7 fl oz) olive oil

450 g (1 lb) onions, skinned and finely sliced

3 garlic cloves, skinned and crushed

397 g (14 oz) can tomatoes, drained or 450 g (1 lb) tomatoes, skinned, seeded and chopped

60 ml (4 tbsp) chopped fresh parsley, plus extra to garnish

3.75 ml ($\frac{3}{4}$ tsp) ground allspice

5 ml (1 tsp) sugar

30 ml (2 tbsp) lemon juice

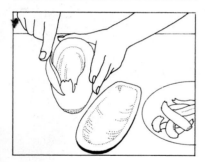

1 Halve the aubergines lengthways. Scoop out the flesh and reserve. Leave a substantial shell so they do not disintegrate.

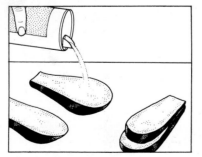

2 Sprinkle the insides of the aubergine shells with salt and invert on a plate for 30 minutes to drain any bitter juices.

3 Heat 45 ml (3 tbsp) olive oil in a saucepan, add the onion and garlic and fry gently for about 15 minutes until soft but not coloured. Add the tomatoes, reserved aubergine flesh, parsley, allspice and salt and pepper to taste. Simmer gently for about 20 minutes until the mixture has reduced and thickened.

4 Rinse the aubergines and pat dry with absorbent kitchen paper. Spoon the filling into each half and place them side by side in a shallow ovenproof dish. They should fit quite closely together.

5 Mix the remaining oil with 150 ml ($\frac{1}{4}$ pint) water, the sugar, lemon juice and salt and pepper to taste. Pour around the aubergines, cover and bake in the oven at 150°C (300°F) mark 2 for at least 1 hour until completely tender.

6 When cooked, remove from the oven, uncover and leave to cool for 1 hour. Chill in the refrigerator for at least 2 hours before serving garnished with lots of chopped parsley.

Menu Suggestion

Imam Bayildi is a Turkish dish, eaten with bread as a first course. Hot pitta bread or crusty French bread are both suitable. Follow with a lamb casserole or kebabs, if you want to continue the Turkish theme.

TARAMASALATA

1.15*	283 cals

* includes 1 hour chilling

Serves 6

225 g (8 oz) smoked cod's roe

1 garlic clove, skinned and crushed

50 g (2 oz) fresh white breadcrumbs

1 small onion, skinned and finely
   chopped

finely grated rind and juice of
   1 lemon

150 ml (¼ pint) olive oil

freshly ground pepper

lemon wedges and pitta or French
   bread or toast, to serve

1 Skin the smoked cod's roe and break it up into pieces. Place in a blender or food processor with the garlic, breadcrumbs, onion, lemon rind and juice and blend to form a purée.

2 Gradually add the oil and blend well after each addition until smooth. Blend in 90 ml (6 tbsp) hot water with pepper to taste.

3 Spoon into a serving dish and chill in the refrigerator for at least 1 hour. To serve, garnish with lemon slices. Serve with pitta, French bread or toast, if liked.

Menu Suggestion

Taramasalata is always popular as a starter for an informal supper party, served with hot white or wholemeal pitta bread. A dry white Retsina wine makes the perfect accompaniment. To continue the Greek theme of the meal, lamb and aubergine moussaka or lamb kebabs make ideal main courses, or you could try the more unusual pork and coriander stew called *afelia*. As a side dish, serve a Greek salad of shredded white cabbage, tomato, onion and black olives dressed with olive oil and lemon juice. Fresh fruit makes a good ending to the meal.

RAMEKINS OF BAKED CRAB

0.45		166 cals

Serves 6

25 g (1 oz) butter or margarine

50 g (2 oz) onion

225 g (8 oz) white crab meat or white and brown mixed

50 g (2 oz) fresh brown breadcrumbs

10 ml (2 tsp) French mustard

150 ml (¼ pint) natural yogurt

45 ml (3 tbsp) single cream or milk

cayenne

salt

about 40 g (1½ oz) Cheddar

lime slices and parsley sprigs, to garnish (optional)

1 Melt the butter in a saucepan. Skin and finely chop the onion and fry it gently in the butter until golden brown.

2 Flake the crab meat, taking care to remove any membranes or shell particles. Mix it into the cooked onions and add the breadcrumbs. Mix well together. Stir in the mustard, yogurt and cream. Sprinkle generously with cayenne, then add salt to taste.

3 Spoon the mixture into 6 individual ramekins or individual soufflé dishes. Grate the cheese thinly over the surface of each dish. Stand the dishes on a baking sheet. Place on the top shelf in the oven and cook at 170°C (325°F) mark 3 for 25–30 minutes, or until really hot. Garnish with lime slices and parsley, if liked.

Menu Suggestion
Serve with triangles of crisp hot granary toast for an informal dinner party starter, or for a tasty lunch or supper snack.

VEGETABLE TARTS

| 1.30 | 🍴 | ✳ | 677 cals |

Makes 4

125 g (5 oz) plain flour

salt and freshly ground pepper

150 g (6 oz) butter or margarine

1 egg yolk

1 small onion, skinned and finely chopped

2 medium courgettes, sliced

a little lightly beaten egg white

142 g (5 oz) full fat soft cheese with herbs and garlic

2 eggs, beaten

20 ml (4 tsp) chopped fresh basil or 10 ml (2 tsp) dried

fresh basil sprigs, to garnish (optional)

1 Make the pastry cases. Sift the flour into a bowl with a pinch of salt. Add 100 g (4 oz) of the butter in pieces and work into the flour with your fingertips.

2 Add the egg yolk and 5–10 ml (1–2 tsp) cold water and work with a palette knife until the dough draws together.

3 Gather the dough into a ball with one hand, then wrap in cling film or foil. Chill in the refrigerator while making the filling.

4 Melt the remaining butter in a heavy-based frying pan, add the onion and fry gently for about 5 minutes until soft and lightly coloured. Add the courgettes and fry over moderate heat for a few minutes, turning them frequently until they are light golden on all sides. Turn into a bowl and leave until cold.

5 Meanwhile, roll out the dough on a lightly floured surface and cut out 4 circles large enough to line 4 individual loose-bottomed 10 cm (4 inch) quiche or tartlet tins.

6 Place the pastry in the tins, prick the bases with a fork, then line with foil and beans. Bake 'blind' in the oven at 190°C (375°F) mark 5 for 10 minutes.

7 Remove the foil and beans, brush the pastry with the egg white and return to the oven for a further 5 minutes.

8 Put the cream cheese mixture in a bowl and beat with a wooden spoon until soft. Add the eggs and beat well to mix, then the courgettes, basil and salt and pepper to taste.

9 Divide the filling equally between the pastry cases, then return to the oven for a further 10–15 minutes, until the filling is set. Leave to stand for at least 15 minutes before serving. Serve warm, garnished with basil sprigs, if liked.

Menu Suggestion
Individual quiches make a most unusual and attractive dinner party starter. They are quite substantial, and need no accompaniment other than a chilled dry white wine such as a French Muscadet.

Served cold, the tarts make excellent cold luncheon or picnic fare, with a selection of crisp, crunchy salads, fresh granary bread or a French stick, and chilled French dry cider.

PROSCIUTTO CON MELONE
(PARMA HAM WITH MELON)

0.20	104 cals

Serves 4

900 g (2 lb) Cantaloupe melon
8 thin slices of Parma ham
freshly ground black pepper

1 Cut the melon in half lengthways. Scoop out the seeds from the centre.

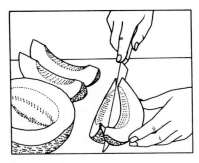

2 Cut each of the melon halves into four even-sized wedge shapes.

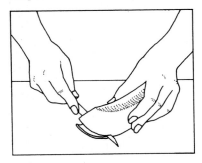

3 With a sharp, pointed knife and using a sawing action, separate the flesh from the skin, keeping it in position on the skin.

4 Cut the flesh across into bite-sized slices, then push each slice in opposite directions.

5 Carefully roll up each of the eight slices of Parma ham. Place two wedges of melon and two rolls of ham on each plate. Grind pepper over the ham before serving.

— VARIATION —

Instead of the melon, use fresh figs in season to make Prosciutto Con Fichi. Only use very fresh, ripe figs in peak condition. In Italy, figs are often served whole and unpeeled, but to help guests who are not used to eating figs as much as the Italians are, it is best to peel them first, then cut them in half. For four people, 8–12 figs is sufficient. Arrange them cut-side up on individual serving plates next to the Parma ham, which may or may not be rolled up, according to how you like it.

BAGNA CAUDA
(HOT ANCHOVY DIP)

| 0.45 | 🍴 | 396 cals |

Serves 6

225 g (8 oz) asparagus, washed, trimmed and freshly cooked

3 globe artichokes, trimmed and freshly cooked

1 small cauliflower

1 large red pepper

1 large green pepper

4 carrots, peeled

6 celery sticks, trimmed

3 courgettes, trimmed

1 bunch radishes

150 ml (¼ pint) olive oil

75 g (3 oz) butter

2 garlic cloves, skinned and finely chopped

two 50 g (2 oz) cans anchovy fillets, drained and finely chopped

1 While the asparagus and artichokes are cooling, prepare the remaining vegetables. Cut the cauliflower into florets, discarding any tough stalks.

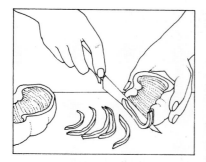

2 Cut the peppers in half lengthways and remove the cores and seeds. Wash the peppers inside and out, dry and cut into strips.

3 Cut the carrots, celery and courgettes into finger-sized sticks. Trim the radishes.

4 Heat the oil and butter in a saucepan until just melted, but not foaming. Add the garlic and cook gently for 2 minutes. Do not allow it to colour.

5 Add the anchovies and cook very gently, stirring all the time, for 10 minutes or until the anchovies dissolve into a paste.

6 To serve. Transfer the dip to an earthenware dish and keep warm over a fondue burner or spirit lamp at the table. Each guest dips the vegetables in the hot anchovy sauce.

TONNO E FAGIOLI
(TUNA FISH WITH BEANS)

2.30*	316 cals

* plus overnight soaking

Serves 4

175 g (6 oz) dried white haricot or
  cannellini beans, soaked in cold
  water overnight

45 ml (3 tbsp) olive oil

15 ml (1 tbsp) wine vinegar

salt and freshly ground pepper

1 small onion, skinned and finely
  sliced

200 g (7 oz) can tuna fish in oil,
  drained and flaked into large
  chunks

chopped fresh parsley, to garnish

1 Drain the beans, rinse under
cold running water, then tip
into a large saucepan and cover
with fresh cold water. Bring to the
boil, then lower the heat and
simmer gently for 1½–2 hours or
until beans are tender. Drain.

2 Whisk together the oil,
vinegar, salt and pepper and
mix with the hot beans. Cool for
15 minutes.

3 Mix in the onion, then the
tuna fish, being careful not to
break it up too much.

4 To serve. Taste and adjust
seasoning, then transfer to a
serving dish. Sprinkle liberally
with chopped fresh parsley just
before serving.

TONNO E FAGIOLI

Both dried white haricot beans
and cannellini are used extensively in Italian cooking—mostly
in salads and soups. Soaking is
essential with dried beans, but if
you forget to soak them overnight, there is an emergency
soaking procedure which works
just as well. Put the beans in a
large saucepan of cold water
(never add salt before cooking
beans as this causes their skins to
toughen) and bring to the boil.
Boil steadily for at least 10
minutes, then remove from the
heat, cover and leave for about 1
hour or until the water has gone
cold. Proceed with the recipe
from step 1.

SMOKED TROUT WITH TOMATOES AND MUSHROOMS.

0.20*	189 cals

* plus 30 minutes to dégorge cucumber

Serves 8 as a starter

700 g (1½ lb) smoked trout
225 g (8 oz) cucumber, skinned
salt and freshly ground pepper
175 g (6 oz) mushrooms, wiped
45 ml (3 tbsp) creamed horseradish
30 ml (2 tbsp) lemon juice
60 ml (4 tbsp) natural yogurt
4 very large Marmande or
   Beefsteak tomatoes, about 350 g
   (12 oz) each
spring onion tops, to garnish

1 Flake the trout flesh, discarding the skin and bones.

2 Finely chop the cucumber, sprinkle with salt and leave for 30 minutes to dégorge. Rinse and drain well, then dry thoroughly with absorbent kitchen paper.

3 Finely chop the mushrooms, combine with the cucumber, horseradish, lemon juice and yogurt. Fold in the trout, then add seasoning to taste.

4 Skin the tomatoes. Pierce each one with a fork in the stalk end and then hold in the flame of a gas hob. Turn the tomato until the skin blisters and bursts, leave until cool enough to handle, then peel off the skin with your fingers.

5 Slice the tomatoes thickly, then sandwich in pairs with the trout mixture.

6 Arrange the tomato 'sandwiches' in a shallow serving dish. Garnish with snipped spring onion tops and chill in the refrigerator until ready to serve.

SMOKED TROUT WITH TOMATOES AND MUSHROOMS

For this recipe, it is important to buy the very large continental-type tomatoes. In the summer months these are widely available, some home-grown as well as the imported types from the Mediterranean. Look for them under the names 'Continental', 'Marmande' and 'Beefsteak' — any of these are suitable, as long as they are not too misshapen or they will not sandwich together. These types of tomatoes are also excellent stuffed.

Snacks and Suppers

PIZZA-IN-THE-PAN

| 0.25 | 1150 cals |

Serves 2

225 g (8 oz) self-raising flour
salt and freshly ground pepper
60 ml (4 tbsp) vegetable oil
60 ml (4 tbsp) water
75 ml (5 tbsp) tomato purée
397 g (14 oz) can tomatoes, drained
  and chopped
175 g (6 oz) Cheddar cheese, grated
chopped fresh herbs
a few black olives

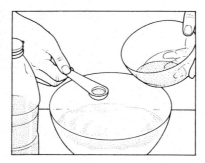

1 Sift the flour and seasoning into a bowl. Make a well in the centre and pour in 30 ml (2 tbsp) of the oil and 60 ml (4 tbsp) of the water. Mix to a soft dough—you will find that it binds together very quickly, although you may need to add a little more water.

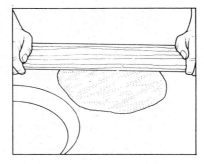

2 Knead the dough lightly on a floured surface, then roll out to a circle that will fit a medium-sized frying pan.

3 Heat half the remaining oil in the pan. Add the circle of dough and fry gently for about 5 minutes until the base is cooked and lightly browned.

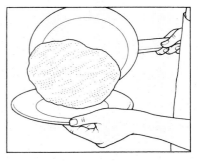

4 Turn the dough out onto a plate and flip it over.

5 Heat the remaining oil in the pan, then slide the dough back into the pan, browned side uppermost. Spread with the tomato purée, then top with the tomatoes and sprinkle over grated cheese, herbs and black olives.

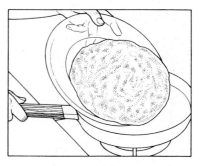

6 Cook for a further 5 minutes until the underside is done, then slide the pan under a preheated grill. Cook for 3–4 minutes until the cheese melts. Serve immediately.

Menu Suggestion
Serve with a mixed salad and an Italian red wine such as Chianti Classico or Valpolicella.

COCOTTE EGGS

0.35	310 cals

Serves 4

25 g (1 oz) butter

1 small onion, skinned and finely chopped

4 rashers of lean back bacon, rinded and finely chopped

100 g (4 oz) button mushrooms, finely chopped

10 ml (2 tsp) tomato purée

10 ml (2 tsp) chopped fresh tarragon or 5 ml (1 tsp) dried tarragon

salt and freshly ground pepper

4 eggs, size 2

120 ml (8 tbsp) double cream

chopped fresh tarragon, to garnish

1 Melt the butter in a small saucepan, add the onion and fry gently until soft. Add the bacon and fry until beginning to change colour, then add the mushrooms and tomato purée. Continue frying for 2–3 minutes until the juices run, stirring constantly.

2 Remove from the heat and stir in the tarragon and seasoning to taste. Divide the mixture equally between 4 cocottes, ramekins or individual soufflé dishes. Make a slight indentation in the centre of each one.

3 Break an egg into each dish, on top of the mushroom and bacon mixture, then slowly pour 30 ml (2 tbsp) cream over each one. Sprinkle with salt and freshly ground pepper to taste.

4 Place the cocottes on a baking tray and bake in the oven at 180°C (350°F) mark 4 for 10–12 minutes until the eggs are set. Serve immediately.

Menu Suggestion
Serve for breakfast, brunch, lunch or supper, with triangles of wholemeal or granary toast and butter.

COCOTTE EGGS

As an alternative to the mushrooms in this recipe, you can use fresh tomatoes. At the end of the summer when they are often overripe, they are best used for cooking rather than in salads, and this baked egg dish is a good way to use them up. Skin them first if you have time as this will make the finished dish more palatable. A quick way to skin a few tomatoes is to pierce one at a time with a fork in the stalk end and then hold in the flame of a gas hob. Turn the tomato until the skin blisters and bursts, leave until cool enough to handle, then peel off the skin with your fingers. To replace the mushrooms, use 4 medium tomatoes, chopped, and substitute basil for the tarragon, if available.

STUFFED BAKED POTATOES

2.00	362 cals

Serves 4

4 medium potatoes, about 250 g (8 oz) each

1 medium onion, skinned

25 g (1 oz) butter or margarine

60 ml (4 tbsp) milk

125 g (4 oz) Cheddar cheese, grated

dash of Worcestershire sauce

salt and freshly ground pepper

snipped fresh chives, to garnish

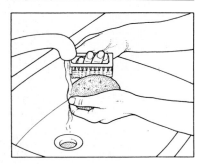

1 Scrub the potatoes with a stiff vegetable brush under cold running water. Pat dry with absorbent kitchen paper and then wrap individually in foil. Bake in the oven at 200°C (400°F) mark 6 for about 1¼–1½ hours, or until just tender. Remove the potatoes from the oven, leaving the oven turned on at the same temperature.

2 Cut the potatoes in half lengthways. Scoop out most of the flesh from the insides, leaving a good rim around the edge of each potato shell. Mash the scooped-out potato in a bowl until free of lumps.

3 Finely chop the onion. Melt the fat in a small saucepan. Add the onion and fry gently until lightly browned. Add the milk and heat gently.

4 Beat this mixture into the mashed potato with half of the grated cheese, the Worcestershire sauce and seasoning to taste.

5 Spoon the potato back into the shells (or pipe with a large, star vegetable nozzle). Sprinkle over the remaining grated cheese.

6 Return to the oven for about 20 minutes, or until golden. Serve immediately, sprinkled with chives.

Menu Suggestion

Serve Stuffed Baked Potatoes on their own for a tasty snack at lunch or supper time. For a more substantial meal, serve with sausages or frankfurters.

——— VARIATIONS ———

Instead of the onion, cheese and Worcestershire sauce, add the following ingredients to the scooped-out mashed potato: **75 g (3 oz) bacon**, roughly chopped and fried, a little **milk**, **salt** and **freshly ground pepper**; or **75 g (3 oz) smoked haddock**, cooked and mashed, **5 ml (1 tsp) chopped fresh parsley**, **5 ml (1 tsp) lemon juice**, a little **milk**, **salt**, **freshly ground pepper** and **grated nutmeg**, or **30–45 ml (2–3 tbsp) cream**, **10 ml (2 tsp) snipped chives**, **salt**.

Pile back into potato skins and serve immediately without returning to the oven.

STUFFED BAKED POTATOES

Baked potatoes, warm and filling, are one of winter's most popular foods—and one of the easiest to cook.

For the best results, buy the varieties recommended for baking. These include Desirée, Kerrs Pink, King Edward, Majestic, Pentland Crown, Pentland Dell and Pentland Ivory. Check before buying that the potatoes are free from disease, mechanical damage and growth shoots, because many people like to eat the skin of jacket-baked potatoes, the most nutritious part. (Potatoes are a rich source of vitamin C, iron, thiamin, riboflavin and nicotinic acid, and the skins also provide dietary fibre.) Also check that the skins are not tinged with green, which is caused by exposure to light and makes the potatoes unpleasant to eat. All potatoes should be stored in the dark to prevent this problem occurring.

MEXICAN BEEF TACOS

| 0.40 | ✳* | 515 cals |

* freeze chilli beef mixture after step 2

Serves 4

30 ml (2 tbsp) vegetable oil

1 onion, skinned and finely chopped

1–2 garlic cloves, skinned and crushed

5–10 ml (1–2 tsp) chilli powder, according to taste

350 g (12 oz) lean minced beef

225 g (8 oz) can tomatoes

15 ml (1 tbsp) tomato purée

2.5 ml ($\frac{1}{2}$ tsp) sugar

salt and freshly ground pepper

283 g (10 oz) can red kidney beans, drained and rinsed

8 taco shells

shredded lettuce and grated Cheddar cheese, to serve

1 Heat the oil in a pan, add the onion, garlic and chilli powder and fry gently until soft. Add the minced beef and fry until browned, stirring and pressing with a wooden spoon to remove any lumps.

2 Stir in the tomatoes with their juice and the tomato purée. Crush the tomatoes well with the spoon, then bring to the boil, stirring. Lower the heat, add the sugar and seasoning to taste, then simmer, uncovered, for 20 minutes until thick and reduced. Stir occasionally during this time to combine the ingredients and prevent them from sticking.

3 Add the kidney beans to the pan and heat through for 5 minutes. Meanwhile, heat the taco shells in the oven according to the instructions on the packet.

4 To serve, divide the meat mixture equally between the taco shells, then top with grated cheese and shredded lettuce. Eat immediately, before the taco shells soften with the heat of the beef.

Menu Suggestion

Crisp taco shells filled with spicy hot beef chilli are perfect for an impromptu snack—teenagers love them. Place warm taco shells on the table with bowls of chilli beef, cheese and lettuce and let everyone make their own. Serve with ice-cold drinks such as cola, root beer or lager.

MEXICAN BEEF TACOS

Take care when adding chilli powder, because strengths vary considerably from one brand to another. Always add the smallest amount specified, then taste before adding more. If you prefer a mild chilli flavour, buy 'chilli seasoning', which is available in small glass bottles at most supermarkets. A blend of chilli powder and other spices, it has less 'fire' than real chilli powder, and can be used in larger amounts.

Mexican taco shells are available in boxes at most large supermarkets. Some packs come with a ready-mixed sauce in a sachet, so make sure it is only the taco shells you are buying.

SAUSAGE BURGERS

0.50	390 cals

Makes 8

450 g (1 lb) pork sausagemeat

125 g (4 oz) fresh white
    breadcrumbs

1 medium onion, skinned and
    finely chopped

60 ml (4 tbsp) chopped fresh
    parsley

1 egg, size 2, beaten

salt and freshly ground pepper

60 ml (4 tbsp) flour

vegetable oil for frying

1 In a bowl or food processor, mix together the sausagemeat, breadcrumbs, onion, parsley, egg and seasoning to taste.

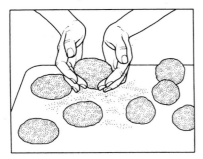

2 Divide the mixture into eight on a floured board. With well-floured hands, shape into rounds about 1 cm (½ inch) thick.

3 Place the burgers on a lightly floured plate and chill in the refrigerator for at least 30 minutes.

4 Heat a little oil in a frying pan, add half of the burgers and fry for 8–10 minutes a side, turning once only. Drain on absorbent kitchen paper and keep hot while frying the remainder.

Menu Suggestion
Serve fresh Sausage Burgers hot in warmed burger baps with a selection of pickles and ketchup. Accompany with a mixed salad of lettuce, tomato and cucumber.

WHOLEWHEAT, APRICOT AND NUT SALAD

0.35*	325–433 cals

* plus overnight soaking and 2 hours chilling

Serves 6–8

225 g (8 oz) wholewheat grain

3 celery sticks, washed and trimmed

125 g (4 oz) dried apricots

100 g (4 oz) Brazil nuts, roughly chopped

50 g (2 oz) unsalted peanuts

60 ml (4 tbsp) olive oil

30 ml (2 tbsp) lemon juice

salt and freshly ground pepper

chopped fresh parsley and cucumber slices, to garnish

1 Soak the wholewheat grain overnight in plenty of cold water. Drain, then tip into a large saucepan of boiling water. Simmer gently for 25 minutes or until the grains have a little bite left.

2 Drain the wholewheat into a colander and rinse under cold running water. Tip into a large serving bowl and set aside.

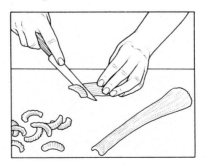

3 Cut the celery into small diagonal pieces with a sharp knife. Stir into the wholewheat.

4 Using kitchen scissors, snip the apricots into small pieces over the wholewheat. Add the nuts and stir well to mix.

5 Mix the oil and lemon juice together with plenty of seasoning, pour over the salad and toss well. Chill in the refrigerator for 2 hours, then toss again and adjust seasoning just before serving.

Menu Suggestion
Serve for a healthy lunch dish with hot granary or wholemeal rolls and a green salad.

WHOLEWHEAT, APRICOT AND NUT SALAD
You can buy the wholewheat grain for this recipe in any good health food shop. Sometimes it is referred to as 'kibbled' wheat, because the grains are cracked in a machine called a 'kibbler', which breaks the grain into little pieces. Do not confuse wholewheat grain with cracked wheat (sometimes also called bulghar or burghul), which is cooked wheat which has been dried and cracked, used extensively in the cooking of the Middle East. Although different, the two kinds of wheat can be used interchangeably in most recipes.

SURPRISE SOUFFLÉ

| 1.15 | 474 cals |

Serves 4

75 g (3 oz) butter
50 g (2 oz) flour
300 ml (½ pint) milk
100 g (4 oz) Gruyère cheese, grated
1.25 ml (¼ tsp) ground mace
salt and freshly ground pepper
5 eggs, separated
225 g (8 oz) button mushrooms, finely sliced

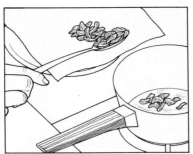

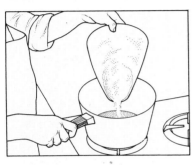

1 Melt 50 g (2 oz) of the butter in a saucepan, sprinkle in the flour and cook for 1–2 minutes, stirring constantly.

2 Remove from the heat and gradually add the milk, beating constantly after each addition. Return to the heat and bring to the boil, stirring, then lower the heat and add the cheese, mace and seasoning to taste. Simmer for about 5 minutes until the cheese melts and the sauce is very thick.

3 Remove from the heat and leave to cool for 5 minutes, then stir in the egg yolks one at a time. Set aside.

4 Melt the remaining butter in a separate pan, add the mushrooms and fry over a high heat for 2 minutes only. Remove from the pan with a slotted spoon; drain on absorbent kitchen paper.

5 Whisk the egg whites until stiff, then fold into the cheese sauce. Spoon three-quarters into a well-buttered 1.5 litre (3 pint) soufflé dish.

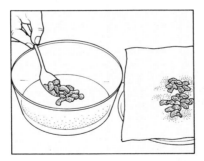

6 Make a well in the centre of the sauce, and spoon in the mushrooms. Cover with the remaining sauce. Bake in the oven at 200°C (400°F) mark 6 for 25–30 minutes until puffed up and golden on top. Serve immediately.

Menu Suggestion
Serve for a supper dish with fresh French bread and a mixed salad tossed in a vinaigrette dressing.

TUNA AND PASTA IN SOURED CREAM

0.25	780 cals

Serves 4

225 g (8 oz) pasta spirals or shells

salt and freshly ground pepper

5 ml (1 tsp) vegetable oil

198 g (7 oz) can tuna, drained

4 eggs, hard-boiled and shelled

25 g (1 oz) butter

150 ml ($\frac{1}{4}$ pint) soured cream

5 ml (1 tsp) anchovy essence

30 ml (2 tbsp) malt vinegar

60 ml (4 tbsp) chopped fresh parsley

1 Cook the pasta in plenty of boiling salted water to which the oil has been added, for about 15 minutes until *al dente* (tender but firm to the bite). Drain well.

2 Meanwhile, flake the tuna fish with 2 forks. Chop the hard-boiled eggs finely.

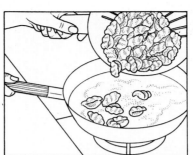

3 Melt the butter in a deep frying pan and toss in the pasta. Stir in the soured cream, anchovy essence and vinegar.

4 Add the tuna and egg to the pan with the parsley. Season well and warm through over low heat, stirring occasionally. Serve immediately.

Menu Suggestion
This rich and filling pasta dish needs a contrasting accompaniment. Serve with a crisp and crunchy green salad of chopped celery, fennel, cucumber and green pepper.

TUNA AND PASTA IN SOURED CREAM

The type of pasta you use for this dish is really a matter of personal taste, although spirals and shells are specified in the ingredients list. As long as the shapes are small *(pasta corta)*, the sauce will cling to them and not slide off—Italians serve short cut pasta with fairly heavy sauces like this one which have chunks of fish or meat in them. Long pasta *(pasta lunga)* such as spaghetti and tagliatelle are best served with smoother sauces. Italian pasta in the shape of shells are called *conchiglie*, and there are many different sizes to choose from. *Farfalle* are shaped like small bow-ties; *fusilli* are spirals, so too are *spirale ricciolo*; *rotelle* are shaped like wheels. There are also many different types of short pasta shaped like macaroni—*penne* are hollow and shaped like quills with angled ends, *rigatoni* have ridges.

Noodles in Walnut Sauce

| 0.20 | 730 cals |

Serves 4

100 g (4 oz) walnut pieces

75 g (3 oz) butter, softened

1 small garlic clove, skinned and
  roughly chopped

30 ml (2 tbsp) flour

300 ml ($\frac{1}{2}$ pint) milk

275 g (10 oz) green tagliatelle

5 ml (1 tsp) vegetable oil

salt and freshly ground pepper

100 g (4 oz) Cheddar cheese,
  grated

freshly grated nutmeg

1 In a blender or food processor, mix together the walnuts, 50 g (2 oz) of the butter and the garlic. Turn into a bowl.

2 Put the remaining 25 g (1 oz) of butter in the blender or food processor. Add the flour and milk and work until evenly mixed.

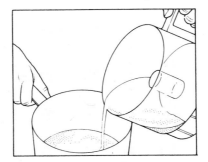

3 Turn the mixture into a saucepan and bring slowly to the boil, stirring. Simmer 6 minutes.

4 Meanwhile, cook the tagliatelle in plenty of boiling salted water, adding the oil to the water (this prevents the pasta from sticking together).

5 For the timing, follow the pack instructions and cook until *al dente* (tender, but firm to the bite). Drain the pasta thoroughly, then return to the pan. Add the nut butter and heat through gently, stirring all the time.

6 Divide the pasta mixture equally between 4 large, individual gratin-type dishes. Add seasoning to the white sauce, then use to coat the pasta.

7 Scatter the grated cheese on top, sprinkle with the nutmeg, then grill for 5–10 minutes until brown and bubbling. Serve immediately.

Menu Suggestion

Serve for a supper dish followed by a tomato and fennel salad dressed with olive oil, lemon juice and chopped fresh basil.

NOODLES IN WALNUT SAUCE

Making velvety smooth sauces is not the easiest of culinary tasks, and most cooks seem to have problems with them at some time or another. Even French chefs have been known to sieve their sauces before serving, to remove lumps! The French method of cooking a roux of butter and flour, then gradually adding milk, requires a certain amount of skill and judgement, whereas the all-in-one method in this recipe is quick and easy to do if you have a blender or food processor—and just about foolproof!

CELERIAC AU GRATIN

1.00	351–527 cals

Serves 4–6

15 ml (1 tbsp) lemon juice

2 heads of celeriac, total weight about 900 g (2 lb)

salt and freshly ground pepper

100 g (4 oz) butter or margarine

150 ml ($\frac{1}{4}$ pint) dry white wine

175 g (6 oz) Gruyère, grated

75 g (3 oz) Parmesan, freshly grated

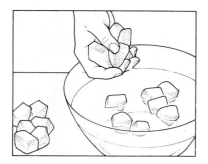

1 Fill a bowl with cold water and add the lemon juice. Peel the celeriac, then cut into chunky pieces. Place the pieces in the bowl of acidulated water as you prepare them, to prevent discoloration.

2 Drain the celeriac, then plunge quickly into a large pan of boiling salted water. Return to the boil and blanch for 10 minutes. Drain thoroughly.

3 Melt the butter in a flame-proof gratin dish. Add the celeriac and turn to coat in the butter. Stir in the wine. Mix together the Gruyère and Parmesan cheeses and sprinkle over the top of the celeriac, with salt and pepper to taste. Bake in the oven at 190°C (375°F) mark 5 for 30 minutes until the celeriac is tender when pierced with a skewer and the topping is golden brown.

Menu Suggestion

Serve for a vegetarian supper dish, with a colourful tomato or red pepper salad, and hot garlic or herb bread.

CELERIAC AU GRATIN

Make the most of celeriac in the winter months; it is a seasonal vegetable which is rarely seen in the shops at other times of year. From the same family as celery, which it resembles in flavour, it is an unusual, quite ugly-looking vegetable, sometimes called "turnip-rooted celery", which is an apt description. Only buy small celeriac, very large specimens tend to be woody and lacking in flavour—and difficult to deal with. This recipe for Celeriac au Gratin has a definite "European" flavour. The French, Swiss and Italians have always used celeriac a lot in their cooking, and on the continent you will come across many different ways of serving it. Steamed or boiled celeriac is usually served as a vegetable accompaniment, simply tossed in melted butter and chopped fresh herbs, or coated in a béchamel or Hollandaise sauce; lightly blanched fingers of celeriac are coated in a vinaigrette dressing while still warm and served as a first course; and grated raw celeriac is served with mayonnaise to make *céléri-rave rémoulade*, a popular French hors d'oeuvre.

The recipe on this page makes a tasty light supper dish, and would make an excellent main course if you are entertaining vegetarians. If you would like to make it more substantial by adding meat, mix 175–225 g (6–8 oz) chopped cooked bacon or ham with the celeriac, before topping with the cheeses.

TURKEY TERRINE

2.00*	✳	311–415 cals

* plus 2 hours cooling and overnight chilling

Serves 6–8

225 g (8 oz) cooked turkey meat

225 g (8 oz) turkey or pig's liver

175 g (6 oz) thinly sliced streaky bacon rashers, rinded

1 medium onion

225 g (8 oz) sausagemeat

1 garlic clove, skinned and crushed

15 ml (1 tbsp) chopped fresh sage or 5 ml (1 tsp) dried

45 ml (3 tbsp) double cream

30 ml (2 tbsp) brandy

1 egg

salt and freshly ground pepper

bay leaf

1 Mince the turkey, liver, 50 g (2 oz) of the bacon and the onion. (Alternatively, work in a food processor.)

2 Put the minced mixture in a bowl. Add the sausagemeat, garlic, sage, cream, brandy, egg and salt and pepper to taste. Mix with a spoon until all the ingredients are evenly combined.

3 Stretch the remaining bacon rashers with the flat side of a blade of a large cook's knife.

4 Use the bacon rashers to line a 1.1 litre (2 pint) terrine or loaf tin, making sure there are no gaps.

5 Spoon the meat mixture into the container and place a bay leaf on top. Cover tightly with foil or a lid, then stand the container in a roasting tin.

6 Pour 3.5 cm (1½ inches) hot water into the roasting tin, then bake in the oven at 170°C (325°F) mark 3 for about 1½ hours. Remove from the water bath and leave to cool for 2 hours. Place heavy weights on top of the terrine and chill in the refrigerator overnight.

7 To serve, turn the terrine out of the container onto a plate and cut into slices.

TURKEY TERRINE

The method of baking a terrine in a roasting tin with hot water, called a *bain marie* or water bath, is essential if the mixture is to cook properly—the hot water distributes the oven heat evenly through the mixture and gives a moist result. Special water baths can be bought at kitchen equipment shops, but an ordinary roasting tin does the job just as well, and can be used in the oven or on top of the cooker according to individual recipe instructions. Always cover the mixture tightly with foil when cooking in a water bath, or the top of the terrine will form an unpleasant hard crust.

*F*ALAFEL
(ISRAELI CHICK PEA PATTIES)

1.40*	186–279 cals

* plus overnight soaking and at least 1 hour chilling

Serves 4–6

225 g (8 oz) chick peas, soaked in cold water overnight

1 medium onion, skinned and roughly chopped

1 garlic clove, skinned and roughly chopped

10 ml (2 tsp) ground cumin

30 ml (2 tbsp) chopped fresh coriander or 5 ml (1 tsp) dried

1.25 ml ($\frac{1}{4}$ tsp) chilli powder

5 ml (1 tsp) salt

plain flour, for coating

1 egg, beaten

vegetable oil, for deep frying

1 Drain the chick peas and rinse well under cold running water. Put in a large saucepan, cover with plenty of fresh cold water and bring slowly to the boil. Skim off any scum with a slotted spoon, then half cover with a lid and simmer for 1 hour, or until the chick peas are tender.

2 Drain the chick peas thoroughly and place in a blender or food processor. Add the onion, garlic, cumin, coriander, chilli powder and salt. Work the mixture until smooth. (Alternatively, work the chick peas, onion and garlic in a mincer or vegetable mill, then mix in the other ingredients.)

3 With floured hands, shape the mixture into 16–18 small flat cakes. Dip them 1 at a time in the beaten egg, then coat them in more flour seasoned with salt and pepper. Chill in the refrigerator for at least 1 hour.

4 Pour enough oil into a deep frying pan to come about 2.5 cm (1 inch) up the sides. Heat until very hot, then fry the falafel in batches for about 3 minutes on each side until golden, turning once. Drain on absorbent kitchen paper while frying the remainder. Serve hot or cold.

Menu Suggestion
Falafel are sold as a snack in Israel, usually eaten stuffed into pockets of pitta bread, with salad.

MEAT LOAF

1.35* ✳	494–659 cals

* plus cooling and overnight chilling
Serves 6–8

900 g (2 lb) boneless leg or shoulder
  of pork, minced

225 g (8 oz) mushrooms, finely
  chopped

225 g (8 oz) streaky bacon, rinded
  and minced

2 medium onions, skinned and
  finely chopped

1 large garlic clove, skinned and
  crushed

125 g (4 oz) fresh breadcrumbs

150 ml ($\frac{1}{4}$ pint) soured cream

45 ml (3 tbsp) dry white wine

5 ml (1 tsp) dried mixed herbs

2.5 ml ($\frac{1}{2}$ tsp) ground allspice

1.25 ml ($\frac{1}{4}$ tsp) grated nutmeg

salt and freshly ground pepper

1 In a large bowl, mix all the
ingredients together until
evenly combined.

2 Pack the mixture into a
1.4 litre ($2\frac{1}{2}$ pint) loaf tin and
cover with foil.

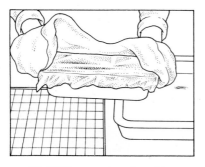

3 Half fill a roasting tin with
water and place the loaf tin
in the water bath. Cook in the
oven at 190°C (375°F) mark 5 for
1 hour.

4 Uncover the tin, increase the
oven temperature to 200°C
(400°F) mark 6 and cook the meat
loaf for a further 30 minutes.

5 Remove the tin from the water
bath and leave to cool for 30
minutes. Cover with foil and place
heavy weights on top. Chill in the
refrigerator overnight.

6 To serve, turn the meat loaf
out of the tin and cut into
slices for serving.

Menu Suggestion
Thickly sliced Meat Loaf is
similar to a pâté or terrine. Serve
as a lunch dish with a potato or
rice salad, and sprigs of
watercress.

SPICY SCOTCH EGGS

0.40*	927 cals

* plus 30 minutes chilling

Makes 4

30 ml (2 tbsp) vegetable oil

1 onion, skinned and very finely
   chopped

10 ml (2 tsp) medium-hot curry
   powder

450 g (1 lb) pork sausagemeat

100 g (4 oz) mature Cheddar
   cheese, finely grated

salt and freshly ground pepper

4 eggs, hard-boiled

plain flour, for coating

1 egg, beaten

100–175 g (4–6 oz) dried
   breadcrumbs

vegetable oil, for deep-frying

1 Heat the 30 ml (2 tbsp) oil in a
small pan, add the onion and
curry powder and fry gently for 5
minutes until soft.

2 Put the sausagemeat and
cheese in a bowl, add the
onion and salt and pepper to taste.
Mix with your hands to combine
the ingredients well together.

3 Divide the mixture into 4
equal portions and flatten out
on a floured board or work surface.

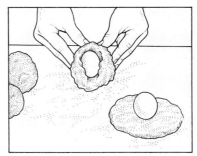

4 Place an egg in the centre of
each piece. With floured
hands, shape and mould the
sausagemeat around the eggs. Coat
lightly with more flour.

5 Brush each Scotch egg with
beaten egg, then roll in the
breadcrumbs until evenly coated.
Chill for 30 minutes.

6 Heat the oil in a deep-fat
fryer to 170°C (325°F). Carefully lower the Scotch eggs into
the oil with a slotted spoon and
deep-fry for 10 minutes, turning
them occasionally until golden
brown on all sides. Drain and cool
on absorbent kitchen paper.

Menu Suggestion
Home-made Scotch eggs are quite
delicious, with far more flavour
than the commercial varieties.
Serve them cut in halves or
quarters with a mixed salad for
lunch, or wrap them individually
in cling film or foil and pack them
for a picnic or packed lunch —
they are easy to eat with the
fingers. Scotch eggs can also be
served hot for a family meal.

MEAT LOAF
The method of cooking meat
loaves, pâtés and terrines in a
roasting tin half filled with water
is called 'au bain-marie' in
French. It is a very simple
method, but an essential one if
the finished meat mixture is to be
moist in texture. If the loaf tin is
placed directly on the oven shelf,
the mixture will dry out and the
top will form a hard, unpleasant
crust. A *bain marie* creates steam
in the oven, which gives a moist
heat. Special tins called water
baths can be bought at kitchen
shops for cooking 'au bain marie',
but an ordinary roasting tin does
the job just as well.

FETA CHEESE PUFFS WITH BASIL

0.25	✳*	274 cals

* freeze after stage 4

Makes 8

225 g (8 oz) Feta cheese, grated

142 g (5 oz) natural yogurt

30 ml (2 tbsp) chopped fresh basil
  or 5 ml (1 tsp) dried

freshly ground pepper

397-g (14-oz) packet frozen puff
  pastry, thawed

beaten egg

fresh basil leaves, to garnish

1 Mix the grated cheese with the yogurt, basil and pepper. (Don't add salt as the cheese adds sufficient.)

2 Roll out the pastry *thinly* and cut out sixteen 10-cm (4-inch) rounds. Fold and reroll the pastry as necessary.

3 Place half the rounds on two baking sheets. Spoon the cheese mixture into the centre of each one.

4 Brush the pastry edges with egg. Cover with remaining rounds, knocking up and pressing the pastry edges together to seal. Make a small slit in the top of each pastry puff.

5 Glaze with beaten egg. Bake in the oven at 220°C (425°F) mark 7 for about 15 minutes or until well browned and crisp. Serve warm, garnished with fresh basil leaves.

FETA CHEESE
Greek Feta cheese can be made from either sheep's or goat's milk. Vacuum packs, which tend to be rather salty, are available at some large supermarkets and good delicatessens, but the best Feta (sold loose in brine) is found in Greek and Middle Eastern stores.

BLUE CHEESE CROQUETTES

1.00*	🍶	✳*	416–623 cals

* plus 2–3 hours chilling; freeze after stage 5

Serves 4–6

100 g (4 oz) celery

75 g (3 oz) butter or margarine

75 g (3 oz) plain flour, plus a little extra for coating

225 ml (8 fl oz) milk

175 g (6 oz) Blue Stilton cheese, grated

30 ml (2 tbsp) snipped fresh chives or 15 ml (1 tbsp) dried

2 eggs

freshly ground pepper

65 g (2½ oz) dried white breadcrumbs

vegetable oil, for deep frying

1 Finely chop the celery; sauté in the butter or margarine for 5–10 minutes until beginning to become brown.

2 Stir in the flour; cook for 1 minute. Off the heat stir in the milk. Bring to the boil, stirring, then cook for 1 minute—the mixture will be *very* thick.

3 Remove from the heat and stir in the grated cheese, chives, one egg and pepper (the cheese will add sufficient salt).

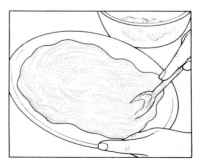

4 Spread the mixture out in a shallow dish, cover with damp greaseproof paper and cool for 30 minutes. Refrigerate for 2–3 hours to firm up.

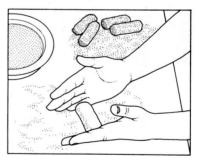

5 Shape the mixture into twelve croquettes then coat lightly in flour, beaten egg and breadcrumbs.

6 Deep fry the croquettes at 180°C (350°F), a few at a time, for 3–4 minutes until golden brown. Serve hot.

KIBBEH
(MIDDLE EASTERN LAMB AND CRACKED WHEAT PATTIES)

| 1.30 | 🍳 🍳 ✳* | 449–748 cals |

* freeze before deep-frying

Serves 4–6

700 g (1½ lb) minced lamb

1 onion, skinned and roughly chopped

225 g (8 oz) cracked wheat (burghul)

salt and freshly ground pepper

vegetable oil, for deep-frying

25 g (1 oz) pine nuts

30 ml (2 tbsp) chopped fresh parsley

1.25 ml (¼ tsp) ground allspice

lemon wedges, to serve

1 Put 550 g (1¼ lb) of the lamb in a blender or food processor with the onion. Work to a smooth, paste-like consistency. (Or work several times through a mincer, fitted with the finest blade.)

2 Put the cracked wheat in a sieve and rinse under cold running water. Turn on to a clean tea towel and wring out as much moisture as possible.

3 Add the wheat to the meat mixture and work again in the machine (or mincer). Add salt and pepper to taste and set aside.

4 Make the filling. Heat 30 ml (2 tbsp) of the oil in a sauce-pan. Add the pine nuts and fry until browned, shaking the pan and tossing the nuts constantly. Remove with a slotted spoon. Add remaining minced lamb to the pan and fry until browned. Cook gently for 15 minutes, stirring frequently. Remove from the heat and stir in the pine nuts, parsley, allspice and salt and pepper.

5 With wet hands, take a small piece of the wheat and meat mixture, about the size of an egg. Hold it in one hand and, with the index finger of the other, make an indent in the centre.

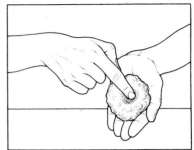

6 Work the kibbeh round in your hand, pressing down with the index finger until the hole in the centre is quite large and the kibbeh is oval or 'torpedo' shaped.

7 Put about 5 ml (1 tsp) of the filling in the centre of the kibbeh, then close the kibbeh around it, wetting the mixture to seal. Roll the kibbeh between wetted palms to ensure a smooth shape, sealing any cracks with water. Repeat with the remaining wheat and meat mixture and the filling until all are used up.

8 Heat the oil in a deep-fat fryer to 190°C (375°F). Deep-fry the kibbeh in batches for about 5 minutes until golden brown on all sides. Drain on absorbent kitchen paper. Serve hot or cold, with lemon for squeezing.

Menu Suggestion
In the Middle East, Kibbeh are traditionally served with a salad. A typical Arabic salad for serving with Kibbeh consists of radishes, green pepper, tomatoes and raw onion. Toss the salad in a dressing made with 60 ml (4 tbsp) tahini paste, the juice of 1 lemon, 150 ml (¼ pint) water, 45 ml (3 tbsp) olive oil and garlic, mint and salt and pepper to taste.

COLD BEEF IN SOURED CREAM

0.30*	318 cals

* plus 2–3 hours chilling

Serves 6

1 large onion, skinned

350 g (12 oz) button mushrooms

700 g (1½ lb) lean rump steak in a thin slice

45 ml (3 tbsp) vegetable oil

salt and freshly ground pepper

7.5 ml (1½ tsp) Dijon mustard

7.5 ml (1½ tsp) chopped fresh thyme or 5 ml (1 tsp) dried

1 large green eating apple

284 ml (10 fl oz) soured cream

15 ml (1 tbsp) lemon juice

crisp lettuce and freshly toasted French bread, to serve

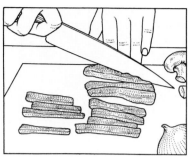

1 Using a sharp knife, finely chop the onion and finely slice the mushrooms. Slice the rump steak into thin strips.

2 Heat the oil in a large frying pan. Quickly brown the steak in a shallow layer, turning occasionally. Don't crowd the pan; cook the meat in two batches if necessary. The beef should remain pink in the centre.

3 Transfer the meat to a bowl using a slotted spoon. Season with salt and pepper.

4 Reheat the fat remaining in the pan. Fry the onion for 5 minutes until golden brown. Add the mushrooms, mustard and thyme. Cook over high heat for 1 minute. Add to beef; allow to cool; refrigerate for 2–3 hours.

5 Quarter and core the apple; slice thinly. Combine with the soured cream and lemon juice.

6 Line a shallow dish with lettuce. Combine the beef and apple mixtures and season. Pile into the centre of the lettuce. Serve with toasted French bread.

SMOKED FISH TIMBALE

0.40*		292 cals

* plus 2–3 hours chilling

Serves 6

350 g (12 oz) long grain rice
15 ml (1 tbsp) ground turmeric
7.5 ml (1½ tsp) salt
350 g (12 oz) smoked haddock or cod fillet
1 small bunch spring onions, washed
2 eggs, hard boiled and shelled
salt and freshly ground pepper
watercress sprigs and fresh prawns, to garnish

1 Cook the rice with the turmeric and salt in a saucepan of water for 10–15 minutes. Drain well and cool.

2 Poach the fish in a little water to just cover for 12–15 minutes. Drain. Flake the fish.

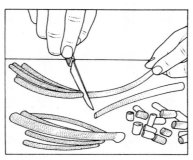

3 Trim the spring onions, then roughly chop them with the hard-boiled eggs, mix with the cold rice and fish, seasoning well.

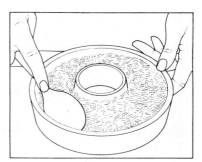

4 Spoon the mixture into an oiled 1.1-litre (2-pint) ring mould. Press down well, cover and chill for 2–3 hours.

5 To serve, unmould the fish ring on to a plate, and garnish with watercress sprigs and prawns.

109

HERBY BRIE QUICHE

1.25	✳	473–709 cals

Serves 4–6

150 g (5 oz) plain flour
5 ml (1 tsp) dried mixed herbs
salt
50 g (2 oz) butter
25 g (1 oz) lard
1 egg yolk
a little beaten egg white
225 g (8 oz) ripe Brie
150 ml (5 fl oz) double cream
3 eggs, lightly beaten
30 ml (2 tbsp) chopped fresh mixed herbs (e.g. thyme, marjoram, parsley, chives)
freshly ground pepper

1 Make the pastry. Sift the flour into a bowl with the herbs and a pinch of salt. Add the butter and lard in small pieces and cut into the flour with a knife.

2 Rub the fat into the flour until the mixture resembles fine breadcrumbs, then stir in the egg yolk. Gather the mixture into a ball of dough, then knead lightly until smooth.

3 Roll out on a floured surface. Use to line a 20-cm (8-inch) plain flan ring set on a baking sheet. Refrigerate for 20 minutes.

4 Prick the base of the dough lightly with a fork, then line with foil and weight down with baking beans. Bake blind in the oven at 200°C (400°F) mark 6 for 10 minutes.

5 Remove the foil and the beans, brush the inside of the pastry case with the beaten egg white, then return to the oven and bake for a further 5 minutes.

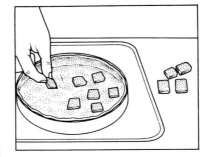

6 Remove the rind from the cheese, cut into squares and place in the base of the pastry case. Soften the cheese with a fork and gradually work in the cream to make a smooth mixture. Whisk in the beaten eggs, then the herbs and salt and pepper to taste.

7 Pour the filling into the pastry case. Bake in the oven at 180°C (350°F) mark 4 for 30 minutes until the filling is just set and the rind from the cheese has formed a golden crust on top. Leave to stand at room temperature for 15 minutes before serving.

BRIE CHEESE

This soft, creamy cheese originated in the province of La Brie in Ile de France, but is now made in factories in other countries besides France—Germany and Denmark, for example, have thriving Brie industries.

Brie is much esteemed by the French, who have called it *roi de fromages*—'the king of cheeses'—since the year 1815 when it was the winner of an international cheese competition in Vienna.

Genuine French Bries often bear the name of their exact place of origin, but this practice is dying out and most simply state the country where they were made. When buying fresh Brie cheese, it is best to buy it freshly cut from a large flat round or wheel at a specialist cheese shop or delicatessen—this is the only way to ensure the cheese is in perfect condition. A ripened cow's milk cheese, a perfect Brie should have a soft, downy rind and a creamy, supple paste. Avoid cheese which has a hard rind or which is either strong-smelling and runny in the centre, or which has a chalky line running through it.

Ripe Brie does not keep well and should be used on the day of purchase. If you need to store it for a few hours, wrap it loosely in foil and place in the least cold part of the refrigerator. Allow to come to room temperature (unwrapped) for 1 hour before required.

SMOKED SALMON QUICHE

1.00*	✳*	336–420 cals

* plus 30 minutes chilling; freeze
for 1 month only

Serves 8–10

225 g (8 oz) plain flour

salt and freshly ground pepper

115 g (4 oz) butter or margarine

1 egg yolk

10 ml (2 tsp) lemon juice

about 30 ml (2 tbsp) cold water

175 g (6 oz) full-fat soft cheese

300 ml (½ pint) single or double
    cream

3 eggs

175 g (6 oz) smoked salmon pieces

finely grated rind of 1 lemon

5 ml (1 tsp) paprika

1 Sift the flour and a pinch of
salt together into a bowl. Cut
the butter into small pieces and
add to the flour.

2 Lightly rub in the butter with
your fingertips until the
mixture resembles fine
breadcrumbs.

3 Add the egg yolk and half of
the lemon juice, then add
enough water to bind the mixture
together in large lumps.

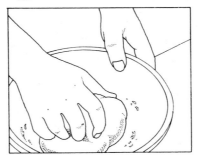

4 With 1 hand, collect the
mixture together to form a
ball. Knead lightly for a few
seconds to give a firm, smooth
dough. Do not overhandle.

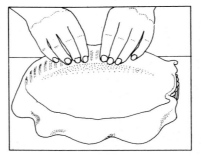

5 Roll out the dough on a
floured surface and use to line
a 25.5 cm (10 inch) loose-bottomed
metal flan tin. Chill in the
refrigerator for 30 minutes.

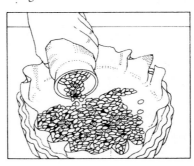

6 Prick the pastry base and then
line with foil and fill with
baking beans. Bake blind on a
preheated baking sheet in the oven
at 200°C (400°F) mark 6 for 10
minutes. Remove the foil and
beans and return to the oven for a
further 5 minutes.

7 Prepare the filling. Put the
cheese in a bowl and gradually
whisk in the cream. When well
mixed and smooth, add the eggs
and beat well to mix.

8 Add the salmon, grated lemon
rind and remaining lemon
juice. Season with a little salt and
plenty of pepper, then add half of
the paprika and beat well to mix.

9 Pour the filling into the baked
flan case and bake in the oven
at 190°C (375°F) mark 5 for 25–30
minutes until set. Sprinkle with
the remaining paprika while very
hot. Serve warm or cold.

WATERCRESS AND RICOTTA QUICHE

| 1.00* | ✳ | 402–536 cals |

* plus 30 minutes chilling

Serves 6–8

pastry made with 225 g (8 oz) flour (see left)

50 g (2 oz) butter or margarine

1 bunch of spring onions, trimmed and finely chopped

2 bunches of watercress

100 g (4 oz) Ricotta or curd cheese

300 ml ($\frac{1}{2}$ pint) single or double cream (or whipping)

3 eggs, beaten

2.5 ml ($\frac{1}{2}$ tsp) grated nutmeg

salt and freshly ground pepper

1 Line a 25.5 cm (10 inch) loose-bottomed metal flan tin with the pastry. Bake blind on a pre-heated baking sheet (see left).

2 Prepare the filling. Melt the butter in a saucepan, add the spring onions and fry gently for about 5 minutes until softened. Add the watercress and fry for a few minutes more, stirring frequently.

3 Transfer the contents of the pan to a blender or food processor. Add the next 4 ingredients with salt and pepper to taste and work until smooth and evenly blended.

4 Pour the filling into the baked flan case and bake in the oven at 190°C (375°F) mark 5 for 25–30 minutes until set. Serve warm or leave until cold.

COURGETTE QUICHE

2.00*	✳	732 cals

* includes 45 minutes chilling and 15 minutes standing time

Serves 4

175 g (6 oz) plain flour

salt

125 g (4 oz) butter or margarine

125 g (4 oz) grated Cheddar cheese

1 egg yolk, beaten

350 g (12 oz) courgettes

3 eggs

150 ml (5 fl oz) double cream

10 ml (2 tsp) chopped fresh basil

finely grated rind of 1 lime (optional)

freshly ground pepper

a little egg white

1 Make the pastry. Sift the flour into a bowl with a pinch of salt. Add the butter in pieces and rub in thoroughly with the finger-tips until the mixture resembles fine breadcrumbs.

2 Stir in the cheese, then the egg yolk. Gather the mixture together with your fingers to make a smooth ball of dough. Wrap and chill the dough in the refrigerator for about 30 minutes.

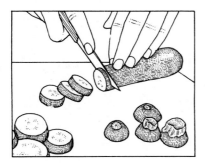

3 Meanwhile, prepare the filling. Trim the ends off the courgettes, then cut the courgettes into 2-cm (¾-inch) chunks.

4 Plunge the courgette pieces into boiling salted water, bring back to the boil, then simmer for 3 minutes. Drain and set aside.

5 Put the eggs in a jug and beat lightly together with the cream. Stir in the basil, lime rind if using, and season to taste. Set aside.

6 Roll out the chilled dough on a floured surface and use to line a loose-bottomed 23-cm (9-inch) flan tin. Refrigerate for 15 minutes.

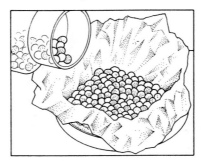

7 Prick the base of the dough with a fork, then line with foil and baking beans. Stand the tin on a preheated baking sheet and bake blind in the oven at 200°C (400°F) mark 6 for 10 minutes.

8 Remove the foil and beans and brush the inside of the pastry case with the egg white to seal. Return to the oven for 5 minutes.

9 Stand the courgette chunks upright in pastry case; slowly pour in egg and cream mixture. Return to oven for 20 minutes.

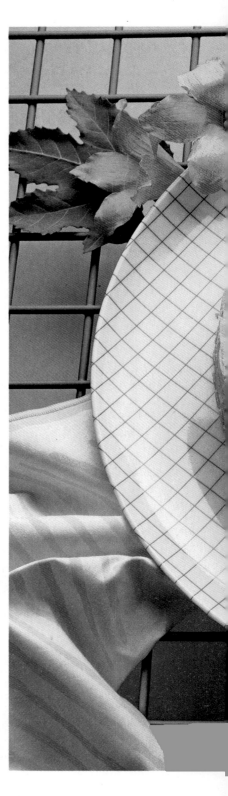

PÂTÉ DE CAMPAGNE WITH BLACK OLIVES

2.20*	475 cals

* plus 2–3 hours chilling and 30 minutes standing time; prepare a day ahead

Serves 8

275 g (10 oz) streaky bacon
75 g (3 oz) black olives
450 g (1 lb) belly pork
275 g (10 oz) pie veal
175 g (6 oz) lamb's liver
2 onions, skinned
1 garlic clove, skinned and crushed
7.5 ml (1½ tsp) salt
freshly ground pepper
5 ml (1 tsp) dried rubbed sage
30 ml (2 tbsp) olive oil
15 ml (1 tbsp) lemon juice
30 ml (2 tbsp) brandy
bay leaves or parsley and black olives, to garnish

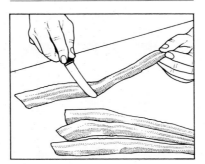

1 Using a sharp knife, cut the rind off the streaky bacon. Stretch the rashers with the back of the knife.

2 Halve, stone and roughly chop the olives. Then pass the belly pork, veal, liver and onions twice through the finest blades of a mincer or food processor. Add the remaining ingredients, except the bacon: mix well.

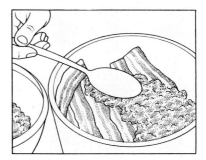

3 Layer the bacon and minced ingredients in a 1.1-litre (2-pint) terrine, topping with the streaky bacon rashers.

4 Cover tightly with foil and lid, if any, and place in a roasting tin, half filled with boiling water. Cook in the oven at 170°C (325°F) mark 3 for about 2 hours until the pâté is firm.

5 Remove the lid and foil. Pour off juices and reserve in the refrigerator. Weight down the pâté and refrigerate overnight.

6 Skim the fat off the jellied juices. Gently warm the juices. Garnish with herbs and black olives, then spoon over the juices. Refrigerate for 2–3 hours to set. Leave to stand at room temperature for 30 minutes.

TURKEY ROQUEFORT SALAD

0.15* 375 cals

* plus 30 minutes chilling

Serves 4

150 ml (¼ pint) soured cream

100 g (4 oz) Roquefort or any other
  blue cheese, crumbled

salt and freshly ground pepper

450 g (1 lb) cold cooked turkey,
  skinned and cut into pieces

lettuce or endive leaves, washed
  and trimmed

snipped chives, to garnish

1 Mix the soured cream and
Roquefort together to make a
dressing. Season to taste. Add the
turkey and coat well in it. Cover
and chill in the refrigerator for 30
minutes.

2 To serve, arrange the lettuce
or endive leaves in a serving
bowl. Spoon the turkey mixture in
the centre and sprinkle with
chives. Serve chilled.

Menu Suggestion
Serve for a summer luncheon with
fresh French bread or rolls and a
bottle of dry sparkling white wine.

HAM AND CHEESE SALAD WITH AVOCADO

0.15	502 cals

Serves 4

2 ripe avocados

60 ml (4 tbsp) natural yogurt

1 garlic clove, skinned and crushed

a few drops of Tabasco sauce

salt and freshly ground pepper

225 g (8 oz) lean cooked ham, cubed

225 g (8 oz) Emmenthal or Gruyère cheese, cubed

1 red pepper, cored, seeded and diced

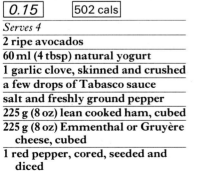

1 Halve the avocados and remove the stones, then peel and mash the flesh. Mix quickly with the yogurt, garlic and Tabasco, seasoning to taste.

2 Fold the ham, cheese and red pepper (reserving some pepper to garnish) into this dressing and pile into a salad bowl. Serve immediately, or the avocado flesh may discolour the dressing. Sprinkle with the reserved red pepper.

Menu Suggestion
This salad is incredibly quick to prepare. Serve it for a healthy lunch, with granary bread rolls.

119

RED FLANNEL HASH

0.45	380 cals

Serves 4

450 g (1 lb) potatoes, scrubbed

salt and freshly ground pepper

225 g (8 oz) salt beef or corned beef, chopped

1 medium onion, skinned and finely chopped

5 ml (1 tsp) garlic salt

225 g (8 oz) cooked beetroot, diced

30 ml (2 tbsp) chopped fresh parsley

50 g (2 oz) beef dripping or lard

1 Cook the potatoes in their skins in lightly salted boiling water for about 20 minutes or until tender when pierced with a fork.

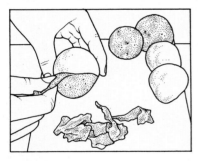

2 Drain the potatoes, leave until cool enough to handle, then peel off the skins with your fingers. Dice the flesh.

3 Put the diced potatoes into a large bowl, add the beef, onion, garlic salt, beetroot and parsley and toss to combine. Add pepper to taste.

4 Heat the dripping or lard in a heavy-based skillet or frying pan until smoking hot. Add the hash mixture and spread evenly with a fish slice or spatula.

5 Lower the heat to moderate and cook the hash, uncovered, for 10–15 minutes. Break up and turn frequently with the slice or spatula, so that the hash becomes evenly browned. Serve hot.

Menu Suggestion

Red Flannel Hash is a traditional dish from New England. Serve it American-style, topped with fried or poached eggs, for a quick evening meal or snack.

SIZZLING STEAK SANDWICHES

0.15	605 cals

Serves 2

2 'flash-fry' steaks, about 75 g (3 oz) each

15 ml (1 tbsp) vegetable oil

salt and freshly ground pepper

4 slices of granary or wholemeal bread, from a large loaf

butter or margarine, for spreading

30 ml (2 tbsp) mayonnaise

about 4 small lettuce leaves, shredded

1 tomato, skinned and sliced

10 ml (2 tsp) Dijon-style mustard

4 Cut each sandwich in half with a serrated knife to make 2 triangles and place on individual plates. Serve immediately.

Menu Suggestion

Steak sandwiches make a protein-packed hot snack at any time of day; they make an especially good quick lunch with glasses of beer, lager or cider.

1 Brush the steaks on one side with half of the oil and sprinkle with pepper to taste. Grill under a preheated hot grill for 3 minutes, then turn them over, brush with the remaining oil, sprinkle with more pepper and grill for a further 3 minutes, or until done to your liking.

2 Meanwhile, toast the bread on both sides, removing the crusts if wished. Spread one side of each slice with butter, then with the mayonnaise. Top 2 slices of toast with the shredded lettuce and sliced tomato and sprinkle with salt and pepper to taste.

3 Place the steaks on top of the salad and spread evenly with the mustard. Cover with the remaining 2 slices of toast.

KEBABS WITH CUMIN

0.30*	*****	280 cals

* plus overnight chilling; freeze after shaping in step 3

Serves 4

350 g (12 oz) finely minced veal or beef

finely grated rind of 1 small lemon

15 ml (1 tbsp) lemon juice

1 garlic clove, skinned and crushed

5 ml (1 tsp) ground cumin

2.5 ml ($\frac{1}{2}$ tsp) salt

2.5 ml ($\frac{1}{2}$ tsp) freshly ground pepper

1 small onion, skinned

vegetable oil, for grilling

lemon wedges, to serve

1 Put the minced meat in a bowl with the lemon rind and juice, the garlic, cumin and salt and pepper. Mix well together, preferably by hand.

2 Grate in the onion and mix again. (The longer the mixture is stirred, the drier it becomes and the easier it is to handle.) Cover the bowl and chill in the refrigerator, preferably overnight.

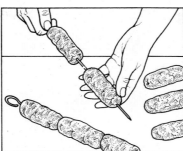

3 Divide the mixture into 12 pieces and form into small sausage shapes. Chill again if possible, then thread on to 4 oiled kebab skewers.

4 Place on a baking sheet. Brush with oil and grill evenly for 10–12 minutes, turning frequently until browned. Serve hot, with lemon wedges.

Menu Suggestion

Serve on a bed of rice or pilaf, or serve in pockets of warm pitta bread with salad.

FRIKADELLER *(DANISH MEAT PATTIES)*

0.30	243 cals

Serves 6

1 egg

300 ml ($\frac{1}{2}$ pint) milk

350 g (12 oz) minced veal

100 g (4 oz) minced pork

1 small onion, skinned and finely chopped

100 g (4 oz) plain flour

15 ml (1 tbsp) chopped fresh thyme or 5 ml ($\frac{1}{2}$ tsp) dried

2.5 ml ($\frac{1}{2}$ tsp) grated nutmeg

salt and freshly ground pepper

45 ml (3 tbsp) vegetable oil

1 Break the egg into a small bowl, add the milk and beat lightly with a fork.

2 Put the minced veal and pork in a separate bowl. Add the onion, flour, thyme, nutmeg and salt and pepper to taste. Mix well together with a wooden spoon.

3 Gradually stir the egg and milk into the meat mixture, then beat well until smooth.

4 Heat the oil in a heavy-based frying pan. Fry heaped table-spoonfuls of the mixture for 5 minutes on each side, or until brown.

5 Remove with a slotted spoon and drain on absorbent kitchen paper. Keep hot while cooking the remainder.

Menu Suggestion

Frikadeller are traditionally served with boiled potatoes.

123

LAMB AND PEPPER KEBABS

1.00*	✳*	404 cals

* plus 4 hours or overnight marinating; freeze in the marinade

Serves 4

700 g (1½ lb) lamb fillet, trimmed of fat

100 ml (4 fl oz) dry white wine

100 ml (4 fl oz) corn oil

50 ml (2 fl oz) lemon juice

2 celery sticks, trimmed and very finely chopped

1 small onion, skinned and grated

2 garlic cloves, skinned and crushed

1 large tomato, skinned and finely chopped

20 ml (4 tsp) chopped fresh thyme or 10 ml (2 tsp) dried thyme

salt and freshly ground pepper

1 medium red pepper

1 medium green pepper

few bay leaves

1 Cut the lamb into cubes and place in a bowl. In a jug, whisk together the wine, oil, lemon juice, celery, onion, garlic, tomato, thyme and salt and freshly ground pepper to taste.

2 Pour the marinade over the lamb and turn the meat until well coated. Cover the bowl and marinate in the refrigerator for 4 hours, preferably overnight.

3 When ready to cook, cut the tops off the peppers and remove the cores and seeds. Cut the flesh into squares.

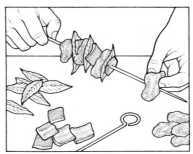

4 Remove the meat from the marinade (reserving the marinade) and thread on to 8 oiled kebab skewers, alternating with the squares of pepper and bay leaves.

5 Cook over charcoal or under a preheated moderate grill for 20–25 minutes until the lamb is tender. Turn the skewers frequently during cooking and brush with the reserved marinade. Serve hot.

Menu Suggestion

For a really quick 'help-yourself' type of meal, serve these kebabs in pockets of hot pitta bread, and accompany with bowls of shredded lettuce or cabbage, sliced tomato and cucumber.

LAMB AND PEPPER KEBABS

Lamb fillet is from the neck of the animal. It is an excellent cut for cutting into cubes for kebabs, casseroles and curries, because it is tender without being dry. Leg of lamb can be boned and cubed, but it is such a lean cut that it tends to dry out on cooking. Shoulder of lamb is also sometimes boned and cubed, but this tends to be more fatty and sinewy. Many large supermarkets sell lamb fillet, but if you are buying it from a butcher, you may have to order in advance.

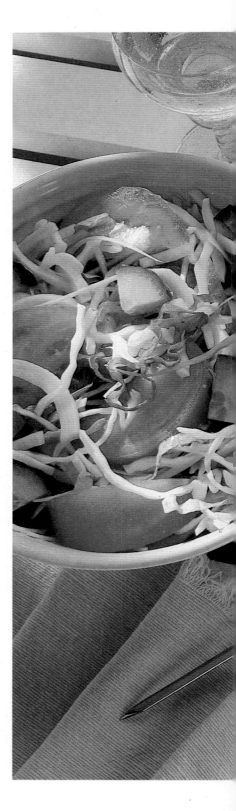

TORTILLA ESPAGNOLA
(SPANISH OMELETTE)

1.00		376 cals

Serves 4

500 ml (17½ fl oz) vegetable or olive oil, for frying

150 g (5 oz) Spanish onion, skinned and thinly sliced

salt and freshly ground pepper

4 medium potatoes, about 500 g (1 lb) total weight, peeled

4 eggs, size 2

1 Heat 60 ml (4 tbsp) of the oil in a large, heavy-based frying pan or omelette pan. Add the sliced onion and a pinch of salt and fry gently, stirring frequently for 10–15 minutes until soft and a light golden brown. Remove with a slotted spoon and drain on absorbent kitchen paper.

2 Cut the potatoes into small wedges. Dry well with a clean tea-towel. Pour the remaining oil into a deep-fat frier and heat to 190°C (375°F). Fry the potatoes in batches for 5 minutes in the hot oil, covering the pan so that they become soft. Remove with a slotted spoon, place on absorbent kitchen paper, sprinkle with salt and leave to drain.

3 Beat the eggs lightly in a large bowl with salt and pepper to taste. Stir in the onion and potatoes.

4 Reheat the oil remaining in the frying pan until smoking. Pour all but 30 ml (2 tbsp) of the egg and potato mixture into the frying pan. Turn the heat down to low and let the mixture run to the sides. Cook for 3–5 minutes until the underneath is just set.

5 Turn the omelette out upside down on to a plate. Heat 15 ml (1 tbsp) of the deep-frying oil in the frying pan.

6 Pour the reserved egg mixture into the pan and tip and tilt the pan so that the egg covers the base and forms a protective layer on which to finish cooking the omelette.

7 Immediately slide in the omelette, set side uppermost. Make the edges neat with a palette knife or spatula and fry for 3–5 minutes until set underneath. Slide on to a serving plate and cut into wedges to serve.

Menu Suggestion
Tortilla Espagnola can be served hot or cold as a main course with a tomato or green salad. It is also delicious cold as an appetiser with drinks before a meal, in which case it should be sliced into thin fingers.

STUFFED AUBERGINES

| 1.30 | 524 cals |

Serves 4

2 medium aubergines

salt and freshly ground pepper

75 ml (5 tbsp) olive oil

1 medium onion, skinned and finely chopped

1–2 garlic cloves, skinned and crushed

1 red or green pepper, cored, seeded and finely diced

175 g (6 oz) button mushrooms, wiped and finely chopped

4 ripe tomatoes, skinned and finely chopped

15 ml (1 tbsp) tomato purée

100 g (4 oz) long grain rice

50 g (2 oz) chopped mixed nuts

30 ml (2 tbsp) chopped fresh parsley

100 g (4 oz) Cheddar cheese, grated

75 g (3 oz) fresh wholemeal breadcrumbs

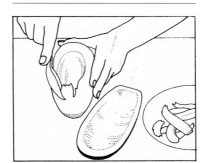

1 Slice the aubergines in half lengthways. Scoop out and reserve the flesh, leaving a narrow margin inside the skin so that the aubergines will hold their shape.

2 Sprinkle the insides of the aubergine shells with salt and stand upside down to drain for 30 minutes.

3 Dice the scooped-out aubergine flesh, then place in a colander, sprinkling each layer with salt. Cover with a plate, place heavy weights on top and leave to dégorge for 30 minutes.

4 Meanwhile, heat 60 ml (4 tbsp) of the oil in a heavy-based saucepan. Add the onion and garlic; fry gently for 5 minutes until soft. Add the diced pepper to the pan and fry gently for 5 minutes.

5 Rinse the diced aubergine under cold running water, then pat dry with absorbent kitchen paper. Add to the pan with the mushrooms, tomatoes and tomato purée. Simmer for about 5 minutes, then add the rice, nuts, parsley and salt and pepper.

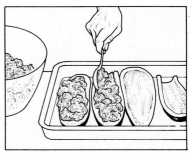

6 Rinse the aubergine cases and pat dry with absorbent kitchen paper. Brush a baking dish with the remaining oil, then stand the aubergine cases in the dish. Fill with the stuffing mixture.

7 Mix the grated cheese and breadcrumbs together, then sprinkle evenly over the top of the aubergines. Bake uncovered in the oven at 180°C (350°F) mark 4 for 45 minutes. Serve hot.

Menu Suggestion
Aubergines stuffed with rice and vegetables make a most nutritious main course dish for a family supper or an informal party.

SWISS STUFFED POTATOES

1.30	346 cals

Serves 4

4 medium baking potatoes

50 g (2 oz) butter or margarine

1 small onion, skinned and finely chopped

450 g (1 lb) fresh spinach, cooked, drained and chopped, or 225 g (8 oz) frozen chopped spinach

100 g (4 oz) full fat soft cheese

1.25 ml ($\frac{1}{4}$ tsp) freshly grated nutmeg

salt and freshly ground pepper

50 g (2 oz) Gruyère or Emmental cheese, grated

pinch of paprika or cayenne

1 Scrub the potatoes under cold running water, then pat dry with absorbent kitchen paper.

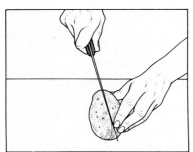

2 With a sharp, pointed knife, score a line in the skin around the middle of each potato.

3 Place the potatoes directly on the oven shelf and bake at 200°C (400°F) mark 6 for 1$\frac{1}{4}$ hours or until tender.

4 About 15 minutes before the end of the cooking time, melt the butter in a heavy-based saucepan, add the onion and fry gently for about 5 minutes until soft and lightly coloured. Add the fresh spinach and cook gently for 2–3 minutes, stirring frequently. (If using frozen spinach, cook for 7–10 minutes until thawed.) Remove from the heat.

5 When the potatoes are cooked, slice in half lengthways. Scoop out the flesh into a bowl and add the spinach mixture, the soft cheese, nutmeg and salt and pepper to taste. Mix well.

6 Spoon the mixture into the potato shells, mounding it up in the centre. Stand the stuffed potatoes on a baking sheet. Sprinkle over the cheese and finally the paprika or cayenne. Return to the oven for 10–15 minutes, until the cheese topping is bubbling and golden. Serve hot.

MEXICAN BAKED POTATOES

| 1.25 | 367 cals. |

Serves 4

4 medium baking potatoes

30 ml (2 tbsp) vegetable oil

1 medium onion, skinned and finely chopped

1 garlic clove, skinned and crushed

397 g (14 oz) can tomatoes

10 ml (2 tsp) tomato purée

2.5 ml ($\frac{1}{2}$ tsp) chilli powder

pinch of granulated sugar

salt and freshly ground pepper

432 g (15.25 oz) can red kidney beans, drained

30 ml (2 tbsp) chopped fresh parsley

50 g (2 oz) mature or farmhouse Cheddar cheese, coarsely grated

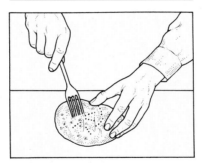

1 Scrub the potatoes under cold running water, then pat dry. Brush with a little vegetable oil, prick all over with a skewer or fork. Bake at 200°C (400°F) mark 6 for 1$\frac{1}{4}$ hours or until tender.

2 Meanwhile, make the stuffing. Heat the remaining oil in a saucepan, add the onion and garlic and fry gently until soft.

3 Add tomatoes with their juice and stir to break up with a wooden spoon. Add the tomato purée, chilli powder, sugar and salt and pepper to taste and bring to the boil, stirring. Simmer, uncovered, for about 20 minutes, stirring occasionally. Add beans and parsley and heat through.

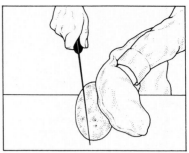

4 When the potatoes are cooked, slice off the top third of each one and reserve for lids. Scoop out some of the potato from the bottom third of each one and add to the tomato sauce.

5 Place 1 potato on each serving plate and spoon the chilli bean mixture into each one, letting it spill out on to the plate. Sprinkle grated cheese on top, then replace the lids at an angle. Serve immediately.

Menu Suggestion
This vegetarian dish is hot, spicy and substantial. Serve for a hearty supper, accompanied by a crisp green salad and glasses of chilled beer or lager.

JACKET BAKED POTATOES

The best potatoes to use for baking are Maris Piper, Desirée and Pentland Squire, although King Edward and Pentland Crown are almost as good. Slightly different methods of baking are used in these 2 recipes. Scoring a line around the middle before baking, as in Swiss Stuffed Potatoes (facing page), makes them easier to cut for stuffing; brushing them with oil, as in Mexican Baked Potatoes (above), gives a crisper skin.

131

QUICK CHICKEN AND MUSSEL PAELLA

0.50	520–780 cals

Serves 4–6

60 ml (4 tbsp) olive oil

about 450 g (1 lb) boneless chicken meat, skinned and cut into bite-sized cubes

1 onion, skinned and chopped

2 garlic cloves, skinned and crushed

1 large red pepper, cored, seeded and sliced into thin strips

3 tomatoes, skinned and chopped

400 g (14 oz) Valencia or risotto rice

1.2 litres ($2\frac{1}{4}$ pints) boiling chicken stock

5 ml (1 tsp) paprika

2.5 ml ($\frac{1}{2}$ tsp) saffron powder

salt and freshly ground pepper

two 150 g (5 oz) jars mussels, drained

lemon wedges, peeled prawns and fresh mussels (optional), to serve

1 Heat the oil in a large, deep frying pan, add the cubes of chicken and fry over moderate heat until golden brown on all sides. Remove from the pan with a slotted spoon and set aside.

2 Add the onion, garlic and red pepper to the pan and fry gently for 5 minutes until softened. Add the tomatoes and fry for a few more minutes until the juices run, then add the rice and stir to combine with the oil and vegetables.

3 Pour in 1 litre ($1\frac{3}{4}$ pints) of the boiling stock (it will bubble furiously), then add half the paprika, the saffron powder and seasoning to taste. Stir well, lower the heat and add the chicken.

4 Simmer, uncovered, for 30 minutes until the chicken is cooked through, stirring frequently during this time to prevent the rice from sticking. When the mixture becomes dry, stir in a few tablespoons of boiling stock. Repeat as often as necessary to keep the paella moist until the end of the cooking time.

5 To serve, fold in the mussels and heat through. Taste and adjust seasoning, then garnish with lemon wedges, mussels in their shells and a sprinkling of the remaining paprika.

Menu Suggestion
Serve for a substantial supper dish with fresh crusty bread and a mixed green salad.

QUICK CHICKEN AND MUSSEL PAELLA

Spain's most famous dish, paella, gets its name from the pan in which it is traditionally cooked — *paellera*. The pan is usually made of a heavy metal such as cast iron, with sloping sides and two flat handles on either side. The *paellera* is not only the best utensil for cooking paella, it is also the most attractive way to serve it, so if you like to make paella fairly frequently it is well worth investing in one — they are obtainable from specialist kitchen shops and some large hardware stores.

CABBAGE AND HAZELNUT CROQUETTES

| 1.00* | 🥛 | ✳ | 141 cals |

* plus 2 hours chilling

Makes 16

450 g (1 lb) potatoes, peeled

salt and freshly ground pepper

900 g (2 lb) cabbage, roughly chopped

45 ml (3 tbsp) milk

50 g (2 oz) butter or margarine

50 g (2 oz) plain flour

50 g (2 oz) hazelnuts, chopped and toasted

2 eggs, beaten

100 g (4 oz) dry white breadcrumbs

vegetable oil, for deep frying

lemon wedges, to serve

1 Boil the potatoes in salted water for about 20 minutes until tender. Drain them well and mash without adding any liquid.

2 Cook the cabbage in boiling salted water for 5–10 minutes or until just tender. Drain well. Purée in a blender or food processor, adding the milk if required—you should have 450 ml ($\frac{3}{4}$ pint) purée.

3 Melt the butter in a saucepan, add the flour and cook gently, stirring, for 1–2 minutes. Gradually blend in the cabbage purée and milk. Bring to the boil, then simmer for 5 minutes.

4 Stir the mashed potatoes and hazelnuts into the sauce, add salt and pepper to taste and mix well. Transfer to a bowl, cool, cover and chill in the refrigerator for at least 1$\frac{1}{2}$ hours or until firm.

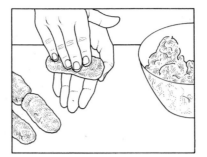

5 With dampened hands, shape the mixture into 16 croquettes. Place on a greased baking sheet and chill again for at least 20 minutes.

6 Coat the croquettes in the beaten eggs and breadcrumbs. Heat the oil to 180°C (350°F) in a deep-fat frier. Deep fry the croquettes in batches for about 4 minutes until crisp and golden. Remove with a slotted spoon and drain on absorbent kitchen paper while frying the remainder. Serve hot, with lemon wedges.

CABBAGE AND HAZELNUT CROQUETTES

Hazelnuts get their name from the Anglo-Saxon word 'haesil', meaning head-dress. This is an apt description, for the outer covering fits over the nut itself. Other names for hazelnuts are filberts and cob nuts, depending on the part of the world in which they are grown. These three nuts are not exactly the same, but they are all close relations of the Corylus family, and are interchangeable in recipes.

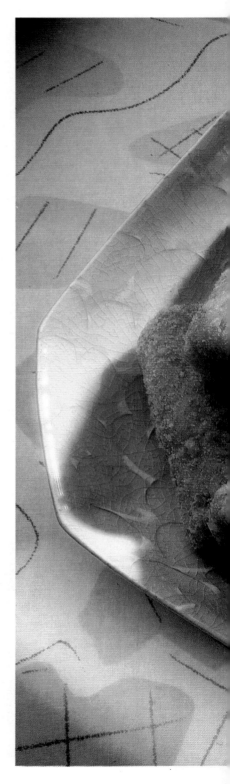

CEVICHE

0.30*   ✳*   307 cals

24 hours refrigeration; freeze after step 4. Defrost in refrigerator overnight, then continue from step 5

Serves 4

500 g (1 lb) haddock fillets

5 ml (1 tsp) coriander seeds

5 ml (1 tsp) black peppercorns

juice of 6 limes

5 ml (1 tsp) salt

30 ml (2 tbsp) olive oil

bunch of spring onions, washed, trimmed and sliced

4 tomatoes, skinned and chopped

dash of Tabasco, or to taste

30 ml (2 tbsp) chopped fresh coriander

1 avocado, to finish

lime slices and fresh coriander, to garnish

1 Skin the haddock fillets. Put the fillets skin-side down on a board and grip the tail end of the skin with fingers dipped in salt. Using a sharp knife, work away from you with a sawing action.

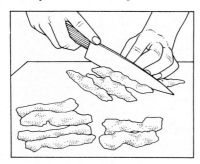

2 Wash the fillets, then pat them dry with absorbent kitchen paper. Cut the fish fillets diagonally into thin, even strips and place in a bowl.

3 Crush the coriander seeds and peppercorns to a fine powder in a mortar and pestle. Mix with the lime juice and salt, then pour over the fish. Cover and chill in the refrigerator for 24 hours, turning the fish occasionally.

4 The next day, heat the oil in a pan, add the spring onions and fry gently for 5 minutes. Add the tomatoes and Tabasco to taste and toss together over brisk heat for 1–2 minutes. Remove from the heat and leave to cool for 20–30 minutes.

5 To serve. Drain the fish from the marinade, discarding the marinade. Combine the fish with the spring onion and tomatoes and the chopped coriander. Taste and adjust seasoning, if necessary.

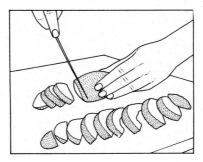

6 Halve the avocado, peel and remove the stone. Slice the flesh crossways. Arrange the slices around the inside of a serving bowl and pile the ceviche in the centre. Garnish with lime slices and coriander leaves. Serve chilled.

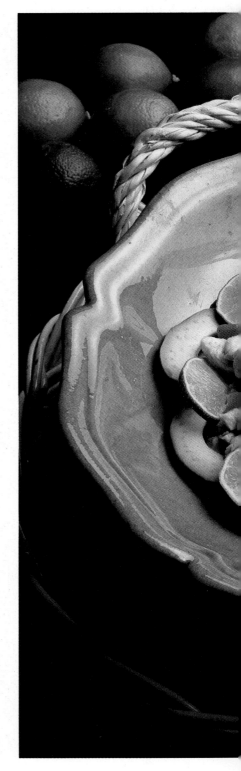

ZUCCHINI ALLA PARMIGIANA
(ITALIAN COURGETTE, PARMESAN AND TOMATO BAKE)

| 1.00 | ✳ | 517 cals |

Serves 4

700 g (1½ lb) courgettes

salt and freshly ground pepper

about 150 ml (¼ pint) vegetable oil

1 medium onion, skinned and finely chopped

450 g (1 lb) tomatoes, skinned and chopped

1 large garlic clove, skinned and crushed

30 ml (2 tbsp) tomato purée

15 ml (1 tbsp) chopped fresh marjoram or 5 ml (1 tsp) dried

two 170 g (6 oz) packets Mozzarella cheese, thinly sliced

75 g (3 oz) freshly grated Parmesan cheese

1 Cut the courgettes into 0.5 cm (¼ inch) thick slices. Sprinkle with salt and leave to dégorge for at least 20 minutes.

2 Heat 30 ml (2 tbsp) of the oil in a saucepan, add the onion and fry for about 5 minutes until just beginning to brown.

3 Stir in the tomatoes, garlic, tomato purée and salt and pepper. Simmer for about 10 minutes, stirring with a wooden spoon to break down the tomatoes. Stir in the marjoram and remove from the heat.

4 Rinse the courgettes and pat dry with absorbent kitchen paper. Heat half of the remaining oil in a frying pan, add half of the courgettes and fry until golden brown. Drain well on kitchen paper while frying the remaining courgettes in the remaining oil.

5 Layer the courgettes, tomato sauce and Mozzarella cheese in a shallow ovenproof dish, finishing with a layer of Mozzarella. Sprinkle with the Parmesan cheese.

6 Bake in the oven at 180°C (350°F) mark 4 for about 40 minutes or until brown and bubbling. Serve hot, straight from the dish.

JERUSALEM ARTICHOKE GRATIN

| 1.20 | ✳* | 725 cals |

* freeze before baking at end of step 10

Serves 4

| 900 g (2 lb) Jerusalem artichokes |
| salt and freshly ground black pepper |
| 225 g (8 oz) small button or pickling onions |
| 3 medium leeks, trimmed |
| 75 g (3 oz) butter or margarine |
| 15 ml (1 tbsp) olive oil |
| 2 garlic cloves, skinned and crushed |
| 150 ml ($\frac{1}{4}$ pint) dry white wine or vegetable stock, or a mixture of both |
| 1.25 ml ($\frac{1}{4}$ tsp) freshly grated nutmeg |
| 225 g (8 oz) fresh or frozen peas |
| 150 ml ($\frac{1}{4}$ pint) double cream |
| 75 g (3 oz) Gruyère cheese, grated |
| 75 g (3 oz) Cheddar cheese, grated |
| 50 g (2 oz) dried wholemeal breadcrumbs |

1 Parboil the Jerusalem artichokes in salted water for 10 minutes. Remove with a slotted spoon and leave until cool enough to handle.

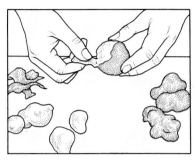

2 Peel the skins off the Jerusalem artichokes and slice the flesh thickly. Set aside.

3 Add the button onions to the water and boil for 2 minutes, then remove with a slotted spoon. Peel off the skins, leaving the root ends intact so that the onions remain whole.

4 Slice the leeks thickly, then wash well under cold running water to remove any grit.

5 Heat 50 g (2 oz) of the butter with the oil in a heavy-based saucepan, add the onions and garlic and toss over moderate heat until the onions are well coated in the butter and oil.

6 Pour in the wine and 150 ml ($\frac{1}{4}$ pint) water and bring to the boil. Add the nutmeg, cover and simmer for 10 minutes.

7 Add the artichokes, leeks and peas and continue simmering for 5 minutes or until all the vegetables are tender. With a slotted spoon, transfer vegetables to a flameproof gratin dish.

8 Boil the cooking liquid rapidly until reduced to about half of its original volume. Lower the heat and stir in the cream.

9 Mix the 2 cheeses together. Stir half of this mixture into the sauce. Add salt and pepper to taste and stir until the cheeses have melted.

10 Pour the cheese sauce over the vegetables in the dish. Mix the remaining cheese with the breadcrumbs, then sprinkle evenly over the top.

11 Dot the remaining butter over the gratin, then bake in the oven at 220°C (425°F) mark 7 for 10 minutes, until the topping is golden brown. Serve hot, straight from the dish.

139

AVOCADO AND LEMON SALAD WITH OMELETTE RINGS

0.30*	412–618 cals

Serves 4–6

4 eggs
50 g (2 oz) Cheddar cheese, grated
salt and freshly ground pepper
25 g (1 oz) butter or margarine
5 ml (1 tsp) whole black peppercorns
5 ml (1 tsp) whole coriander seeds
90 ml (6 tbsp) olive or vegetable oil
45 ml (3 tbsp) lemon juice
2 ripe avocados
parsley sprigs, to garnish (optional)

1 Put the eggs in a bowl with the cheese, 15 ml (1 tbsp) water and salt and pepper to taste. Whisk together.

2 Melt a quarter of the butter in an omelette pan or small non-stick frying pan. When foaming, pour in a quarter of the egg mixture. After a few seconds, push the set egg mixture into the centre of the pan to allow the uncooked egg to run to the edges. Cook until just set.

3 Brown the omelette under a preheated hot grill. Turn out on to a plate. Repeat with the remaining egg mixture to make another 3 omelettes.

4 While the omelettes are still warm, roll them up loosely. Wrap in greaseproof paper and leave to cool.

5 Meanwhile, crush the peppercorns and coriander seeds coarsely with a pestle and mortar, or with the end of a rolling pin in a sturdy bowl.

6 In a bowl, whisk together the oil, lemon juice, crushed spices and salt and pepper to taste. Halve, stone and peel the avocados, then slice thickly into the dressing. Toss gently to coat completely.

7 Slice the omelettes thinly. Arrange the omelette rings and avocado slices on individual serving plates. Spoon over the dressing and garnish with sprigs of parsley, if liked. Serve immediately.

Menu Suggestion
Omelette rings and avocado slices combine together to make this a substantial and nutritious salad. Serve for a main course at lunchtime, with wholemeal French-style bread, or as a light supper.

Meat

CROWN ROAST OF LAMB

2.15			427–640 cals

Serves 4–6

2 best end necks of lamb, chined, each with 6–8 cutlets
75 g (3 oz) long grain rice
salt and freshly ground pepper
25 g (1 oz) butter or margarine
1 small onion, skinned and finely chopped
3 celery sticks, trimmed and finely chopped
1 eating apple, peeled, cored and finely chopped
1 small garlic clove, skinned and crushed
10 ml (2 tsp) curry powder
225 g (8 oz) fresh breadcrumbs, toasted
30 ml (2 tbsp) chopped fresh parsley
1 egg
50 g (2 oz) lard
30 ml (2 tbsp) plain flour
450 ml (¾ pint) beef stock

1 With a sharp, pointed knife, trim each cutlet bone to a depth of 2.5 cm (1 inch).

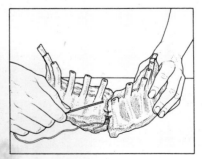

2 Bend the joints around, fat side inwards, and sew together using strong cotton or fine string to form a crown. Cover the exposed bones with foil.

3 Put the rice in a large saucepan of boiling salted water and cook for 12–15 minutes or until tender. Drain, then rinse well under cold running water.

4 Melt the butter in a saucepan, add the onion, celery, apple, garlic and curry powder and cook gently until the vegetables are softened.

5 Remove from the heat and stir in the breadcrumbs, parsley, cooked rice, egg and salt and pepper to taste. Allow to cool, then spoon into the centre of the crown roast. Weigh the joint and calculate the cooking time, allowing 25 minutes per 450 g (1 lb) plus an extra 25 minutes.

6 Melt the lard in a roasting tin then stand the lamb joint in the tin. Roast in the oven at 180°C (350°F) mark 4 for the calculated cooking time, basting occasionally. Cover the joint lightly with foil if the stuffing becomes too brown during roasting.

7 Transfer the crown roast to a warmed serving dish and keep hot. Pour off all but 30 ml (2 tbsp) of the fat from the roasting tin, place the tin on top of the cooker and sprinkle in the flour. Blend well with a wooden spoon, then cook for 2–3 minutes, stirring continuously until golden brown. Gradually stir in the stock and bring to the boil. Simmer for 2–3 minutes, then add salt and pepper to taste. Pour into a gravy boat or jug and serve hot with the joint.

Menu Suggestion
Serve Crown Roast of Lamb for a special occasion meal. With its mildly curried stuffing, it goes well with a medley of courgettes and button onions, or an exotic vegetable such as aubergines or peppers stuffed with a mixture of spiced rice, nuts and raisins.

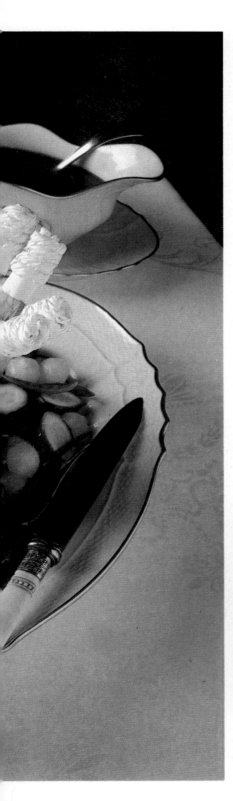

LAMB WITH ROSEMARY AND GARLIC

| 3.15* | ✳* | 305 cals |

* plus 12 hours standing; freeze after stage 3

Serves 6

2-kg (4¼-lb) leg of lamb

2 large garlic cloves, skinned

50 g (2 oz) butter, softened

15 ml (1 tbsp) chopped fresh rosemary or 5 ml (1 tsp) dried

salt and freshly ground pepper

30 ml (2 tbsp) plain flour

450 ml (¾ pint) chicken stock

fresh rosemary sprigs, to garnish

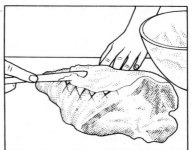

3 Mix the butter with the rosemary and seasoning and then spread all over the lamb. Place the joint in a shallow dish, cover tightly with cling film and refrigerate for at least 12 hours.

4 Uncover the lamb and transfer it to a medium roasting tin. Place in the oven and cook at 180°C (350°F) mark 4 for about 2¼ hours, basting occasionally as the fat begins to run. Pierce the joint with a fine skewer; when done the juices should run clear at first, then with a hint of red.

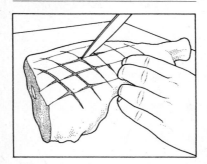

1 Using a sharp knife, score the surface of the lamb into a diamond pattern to the depth of about 12 mm (½ inch).

5 Place the joint on a serving plate, cover loosely and keep warm in a low oven. Pour all excess fat out of the roasting tin leaving about 45 ml (3 tbsp) fat with the meat juices. Sprinkle the flour into the roasting tin and stir until evenly mixed. Cook over a gentle heat for 2–3 minutes until well browned, stirring frequently.

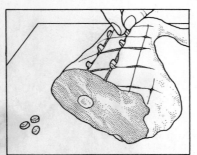

2 Cut the cloves of garlic into wafer thin slices. Push the slices into the scored surface of the lamb with your fingers.

6 Add the stock and seasoning and bring to the boil, stirring. Simmer for 3–4 minutes, adjust the seasoning. To serve, garnish the lamb with rosemary and serve the gravy separately.

LAMB KORMA

| 2.15 | ✳ | 348 cals |

Serves 4

2 onions, skinned and chopped

2.5 cm (1 inch) piece fresh root ginger, peeled

40 g (1½ oz) blanched almonds

2 garlic cloves, skinned

90 ml (6 tbsp) water

5 ml (1 tsp) ground cardamom

5 ml (1 tsp) ground cloves

5 ml (1 tsp) ground cinnamon

5 ml (1 tsp) ground cumin

5 ml (1 tsp) ground coriander

1.25 ml (¼ tsp) cayenne pepper

45 ml (3 tbsp) vegetable oil or ghee

900 g (2 lb) boned tender lamb, cubed

300 ml (½ pint) natural yogurt

salt and freshly ground pepper

cucumber and lime slices, to garnish

1 Put the onions, ginger, almonds and garlic in a blender or food processor with the water and blend to a smooth paste. Add the spices and mix well.

2 Heat the oil or ghee in a heavy-based saucepan and fry the lamb for 5 minutes until browned on all sides.

3 Add the paste mixture and fry for about 10 minutes, stirring, until the mixture is lightly browned. Stir in the yogurt 15 ml (1 tbsp) at a time and season.

4 Cover with a tight-fitting lid, reduce the heat and simmer for 1¼–1½ hours or until the meat is really tender.

5 Transfer to a warmed serving dish and serve garnished with cucumber and lime slices.

Menu Suggestion
Serve with plain boiled or pilau rice, poppadoms, cucumber and yogurt raita, and a sag aloo (spinach and potato curry).

LAMB KORMA

Mild in flavour, creamy in texture, the Indian korma is a very special dish, which was originally only served on special occasions such as feast days and holidays. Our version is relatively simple compared with some of the korma recipes which were devised for celebrations. These often contained such luxurious ingredients as saffron (the most expensive spice in the world), cashew nuts and double cream. If you want to make a richer korma for a dinner party main course, then add powdered saffron or infused saffron liquid with the ground spices in step 1, and stir in 50 g (2 oz) chopped unsalted cashew nuts just before serving. Substitute double cream for the yogurt and swirl more cream over the top of the korma before garnishing.

LAMB CUTLETS EN CROÛTE

$1.00*$ | ✳ | 890 cals

* freeze after cooking only if serving
cold

Serves 6

| 25 g (1 oz) butter |
| 1 onion, skinned and chopped |
| 25 g (1 oz) fresh white breadcrumbs |
| 1 egg, beaten |
| 30 ml (2 tbsp) chopped fresh mint |
| salt and freshly ground pepper |
| squeeze of lemon juice |
| 12 lamb cutlets, trimmed |
| 450 g (1 lb) puff pastry or two 368-g (13-oz) packets frozen puff pastry, thawed |
| beaten egg, to glaze |
| sprig of fresh mint, to garnish |

1 Make the stuffing. Melt the
butter in a pan and fry the
onion for about 5 minutes until
soft but not brown. Remove from
the heat. Stir in the breadcrumbs
and bind with the beaten egg. Mix
in the mint, salt, freshly ground
pepper and lemon juice.

2 Grill or fry the cutlet for 3
minutes on both sides. They
should be browned, but pink inside. Leave to cool.

3 Roll out each piece of pastry
thinly and cut each one into
six squares.

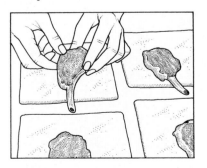

4 Place each of the lamb cutlets
on a square of pastry so that
the bone extends over the edge of
the pastry.

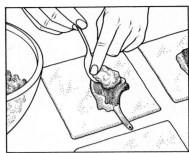

5 Press even amounts of stuffing
on the eye of each cutlet.
Dampen the pastry edges, wrap the
pastry over the cutlets and seal.

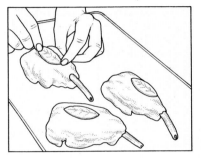

6 Place on a dampened baking
tray, folded sides underneath.
Use any pastry trimmings to decorate the cutlets. Brush with a little
beaten egg.

7 Bake in the oven at 220°C
(425°F) mark 7 for 15–20
minutes, then reduce the oven
temperature to 190°C (375°F)
mark 5 and bake for a further 15
minutes until the pastry is golden.
Serve hot or cold, garnished with
a sprig of fresh mint, if wished.

TANGY CHOPS

| 0.45 | 526 cals |

Serves 4

30 ml (2 tbsp) vegetable oil

4 lamb chump chops

salt and freshly ground pepper

finely grated rind and juice of 1
  lemon

30 ml (2 tbsp) chopped fresh
  parsley or 10 ml (2 tsp)
  dried parsley

15 ml (1 tbsp) chopped fresh mint
  or 5 ml (1 tsp) dried mint

5 ml (1 tsp) sugar

150 ml ($\frac{1}{4}$ pint) beef or chicken stock

1 Heat the oil in a sauté pan or
frying pan, add the chops and
fry over brisk heat until browned
on both sides. Lower the heat and
season the chops with salt and
pepper to taste.

2 Mix the remaining ingredients
together. Spoon this mixture
over the chops and pour in the
stock. Cover the pan tightly and
simmer gently for 30 minutes or
until the meat is tender. Serve hot
on a warmed dish, with the juices
poured over.

Menu Suggestion
Serve for an informal family meal
with grilled or oven-baked
tomatoes, potatoes and a seasonal
green vegetable.

SPICED LENTIL BAKE

| 2.30 | 630 cals |

Serves 4

45 ml (3 tbsp) vegetable oil

8 middle neck lamb chops, total weight about 1.1 kg (2½ lb), trimmed of excess fat

2 medium onions, skinned and thinly sliced

15 ml (1 tbsp) turmeric

5 ml (1 tsp) paprika

5 ml (1 tsp) ground cinnamon

75 g (3 oz) red lentils

salt and freshly ground pepper

450 g (1 lb) potatoes, peeled and thinly sliced

450 g (1 lb) swede, peeled and thinly sliced

300 ml (½ pint) lamb or chicken stock

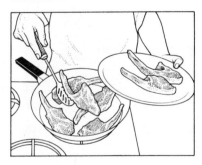

1 Heat the oil in a large sauté or frying pan, add the chops and brown well on both sides. Remove from the pan with a slotted spoon.

2 Add the onions to the pan with the turmeric, paprika, cinnamon and lentils. Fry for 2–3 minutes. Add plenty of salt and pepper and spoon into a shallow 2 litre (3½ pint) ovenproof dish.

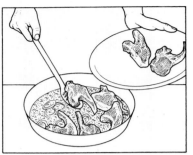

3 Place the chops on top of the onion and lentil mixture. Arrange the vegetable slices on top of the chops, then season and pour over the stock.

4 Cover the dish tightly and cook in the oven at 180°C (350°F) mark 4 for about 1½ hours, or until the chops are tender. Uncover and cook for a further 30 minutes, or until lightly browned on top. Serve hot, straight from the dish.

Menu Suggestion

Spiced Lentil Bake is a complete meal in itself, with lamb chops, lentils, potatoes and swede baked together in one dish. Serve with a crisp green salad or a seasonal green vegetable.

SPICED LENTIL BAKE

The different kinds of lentils available can be confusing, especially in health food shops where there is always such a large selection. The red lentils used in this recipe are the most common kind, sometimes also described as 'split red lentils' or even 'Egyptian lentils'. They do not need soaking and are quick-cooking, but they tend to lose their shape. 'Continental lentils' are green, brown or reddish-brown in colour, and are whole rather than split. These varieties keep their shape and have a nuttier texture than red lentils, but take longer to cook.

ORIENTAL LAMB

| 1.00 | 493 cals |

Serves 4

1.4 kg (3 lb) lean shoulder of lamb
450 g (1 lb) small new potatoes
225 g (8 oz) small pickling onions
30 ml (2 tbsp) vegetable oil
25 g (1 oz) butter or margarine
15 ml (1 tbsp) flour
5 ml (1 tsp) ground ginger
300 ml ($\frac{1}{2}$ pint) chicken stock
15 ml (1 tbsp) Worcestershire sauce
30 ml (2 tbsp) soy sauce
salt and freshly ground pepper
2 caps canned pimento, diced

1 Slice all the meat off the bone, discarding any excess fat, and cut into 2.5 cm (1 inch) pieces about 5 mm ($\frac{1}{4}$ inch) thick.

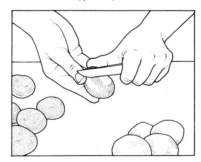

2 Wash the new potatoes and scrub them with a vegetable brush, or scrape with a knife.

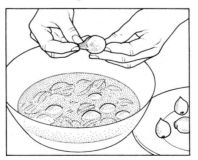

3 Skin the onions. Put them in a bowl and pour in enough boiling water to cover. Leave to stand for 2 minutes, then drain and plunge into a bowl of cold water. Peel off the skin with your fingers.

4 Heat the oil and fat in a large sauté pan and brown the meat in it a few pieces at a time. Remove from the pan with a slotted spoon.

5 Add the potatoes and onions to the residual fat in the pan and fry them until lightly browned, turning frequently.

6 Return the meat to the pan, sprinkle in the flour and ginger and stir well. Cook gently, stirring, for 2 minutes.

7 Add the stock, Worcestershire sauce, soy sauce and seasoning to taste. Bring to the boil, stirring, then cover and simmer for 30 minutes or until the meat is tender.

8 Add the pimentos and stir over low heat to bring to serving temperature. Taste and adjust seasoning, then transfer to a warmed serving dish. Serve hot.

Menu Suggestion
This casserole has its own vegetables included with the meat. Serve with a simple green salad, or a seasonal green vegetable such as courgettes, if liked.

LAMB NOISETTES WITH RED WINE SAUCE

1.00	617 cals

Serves 6

12 lamb noisettes

flour, for coating

25 g (1 oz) butter

60 ml (4 tbsp) vegetable oil

2 large onions, skinned and sliced

1 garlic clove, skinned and finely
  chopped

225 g (8 oz) button mushrooms,
  wiped

300 ml (½ pint) red wine

150 ml (¼ pint) chicken stock

15 ml (1 tbsp) tomato purée

2 bay leaves

salt and freshly ground pepper

2 Add the onion and garlic to the casserole and fry for about 5 minutes until golden. Add the mushrooms and fry for a further 2–3 minutes. Stir in the red wine, stock, tomato purée and bay leaves. Season well with salt and freshly ground pepper.

3 Replace the noisettes and bring to the boil, then cover and simmer gently for about 40 minutes until tender, turning the meat once during this time.

4 Lift the noisettes out of the sauce and remove the string. Place the noisettes on a warmed serving dish and keep warm. Boil the remaining liquid rapidly for 5–10 minutes to reduce the sauce. Taste and adjust the seasoning, then pour over the noisettes. Serve immediately.

1 Lightly coat the lamb noisettes with flour. Heat the butter and oil in a large flameproof casserole. Add the noisettes, a few at a time, and brown quickly on both sides. Remove from the casserole with a slotted spoon and set aside.

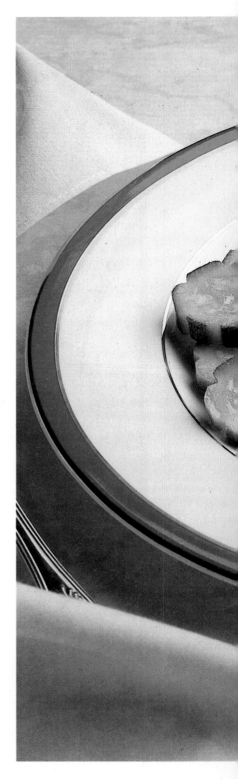

LAMB NOISETTES WITH RED WINE SAUCE

Lamb noisettes are a very special cut of meat. You can buy them ready-prepared at some large supermarkets, or ask your butcher to prepare them for you as they are a little tricky to do yourself. Lamb noisettes are cut from the best end of neck. This is the same cut which is used for making Guard of Honour, except that the bones are removed from the whole rack, then the meat is rolled up and tied at intervals according to how many cutlets there were in the rack—usually six or eight.

ROLLED STUFFED BREASTS OF LAMB

| 1.55 | ❄* | 925 cals |

* freeze at end of step 4

Serves 4

25 g (1 oz) butter or margarine

1 medium onion, skinned and chopped

25 g (1 oz) streaky bacon, rinded and chopped

226 g (8 oz) packet frozen leaf spinach, thawed

75 g (3 oz) fresh breadcrumbs

45 ml (3 tbsp) chopped fresh parsley

finely grated rind of ½ lemon

15 ml (1 tbsp) lemon juice

pinch of grated nutmeg

1 egg, beaten

salt and freshly ground pepper

2 large breasts of lamb, boned and trimmed, total weight about 1.1 kg (2½ lb)

45 ml (3 tbsp) vegetable oil

watercress, to garnish

1 Melt the butter in a saucepan, add the onion and bacon and fry for about 5 minutes until lightly browned.

2 Drain the spinach and chop roughly. Place in a bowl with the onion and bacon, bread-crumbs, parsley, lemon rind and juice, nutmeg and egg. Mix together well, adding salt and pepper to taste.

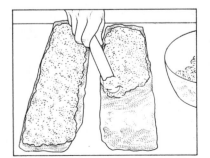

3 Lay the breasts of lamb fat side down on a work surface and spread the stuffing evenly over them with a palette knife.

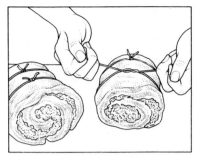

4 Roll up the lamb breasts loosely and tie in several places with string to hold their shape.

5 Weigh each joint and calculate the cooking time, allowing 25 minutes per 450 g (1 lb) plus 25 minutes for each joint. Heat the oil in a roasting tin and place the joints in the tin. Roast in the oven at 180°C (350°F) mark 4 for the calculated cooking time, basting occasionally. Serve hot, garnished with watercress.

Menu Suggestion

Breast of lamb makes an economical midweek roast. This recipe has a spinach stuffing, therefore only one or two additional vegetables is necessary. New potatoes tossed in mint butter would go well, with glazed carrots.

ROLLED STUFFED BREASTS OF LAMB

Breast of lamb is one of the fattier cuts, but it is excellent cooked in this way with a tasty and substantial stuffing. When buying breasts of lamb, look for the leanest ones possible — not all lamb breasts are very fatty. Any visible fat should be white and dry, whereas the meat should be pink and moist. Most lambs are aged between 3 and 6 months at the time of slaughtering, after this time the meat darkens in colour and becomes more coarsely grained.

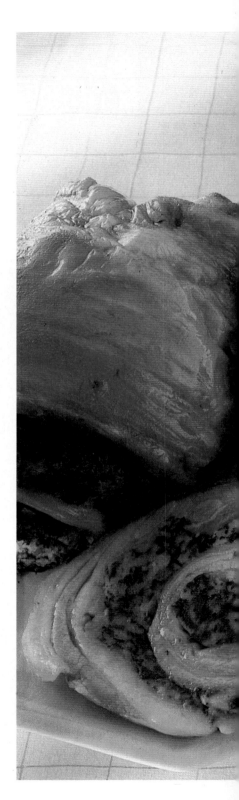

LANCASHIRE HOT POT

| 2.40 | ✳ | 427 cals |

Serves 4

8 middle neck lamb chops
2 lamb's kidneys
8 shelled oysters (optional—see box)
2 medium onions, skinned and sliced
125 g (4 oz) mushrooms, sliced
5 ml (1 tsp) dried thyme
salt and freshly ground pepper
450 g (1 lb) potatoes, peeled and thinly sliced
450 ml (¾ pint) lamb or beef stock
25 g (1 oz) lard or dripping

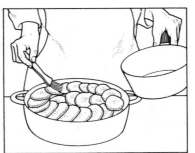

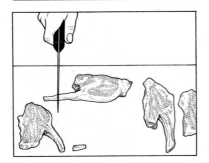

1 Remove any excess fat from the lamb. Select a large, deep casserole. If it is not deep enough to hold the meat, chop the ends off the bones.

2 Skin, halve and core the kidneys and divide each half into 3–4 pieces.

3 Layer the meat in the casserole with the oysters, if using, the kidneys, onions and mushrooms. Sprinkle each layer with thyme and salt and pepper to taste. If the casserole has a narrow top, add some of the potatoes at this stage. Pour in the stock.

4 Arrange a layer of overlapping potato slices on top. Melt the lard and brush over the potatoes. Cover and cook in the oven at 170°C (325°F) mark 3 for 2 hours, or until both the meat and the potatoes are tender when tested with a skewer.

5 Remove the lid carefully, increase the oven temperature to 220°C (425°F) mark 7 and continue cooking for about 20 minutes, or until the potatoes are golden brown and crisp. Serve hot.

Menu Suggestion
Lancashire Hot Pot makes a filling family meal. It is especially good in cold weather, with a nourishing vegetable dish like 'mushy' peas or mashed root vegetables. Pickled red cabbage was the traditional accompaniment, but ordinary red cabbage tastes just as good.

LANCASHIRE HOT POT

One of the best known of Lancashire dishes, the hot pot takes its name from the tall earthenware dish in which it was traditionally cooked. The long boned chops from the Pennine sheep could be stood vertically around the pot and the centre filled with vegetables, kidneys, mushrooms and, in the days when they were cheap, oysters. A thatch of sliced potatoes completed the dish.

MOUSSAKA

1.40*	🍷	❋*	632–948 cals

* plus 30 minutes to dégorge the aubergines and 15 minutes standing; freeze before baking at step 8

Serves 4–6

2 medium aubergines

salt and freshly ground pepper

about 150 ml (¼ pint) olive or vegetable oil, or a mixture of both

1 large onion, skinned and roughly chopped

1–2 garlic cloves, skinned and crushed

450 g (1 lb) minced lamb

227 g (8 oz) can tomatoes

30 ml (2 tbsp) tomato purée

10 ml (2 tsp) dried oregano

5 ml (1 tsp) ground allspice

2 bay leaves

410 g (14½ oz) can evaporated milk

40 g (1½ oz) cornflour

25 g (1 oz) butter or margarine

25 g (1 oz) plain flour

pinch of grated nutmeg

1 egg, beaten

1 Slice the aubergines thinly and place in a colander, sprinkling each layer with salt. Cover with a plate, place heavy weights on top and leave the aubergines to dégorge for 30 minutes.

2 Meanwhile, heat 30 ml (2 tbsp) of the oil in a heavy-based saucepan, add the onion and garlic and fry gently for 5 minutes until soft and lightly coloured. Add the minced lamb and fry until well browned, stirring and pressing with a wooden spoon to break up any lumps.

3 Add the tomatoes with their juice, the tomato purée, oregano, allspice and salt and pepper to taste, then add the bay leaves. Cover and simmer for about 20 minutes, stirring occasionally to break up the tomatoes.

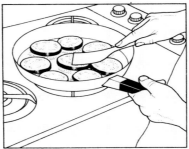

4 Meanwhile, rinse the aubergines under cold running water, then pat dry with absorbent kitchen paper. Pour enough oil into a heavy-based frying pan to just cover the base. Heat until very hot, then add a layer of aubergine slices. Fry until golden on both sides, turning once, then remove with a spatula and drain on absorbent kitchen paper. Continue frying and draining all the aubergine slices in this way, adding more oil to the pan as necessary.

5 Make the sauce for the topping. Dilute the evaporated milk with water to make up to 1 litre (1¾ pints) as directed on the can. In a jug, mix the cornflour to a smooth paste with a few spoonfuls of the milk.

6 Melt the butter in a saucepan, add the flour and cook gently, stirring, for 1–2 minutes. Remove from the heat and gradually blend in the milk. Bring to the boil, stirring constantly, then simmer for 3 minutes.

7 Stir in the cornflour paste and continue simmering and stirring until the sauce is thick. Remove the pan from the heat, add the nutmeg and salt and pepper to taste, then stir in the beaten egg.

8 Arrange the meat and aubergines in layers in a baking dish, then pour over the sauce. Bake, uncovered, in the oven at 180°C (350°F) mark 4 for 40 minutes. Leave to stand at room temperature for at least 15 minutes before serving.

Menu Suggestion

Greek Moussaka is an extremely filling dish. Serve for a family meal, or even for an informal supper party, with Greek sesame seed bread and a mixed salad. Retsina wine is the ideal drink to accompany Greek food.

GREEK LAMB

| 2.20 | ✳ | 673–1011 cals |

Serves 4–6

60 ml (4 tbsp) olive oil

900 g (2 lb) small new potatoes, scraped, or old potatoes, peeled and cut into cubes

1.1 kg (2½ lb) boned lean shoulder of lamb, trimmed of fat and cubed

2 large onions, skinned and sliced

15 ml (1 tbsp) plain flour

300 ml (½ pint) dry white wine

350 g (12 oz) tomatoes, skinned and chopped

30 ml (2 tbsp) wine vinegar

2 cinnamon sticks

2 bay leaves

10 ml (2 tsp) chopped fresh thyme or 5 ml (1 tsp) dried

salt and freshly ground pepper

thyme sprigs, to garnish

1 Heat 30 ml (2 tbsp) of the oil in a large flameproof casserole. Pierce each potato (or potato cube) with a sharp knife, add to the casserole and fry over moderate heat until golden on all sides. Remove from the oil with a slotted spoon and drain on absorbent kitchen paper.

2 Heat the remaining oil in the casserole, add the lamb and onions in batches and fry over moderate heat until browned on all sides. Sprinkle in the flour and fry 1 further minute, stirring until it is absorbed.

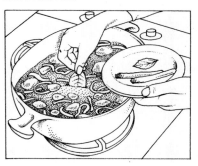

3 Pour the wine into the casserole and add the tomatoes and wine vinegar. Bring slowly to boiling point, then lower the heat and add the cinnamon, bay leaves, thyme and seasoning to taste. Cover and simmer gently for 1 hour, stirring occasionally.

4 Add the fried potatoes to the casserole and continue simmering for 1 further hour or until the lamb and potatoes are tender. Remove the cinnamon sticks and bay leaves, then taste and adjust seasoning. Garnish with thyme sprigs and serve the casserole immediately.

Menu Suggestion
Serve with a Greek-style salad of tomato, shredded white cabbage, raw onion, black olives and chopped fresh coriander.

GREEK LAMB

A rich and pungent dish, Greek Lamb is given its authentic flavour with the combination of olive oil, white wine, tomatoes, cinnamon and fresh thyme. Greek olive oil from the first cold pressing of the olives is thick and green, often with flecks of olives floating in it. Look for it in Greek and Cypriot food shops—its superb flavour and texture make it good for salads as well as cooking.

165

LAMB IN TOMATO SAUCE WITH HERB BREAD

| 2.40 | ✳* | 747 cals |

* freeze lamb in tomato sauce only, without French bread

Serves 4

30 ml (2 tbsp) vegetable oil

1 kg (2¼ lb) boned lean shoulder of lamb, trimmed of fat and cubed

1 medium onion, skinned and sliced

20 ml (4 tsp) plain flour

397 g (14 oz) and 227 g (8 oz) can tomatoes

30 ml (2 tbsp) tomato purée

pinch of granulated sugar

2.5 ml (½ tsp) dried rosemary

60 ml (4 tbsp) red wine (optional)

salt and freshly ground pepper

lamb or beef stock, if necessary

40 g (1½ oz) butter

15 ml (1 tbsp) snipped fresh chives

eight 1 cm (½ inch) slices of French bread

1 Heat the oil in a flameproof casserole, add the lamb and fry over high heat until browned on all sides. Remove from the casserole with a slotted spoon and set aside.

2 Add the onion to the pan and fry for 5 minutes until soft. Stir in the flour and cook for 1 minute. Add the tomatoes with their juice, the tomato purée, sugar, rosemary and wine, if using. Bring to the boil, stirring all the time.

3 Return the meat to the pan and add salt and pepper to taste. Add a little stock, if necessary, to cover the meat. Cover the casserole and cook in the oven at 170°C (325°F) mark 3 for about 1¼ hours.

4 Meanwhile, make the herb butter. Beat the butter until smooth, then beat in the chives and salt and pepper to taste.

5 Spread the butter on to the slices of French bread. Uncover the casserole and place the bread, butter side up, on top. Cook for 1 further hour, or until the meat is tender. Serve hot.

Menu Suggestion
With its garnish of herb bread, this lamb casserole is quite a substantial dish. Serve simply, with a seasonal green vegetable.

LAMB IN TOMATO SAUCE WITH HERB BREAD
Shoulder of lamb is an excellent cut for casseroles such as this one, because it is so economical. It can be fatty, however, especially if the lamb is not an early-season, young animal. Check with your butcher before buying. An alternative cut of lamb which tends to be less fatty is the fillet. This cut comes from the middle neck and scrag; it is quite lean and tender, yet it does not become dry in casseroles as with the more expensive leg of lamb, which is too lean.

SAG GOSHT
(INDIAN LAMB AND SPINACH CURRY)

2.00	✳	589 cals

Serves 4

1–2 garlic cloves, skinned and roughly chopped

2.5 cm (1 inch) piece of fresh root ginger, peeled and roughly chopped

15 ml (1 tbsp) mustard seeds

15 ml (1 tbsp) coriander seeds

5 ml (1 tsp) turmeric

2.5 ml ($\frac{1}{2}$ tsp) chilli powder or to taste

salt

65 g ($2\frac{1}{2}$ oz) ghee or butter

3 medium onions, skinned and thinly sliced

900 g (2 lb) boneless lamb fillet, trimmed of fat and cut into cubes

300 ml ($\frac{1}{2}$ pint) natural yogurt

450 g (1 lb) fresh spinach, trimmed and washed, or 225 g (8 oz) frozen leaf spinach, thawed

1 Put the garlic and ginger in a mortar and pestle with the mustard seeds and coriander. Pound until well crushed, then mix in the turmeric, chilli powder and 5 ml (1 tsp) salt.

2 Melt 50 g (2 oz) of the ghee in a flameproof casserole, add two-thirds of the onions and fry gently for about 10 minutes until softened and lightly coloured.

3 Add the crushed spice mixture and fry gently, stirring, for a few minutes. Add the lamb in batches, increase the heat and fry until well browned on all sides.

4 Return all the lamb to the casserole. Add the yogurt to the meat, 15 ml (1 tbsp) at a time. Stir-fry after each addition to mix with the meat, then cover and cook gently for 1 hour or until the lamb is tender.

5 Add the spinach to the casserole, stir well to mix with the meat and continue cooking for a further 5 minutes.

6 Meanwhile, melt the remaining ghee in a small frying pan, add the remaining sliced onion and fry, stirring constantly, over moderate heat until the onion is softened and golden.

7 Taste the curry and add more salt, if necessary. Turn into a warmed serving dish and sprinkle the golden onion slices over the top. Serve hot.

Menu Suggestion
The rich combination of spinach and lamb needs a plain accompaniment. Serve with boiled basmati rice, a yogurt and cucumber or onion raita, crispy poppadoms and chutneys.

RAAN
(INDIAN SPICED LAMB)

4.00*		685 cals

* plus 2–3 days marinating and 1 hour coming to room temperature

Serves 6

1.8 kg (4 lb) leg of lamb, skin and H-bone removed

6 large garlic cloves, skinned and roughly chopped

1 large piece of fresh root ginger, weighing about 50 g (2 oz), peeled and roughly chopped

300 ml ($\frac{1}{2}$ pint) natural yogurt

thinly pared rind and juice of 1 lemon

15 ml (1 tbsp) cumin seeds

seeds of 6 cardamom pods

6 whole cloves

150 g (5 oz) blanched almonds

10 ml (2 tsp) salt

5 ml (1 tsp) turmeric

5–10 ml (1–2 tsp) chilli powder, according to taste

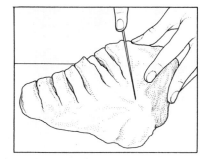

1 Make deep slashes all over the leg of lamb with a sharp, pointed knife. Set aside while making the marinade.

2 Put the garlic and ginger in a blender or food processor with 60 ml (4 tbsp) of the yogurt, the lemon rind and juice, the cumin seeds, cardamom pods and cloves. Work to a paste.

3 Roughly chop 100 g (4 oz) of the almonds, then add to the machine with a few more spoonfuls of yogurt. Work again, then add the remaining yogurt with the salt, turmeric and chilli powder. Work until all the ingredients are thoroughly combined.

4 Put the leg of lamb in a roasting tin and spread all over with the spiced yogurt paste. Work the paste into the cuts in the meat as much as possible. Cover the lamb loosely with foil and marinate in the refrigerator for 2–3 days.

5 When ready to cook, uncover the lamb and allow the meat to come to room temperature for about 1 hour. Roast in the oven at 220°C (425°F) mark 7 for 30 minutes.

6 Lower the oven temperature to 180°C (350°F) mark 4 and roast for a further 1 hour, then lower the temperature to 170°C (325°F) mark 3 and roast for a further 2 hours, or until the meat is very tender and almost falling off the bone.

7 Remove the lamb from the roasting tin and place on a warmed serving platter. Cover loosely with foil and keep warm in a low oven.

8 Pour off the excess fat from the roasting tin, then place the tin on top of the cooker. Boil the sediment and juices to reduce, stirring and scraping the pan with a wooden spoon.

9 Uncover the lamb and pour over the pan juices. Arrange the remaining almonds over the lamb in a decorative 'flower' pattern. Serve hot.

Menu Suggestion
Raan is quite a spectacular dish to serve, either for a dinner party or for a special Sunday roast. Saffron rice looks good as an accompaniment, and *sag bhaji* (curried spinach) complements the flavour of the lamb well. Alternatively, serve with *sag aloo* (spinach and potato curry) instead of separate dishes of rice and spinach.

LAMB AND SPINACH LASAGNE

1.45	🍳	✳*	799 cals

* freeze at the end of step 6

Serves 6

450 g (1 lb) fresh spinach, washed

30 ml (2 tbsp) vegetable oil

1 medium onion, skinned and chopped

450 g (1 lb) minced lamb

227 g (8 oz) can tomatoes

1 garlic clove, skinned and crushed

30 ml (2 tbsp) chopped fresh mint

5 ml (1 tsp) ground cinnamon

freshly grated nutmeg

salt and freshly ground pepper

50 g (2 oz) butter or margarine

50 g (2 oz) plain flour

900 ml (1½ pints) milk

150 ml (¼ pint) natural yogurt

12–15 sheets oven-ready lasagne

175 g (6 oz) Feta or Cheddar cheese, grated

1 Put the spinach in a saucepan with only the water that clings to the leaves and cook gently for about 4 minutes. Drain well and chop finely.

2 Heat the oil in a large saucepan, add the onion and fry gently for 5 minutes until softened. Add the lamb and brown well, then drain off all the fat.

3 Stir in the spinach with the tomatoes and their juice, the garlic, mint and cinnamon. Season with nutmeg, salt and pepper to taste. Bring to the boil and simmer, uncovered, for about 30 minutes. Leave to cool while making the white sauce.

4 Melt the butter in a saucepan, add the flour and cook gently, stirring, for 1–2 minutes. Remove from the heat and gradually blend in the milk. Bring to the boil, stirring constantly, then simmer for 3 minutes until thick and smooth. Add the yogurt and salt and pepper to taste.

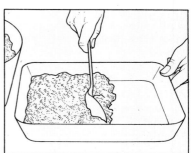

5 Spoon one-third of the meat mixture over the base of a rectangular baking dish.

6 Cover with 4–5 sheets of lasagne and spread over one-third of the white sauce. Repeat these layers twice more, finishing with the sauce, which should completely cover the lasagne. Sprinkle the cheese on top.

7 Stand the dish on a baking sheet. Bake in the oven at 180°C (350°F) mark 4 for 45–50 minutes, or until the top is well browned and bubbling. Serve hot.

Menu Suggestion

Lamb and Spinach Lasagne is rich and filling. Serve with a tomato salad dressed with oil, lemon juice and raw onion rings, chopped spring onion or snipped fresh chives.

STEAK AND MUSHROOM PIE

*3.00** | 562 cals

* plus 1 hour cooling

Serves 4

700 g (1½ lb) stewing steak, cut into 2.5 cm (1 inch) cubes

30 ml (2 tbsp) plain flour

1 medium onion, skinned and sliced

450 ml (¾ pint) beef stock

100 g (4 oz) button mushrooms

212 g (7½ oz) packet frozen puff pastry, thawed

beaten egg, to glaze

1 Coat the meat with the flour, then put in a heavy-based saucepan with the sliced onion. Pour in the beef stock.

2 Bring to the boil, then lower the heat and simmer for 1½–2 hours, until the meat is tender. (Alternatively, the meat can be cooked in a covered casserole in the oven at 170°C (325°F) mark 3 for 2 hours.) Leave for about 1 hour, until cold.

3 Using a slotted spoon, transfer the meat to a 1 litre (2 pint) pie dish. Mix in the mushrooms.

4 Slowly pour in enough of the cold cooking liquid to half fill the pie dish.

5 Roll out the pastry 2.5 cm (1 inch) larger than the top of the dish. Cut off a 1 cm (½ inch) strip from round the edge of the pastry and put this strip round the dampened rim of the dish.

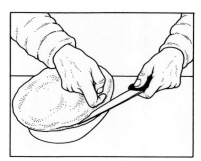

6 Dampen the edges of the pastry with water and put on the top of the pie, without stretching the pastry; trim if necessary and knock up the edges. Use the trimmings to make decorations, if wished. Brush the top of the pie with beaten egg to glaze the pastry.

7 Bake the pie in the oven at 220°C (425°F) mark 7 for 20 minutes. Reduce the heat to 180°C (350°F) mark 4 and cook for a further 20 minutes. Serve hot, straight from the dish.

Menu Suggestion

Steak and Mushroom Pie is a traditional English dish. Serve with boiled or creamed potatoes and seasonal vegetables for a substantial family meal

---

STEAK AND MUSHROOM PIE

There are lots of ways in which you can vary this pie. For everyday family meals, it can be made more colourful with the addition of 2–3 carrots, peeled and sliced, which should be cooked with the beef in steps 1 and 2. Parsnips could also be used to add bulk; they taste really good with beef and also add a touch of sweetness to the gravy. For those who like them, 100 g (4 oz) lambs' kidneys can be added, which will increase the nutritional value of the dish — kidneys are rich in iron and vitamin B. Steak and Mushroom Pie also makes a delicious main course for a dinner party with a traditional English theme. Make it more special by using half red wine and half beef stock, and by including a few fresh or smoked oysters or fresh scallops.

BRAISED BEEF

3.00	703 cals

Serves 6

1.4 kg (3 lb) piece of silverside

2 medium carrots, peeled

2 medium parsnips, peeled

3 celery sticks

2 small turnips, peeled

2 medium onions, skinned

30 ml (2 tbsp) vegetable oil or dripping

75 g (3 oz) streaky bacon rashers, rinded and chopped

1 bay leaf

salt and freshly ground pepper

150 ml ($\frac{1}{4}$ pint) beef stock

150 ml ($\frac{1}{4}$ pint) cider

15 ml (1 tbsp) arrowroot

chopped fresh parsley, to garnish

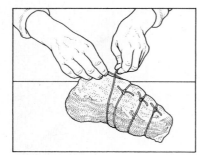

1 Tie up the meat to form a neat joint. Cut the carrots and parsnips into slices about 1 cm ($\frac{1}{2}$ inch) thick, halving them if large. Cut the celery and turnip into similar-sized pieces. Cut the onions in half and slice thickly.

2 Heat the oil in a deep 3.4 litre (6 pint) flameproof casserole. Add the bacon and fry until beginning to brown. Remove with a slotted spoon and reserve.

3 Reheat the oil in the casserole for a few seconds. Add the meat and fry until browned all over, then remove from the casserole and set aside.

4 Add the vegetables to the casserole and fry over high heat. Return the bacon to the casserole, add the bay leaf and plenty of salt and pepper.

5 Place the joint in the centre of the bed of vegetables. Pour in the stock and cider and bring to the boil.

6 Fit a piece of foil over the meat and vegetables to form a 'tent', then cover with a close-fitting lid.

7 Cook the joint in the oven at 160–170°C (300–325°F) mark 2–3 for 2–2½ hours. Halfway through the cooking time, turn the joint over and re-cover firmly. Test the meat after 2 hours; if it is done, a fine skewer will glide easily and smoothly into the joint.

8 Lift the joint on to a board and cut into slices no more than 0.5 cm ($\frac{1}{4}$ inch) thick. Remove the vegetables from the casserole with a slotted spoon and place on a shallow serving dish. Arrange the meat over the vegetables, cover with foil and place in a low oven.

9 Mix the arrowroot to a smooth paste with 45 ml (3 tbsp) water. Skim off the excess fat from the cooking juices, then stir in the arrowroot.

10 Place the casserole on top of the cooker and bring slowly to the boil, stirring. Boil for 1 minute, then taste and adjust seasoning. Spoon a little gravy over the meat and sprinkle with parsley. Serve the remaining gravy separately in a sauceboat.

Menu Suggestion

With its own vegetables and gravy, this joint of braised silverside needs no accompaniment other than creamed or boiled potatoes.

BRAISED BEEF

Braising is the perfect cooking method for a joint of silverside. The long, slow cooking breaks down tough fibres and ensures tender meat, and the simmering in vegetables and liquid gives both flavour and succulence. With braising, it is important to choose a casserole dish which fits the joint snugly, and to keep it tightly covered during cooking. This is so that none of the juices can escape and the flavours of the different vegetables and liquid can concentrate as much as possible. Frying the meat and vegetables first also helps accentuate flavour.

BEEF WITH STOUT

| 2.30 | ✳ | 509 cals |

Serves 4

700 g (1½ lb) stewing beef
30 ml (2 tbsp) vegetable oil
2 large onions, skinned and sliced
15 ml (1 tbsp) flour
275 ml (9.68 fl oz) can stout
200 ml (7 fl oz) beef stock
30 ml (2 tbsp) tomato purée
100 g (4 oz) stoned prunes
225 g (8 oz) carrots, peeled and sliced
salt and freshly ground pepper
croûtons, to garnish

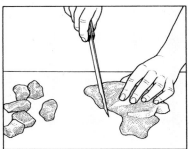

1 Cut the meat into 4 cm (1½ inch) cubes, trimming off all fat. Heat the oil in a flameproof casserole, add the meat and fry until well browned on all sides. Remove with a slotted spoon.

2 Add the onions to the remaining oil in the pan and fry gently until lightly browned. Stir in the flour and cook for 1 minute. Stir in the stout, stock, tomato purée, prunes and carrots. Bring to the boil and season well.

3 Replace the meat, cover and cook in the oven at 170°C (325°F) mark 3 for 1½–2 hours until tender. Adjust seasoning. Serve garnished with croûtons.

BOEUF STROGANOFF
(BEEF WITH MUSHROOMS AND SOURED CREAM)

0.25	538 cals

Serves 4

700 g (1½ lb) rump steak, thinly
   sliced

45 ml (3 tbsp) flour

salt and freshly ground pepper

50 g (2 oz) butter

1 onion, skinned and thinly sliced

225 g (8 oz) mushrooms, wiped and
   sliced

150 ml (¼ pint) soured cream

10 ml (2 tsp) tomato purée
   (optional)

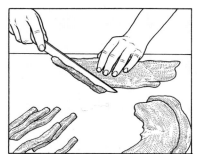

2 Trim the fat off the steak and
discard. Cut the meat across
the grain into thin strips.

3 Coat the strips of steak in the
flour seasoned with salt and
pepper. Melt half the butter in a
sauté pan, add the meat and fry
for 5–7 minutes, tossing
constantly until golden brown.

4 Add the remaining butter, the
onion and mushrooms and fry,
stirring, for 3–4 minutes. Stir in
the soured cream and tomato
purée (if liked), and season well,
using plenty of pepper. Heat
through gently, without boiling.
Transfer to a warmed serving dish
and serve immediately.

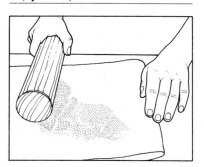

1 Beat the steak with a meat
mallet or rolling pin between
two sheets of greaseproof paper.

BOEUF STROGANOFF

The story goes that this dish was
created in the nineteenth century
by a French chef for a Russian
nobleman called Count
Stroganoff. The chef worked for
the Count, who was something
of a gourmet. In the freezing
temperatures of the Russian
winter, there were always
problems cutting meat, which
was more or less permanently
frozen. On one occasion when
the Count ordered beef, the chef
hit upon the idea of cutting it
into wafer-thin slices—this way
it was easier to cut and it also
cooked more quickly. The result
of this experiment has since
become a famous, classic dish, so
it must have met with the
Count's approval!

GOULASH
(BEEF STEW WITH PARAPRIKA)

| 3.10 | ✳ | 354 cals |

Serves 8

1.4 kg (3 lb) stewing veal or braising steak

75 g (3 oz) butter or margarine

700 g (1½ lb) onions, skinned and thinly sliced

450 g (1 lb) carrots, peeled and thinly sliced

45–60 ml (3–4 tbsp) paprika

30 ml (2 tbsp) plain flour

900 ml (1½ pints) chicken stock

60 ml (4 tbsp) dry white wine

salt and freshly ground pepper

142 ml (5 fl oz) soured cream

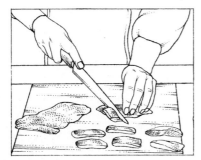

1 Cut the meat into 4 cm (1½ inch) pieces. Melt the fat in a frying pan and fry the meat, a little at a time, until browned. Drain and place in a shallow oven-proof dish.

2 Fry the onions and carrots in the fat remaining in the pan for about 5 minutes until lightly browned. Add the paprika and flour and fry for 2 minutes. Gradually stir in the stock, wine and seasoning. Bring to the boil and pour over the meat.

3 Cover tightly and cook in the oven at 150°C (300°F) mark 2 for 2¾ hours until tender. When cooked, pour the soured cream over the goulash and serve.

Menu Suggestion
Goulash is traditionally served with dumplings or noodles. An unusual alternative to these accompaniments is a dish of boiled new potatoes and sautéed button mushrooms, tossed together with chopped fresh herbs and some melted butter.

GOULASH
This recipe for goulash is simple and straightforward — typical of the kind of goulash to be found in Austria. Hearty and warming, it is the ideal dish to serve in cold weather, especially in the depths of winter when snow is on the ground — the Austrians frequently eat goulash or bowls of goulash soup to keep them warm at lunchtime after a morning's skiing. Goulash is also very popular in Hungary, where it is often made with extra ingredients such as red and green peppers, mushrooms and tomatoes, resulting in a more flamboyant-looking dish with a stronger flavour. When buying paprika to make goulash, look for the variety in the silver sachet from Hungary which is labelled *süss* (sweet).

SUSSEX STEW

3.00	✳	533 cals

Serves 4

30 ml (2 tbsp) plain flour
5 ml (1 tsp) dried thyme
salt and freshly ground pepper
900 g (2 lb) stewing steak, in one
  piece
30 ml (2 tbsp) beef dripping or lard
1 large onion, skinned and sliced
300 ml (½ pint) sweet stout
30 ml (2 tbsp) mushroom ketchup
thyme sprigs, to garnish

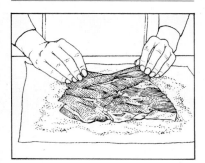

1 Mix the flour with the thyme and salt and pepper and spread out on a large flat plate or sheet of greaseproof paper. Coat the meat in the flour.

2 Melt the dripping or lard in a flameproof casserole. Add the onion slices and fry gently for 5 minutes until soft but not coloured. Remove with a slotted spoon and set aside. Add the beef to the casserole, increase the heat and fry quickly until browned on both sides.

3 Return the onion slices to the casserole, then pour in the stout mixed with the mushroom ketchup. Bring slowly to boiling point, then cover with a lid and cook in the oven at 150°C (300°F) mark 2 for 2–2½ hours until tender. Taste and adjust seasoning. Serve the casserole garnished with thyme sprigs.

Menu Suggestion
Sussex Stew has plenty of thick, rich gravy. Accompanied by creamed potatoes and carrots tossed in chopped fresh herbs, it makes a perfectly balanced family meal.

SUSSEX STEW

Sussex Stew is an old, traditional English dish, in which stewing beef is slowly braised in sweet stout and mushroom ketchup until wonderfully succulent and full of flavour. Although an everyday family dish, take care with your choice of ingredients for best results. Sweet stout rather than ordinary stout or ale is essential for the richness of the gravy, and mushroom ketchup gives it a special tang, which helps offset the sweetness of the stout. Mushroom ketchup is easy to find in large supermarkets and delicatessens; sold in bottles, it keeps indefinitely, so is well worth buying as it can be used in other dishes.

COTTAGE PIE

| 1.45 | ✳* | 592 cals |

* freeze before cooking in step 4

Serves 4

900 g (2 lb) potatoes, peeled

salt and freshly ground pepper

45 ml (3 tbsp) milk

knob of butter or margarine

15 ml (1 tbsp) vegetable oil

1 large onion, skinned and chopped

450 g (1 lb) minced beef

30 ml (2 tbsp) plain flour

300 ml ($\frac{1}{2}$ pint) beef stock

30 ml (2 tbsp) chopped fresh parsley or 10 ml (2 tsp) dried mixed herbs

1 Cook the potatoes in boiling salted water for 15–20 minutes, then drain and mash with the milk, butter and salt and pepper to taste.

2 Heat the oil in a frying pan, add the onion and fry for about 5 minutes until browned. Stir in the minced beef and fry for a further 5–10 minutes until browned, stirring occasionally.

3 Add the flour and cook for 2 minutes, then stir in the stock, parsley and salt and pepper to taste. Bring to the boil and simmer for 30 minutes.

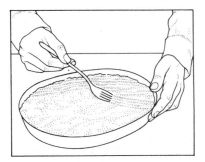

4 Spoon into an ovenproof dish and cover with mashed potato. Bake in the oven at 190°C (375°F) mark 5 for 25–30 minutes.

Menu Suggestion
Serve with seasonal vegetables, and gravy for those who like it.

BEEF AND RED BEAN GRATIN

| 1.30 | ✳* | 436 cals |

* freeze before baking

Serves 4

| 100 g (4 oz) dried red kidney beans, soaked in cold water overnight |
| 75 g (3 oz) butter or margarine |
| 1 small onion, skinned and thinly sliced |
| 225 g (8 oz) minced beef |
| 65 g (2½ oz) plain flour |
| 200 ml (7 fl oz) beef stock |
| cayenne pepper |
| salt and freshly ground pepper |
| 225 g (8 oz) tomatoes, skinned and chopped |
| 15 ml (1 tbsp) tomato purée |
| 5 ml (1 tsp) chopped fresh mixed herbs or 2.5 ml (½ tsp) dried |
| 250 ml (9 fl oz) milk |
| 50 g (2 oz) Cheddar cheese, grated |
| 1.25 ml (¼ tsp) made English mustard |

1 Drain the beans and put them into a large saucepan. Cover with fresh cold water and bring to the boil. Boil rapidly for a full 10 minutes, then lower the heat and boil gently for about 45 minutes or until tender. Drain.

2 Melt 25 g (1 oz) of the butter in a heavy-based saucepan, add the onion and minced beef and brown over high heat, stirring.

3 Stir in 40 g (1½ oz) of the flour, the stock and cayenne, salt and pepper to taste. Bring to the boil and cook for 2–3 minutes until very thick. Transfer to a deep 1.7 litre (3 pint) ovenproof dish.

4 Melt another 25 g (1 oz) of the butter in the saucepan, add the tomatoes and cook for about 10 minutes until they are soft and broken up. Stir in the beans, tomato purée and herbs and simmer until reduced and thickened. Spread over the meat.

5 Melt the remaining butter in a clean saucepan and add the remaining flour. Cook, stirring, for 2 minutes. Remove from the heat and gradually blend in the milk, stirring after each addition to prevent lumps forming. Bring to the boil slowly and continue to cook, stirring all the time, until the sauce comes to the boil and thickens.

6 Stir in half of the cheese, the mustard and salt and pepper to taste. Pour the sauce over the bean layer and sprinkle the remaining cheese on top. Bake in the oven at 200°C (400°F) mark 6 for about 25 minutes until golden brown on top. Serve hot.

Menu Suggestion
This dish is very substantial and therefore needs only a light accompaniment such as a mixed or green salad.

MEAT LOAF WITH ONION SAUCE

2.00	511 cals

Serves 4

50 g (2 oz) butter or margarine

2 medium onions, skinned and finely chopped

5 ml (1 tsp) paprika

450 g (1 lb) minced beef

65 g (2½ oz) fresh breadcrumbs

1 garlic clove, skinned and crushed

60 ml (4 tbsp) tomato purée

15 ml (1 tbsp) chopped fresh mixed herbs or 5 ml (1 tsp) dried

salt and freshly ground pepper

1 egg, beaten

15 g (½ oz) plain flour

300 ml (½ pint) milk

1 Grease a 450 g (1 lb) loaf tin, then line the base with greased greaseproof paper. Set aside.

2 Melt 25 g (1 oz) of the butter in a frying pan, add half of the onions and cook until softened. Add the paprika and cook for 1 minute, stirring, then turn the mixture into a large bowl.

3 Add the beef, breadcrumbs, garlic, tomato purée, herbs and salt and pepper to taste. Stir thoroughly until evenly mixed, then bind with the beaten egg.

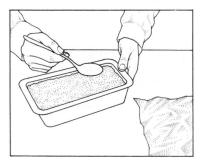

4 Spoon the mixture into the loaf tin, level the surface and cover tightly with foil. Stand the tin in a roasting tin and pour in water to a depth of 2.5 cm (1 inch). Bake in the oven at 180°C (350°F) mark 4 for 1½ hours.

5 Meanwhile, melt the remaining butter in a saucepan. Add the rest of the onion and cook over low heat, stirring occasionally, for 10 minutes until soft but not coloured. Add the flour and cook over low heat, stirring, for 2 minutes.

6 Remove the pan from the heat and gradually blend in the milk, stirring after each addition to prevent lumps forming.

7 Bring to the boil slowly and continue to cook, stirring all the time, until the sauce comes to the boil and thickens. Simmer very gently for a further 2–3 minutes, then add salt and pepper to taste.

8 To serve, turn out the meat loaf on to a warmed serving plate and peel off the lining paper. Serve immediately, with the hot onion sauce.

Menu Suggestion

Serve for a family supper with creamed potatoes and a cucumber and dill salad.

MEAT LOAF

Meat Loaf is a traditional Jewish dish called Klops, and just about every Jewish family have their own favourite version. Some cooks include matzo meal amongst the ingredients, to bind the mixture and help 'stretch' the meat in the same way as breadcrumbs. Onion sauce is traditional with Meat Loaf, and sometimes mushrooms are added. For this quantity of sauce, use 100 g (4 oz) button mushrooms, sliced, and add them to the sauce at the end of step 7.

BEEF KEBABS WITH HORSERADISH DIP

0.45	501 cals

Serves 4

75 ml (3 fl oz) whipping cream
150 ml (¼ pint) soured cream
30 ml (2 tbsp) grated fresh
  horseradish
5 ml (1 tsp) white wine vinegar
2.5 ml (½ tsp) sugar
salt and freshly ground pepper
450 g (1 lb) minced beef
1 small onion, skinned
25 g (1 oz) fresh white or brown
  breadcrumbs
30 ml (2 tbsp) chopped fresh
  coriander or parsley
10 ml (2 tsp) ground cumin
1.25 ml (¼ tsp) cayenne pepper
5 ml (1 tsp) salt
1 egg, beaten
8 cherry tomatoes or 2 tomatoes,
  quartered
12 bay leaves
vegetable oil, for brushing
chopped coriander leaves, to
  garnish

1 First make the dip. Whip the
creams together, then fold in
the horseradish, vinegar and sugar.
Add salt and pepper to taste, then
spoon into a serving bowl and chill
in the refrigerator.

2 Put the minced beef in a bowl.
Grate in the onion, then add
the breadcrumbs, coriander,
cumin, cayenne and the salt.

3 Mix the ingredients well with
your hands until evenly
combined. Bind with the egg.

4 With wetted hands, form the
mixture into 16 balls. Thread 4
balls on each of 4 oiled kebab
skewers, alternating with tomatoes
and bay leaves.

5 Brush the kebabs with oil, then
grill under a preheated
moderate grill for 10 minutes,
turning them frequently and
brushing with more oil so that
they cook evenly.

6 Serve the beef kebabs hot on
individual plates, garnish with
coriander leaves and serve the
horseradish dip separately.

Menu Suggestion
These spicy kebabs and creamy
dip make an interesting family
supper dish. Serve on a bed of
long grain rice. A crunchy mixed
salad is the only other
accompaniment needed.

ITALIAN-STYLE MEATBALLS

1.00	🍳	✳	557 cals

Serves 4

30 ml (2 tbsp) olive oil

1 large onion, skinned and finely
  chopped

2 garlic cloves, skinned and
  crushed

397 g (14 oz) can chopped
  tomatoes

10 ml (2 tsp) dried mixed herbs

10 ml (2 tsp) dried oregano

salt and freshly ground pepper

450 g (1 lb) minced beef

50 g (2 oz) fresh white
  breadcrumbs

50 g (2 oz) Parmesan cheese,
  freshly grated

1 egg, beaten

20 small black olives, stoned

vegetable oil, for deep frying

100 ml (4 fl oz) red or white dry
  Italian wine

1 Heat the oil in a heavy-based
saucepan, add the onion and
half of the crushed garlic and fry
gently for about 5 minutes until
soft and lightly coloured.

2 Add the tomatoes, half of the
herbs and salt and pepper to
taste. Bring to the boil, stirring,
then lower the heat, cover and
simmer for about 20 minutes.

3 Meanwhile, make the
meatballs. Put the minced beef
in a bowl with the breadcrumbs,
Parmesan, remaining garlic and
herbs. Mix well with your hands,
then add salt and pepper to taste
and bind with the beaten egg.

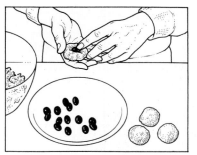

4 Pick up a small amount of the
mixture about the size of a
walnut. Press 1 olive in the centre,
then shape the mixture around it.
Repeat with the remaining olives
and meat to make 20 meatballs
altogether.

5 Heat the oil in a deep-fat fryer
to 190°C (375°F). Deep-fry
the meatballs in batches for
2–3 minutes until lightly browned,
then drain thoroughly on
absorbent kitchen paper.

6 Stir the wine into the tomato
sauce, then add 300 ml (½ pint)
water and the meatballs. Shake the
pan to coat the balls in the sauce,
adding more water if necessary.
Cover and simmer for a further
15 minutes, then taste and adjust
seasoning. Serve hot.

Menu Suggestion
Serve for a family supper with
tagliatelle or spaghetti, and hand
round a bowl of freshly grated
Parmesan for sprinkling on top.

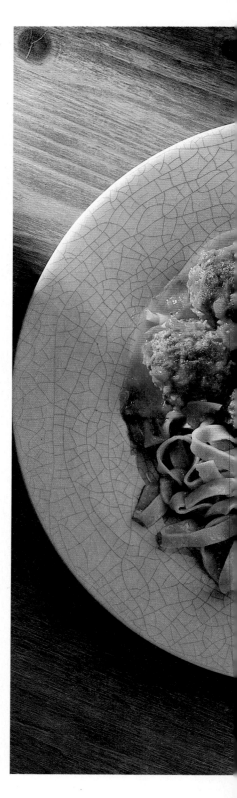

PASTITSIO

1.00	447–671 cals

Serves 4–6

30 ml (2 tbsp) olive oil

1 medium onion, skinned and finely chopped

1 garlic clove, skinned and crushed

450 g (1 lb) minced beef

397 g (14 oz) can tomatoes

10 ml (2 tsp) chopped fresh marjoram or 5 ml (1 tsp) dried

5 ml (1 tsp) ground allspice

salt and freshly ground pepper

225 g (8 oz) macaroni

2 eggs

300 ml ($\frac{1}{2}$ pint) natural yogurt

1 Heat the oil in a heavy-based saucepan, add the onion and garlic and fry gently for about 5 minutes until soft and lightly coloured.

2 Add the minced beef in batches and fry until browned, pressing the meat with the back of a wooden spoon to remove any lumps.

3 Add the tomatoes, marjoram, half of the allspice and salt and pepper to taste. Bring to the boil, stirring, then lower the heat, cover and simmer for 20 minutes.

4 Meanwhile, bring a large pan of salted water to the boil. Add the macaroni and boil for 10 minutes. Drain well.

5 Put the macaroni and minced beef mixture in an ovenproof dish. Mix well together, then taste and adjust seasoning.

6 In a bowl, beat the eggs with the yogurt and remaining allspice. Pour over the beef and macaroni. Bake in the oven at 190°C (375°F) mark 5 for 30 minutes. Serve hot.

Menu Suggestion
This Greek dish goes well with a salad of unpeeled cucumber cut into chunks, stoned black olives dressed with olive oil and lemon juice, and chopped fresh mint.

PASTITSIO

There are many variations of this Greek dish, which is immensely popular throughout mainland Greece as well as on the islands—if you have visited Greece on holiday you are sure to have eaten Pastitsio in one form or another. In many ways it bears a close resemblance to that other, more famous, Greek dish, moussaka, in that it has the same flavourings of tomatoes and allspice, and a similar thick topping made from natural yogurt and eggs. In Greece, this type of dish is almost always served lukewarm. The custard topping sets on standing, and the dish is them cut into slices or wedges like a cake.

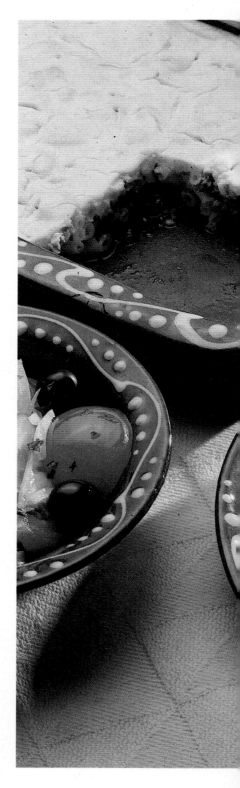

VEAL IN TOMATO AND WINE SAUCE

2.30	✳	414 cals

Serves 4

25 g (1 oz) butter
30 ml (2 tbsp) olive oil
3 onions, skinned and chopped
2 carrots, peeled and chopped
1–2 celery stalks, trimmed and chopped
1 garlic clove, skinned and crushed
4 pieces shin of veal, 900 g (2 lb) total weight
plain flour, for coating
salt and freshly ground pepper
300 ml ($\frac{1}{2}$ pint) dry white wine
350 g (12 oz) tomatoes, skinned and chopped, or 396 g (14 oz) can tomatoes
150 ml ($\frac{1}{4}$ pint) chicken stock
2 strips of lemon peel
1 bay leaf
15 ml (1 tbsp) chopped fresh parsley
2.5 ml ($\frac{1}{2}$ tsp) dried basil
1.25 ml ($\frac{1}{4}$ tsp) dried thyme

1 Melt the butter with the oil in a large frying pan. Add the chopped vegetables and the garlic and fry gently for 5 minutes until lightly coloured.

2 With a slotted spoon, transfer the vegetables to a large flame-proof casserole which will hold the pieces of veal in one layer.

3 Coat the pieces of veal in flour seasoned with salt and pepper. Add to the frying pan and fry over moderate heat until browned on all sides.

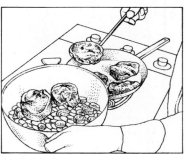

4 Place the pieces of browned veal on top of the vegetables in the casserole.

5 Pour the wine into the frying pan and bring to boiling point. Stir constantly with a wooden spoon, scraping base and sides of pan to dislodge any sediment.

6 Add the remaining ingredients and simmer, stirring, until the tomatoes are broken down. Add seasoning to taste, then pour over the veal in the casserole.

7 Cover and cook in the oven at 180°C (350°F) mark 4 for about 2 hours or until the veal is tender. Taste and adjust seasoning before serving.

Menu Suggestion
Serve with Italian risotto for a dinner party main course with a difference. A chilled dry Italian white wine such as Orvieto, Frascati or Soave would be an ideal drink.

VEAL IN CREAM SAUCE

| 1.45 | 🍴 | 469 cals |

Serves 6

900 g (2 lb) stewing veal or braising
    steak, cubed
450 g (1 lb) carrots, peeled and cut
    into fingers
225 g (8 oz) button onions, skinned
bouquet garni
150 ml ($\frac{1}{4}$ pint) white wine
900 ml ($1\frac{1}{2}$ pints) water
salt and freshly ground pepper
chicken stock, if necessary
50 g (2 oz) butter
50 g (2 oz) plain flour
300 ml ($\frac{1}{2}$ pint) single cream
lemon slices and grilled bacon
    rolls, to garnish

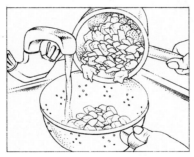

1 Cover the meat with cold
water, bring to the boil and
boil for 1 minute. Strain in a
colander and rinse under cold
running water to remove all scum.
Place the meat in a flameproof
casserole.

2 Add the carrots and onions to
the casserole with the bouquet
garni, wine, water and plenty of
seasoning. Bring slowly to the
boil, cover and simmer gently for
about $1\frac{1}{4}$ hours or until the meat
is tender.

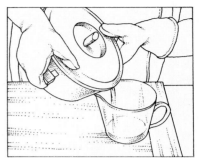

3 Strain off the cooking liquor,
make up to 750 ml ($1\frac{1}{4}$ pints)
with stock if necessary, reserve.
Keep the meat and vegetables
warm in a covered serving dish.

4 Melt the butter in a saucepan
and stir in the flour, cook
gently for 1 minute. Remove from
the heat and stir in the strained
cooking liquor; season well. Bring
to the boil, stirring all the time,
and cook gently for 5 minutes.

5 Take the sauce off the heat
and stir in the cream. Warm
very gently, without boiling, until
the sauce thickens slightly. Adjust
the seasoning. Pour the sauce over
the meat. Garnish with lemon
slices and bacon rolls.

Menu Suggestion
Veal in Cream Sauce is a very rich
dinner party dish. Serve with
plain boiled rice and a green salad
tossed in a vinaigrette dressing.

SWEDISH VEAL MEATBALLS

| 1.15* | ☐ | ✳* | 492 cals |

*plus 1 hour chilling; freeze after step 5

Serves 4

450 g (1 lb) lean veal, pork or beef (or a mixture of these)

100 g (4 oz) smoked streaky bacon, rinded

½ small onion, skinned

50 g (2 oz) stale brown bread

2.5 ml (½ tsp) ground allspice

salt and freshly ground pepper

75 g (3 oz) unsalted butter

450 ml (¾ pint) chicken stock

juice of ½ lemon

10 ml (2 tsp) chopped fresh dill or 5 ml (1 tsp) dried

142 ml (5 fl oz) soured cream

dill sprigs, to garnish (optional)

1 Put the meat, bacon, onion and bread through the blades of a mincer twice so that they are minced very fine. (Or work them in a food processor.)

2 Add the allspice to the mixture with seasoning to taste, then mix in with the fingertips to bind the mixture. (Pick up a handful and press firmly in the hand—it should cling together, but not be too wet.) Chill in the refrigerator for 1 hour.

3 Melt the butter gently in a large flameproof casserole. Dip a tablespoon in the butter, then use to shape a spoonful of the minced mixture.

4 Add the meatball to the casserole and then continue dipping the spoon in the butter and shaping meatballs until there are 12–14 altogether.

5 Fry the meatballs half at a time, if necessary, over moderate heat until they are browned on all sides. Return all the meatballs to the casserole, pour in the stock and lemon juice and bring slowly to boiling point. Lower the heat, add the dill and seasoning to taste, then cover the casserole and simmer gently for 30 minutes.

6 Stir the soured cream into the casserole and mix gently to combine evenly with the meatballs and cooking liquid. Taste and adjust the seasoning of the sauce and then garnish with dill sprigs, if liked. Serve hot.

Menu Suggestion
In Sweden and other parts of Scandinavia, these meatballs are traditionally served with boiled potatoes and creamed spinach.

SWEDISH VEAL MEATBALLS

Egg-shaped meatballs like these are popular all over Scandinavia, where they are served for the evening meal with hot vegetables. Our version are casseroled, but they are often served simply fried in butter, with a gravy made from the pan juices. In Denmark, these are known as frikadeller, and are immensely popular. The Danes use minced pork to make them, and sometimes they add a little smoked bacon to the mixture, for extra flavour. Some Scandinavian cooks stir a little soda water into the meat mixture before it is shaped. If you have soda water to hand, you can add up to 45 ml (3 tbsp) for a lighter result.

PORK ESCALOPES WITH SAGE

0.20	✳*	444 cals

* freeze at the end of stage 3

Serves 4

450 g (1 lb) pork fillet

1 egg, beaten

100 g (4 oz) fresh brown
   breadcrumbs

30 ml (2 tbsp) fresh sage or 10 ml
   (2 tsp) dried

grated rind of 1 lemon

75 g (3 oz) butter, melted

lemon wedges, to serve

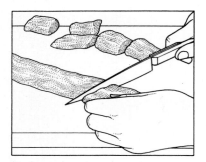

1 Using a sharp knife, trim any excess fat from the pork fillet and cut the meat into 5-mm ($\frac{1}{4}$-inch) slices.

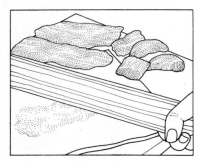

2 Beat out into even thinner slices between two sheets of greaseproof paper, using a meat cleaver or a wooden rolling pin.

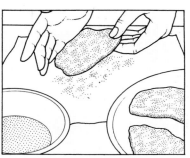

3 Coat the escalopes with the beaten egg. Then mix together the breadcrumbs, sage and grated lemon rind and coat the pork escalopes.

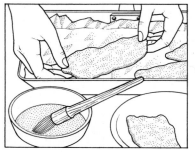

4 Lay in the base of a grill pan lined with foil (this quantity will need to be grilled in two batches). Brush with melted butter. Grill for about 3 minutes each side. Serve with lemon wedges.

PORK CHOPS IN ORANGE JUICE

| 1.00 | ✳* | 395 cals |

* freeze after step 5

Serves 4

30 ml (2 tbsp) plain flour, for coating

2.5 ml ($\frac{1}{2}$ tsp) ground mixed spice

salt and freshly ground pepper

4 loin pork chops, trimmed of rind and fat

15 g ($\frac{1}{2}$ oz) butter

30 ml (2 tbsp) vegetable oil

1 medium onion, skinned and chopped

half 170 ml (6 fl oz) can frozen concentrated orange juice

Tabasco sauce, to taste

1 bay leaf

30–45 ml (2–3 tbsp) shredded orange rind, to garnish

1 Place the flour in a bowl. Add the spice and seasoning. Dip the chops in the seasoned flour, ensuring that they are evenly coated on both sides.

2 Melt the butter with the oil in a large flameproof casserole. Add the chops and fry over moderate heat until browned on all sides. Remove from the casserole with a slotted spoon and drain on absorbent kitchen paper.

3 Add the onion to the casserole with any flour remaining from the chops and fry gently for 5 minutes until onion is soft but not coloured.

4 Dilute the orange juice with 200 ml (7 fl oz) water, then pour into the casserole and stir to combine with the onion.

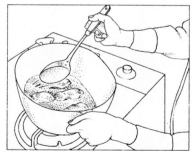

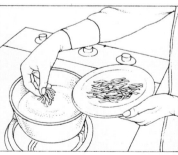

7 Transfer the chops to a warmed serving dish, then remove the bay leaf and taste and adjust the seasoning of the orange sauce. Pour the sauce over the chops, sprinkle with the blanched orange rind and serve at once.

Menu Suggestion
A colourful, fruity main course for a dinner party. Serve with buttered noodles and a crisp green salad or seasonal green vegetable.

5 Return the chops to the casserole and bring slowly to boiling point. Lower heat, add bay leaf and Tabasco to taste. Cover and simmer for 45 minutes until the chops are tender. Baste occasionally during this time.

6 A few minutes before the end of the cooking time, blanch the orange rind for 1 minute in boiling water. Drain, rinse under cold running water (to preserve a good colour), then dry on absorbent kitchen paper.

STIR-FRIED PORK AND VEGETABLES

| 0.50 | 433 cals |

Serves 4

700 g (1½ lb) pork fillet or
  tenderloin, trimmed of fat
60 ml (4 tbsp) dry sherry
45 ml (3 tbsp) soy sauce
10 ml (2 tsp) ground ginger
salt and freshly ground pepper
1 medium cucumber
30 ml (2 tbsp) vegetable oil
1 bunch of spring onions, trimmed
  and finely chopped
1–2 garlic cloves, skinned and
  crushed (optional)
30 ml (2 tbsp) cornflour
300 ml (½ pint) chicken stock
175 g (6 oz) beansprouts

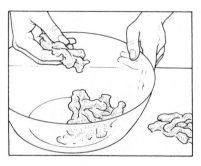

1 Cut the pork in thin strips and
place in a bowl. Add the
sherry, soy sauce, ginger and salt
and pepper to taste, then stir well
to mix. Set aside.

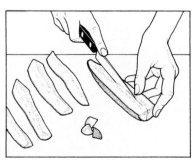

2 Prepare the cucumber sticks.
Cut the cucumber in half, then
cut into quarters lengthways, discarding the rounded ends. Leave
the skin on, to add colour.

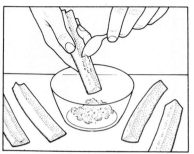

3 Using a sharp-edged teaspoon,
scoop out the seeds and
discard. Cut the cucumber
quarters lengthways again, then
slice across into strips about
2.5 cm (1 inch) long.

4 Heat the oil in a wok or large,
heavy-based frying pan, add
the spring onions and garlic, if
using, and fry gently for about 5
minutes until softened.

5 Add the pork to the pan,
increase the heat and stir-fry
for 2–3 minutes until lightly
coloured, tossing constantly so
that it cooks evenly.

6 Mix the cornflour with the
cold chicken stock and set
aside.

7 Add the cucumber, spring
onions and beansprouts to the
pork, with the cornflour and stock.
Stir-fry until the juices thicken
and the ingredients are well
combined. Taste and adjust
seasoning, then turn into a
warmed serving dish. Serve
immediately.

Menu Suggestion
Both meat and vegetables are
cooked together in this Chinese-
style dish. For a simple meal,
serve on a bed of egg noodles or
plain boiled rice.

CIDER PORK SAUTÉ

1.45	536 cals

Serves 4

450 g (1 lb) green dessert apples

450 g (1 lb) floury old potatoes
   (eg King Edwards)

salt and freshly ground pepper

50 g (2 oz) butter

450 g (1 lb) pork escalope

15 ml (1 tbsp) vegetable oil

1 small onion, skinned and finely
   chopped

15 ml (1 tbsp) plain flour

300 ml ($\frac{1}{2}$ pint) dry cider

30 ml (2 tbsp) capers

beaten egg, to glaze

1 Peel half of the apples. Halve, core and slice thickly. Peel the potatoes, then cut them into small chunks.

2 Cook the prepared apples and potatoes together in a saucepan of salted water for 20 minutes or until the potatoes are tender. Drain well.

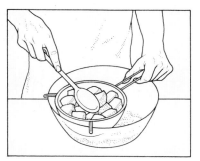

3 Press the apples and potatoes through a sieve into a bowl. Beat in 25 g (1 oz) of the butter, then add salt and pepper to taste.

4 Spoon or pipe the mixture down both ends of a 1.4 litre (2$\frac{1}{2}$ pint) shallow ovenproof dish.

5 Meanwhile, cut the pork escalope into fine strips. Quarter and core the remaining apples (but do not peel them). Slice them thickly into a bowl of cold water.

6 Heat the remaining butter and the oil in a large frying pan, add the pork strips, a few at a time, and fry until browned. Remove with a slotted spoon.

7 Add the onion to the pan and fry for 2–3 minutes. Return all the pork strips and stir in the flour. Cook, stirring, for 1–2 minutes, then blend in the cider and bring to the boil.

8 Drain the apple slices and stir into the pork. Simmer gently for 4–5 minutes, or until the pork is tender but the apple still holds its shape. Stir in the capers, with salt and pepper to taste.

9 Spoon the mixture into the centre of the dish. Brush the potato with beaten egg. Bake in the oven at 200°C (400°F) mark 6 for 25–30 minutes until golden. Serve hot, straight from the dish.

Menu Suggestion
Cider Pork Sauté is ideal for mid-week entertaining. Potatoes are included, so all you need is a seasonal vegetable like creamed spinach or a purée of sprouts.

CHINESE PORK AND GINGER CASSEROLE

| 1.25 | ✳* | 448 cals |

* freeze after step 4

Serves 4

30 ml (2 tbsp) vegetable oil

1 small onion, skinned and finely chopped

2.5 cm (1 inch) piece fresh root ginger

700 g (1½ lb) boneless lean pork (e.g. shoulder or sparerib), cubed

30 ml (2 tbsp) dry sherry

15 ml (1 tbsp) soy sauce

300 ml (½ pint) dry or American ginger ale

2.5 ml (½ tsp) five-spice powder

salt and freshly ground pepper

50 g (2 oz) stem ginger, sliced

½ red pepper, cored, seeded and sliced

½ yellow pepper, cored, seeded and sliced

1 Heat the oil in a flameproof casserole, add the onion and fry gently for 5 minutes until soft but not coloured.

2 Meanwhile, skin the root ginger and then crush the flesh with a mortar and pestle.

3 Add the crushed ginger to the casserole with the pork, increase the heat and fry until the meat is browned on all sides.

4 Stir in the sherry and soy sauce, then the ginger ale, five-spice powder and seasoning to taste. Bring slowly to boiling point, stirring, then lower the heat, cover and simmer for about 1 hour until the pork is just tender.

5 Add the stem ginger and pepper slices to the casserole and continue cooking for a further 10 minutes. Serve hot.

Menu Suggestion

An informal supper party dish. Serve with Chinese egg noodles and stir-fried vegetables such as grated carrots, finely sliced celery, green pepper and beansprouts.

SWEET AND SOUR SPARE RIB CHOPS

1.15*	✳*	372 cals

* plus 4 hours marinating; freeze in the marinade before cooking

Serves 4

30 ml (2 tbsp) wine vinegar

30 ml (2 tbsp) soy sauce

30 ml (2 tbsp) soft brown sugar

15 ml (1 tbsp) Worcestershire sauce

5 ml (1 tsp) garlic salt

1.25 ml ($\frac{1}{4}$ tsp) chilli powder

4 spare rib pork chops (see box)

45 ml (3 tbsp) vegetable oil

300 ml ($\frac{1}{2}$ pint) chicken stock or water

1 small bunch of spring onions, to finish

1 Make the marinade. Mix the first six ingredients together in a shallow dish. Add the chops and turn to coat, then cover and leave to marinate for 4 hours. Turn the chops in the marinade occasionally during this time.

2 Remove the chops from the marinade. Heat 30 ml (2 tbsp) of the oil in a flameproof casserole, which is large enough to hold the chops in a single layer. Add the chops and fry over brisk heat until browned on all sides.

3 Mix the marinade with the stock or water, then pour over the chops. Bring slowly to boiling point, then lower the heat, cover and simmer gently for 45 minutes or until the chops are tender.

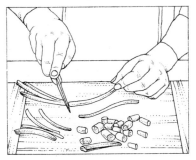

4 Ten minutes before serving, chop the spring onions, reserving the tops for the garnish. Heat the remaining oil in a small pan, add the chopped onions and fry gently for a few minutes until softened. Sprinkle over the dish just before serving and garnish with the reserved tops.

Menu Suggestion

Serve these spare rib chops for an informal supper party with a medley of fried rice, diced pepper and spring onions. Follow with a mixed salad.

SWEET AND SOUR SPARE RIB CHOPS

Take care to buy the right cut of pork for this recipe. Spare rib chops are from the neck end of the pig; thick and meaty, they become succulent and tender when casseroled, and yet they are inexpensive to buy compared with the leaner loin chops, that are better suited to a quick-cooking method such as grilling. Do not confuse spare rib chops with spare ribs, which are cut from inside the thick end of the belly—these are the kind used in Chinese cookery, most often served in a sweet and sour sauce.

CHILLI PORK AND BEANS

| 3.30* | 465–698 cals |

* plus overnight soaking

Serves 4–6

30 ml (2 tbsp) vegetable oil

900 g (2 lb) boneless pork shoulder, trimmed of fat and cut into cubes

1 large onion, skinned and roughly chopped

2 celery sticks, trimmed and sliced

1–2 garlic cloves, skinned and crushed

175 g (6 oz) red kidney beans, soaked in cold water overnight

15 ml (1 tbsp) black treacle

15 ml (1 tbsp) French mustard

5 ml (1 tsp) chilli powder

salt and freshly ground pepper

1 Heat 15 ml (1 tbsp) of the oil in a flameproof casserole, add the pork in batches and fry over high heat until coloured on all sides. Remove with a slotted spoon and drain on absorbent kitchen paper.

2 Lower the heat, then add the remaining oil to the pan with the onion, celery and garlic. Fry gently for 10 minutes until softened.

3 Drain the kidney beans and add to the pan with 1.1 litres (2 pints) water. Bring to the boil, stirring, then boil rapidly for 10 minutes to destroy any toxins in the beans.

4 Lower the heat, return the pork to the pan and add the black treacle, mustard, chilli powder and pepper to taste. Stir well to mix.

5 Cover the casserole and cook in the oven at 150°C (300°F) mark 2 for 3 hours. Stir the pork and beans occasionally during the cooking time and add more water if dry. Add 5 ml (1 tsp) salt half-way through, then taste and adjust seasoning before serving, adding more chilli powder if a hotter flavour is liked.

Menu Suggestion
Serve this hot Mexican-style dish for a family supper, with plain boiled rice and a salad of sliced avocado and tomato dressed with oil and lemon juice. A bowl of natural yogurt can also be served, to cool and refresh the palate.

PORK PAPRIKASH

2.30	✳✳	653 cals

* freeze at the end of step 3

Serves 4

50 g (2 oz) butter or margarine

30 ml (2 tbsp) olive oil

900 g (2 lb) boneless pork sparerib, trimmed of excess fat and cut into cubes

450 g (1 lb) Spanish onions, skinned and thinly sliced

2 garlic cloves, skinned and crushed (optional)

15 ml (1 tbsp) paprika

10 ml (2 tsp) caraway seeds

450 ml ($\frac{3}{4}$ pint) chicken stock

salt and freshly ground pepper

about 150 ml ($\frac{1}{4}$ pint) soured cream and snipped chives, to finish

1 Heat half of the butter with the oil in a flameproof casserole, add the cubes of pork and fry over high heat for about 5 minutes until coloured on all sides. Remove with a slotted spoon to a plate.

2 Reduce the heat to very low and melt the remaining butter in the pan. Add the onions and garlic, if using, and fry very gently for about 30 minutes until very soft and golden, stirring frequently to prevent catching and burning.

3 Stir the paprika and caraway seeds into the onions, then add the pork and juices and mix well. Pour in the stock, add salt and pepper to taste and bring slowly to the boil, stirring. Cover and cook gently for about 1$\frac{1}{2}$ hours until the pork is tender.

4 Before serving, taste and adjust seasoning. Drizzle over soured cream and sprinkle with chives. Serve hot.

Menu Suggestion
Pork Paprikash is best served on a bed of noodles or rice. Accompany with a green vegetable such as broccoli, courgettes or French beans, or follow with a colourful mixed salad of shredded lettuce or endive, red and green pepper rings and sliced cucumber.

CHINESE RED-COOKED PORK

2.30	887–1330 cals

Serves 4–6

1.8 kg (4 lb) rolled neck end of pork
  with skin

450 ml (¾ pint) chicken stock or
  water

200 ml (⅓ pint) soy sauce

4 garlic cloves, skinned and sliced

5 cm (2 inch) piece of fresh root
  ginger, peeled and sliced

10 ml (2 tsp) Chinese five-spice
  powder (see box)

60 ml (4 tbsp) sugar

150 ml (¼ pint) dry sherry

1 Bring a large saucepan of
water to the boil. Add the pork
and remove immediately, to scald
it. Drain and pat dry.

2 Pour the stock into a large
flameproof casserole. Add the
soy sauce, garlic, ginger, five-spice
powder and sugar. Bring to the
boil, then lower the heat and
simmer for 5 minutes.

3 Add the pork, skin side down,
to the casserole and baste well.
Cover and cook in the oven at 180°C
(350°F) mark 4 for 1½ hours.

4 Remove the lid of the
casserole, turn the meat skin
side up and baste well with the
juices. Return to the oven,
uncovered, for another 30 minutes
or until the pork is very tender,
basting regularly.

5 Transfer the casserole to the
top of the cooker. Add the
dry sherry and then bring the
juices to the boil.

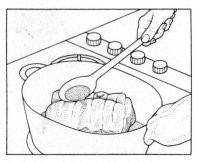

6 Boil rapidly for about 15
minutes, continually basting
the meat until glazed. Take care
that the meat does not catch or
burn. Serve the meat sliced, hot or
cold, with any remaining sauce.

Menu Suggestion
Red-Cooked Pork is rich and
spicy. Serve with a contrasting
plain accompaniment such as
boiled rice, and follow with stir-
fried crisp spring vegetables.

SWEET AND SOUR PORK

0.30	447 cals

Serves 4

700 g (1½ lb) boneless leg or
  shoulder of pork

20 ml (4 tsp) cornflour

salt and freshly ground pepper

vegetable oil for deep-frying,
  plus 15 ml (1 tbsp)

1 green pepper, cored, seeded
  and thinly sliced

30 ml (2 tbsp) sugar

30 ml (2 tbsp) white wine vinegar

30 ml (2 tbsp) tomato purée

30 ml (2 tbsp) pineapple juice

30 ml (2 tbsp) soy sauce

2 fresh or canned pineapple rings,
  finely chopped

1 Trim the fat off the pork, then
cut the meat into 2.5 cm
(1 inch) cubes. Coat in the cornflour, reserving 5 ml (1 tsp) for the
sauce. Add salt to taste.

2 Heat the vegetable oil in a
deep-fat fryer to 180°C
(350°F). Add half of the pork and
deep-fry for 8–9 minutes or until
tender. Remove with a slotted
spoon and drain on absorbent
kitchen paper. Keep hot while
frying the remaining pork.

3 Make the sauce. Heat the
15 ml (1 tbsp) vegetable oil in a
wok or frying pan, add the green
pepper and stir-fry for 1 minute.
Stir in the remaining ingredients
with the reserved cornflour. Stir-
fry for 1–2 minutes.

4 Add the pork and stir-fry for
1 minute. Taste and adjust
seasoning, then turn into a
warmed serving bowl. Serve hot.

Menu Suggestion
For a Chinese-style meal, serve
Sweet and Sour Pork with white
rice. Boil the rice, drain, then toss
in a little sesame oil for an
authentic flavour. Follow with a
salad of raw beansprouts, grated
carrot, shredded Chinese leaves
and strips of cucumber. Toss the
salad in an oil and vinegar dressing
flavoured with soy sauce.

**CHINESE RED-COOKED
PORK**
Five-spice powder is so called
because it is a mixture of five
different spices. Cinnamon,
cloves, fennel, star anise and
Szechuan peppercorns is the
usual combination, but the blend
can vary from one brand to
another, so that not all five-spice
powder tastes the same. Look for
it in packets and small jars in
Chinese specialist shops, and in
some large supermarkets and
delicatessens. It is not absolutely
essential for this dish if you are
unable to obtain it, ground mixed
spice can be used instead.

HUNTINGDON FIDGET PIE

1.15*   686 cals

* plus 30 minutes chilling

Serves 4

250 g (9 oz) plain flour

100 g (4 oz) butter or margarine

salt and freshly ground pepper

225 g (8 oz) streaky bacon, rinded
  and roughly chopped

1 medium onion, skinned and
  roughly chopped

225 g (8 oz) cooking apples, peeled,
  cored and roughly chopped

15 ml (1 tbsp) chopped parsley

150 ml (¼ pint) medium cider

beaten egg, to glaze

1 Make the pastry. Sift 225 g
(8 oz) of the flour and a pinch
of salt into a bowl. Cut the
butter into small pieces and rub
into the flour until the mixture resembles breadcrumbs. Add enough
water to mix to a firm dough.

2 Gather the dough into a ball
and knead lightly. Wrap in foil
and chill for 30 minutes.

3 Meanwhile, combine the
bacon, onion and apples in a
600 ml (1 pint) pie dish. Add the
parsley and salt and pepper.

4 Blend the remaining flour with
the cider, a little at a time, and
pour into the pie dish.

5 Roll out the pastry. Cut out a
thin strip long enough to go
around the rim of the pie dish.
Moisten the rim with water and
place the pastry strip on the rim.

6 Roll out the remaining pastry
for a lid, moisten the strip of
pastry, then place the lid on top
and press to seal. Knock up and
flute the edge.

7 Make a diagonal cross in the
centre almost to the edges of
the dish, then fold back to reveal
the filling.

8 Brush the pastry with the
beaten egg. Bake in the oven at
190°C (375°F) mark 5 for about 45
minutes, or until the pastry is
golden and the filling is cooked.

Menu Suggestion
Serve with seasonal vegetables for
an economical, yet tasty family
supper. Tankards of beer, lager or
cider make ideal drinks.

**HUNTINGDON
FIDGET PIE**
Fidget or Fitchett Pie was
traditionally made at harvest
time to feed the hungry workers.
Potatoes can be added to the
filling.

BACON IN CIDER WITH SAGE AND ONION DUMPLINGS

2.30	858 cals

Serves 6

1.1 kg (2½ lb) smoked collar of bacon

4 cloves

300 ml (½ pint) dry cider

1 bay leaf

125 g (4 oz) fresh white
  breadcrumbs

175 g (6 oz) self raising flour

50 g (2 oz) shredded suet

5 ml (1 tsp) rubbed sage

25 g (1 oz) butter or margarine

2 medium onions, skinned

salt and freshly ground pepper

parsley sprigs, to garnish

1 Place the bacon in a saucepan and cover with cold water. Bring slowly to the boil. Drain off the water. Pat the bacon dry.

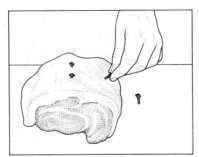

2 Slice off the rind if it is not cooked enough to peel away. Stud the fat with cloves.

3 Put the bacon in a shallow casserole with the cider and bay leaf. Cover tightly and cook in the oven at 180°C (350°F) mark 4 for 2¼ hours.

4 Meanwhile, mix the breadcrumbs, flour, suet and sage together in a bowl. Rub in the butter with your fingertips.

5 Coarsely grate in the onions. Bind to a soft dough with water, then add a little salt and freshly ground pepper.

6 Shape the dough into 12 dumplings. Forty-five minutes before the end of the cooking time, add the dumplings to the juices surrounding the bacon. Cover again and finish cooking. Serve the bacon sliced, with a little of the cooking liquid spooned over, surrounded by the dumplings. Garnish with parsley sprigs.

Menu Suggestion
With its sage and onion dumplings, this bacon dish is very substantial—ideal for a winter family supper. Serve with a seasonal green vegetable such as Brussels sprouts or spinach.

PEANUT GLAZED BACON HOCK

| 2.45 | 518 cals |

Serves 6

1.1 kg (2½ lb) bacon hock
1 medium carrot, peeled and sliced
1 medium onion, skinned and quartered
1 bay leaf
30 ml (2 tbsp) lemon marmalade
30 ml (2 tbsp) demerara sugar
10 ml (2 tsp) lemon juice
dash of Worcestershire sauce
25 g (1 oz) salted peanuts, chopped

1 Put the bacon in a casserole with the carrot, onion and bay leaf. Pour in enough water to come half-way up the joint. Cover and cook in the oven at 180°C (350°F) mark 4 for about 2¼ hours.

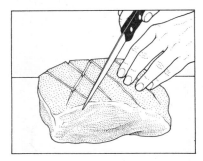

2 Remove the bacon from the casserole, carefully cut off and discard the rind, then score the fat with a sharp knife.

3 Put the marmalade, sugar, lemon juice and Worcestershire sauce in a bowl and mix well together with a wooden spoon.

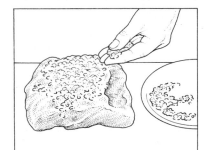

4 Spread the mixture over the surface of the joint. Sprinkle on the chopped peanuts.

5 Place the joint in a roasting tin. Increase the oven temperature to 220°C (425°F) mark 7 and return the joint to the oven for 15 minutes to glaze. Serve sliced.

Menu Suggestion
Glazed bacon is good for a family meal, served hot with seasonal vegetables. Alternatively, serve it sliced cold for a buffet party, with a selection of salads.

POT ROAST OF PORK AND RED CABBAGE

2.15	531 cals

Serves 4

45 ml (3 tbsp) red wine vinegar

450 g (1 lb) red cabbage

225 g (8 oz) cooking apple

15 ml (1 tbsp) demerara sugar

15 ml (1 tbsp) plain flour

salt and freshly ground pepper

700 g (1½ lb) boneless pork shoulder, rinded

coriander sprigs, to garnish

1 Bring a large saucepan of water to the boil, to which 15 ml (1 tbsp) of the vinegar has been added.

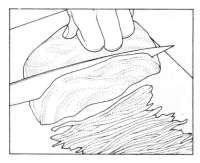

2 Meanwhile, shred the red cabbage. When the water is boiling, add the cabbage, bring back to the boil, then drain well.

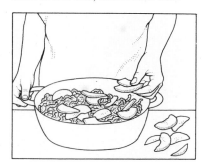

3 Peel, core and slice the apple and place with the cabbage in a casserole just wide enough to take the pork joint.

4 Add the sugar, the remaining vinegar, the flour and salt and pepper to taste. Stir well together.

5 Slash the fat side of the joint several times and sprinkle with plenty of salt and pepper. Place on top of the cabbage and cover the casserole.

6 Cook in the oven at 190°C (375°F) mark 5 for about 1¾ hours, or until pork is tender. Serve the pork sliced on a warmed serving platter, surrounded by cabbage. Garnish with coriander and serve the remaining cabbage in a serving dish.

Menu Suggestion
This tasty dish is good served for an everyday evening meal, with a plain accompaniment such as creamed potatoes.

GLAZED GAMMON STEAKS

0.25	753 cals

Serves 4

15 ml (1 tbsp) soy sauce

2.5 ml (½ tsp) dry mustard

15 ml (1 tbsp) golden syrup

1.25 ml (¼ tsp) ground ginger

90 ml (6 tbsp) orange juice

garlic salt

freshly ground black pepper

15 ml (1 tbsp) cornflour

15 ml (1 tbsp) lemon juice

8 bacon chops or 4 gammon steaks

1 In a small saucepan, combine the first five ingredients, with garlic salt and pepper to taste.

2 Blend the cornflour with the lemon juice, stir in a little of the mixture from the pan and then return it all to the pan. Bring to the boil, stirring all the time, until the mixture has thickened to a glaze. Remove from the heat.

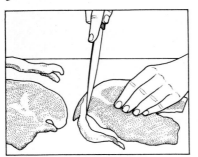

3 Cut most of the fat from the bacon chops or gammon steaks and then brush half of the glaze on one side.

4 Grill under moderate heat for 15 minutes, until the meat is cooked right through, brown and bubbling. Turn several times and brush with the remaining glaze during cooking. Serve hot.

Menu Suggestion

Serve with sauté potatoes and a medley of frozen vegetables such as peas, sweetcorn and peppers. Frozen stir-fried vegetables (available in packets from most supermarkets) make a good standby accompaniment when you are preparing a last-minute meal such as this one.

GLAZED GAMMON STEAKS

For everyday family meals and informal entertaining, bacon chops and gammon steaks are a good buy because they cook so quickly. They are also economical in that they have very little wastage in the form of fat or bone. For this recipe, a small amount of fat around the edges of the meat will help keep the meat moist during grilling. If you are using gammon steaks, it is a good idea to cut the fat at regular intervals to help prevent curling. Simply snip through the fat with sharp kitchen scissors, allowing about 5 mm (¼ inch) between cuts. This will give the finished dish an attractive professional touch, as well as helping the meat to cook more evenly.

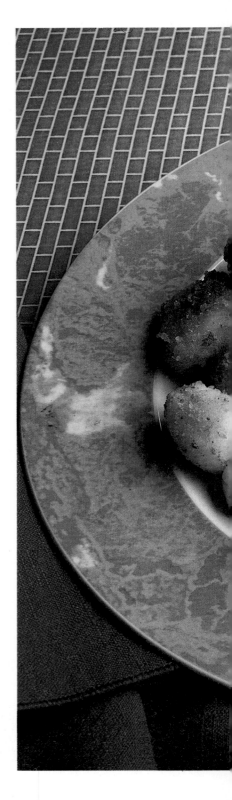

BRAISED OXTAIL

4.30	✳	256 cals

Serves 4

2 small oxtails cut up, about 1.4 kg (3 lb) total weight

30 ml (2 tbsp) plain flour

salt and freshly ground pepper

40 g (1½ oz) lard

350 g (12 oz) onions, skinned and sliced

900 ml (1½ pints) beef stock

150 ml (¼ pint) red wine

15 ml (1 tbsp) tomato purée

pared rind of ½ lemon

2 bay leaves

225 g (8 oz) carrots, peeled and thickly sliced

450 g (1 lb) parsnips, peeled and cut into chunks

chopped fresh parsley, to garnish

1 Coat the oxtails in the flour seasoned with salt and pepper. Heat the lard in a large flameproof casserole and brown the oxtail pieces, a few at a time. Remove from the casserole.

2 Fry the onions in the casserole for 5 minutes until lightly browned. Stir in any remaining flour, the stock, wine, tomato purée, lemon rind, bay leaves and season well. Bring to the boil and replace the meat.

3 Cover the pan with a tight-fitting lid and simmer the contents for 2 hours; skim well to remove any excess fat.

4 Stir the carrots and parsnips into the casserole. Cover and simmer for a further 2 hours or until the meat is tender.

5 Skim all fat off the surface of the casserole, adjust the seasoning and garnish with chopped parsley.

Menu Suggestion

Braised oxtail is a rich, satisfying dish for a midweek meal in winter. Serve with plain boiled or mashed potatoes and crisply cooked winter cabbage.

BRAISED OXTAIL

Oxtail is an inexpensive cut of beef with an excellent 'meaty' flavour and wonderfully succulent texture if cooked slowly as in this recipe. The main problem with oxtail, however, is its fattiness, which many people find off-putting, and yet there is a simple solution. Cook the casserole the day before required and leave it until completely cold. Chill it in the refrigerator overnight, at the end of which time the fat will have risen to the surface and formed a solid layer. Simply lift off this layer and you will find a thick, gelatinous gravy underneath, which becomes rich and flavoursome on reheating.

LIVER GOUJONS WITH ORANGE SAUCE

0.40	607 cals

Serves 4

350 g (12 oz) lamb's liver, sliced

75 ml (5 tbsp) plain flour

salt and freshly ground pepper

1 egg, beaten

125 g (4 oz) medium oatmeal

50 g (2 oz) butter or margarine

1 medium onion, sliced

300 ml ($\frac{1}{2}$ pint) lamb or beef stock

finely grated rind and juice of 1 medium orange

5 ml (1 tsp) dried sage

few drops of gravy browning

60 ml (4 tbsp) vegetable oil

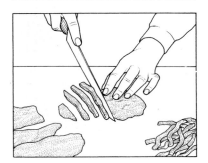

1 Cut the liver into 5 cm (2 inch) pencil-thin strips. Coat evenly in 45 ml (3 tbsp) of the flour, liberally seasoned with salt and freshly ground pepper.

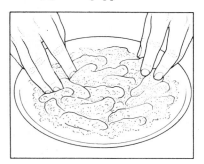

2 Dip the liver in the beaten egg, then roll in the oatmeal to coat. Chill in the refrigerator while preparing the sauce.

3 Melt 25 g (1 oz) of the butter in a saucepan, add the onion and fry gently until golden brown. Add the remaining flour and cook gently, stirring, for 1–2 minutes.

4 Gradually blend in the stock, orange rind and juice, sage and salt and pepper to taste. Bring to the boil, stirring constantly, then simmer for 10–15 minutes. Add the gravy browning and taste and adjust seasoning.

5 Heat the remaining butter and the oil in a frying pan, add the liver goujons and fry gently for 1–2 minutes until tender.

6 Arrange the goujons on a warmed serving platter and pour over a little of the sauce. Hand the remaining sauce separately in a sauceboat or jug.

Menu Suggestion

Serve on a bed of tagliatelle or Chinese noodles, and accompany with a green vegetable, or crunchy salad of raw beansprouts, celery and finely chopped walnuts, unsalted peanuts or cashews.

LIVER GOUJONS

The French word *goujon* is used in cooking to describe small strips or thin slivers of food; fish is often cut into goujons, then coated in egg and breadcrumbs before deep-frying. In this recipe, goujons of liver are coated in egg and oatmeal, which gives a nutty crunch to the coating, contrasting well with the soft texture of the liver inside. Orange is a popular flavour with liver in France, so too is vermouth. To give the dish an added 'kick', add a splash of dry vermouth with the orange juice in step 4.

LIVER AND BACON WITH POTATO PANCAKES

| 1.00 | 🍳 | 662 cals |

Serves 4

2 large potatoes, peeled

1 egg, beaten

60 ml (4 tbsp) self raising flour

salt and freshly ground pepper

vegetable oil and butter (optional), for frying

450 g (1 lb) lamb's liver, cut thickly

25 g (1 oz) plain flour

8 rashers of back bacon

2 medium onions, skinned and finely sliced

10 ml (2 tsp) wine vinegar

30 ml (2 tbsp) chopped fresh parsley, to garnish

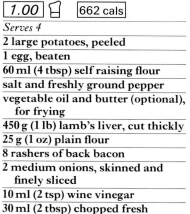

1 Grate the potatoes finely. Place in a sieve and rinse under cold water. Leave to drain for about 15 minutes. Wrap the potato in a clean tea towel and squeeze out any excess moisture.

2 Put the grated potatoes in a bowl. Add the egg, self raising flour and salt and pepper to taste, then mix well together.

3 Heat enough oil in a frying pan to come 0.5 cm ($\frac{1}{4}$ inch) up the sides. When hot, add large spoonfuls of potato mixture, pressing them into flat pancakes with a spatula or fish slice.

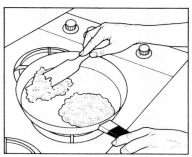

4 Cook the pancakes for about 5 minutes on each side until golden brown. Remove from the pan and drain on absorbent kitchen paper. Keep hot in the oven while cooking the liver.

5 Remove any ducts from the liver and discard. Dip the liver in the plain flour seasoned with salt and pepper. Heat a little oil or butter in a frying pan, add the liver and fry for 3–4 minutes on each side (it should still be slightly pink inside). Cover and keep hot.

6 Add the bacon to the pan and fry over brisk heat until crisp. Keep hot, but do not cover as it will become soggy.

7 Add the onions to the pan and cook for 5 minutes until just beginning to brown. Remove from the pan and arrange on a serving dish. Top with the liver and bacon and keep warm.

8 Add the vinegar and 45 ml (3 tbsp) water to the frying pan. Bring to the boil, scraping up any sediment from the bottom of the pan. Pour over the liver and bacon, then garnish with chopped parsley. Serve with the pancakes.

Menu Suggestion

This dish of fried liver, bacon and onions has its own accompaniment in the potato pancakes. Serve with colourful vegetables such as grilled tomatoes and peas.

PAN-FRIED LIVER AND TOMATO

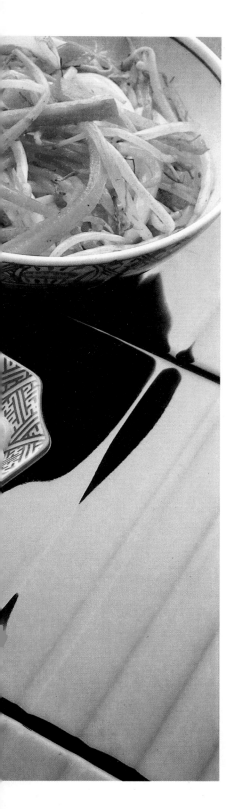

| 0.15* | 290 cals |

* plus several hours marinating

Serves 4

450 g (1 lb) lamb's liver, sliced

30 ml (2 tbsp) Marsala or sweet
   sherry

salt and freshly ground pepper

225 g (8 oz) tomatoes, skinned

30 ml (2 tbsp) vegetable oil

2 medium onions, skinned and
   finely sliced

pinch of ground ginger

150 ml ($\frac{1}{4}$ pint) chicken stock

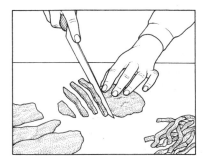

1 Using a very sharp knife, cut
   the liver into wafer-thin strips.
Place in a shallow bowl with the
Marsala or sweet sherry. Sprinkle
with freshly ground pepper to
taste. Cover and leave to marinate
for several hours.

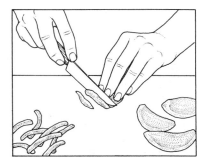

2 Cut the tomatoes into quarters
   and remove the seeds, reserving the juices. Slice the flesh into
fine strips and set aside.

3 Heat the oil in a sauté pan or
   non-stick frying pan. When
very hot, add the liver strips, a few
at a time. Shake the pan briskly
for about 30 seconds until pearls
of blood appear.

4 Turn the slices and cook for a
   further 30 seconds only (liver
hardens if it is overcooked).
Remove from the pan with a
slotted spoon and keep warm
while cooking the remaining
batches.

5 Add the onions and ginger to
   the residual oil in the pan and
cook, uncovered, for about 5
minutes. Add the stock and
seasoning to taste, return the liver
to the pan and add the tomatoes
and their juice. Bring just to the
boil, then turn into a warmed
serving dish and serve
immediately.

Menu Suggestion
Serve with Chinese egg noodles
and a stir-fried vegetable dish of
onion, ginger, beansprouts and
carrots.

PAN-FRIED LIVER
AND TOMATO
The Marsala used in this
recipe is an Italian fortified
white wine, available at good off
licences and some large supermarkets with good wine depart-
ments. The wine is named after
the town of Marsala, in the
western part of the island of
Sicily in the Mediterranean,
where it has been made for over
two hundred years. It was first
introduced into Britain by a
Liverpool merchant, John
Woodhouse, who set up a
thriving business importing
Marsala from Sicily—he even
supplied Lord Nelson's fleet
with it! There are different
types of Marsala, from very dry
to sweet. For this recipe, use one
of the dry varieties.

LIVER AND BACON ROULADES

0.25*	226–301 cals

* plus 1 hour marinating

Serves 3–4

4 rashers streaky bacon, about 100 g (4 oz) total weight

225 g (8 oz) lamb's liver

60 ml (4 tbsp) orange juice

30 ml (2 tbsp) brandy

15 ml (1 tbsp) chopped fresh marjoram or oregano or 5 ml (1 tsp) dried

salt and freshly ground pepper

1 Cut the rind off each rasher and stretch the rashers with a blunt-edged knife. Cut each rasher across into three pieces.

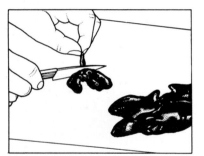

2 Divide the liver into twelve even-sized pieces, removing any skin and ducts.

3 Roll a piece of bacon around each piece of liver and secure with a cocktail stick. Place in the base of a foil-lined grill pan.

4 Mix the orange juice, brandy, herbs and seasoning together and spoon over the bacon rolls. Leave to marinate in a cool place for 1 hour or longer.

5 Cook under a moderate grill for 12–15 minutes, turning and basting occasionally. Remove cocktail sticks before serving, replacing them with fresh ones if liked. Serve hot.

LIVER AND BACON ROULADES

The French word *roulade* means a roll or a rolled slice in culinary terms, and here it is used to describe the way in which bacon is rolled around pieces of lamb's liver. The method of marinating meat in a mixture of alcohol, fruit juice, herbs and seasonings is a very common one in French cookery—the purpose of a marinade is to tenderize the meat and make it flavoursome.

Some meats are left to marinate for as long as 2–3 days, but most marinades are left for an hour or so, overnight at the most. The combination of alcohol and an acid liquid such as juice from citrus fruit helps break down any tough fibres and sinews in meat, so it is a process which is well worth doing if it is specified in a recipe, especially if the meat is one of the inexpensive, tougher cuts. Any alcohol can be used, but red or white wine and brandy are popular.

Wine vinegar and lemon juice are the usual acid ingredients, although orange juice as specified in this recipe has much the same effect. Fresh pineapple juice is another popular marinade ingredient; it contains an enzyme which breaks down tough fibres in tough cuts of meat.

KIDNEYS AND MUSHROOMS IN RED WINE

0.30	294–392 cals

Serves 3–4

50 g (2 oz) butter

2 onions, skinned and chopped

10 lamb's kidneys

45 ml (3 tbsp) plain flour

150 ml (¼ pint) red wine

150 ml (¼ pint) beef stock

bouquet garni

30 ml (2 tbsp) tomato purée

salt and freshly ground pepper

100 g (4 oz) mushrooms, sliced

chopped fresh parsley, to garnish

1 Melt the butter in a saucepan or a frying pan and fry the onions for about 5 minutes until golden brown.

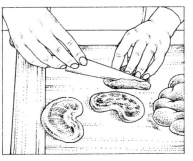

2 Wash, skin and core the kidneys and cut them into halves lengthways. Add to the pan and cook for 5 minutes, stirring occasionally.

3 Stir in the flour, pour in the wine and stock and bring slowly to the boil. Stir in the bouquet garni, tomato purée, seasoning and mushrooms. Cover and simmer for about 15 minutes until the kidneys are tender.

4 Remove the bouquet garni and adjust the seasoning. Serve sprinkled with chopped parsley.

Menu Suggestion

Serve for an informal supper party with boiled long-grain rice and a mixed salad tossed in plenty of vinaigrette dressing.

Sausage and Bean Ragout

2.30*	✳	710 cals

* plus overnight soaking

Serves 4

125 g (4 oz) haricot beans, soaked
  overnight

125 g (4 oz) red kidney beans,
  soaked overnight

30 ml (2 tbsp) vegetable oil

450 g (1 lb) pork sausages

175 g (6 oz) onions, skinned and
  sliced

227 g (8 oz) can tomatoes

15 ml (1 tbsp) cornflour

15 ml (1 tbsp) chilli seasoning

30 ml (2 tbsp) tomato purée

350 ml (12 fl oz) dry cider

salt and freshly ground pepper

1 Drain the haricot and kidney
beans and place in a saucepan.
Cover with cold water, bring to
the boil and boil rapidly for 10
minutes, then drain again.

2 Heat the oil in a large flameproof casserole and fry the
sausages for about 5 minutes until
browned. Remove from the
casserole and cut each sausage in
half crossways.

3 Add the onions to the casserole
and fry for 5 minutes until
golden brown. Return the
sausages to the casserole together
with the beans and tomatoes.

4 Blend the cornflour, chilli
seasoning and tomato purée
with a little cider until smooth,
then stir in the rest of the cider.
Pour into the casserole, mix well
and add pepper to taste.

5 Cover tightly and cook in the
oven at 170°C (325°F) mark 3
for about 2 hours or until beans
are tender. Add salt before
serving the ragout.

Menu Suggestion
A filling midweek family meal,
Sausage and Bean Ragout may be
served with fresh French bread,
boiled rice or creamed potatoes.
Follow with a green salad and
fresh fruit to complete the meal.

TOAD IN THE HOLE

0.45	483–643 cals

Serves 3–4

450 g (1 lb) pork sausages
25 g (1 oz) lard or dripping
225 ml (8 fl oz) milk
100 g (4 oz) plain flour
pinch of salt
1 egg

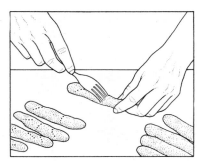

1 Prick the sausages all over with a fork. Put the lard in a Yorkshire pudding tin or small roasting tin and add the sausages.

2 Bake in the oven at 220°C (425°F) mark 7 for 10 minutes until the lard is hot.

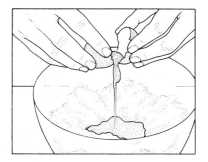

3 Meanwhile, make the batter. Mix the milk and 50 ml (2 fl oz) water together in a jug. Put the flour and salt in a bowl. Make a hollow in the centre and break the egg into it.

4 Mix the flour and egg together gradually, then add the milk and water, a little at a time, and beat until the mixture is smooth.

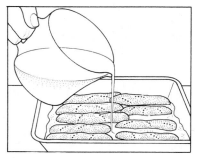

5 Pour the batter into the tin. Bake for about 30 minutes, or until golden brown and well risen. Do not open the oven door during baking or the batter might sink. Serve at once.

Menu Suggestion
Serve for an everyday family supper, with a crisply cooked green vegetable. Children will probably like Toad in the Hole with baked beans, which are just as nutritious as green vegetables.

TOAD IN THE HOLE
One of northern England's most famous dishes, Toad in the Hole is simply a Yorkshire pudding batter cooked with pork sausages. Years ago in Victorian times, when larger quantities of meat were eaten than they are today, Toad in the Hole was made with rump steak. Some cooks even added oysters and mushrooms to the steak, and there is even a recipe for Toad in the Hole made with a boned, stuffed chicken! Kidneys were also a favourite ingredient in those days and, if you like their flavour, they make a good combination with the sausages. You will need about 3 lamb's kidneys, which should be sliced and cooked with the sausages before pouring in the batter.

BAKED STUFFED LAMB'S HEARTS

3.20–3.50	425 cals

Serves 4

4 small lamb's hearts, total weight about 550 g (1¼ lb)

2 large onions, skinned

60 ml (4 tbsp) vegetable oil

50 g (2 oz) streaky bacon, rinded and chopped

50 g (2 oz) button mushrooms, chopped

50 g (2 oz) fresh breadcrumbs

finely grated rind of ½ lemon

15 ml (1 tbsp) lemon juice

30 ml (2 tbsp) chopped fresh parsley

salt and freshly ground pepper

2 carrots, peeled and sliced

300 ml (½ pint) lamb or chicken stock

15 ml (1 tbsp) tomato purée

chopped parsley and blanched julienne of lemon zest, to garnish

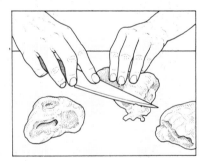

1 Wash the hearts thoroughly under cold running water. Trim them and remove any ducts.

2 Cut 1 of the onions in half and chop 1 half finely. Heat half of the oil in a frying pan, add the chopped onion, bacon and mushrooms and fry for about 5 minutes until the onion is softened. Turn into a bowl, add the breadcrumbs, lemon rind and juice, parsley and salt and pepper to taste. Mix well together. Leave to cool for 10 minutes.

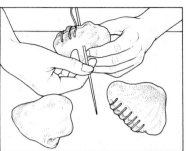

3 Use the stuffing to fill the hearts and sew up neatly to hold in the stuffing.

4 Chop the remaining onions roughly. Heat the remaining oil in a flameproof casserole, add the hearts, carrot and chopped onion and fry for about 5 minutes until lightly browned.

5 Stir in the stock, tomato purée, and salt and pepper. Bring to the boil. Cover tightly and cook in the oven at 170°C (325°F) mark 3 for 2½–3 hours, or until tender. Serve the hearts whole or sliced and pour the skimmed juices over. Garnish with chopped parsley and blanched julienne of lemon zest.

Menu Suggestion

Economical and filling, these stuffed lamb's hearts make a deliciously different family meal. Serve with a colourful vegetable macédoine and creamed potatoes.

BAKED STUFFED LAMB'S HEARTS

Lamb's hearts vary in size quite considerably, depending on the time of year. Very young lamb's hearts are small, weighing only about 75 g (3 oz) each, whereas the more mature hearts can weigh as much as double this. For this recipe, look for hearts weighing around 150 g (5 oz) each. Alternatively, if only the small hearts are available, buy 6 and slice them before serving.

Poultry and Game

CHICKEN WITH GARLIC

2.15	208 cals

Serves 6

60 ml (4 tbsp) olive or corn oil

1.8 kg (4 lb) chicken

1 sprig each of rosemary, thyme, savory and basil or 2.5 ml ($\frac{1}{2}$ tsp) dried

1 bay leaf

40 garlic cloves

salt and freshly ground pepper

grated nutmeg

300 ml ($\frac{1}{2}$ pint) hot water

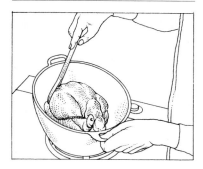

1 Heat the oil in a flameproof casserole and fry the chicken for about 8 minutes until browned on all sides. Remove chicken from the casserole.

2 Place the herbs in the base of the casserole. Arrange the garlic, unpeeled, in one layer over them. Place the chicken on top and season well with salt, pepper and nutmeg.

3 Cover and cook over a very low heat for $1\frac{1}{4}$–$1\frac{3}{4}$ hours until tender, adding a little hot water if necessary.

4 When cooked, remove the chicken and place on a warmed serving dish. Set aside and keep hot until required.

5 Strain the sauce into a bowl, pushing the garlic cloves through the sieve, using the back of a wooden spoon.

6 Add the hot water to the casserole and stir to lift the sediment. Return the sauce, taste and adjust seasoning, and simmer for 2 minutes or until hot. Transfer to a warm sauceboat and serve with the chicken.

Menu Suggestion
This French main course dish is traditionally served with rounds of French bread. A crisp green salad is usually served afterwards, to refresh the palate.

CHICKEN WITH GARLIC

In France, Poulet aux Quarantes Gousses d'Ail, is a popular recipe, and it's surprising how such a large number of garlic cloves tastes so mild. Any garlic residue can be used in the classic French potato dish Gratin Dauphinois, or another favourite French way of serving it is to spread it on slices of toasted baguette (French stick). This garlic-spread bread is then offered as an accompaniment to the chicken dish, and is considered a great delicacy by the French.

241

CHICKEN TERIYAKI

| 0.30* | ✳* | 220 cals |

* plus overnight marinating; freeze after step 2

Serves 4

4 boneless chicken breasts, skinned

90 ml (6 tbsp) soy sauce, preferably *shoyu* **(Japanese light soy sauce)**

90 ml (6 tbsp) *sake* **(Japanese rice wine) or dry sherry**

25 g (1 oz) sugar

2 garlic cloves, skinned and crushed

2.5-cm (1-inch) piece of fresh root ginger, peeled and crushed

salt and freshly ground pepper

15–30 ml (1–2 tbsp) vegetable oil

1 Cut the chicken breasts into bite-size pieces. Place the pieces in a shallow bowl.

2 Mix together half the soy sauce, *sake* and sugar, then add half the garlic and ginger with salt and pepper to taste. Pour over the chicken, cover and leave to marinate overnight.

3 Turn the chicken pieces in the marinade occasionally during the marinating time.

4 Thread the cubes of chicken on to oiled kebab skewers. Brush with oil. Barbecue or grill under moderate heat for about 10 minutes until the chicken is tender. Baste the chicken with the marinade and turn frequently during cooking.

5 While the chicken is cooking, put the remaining soy sauce, *sake* and sugar in a small pan with the remaining garlic and ginger. Add salt and pepper to taste and heat through.

6 Serve the chicken hot, with the warmed soy sauce mixture poured over to moisten.

Menu Suggestion
Spicy and sweet, this Japanese skewered chicken looks good on a bed of saffron rice. For an exotic touch, follow with a mixed salad of oriental vegetables such as beansprouts, bamboo shoots, spring onions and fresh root ginger.

CHICKEN TERIYAKI

This is a classic Japanese dish in which pieces of chicken are marinated overnight to tenderise and flavour them, then threaded onto skewers, grilled and served with a hot spicy sauce.

The marinade contains the Japanese rice wine, known as *sake*, which is sold in oriental stores. For a really authentic touch, try using bamboo skewers instead of metal ones—they will need soaking in hot water for about 15 minutes before use.

Pork fillet can be used in place of the chicken.

GINGERED JAPANESE CHICKEN

1.00	🥘	361 cals

Serves 4

1.4-kg (3-lb) oven-ready chicken
15 ml (1 tbsp) plain flour
15 ml (1 tbsp) ground ginger
60 ml (4 tbsp) vegetable oil
1 onion, skinned and sliced
283-g (10-oz) can bamboo shoots
1 red pepper, halved, seeded and
    sliced
150 ml ($\frac{1}{4}$ pint) chicken stock
45 ml (3 tbsp) soy sauce
45 ml (3 tbsp) medium dry sherry
salt and freshly ground pepper
100 g (4 oz) mushrooms, sliced

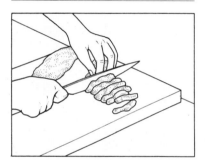

1 Cut all the flesh off the chicken and slice into chunky 'fingers', discarding the skin.

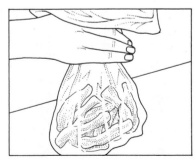

2 Mix the flour and ginger to-gether in a polythene bag and toss the chicken in it to coat.

3 Heat the oil in a very large sauté or deep frying pan and fry the chicken and sliced onion together for 10–15 minutes until they are both golden.

4 Cut up the canned bamboo shoots into 1-cm ($\frac{1}{2}$-inch) strips; add to the pan, together with the sliced pepper. Then stir in stock, soy sauce, sherry and seasoning. Bring to boil, cover, simmer 15 minutes.

5 Add the sliced mushrooms, cover again with lid and cook for a further 5–10 minutes, or until the chicken is tender.

BAMBOO SHOOTS

These are used extensively in oriental cooking, although the Chinese and Japanese use fresh shoots rather than the canned ones specified in this recipe. If fresh bamboo shoots are not obtainable, buy canned ones which are available at oriental specialist stores, large super-markets and delicatessens. These make a very convenient substi-tute—they are pre-cooked, so all they need is draining and heating through.

The flavour of bamboo shoots is very difficult to describe. Some say they taste like mild asparagus, although asparagus afficionadoes would probably disagree! Look for those canned in water rather than those canned in vinegar—they will have a milder flavour.

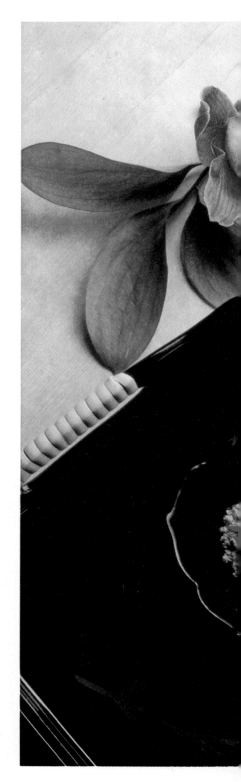

CHICKEN WITH SAFFRON

1.15	🍴	316 cals

Serves 6

6 chicken breasts about 175 g (6 oz) each
30 ml (2 tbsp) plain flour
salt and freshly ground pepper
40 g (1½ oz) butter
200 ml (⅓ pint) chicken stock
30 ml (2 tbsp) dry white wine
large pinch of saffron strands
2 egg yolks
60 ml (4 tbsp) single cream
vegetable julienne, to garnish

4 Sprinkle in the saffron, pushing it down under the liquid. Bring up to the boil, cover tightly, and bake in the oven at 180°C (350°F) mark 4 for about 50 minutes until cooked.

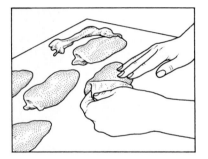

1 Skin the chicken breasts and remove any fat. Lightly coat the chicken in the flour, seasoned with salt and pepper.

2 Melt the butter in a medium flameproof casserole. Fry the chicken pieces, half at a time, for 5–10 minutes until golden brown.

3 Return all the chicken pieces to the pan with any remaining flour and pour in the chicken stock and white wine.

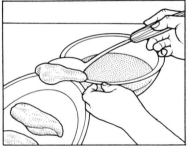

5 Lift the chicken out of the juices and place in an edged serving dish. Cover and keep warm in a low oven.

6 Strain the cooking juices into a small saucepan. Mix the egg yolks and cream together and off the heat stir into the cooking juices until evenly mixed.

7 Cook gently, stirring all the time until the juices thicken slightly. Do not boil. To serve, adjust seasoning, spoon over the chicken and garnish with vegetable julienne. Serve immediately.

NORMANDY CHICKEN

1.20		622 cals

Serves 4

30 ml (2 tbsp) vegetable oil
40 g (1½ oz) butter
4 chicken portions
6 eating apples
salt and freshly ground pepper
300 ml (½ pint) dry cider
60 ml (4 tbsp) Calvados
**60 ml (4 tbsp) double cream
(optional)**

1 Heat the oil with 25 g (1 oz) of the butter in a large flame-proof casserole. Add the chicken portions and fry over moderate heat until golden brown on all sides. Remove from the pan and drain on absorbent kitchen paper.

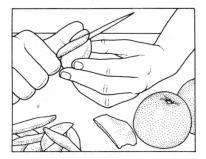

2 Peel, core and slice four of the apples. Add to the pan and fry gently, tossing constantly, until lightly coloured.

3 Return the chicken portions to the pan, placing them on top of the apples. Sprinkle with salt and pepper to taste, then pour in the cider. Bring to the boil, then cover and cook in the oven at 180°C (350°F) mark 4 for 45 minutes or until the chicken portions are tender.

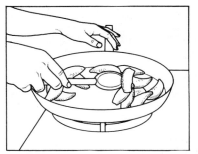

4 Meanwhile, peel, core and slice the remaining apples. Melt the 15 g (½ oz) butter in a frying pan, add the apple slices and toss to coat in the fat. Fry until lightly coloured, then spoon over chicken.

5 Warm the Calvados gently in a ladle or small pan, then ignite and pour over the chicken and apples. Serve as soon as the flames have died down, drizzled with cream, if liked.

Menu Suggestion
Calvados and cider combine together to make this main course dish quite heady. Serve with plain boiled potatoes sprinkled with melted butter and chopped fresh herbs, with a green salad tossed in a sharp vinaigrette dressing to follow. French dry cider would make an unusual drink to serve instead of wine.

CHICKEN PUFF PIE

2.15*	✳*	409–613 cals

* plus about 30 minutes cooling;
freeze after step 8

Serves 4–6

900 g (2 lb) chicken

1 bay leaf

**2 sprigs of fresh rosemary or
    marjoram, or 10 ml (2 tsp) dried**

salt and freshly ground pepper

**4 leeks, trimmed, washed and cut
    into 2-cm (¾-inch) lengths**

**2 large carrots, peeled and thickly
    sliced**

**100 g (4 oz) boiled ham, cut into
    bite-size pieces**

25 g (1 oz) butter or margarine

**1 medium onion, skinned and
    chopped**

45 ml (3 tbsp) flour

150 ml (¼ pint) milk

60 ml (4 tbsp) double cream

**225 g (8 oz) frozen puff pastry,
    defrosted**

1 egg, beaten, to glaze

1 Put the chicken in a large
    saucepan with the herbs and
salt and pepper to taste. Cover
with water and bring to the boil,
then cover with a lid and simmer
for 45–60 minutes until the
chicken is tender.

2 Remove the chicken from the
    liquid and leave to cool
slightly. Meanwhile, add the leeks
and carrots to the liquid, bring to
the boil and simmer for about 7
minutes until tender but still
crunchy. Remove from the pan
with a slotted spoon.

3 Remove the chicken meat
    from the bones, discarding the
skin. Cut into bite-size chunks.

4 Mix the chicken with the ham
    and cooked leeks and carrots in
a 1.1-litre (2-pint) pie dish.

5 Melt the fat in a clean sauce-
    pan, add the onion and fry
gently until soft. Sprinkle in the
flour and cook for 1–2 minutes,
stirring, then gradually add 600 ml
(1 pint) of the cooking liquid (discarding the bay leaf and herb
sprigs, if used). Bring to the boil
and simmer, stirring, until thick,
then stir in the milk and cream
with salt and pepper to taste. Pour
into the pie dish and leave for
about 30 minutes until cold.

6 Roll out the pastry on a
    floured work surface until
about 2.5 cm (1 inch) larger all
round than the pie dish.

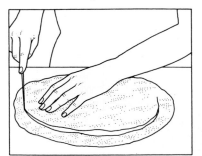

7 Cut off a strip from all round
    the edge of the pastry. Place
the strip on the moistened rim of
the pie dish, moisten the strip,
then place the pastry lid on top.

8 Press the edge firmly to seal,
    then knock up and flute. Make
a hole in the centre of the pie and
use the pastry trimmings to make
decorations, sticking them in place
with water.

9 Brush the pastry with beaten
    egg, then bake in the oven at
190°C (375°F) mark 5 for 30
minutes until puffed up and
golden brown. Serve hot.

Menu Suggestion
Ideal for a midweek family meal,
this filling chicken pie needs no
further accompaniment other than
a freshly cooked green vegetable
such as French beans or spinach.

—————— VARIATIONS ——————

Replace the leeks with **6 sticks of
celery**, cleaned and cut in the
same way. Add them to the pan 3
minutes after adding the carrots.

    Replace all of the leeks with **8
Jerusalem artichokes**, peeled
and thickly sliced.

    Replace one of the carrots with
1 medium turnip, peeled and
roughly cubed.

    Replace the carrots with **1
medium celeriac**, peeled and
cubed.

    Replace the puff pastry with the
same weight of shortcrust pastry.

    Add **100 g (4 oz) thickly sliced
mushrooms** and **5 ml (1
teaspoon) celery seeds** at step 5
when frying the onion.

STIR-FRIED CHICKEN WITH WALNUTS

0.20*	358 cals

* plus at least 1 hour marinating

Serves 4

4 boneless chicken breasts, skinned and cut into thin strips

5-cm (2-inch) piece of fresh root ginger, peeled and thinly sliced

60 ml (4 tbsp) soy sauce

60 ml (4 tbsp) dry sherry

5 ml (1 tsp) five-spice powder

45 ml (3 tbsp) sesame or vegetable oil

30 ml (2 tbsp) cornflour

150 ml ($\frac{1}{4}$ pint) chicken stock

salt and freshly ground pepper

75 g (3 oz) walnut pieces

$\frac{1}{4}$ cucumber, cut into chunks

spring onion tassels, to garnish

1 Put the chicken in a bowl with the ginger, soy sauce, sherry and five-spice powder. Stir well to mix, then cover and marinate for at least 1 hour.

2 Remove the chicken and ginger from the marinade with a slotted spoon. Reserve marinade.

3 Heat 30 ml (2 tbsp) of the oil in a wok or large heavy-based frying pan. Add the chicken and stir-fry over brisk heat for 5 minutes until well browned.

4 Mix the marinade with the cornflour then stir in the stock. Pour into the pan and bring to the boil, then add salt and pepper to taste and stir-fry for a further 5 minutes or until the chicken strips are tender.

5 Heat the remaining oil in a separate small pan, add the walnuts and cucumber and stir-fry briefly to heat through.

6 Transfer the chicken mixture to a warmed serving dish and top with the walnuts and cucumber. Garnish with spring onion tassels and serve.

Menu Suggestion
Serve with Chinese egg noodles, followed by a mixed salad of beansprouts, grated carrot, chopped celery and onion tossed in a dressing of oil, lemon juice and soy sauce.

CHICKEN FLORENTINE

1.00	527 cals

Serves 4

450 g (1 lb) fresh spinach
salt and freshly ground pepper
4 boneless chicken breasts, skinned
75 g (3 oz) butter or margarine
15 ml (1 tbsp) vegetable oil
1.25 ml ($\frac{1}{4}$ tsp) freshly grated
    nutmeg
25 g (1 oz) flour
450 ml ($\frac{3}{4}$ pint) milk

100 g (4 oz) Cheddar or Double
    Gloucester cheese, grated
pinch of ground mace
a little paprika

1 Wash the spinach, put into a pan with a pinch of salt. Cook over low heat for 7 minutes until just tender. Drain well.

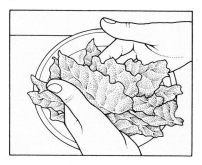

2 Meanwhile, cut each chicken breast in two horizontally. Melt 25 g (1 oz) of the fat in a frying pan with the oil. Fry the chicken for 3 minutes on each side.

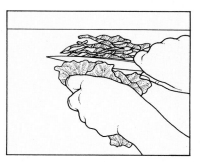

3 Chop the drained spinach. Mix with half of the remaining fat, the nutmeg and salt and pepper to taste. Put the spinach in the base of an ovenproof dish, then arrange the chicken on top.

4 Melt the remaining fat in a pan. Add the flour and stir for 2 minutes. Gradually add the milk, then the cheese, mace and seasoning. Simmer until thick.

5 Pour over the chicken, then sprinkle with the remaining cheese and a little paprika. Bake at 190°C (375°F) mark 5 for 30 minutes.

Menu Suggestion
Serve with mashed potatoes.

CHICKEN CROQUETTES

| 0.20* | ✳* | 642 cals |

* plus 30 minutes cooling and at least
2–3 hours chilling; freeze after step 3

Serves 2

50 g (2 oz) butter or margarine

60 ml (4 tbsp) flour

200 ml ($\frac{1}{3}$ pint) milk

$\frac{1}{2}$ lemon

15 ml (1 tbsp) capers, chopped

175 g (6 oz) cooked chicken, minced

15 ml (1 tbsp) chopped fresh
  parsley

salt and freshly ground pepper

1 egg, beaten

50 g (2 oz) dry white breadcrumbs

vegetable oil, for frying

lemon wedges, to garnish

1 Melt the fat in a saucepan.
Add the flour and cook gently,
stirring, for 3 minutes. Remove
from the heat and gradually stir in
the milk. Bring to the boil and
cook for about 5 minutes, stirring
all the time, until the sauce is
smooth and thick.

2 Grate in the lemon rind. Add
the capers and chicken with
the parsley and seasoning. Mix
well together. Cool for 30 minutes,
then chill in the refrigerator for
2–3 hours or preferably overnight.

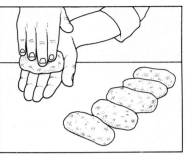

3 Shape the mixture into six
even-sized croquettes. Dip in
the beaten egg, then roll in the
breadcrumbs to coat.

4 Deep-fry at 180°C (350°F) or
shallow fry in hot oil for about
10 minutes or until golden brown.
Serve hot, with lemon wedges.

Menu Suggestion
Serve Chicken Croquettes hot
with French fries and a colourful
medley of mixed vegetables such
as peas, sweetcorn and red
peppers, or a tomato salad.

CHICKEN CROQUETTES
Croquettes come in all shapes
and sizes. Although they are
most often made into sausage
shapes as here, you can also try
making them into rectangles,
balls, egg shapes or flat cakes.
Traditionally, they were often
served as an entrée, or made very
small and used as a garnish for
roast meat or game.
  The basic mixture can be
varied by replacing the sauce
with egg-enriched rice or potato
purée, seasoned and mixed with
any variety of flavourings and
finely chopped or minced meat,
fish or vegetable. Croquettes can
also be made from thin pancakes
stuffed and rolled up, then
sliced, dipped in egg and breadcrumbs and deep-fried.

CHICKEN CORDON BLEU

| 0.45* | ⬚ | ✳* | 452 cals |

* plus 30 minutes chilling; freeze after
step 5

Serves 4

**4 boneless chicken breasts,
  skinned**

4 thin slices of boiled ham

4 thin slices of Gruyère cheese

salt and freshly ground pepper

about 25 g (1 oz) flour

1 egg, beaten

75 g (3 oz) dried white breadcrumbs

60 ml (4 tbsp) vegetable oil

50 g (2 oz) butter

**lemon twists and sprigs of fresh
  herbs, to garnish**

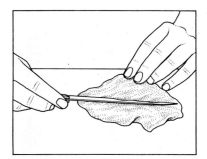

1 Slit along one long edge of
each chicken breast, then carefully work knife to the opposite
edge, using a sawing action.

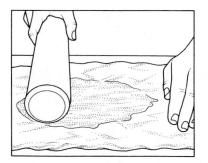

2 Open out the chicken breast,
place between two sheets of
damp greaseproof paper or cling
film and beat with a meat bat or
rolling pin to flatten slightly.

3 Place a slice of ham on top of
each piece of chicken, then a
slice of cheese. Fold the chicken
over to enclose ham and cheese.

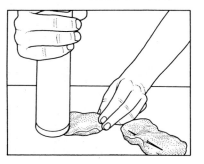

4 Pound the open edge of the
parcels so that they stay together, then secure with wooden
cocktail sticks.

5 Sprinkle the chicken parcels
with salt and pepper to taste,
then coat lightly in flour. Dip in
the beaten egg, then in the breadcrumbs. Press the breadcrumbs on
firmly so that they adhere evenly
and completely coat the chicken.
Refrigerate for about 30 minutes.

6 Heat the oil and butter together in a large heavy-based
frying pan (you may need to use
two if the chicken parcels are
large), then fry the chicken for 10
minutes on each side until crisp
and golden. Drain on absorbent
paper, remove the cocktail sticks,
then arrange the chicken on a
warmed serving platter and
garnish with lemon and herbs.

Menu Suggestion
Crunchy on the outside, meltingly
delicious on the inside, Chicken
Cordon Bleu goes well with
vegetables such as mushrooms, or
French beans, spinach, courgettes
and mange-touts. Sauté potatoes
can also be served, for hungry
guests!

CIRCASSIAN CHICKEN

| 1.30 | 366–549 cals |

Serves 4–6

1.8 kg (4 lb) chicken

1 medium onion, skinned and sliced

2 sticks of celery, roughly chopped

1 carrot, peeled and roughly chopped

few sprigs of parsley

salt and freshly ground pepper

100 g (4 oz) shelled walnuts

40 g (1½ oz) butter

45 ml (3 tbsp) vegetable oil

1.25 ml (¼ tsp) ground cinnamon

1.25 ml (¼ tsp) ground cloves

5 ml (1 tsp) paprika

1 Put the chicken in a large saucepan with the vegetables, parsley, 5 ml (1 tsp) salt and pepper to taste. Cover the chicken with water and bring to the boil. Lower heat, half cover pan with a lid and simmer for 40 minutes.

2 Remove the chicken from the pan, strain the cooking liquid and set aside. Cut the chicken into serving pieces, discarding the skin.

3 Pound the walnuts with a pestle in a mortar until very fine, or grind them in an electric grinder or food processor.

4 Melt the butter with 15 ml (1 tbsp) oil in a large frying pan. Add the chicken pieces and fry over moderate heat for 3–4 minutes until well coloured.

5 Add 450 ml (¾ pint) of the cooking liquid, the walnuts, cinnamon and cloves. Stir well to mix, then simmer uncovered for about 20 minutes or until the chicken is tender and the sauce thickly coats the chicken. Stir the chicken and sauce frequently during this time.

6 Just before serving, heat the remaining oil in a separate small pan. Sprinkle in the paprika, stirring to combine with the oil.

7 Taste and adjust the seasoning of the walnut sauce. Arrange the chicken and sauce on a warmed serving platter and drizzle with the paprika oil. Serve at once.

Menu Suggestion
For a Middle-Eastern style meal, serve the chicken and walnut sauce in a ring of saffron rice. Follow with a tomato, onion and black olive salad sprinkled with olive oil and lemon juice.

KOTOPOULO KAPANICI

1.00	✳	416 cals

Serves 4

4 chicken portions, skinned

salt and freshly ground pepper

45 ml (3 tbsp) olive oil

15 g ($\frac{1}{2}$ oz) butter

1 small onion, skinned and chopped

3 garlic cloves, skinned and crushed

100 ml (4 fl oz) dry white wine

450 g (1 lb) ripe tomatoes, skinned, seeded and chopped

15 ml (1 tbsp) tomato purée

1 cinnamon stick

4 cloves

6 allspice berries

150 ml ($\frac{1}{4}$ pint) water

175-g (6-oz) can or jar artichoke hearts, drained (optional)

15–30 ml (1–2 tbsp) chopped fresh parsley or coriander

1 Sprinkle the chicken liberally with salt and pepper. Heat the oil with the butter in a large flame-proof casserole, add the chicken and fry over moderate heat for about 5 minutes until well coloured on all sides. Remove from the pan with a slotted spoon and set aside.

2 Add the onion and garlic to the pan and fry gently for about 5 minutes until soft.

3 Return the chicken to the pan, pour in the wine, then add the tomatoes and tomato purée and mix well. Let the mixture bubble for a few minutes.

4 Meanwhile, pound the spices with a pestle in a mortar. Add to the casserole with the water and stir well to mix. Cover the pan and simmer for about 45–60 minutes until the chicken is tender

5 Add the artichokes (if using) about 10 minutes before the end of cooking time, to heat through. Taste and adjust seasoning, stir in the parsley or coriander and serve immediately.

Menu Suggestion

This Greek chicken casserole with its spicy tomato sauce goes well with plain boiled rice or a Greek potato dish made by tossing new potatoes in their skins in a mixture of olive oil, white wine and crushed coriander seeds. Follow with a salad of raw shredded white cabbage and lettuce, sliced onion, black olives and crumbled Feta cheese tossed in an olive oil and lemon juice dressing.

KOTOPOULO KAPANICI

This spicy chicken casserole comes from Greece. The Greeks would choose a boiling fowl rather than a young chicken, which would be reserved for grilling, or any other quick method of cooking. The chicken is simmered gently in a rich tomato and wine mixture until very tender and juicy. What makes it different from other chicken casseroles is the addition of cinnamon, cloves and allspice which give the finished dish a distinctive warm and spicy flavour. Although all these spices are available ground, the flavour is far superior if you buy them whole and grind your own just before using.

Cinnamon is the aromatic bark of a type of laurel tree, native to India, while allspice 'berries' are the dried fruit of the pimento tree, native to the West Indies. Cloves are the dried flower buds of the clove tree, most often associated with baking.

261

SPANISH CHICKEN

| 1.15 | ✳ | 513 cals |

Serves 4

60 ml (4 tbsp) olive oil

1 onion, skinned and chopped

2 garlic cloves, skinned and crushed

4 chicken portions

60 ml (4 tbsp) brandy

2 small peppers (1 red and 1 green or yellow), cored, seeded and sliced

4 large tomatoes, skinned and chopped

150 ml (¼ pint) dry white wine

150 ml (¼ pint) chicken stock or water

10 ml (2 tsp) chopped fresh rosemary or 5 ml (1 tsp) dried

salt and freshly ground pepper

1 Heat the oil in a flameproof casserole, add the onion and garlic and fry gently for 5 minutes until soft but not coloured.

2 Add the chicken portions and fry for a few minutes more, turning the chicken constantly so that the pieces become browned on all sides.

3 Warm the brandy gently in a small pan or ladle. Remove the casserole from the heat, pour the brandy over the chicken and set it alight with a match.

4 When the flames have died down, return the casserole to the heat and add the peppers and tomatoes. Fry over moderate heat for about 10 minutes, mashing the tomatoes down to a purée with a wooden spoon.

5 Pour in the wine and stock and bring slowly to boiling point. Lower the heat, add the rosemary and seasoning to taste, then cover and simmer for 30 minutes or until the chicken is tender when pierced with a skewer. Taste and adjust seasoning before serving.

Menu Suggestion

A quick-to-make main course for an informal dinner party, Spanish Chicken is best served with saffron rice or hot herb bread. Follow with a salad of shredded lettuce and finely chopped onion tossed in olive oil, lemon juice and salt and freshly ground pepper.

SPANISH CHICKEN

Olive oil, onion, garlic, peppers and tomatoes are all ingredients which conjure up a vivid image of colourful Spanish cookery. Wine and spirits also play quite a large part in the cuisine of Spain, although this is less well known than with French cookery, for example.

Don't worry about the high alcohol content of this recipe, which combines both brandy and wine together—a popular

Spanish combination. The actual alcohol content is burnt off by the flaming of the brandy, and evaporated by the heating of the wine, as long as the cooking time is at least 20 minutes, which it is in the case of the recipe above. If the alcohol were not eliminated in this way, the flavour of the finished dish would be raw and harsh. In this recipe the alcohol gives body and richness to the sauce.

CHICKEN DHANSAK

| *1.15* | ✳ | 568 cals |

Serves 4

40 g (1½ oz) ghee or clarified butter

1 onion, skinned and chopped

2.5 cm (1 inch) piece fresh root ginger, skinned and crushed

1–2 garlic cloves, skinned and crushed

4 chicken portions

5 ml (1 tsp) ground coriander

2.5 ml (½ tsp) chilli powder

2.5 ml (½ tsp) ground turmeric

1.25 ml (¼ tsp) ground cinnamon

salt

225 g (8 oz) red lentils, rinsed and drained

juice of 1 lime or lemon

fresh lime slices and coriander leaves, to garnish

1 Melt the ghee or butter in a flameproof casserole, add the onion, ginger and garlic and fry gently for 5 minutes until soft but not coloured.

2 Add the chicken portions and spices and fry for a few minutes more, turning the chicken constantly so that the pieces become coloured on all sides.

3 Pour enough water into the casserole to just cover the chicken. Add salt to taste, then the red lentils.

4 Bring slowly to boiling point, stirring, then lower the heat and cover the casserole. Simmer for 40 minutes or until the chicken is tender when pierced with a skewer. During cooking, turn the chicken in the sauce occasionally, and check that the lentils have not absorbed all the water and become too dry—add water if necessary.

5 Remove the chicken from the casserole and leave until cool enough to handle. Take the meat off the bones, discarding the skin. Cut the meat into bite-sized pieces, return to the casserole and heat through thoroughly. Stir in the lime or lemon juice; taste and add more salt if necessary. Garnish with fresh lime slices and coriander leaves before serving.

Menu Suggestion
Serve this hot Indian curry with boiled or fried basmati rice and a yogurt and cucumber salad (raita) for a cooling effect. Indian bread such as paratha or puri (packet mixes are now widely available) can also be served as an appetising accompaniment.

CHICKEN DHANSAK

Ghee or clarified butter is used frequently in Asian cookery. To make it, simmer melted butter in a heavy pan until a thick froth forms on top. Lower the heat and continue simmering until froth starts to separate and sediment settles at the bottom. Cool slightly, then strain through a metal sieve lined with muslin or a clean tea-towel. Discard sediment. Store ghee in refrigerator.

CARIBBEAN CHICKEN

0.50* | 447 cals

* plus overnight marinating

Serves 4

4 boneless chicken breasts, skinned

15 ml (1 tbsp) vinegar

425 g (15 oz) can pineapple slices in natural juice

10 ml (2 tsp) soft brown sugar

salt and freshly ground pepper

45 ml (3 tbsp) vegetable oil

175 g (6 oz) long grain rice

1½ green, red or yellow peppers, cored, seeded and sliced

Tabasco sauce, to taste

60 ml (4 tbsp) dark rum

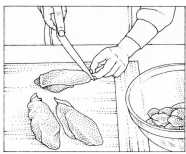

1 Cut the chicken into bite-sized pieces and place in a bowl. Make the marinade. Mix together the vinegar, pineapple juice, sugar, 10 ml (2 tsp) salt and pepper to taste. Pour over the chicken, cover and leave to marinate overnight. Turn the chicken in the marinade occasionally during this time.

2 Drain the chicken and reserve the marinade. Make the marinade up to 600 ml (1 pint) with water and set aside.

3 Heat the oil in a flameproof casserole, add the chicken and fry over moderate heat until turning colour on all sides. Add the rice and most of the pepper and fry for 5 minutes, stirring.

4 Pour in the marinade and bring slowly to the boil. Stir once, then shake in Tabasco sauce to taste and lower the heat. Cover and simmer for 20 minutes or until the chicken and rice are tender and most of the liquid has been absorbed.

5 Chop the pineapple and add to the casserole with the rum. Fold in gently and heat through. Taste and adjust seasoning before serving. Garnish with remaining pepper slices.

Menu Suggestion

Caribbean Chicken combines meat, vegetables and rice in one dish. Serve with hot French bread and follow with a green salad, for an informal meal.

265

STOVED CHICKEN

2.15	586 cals

Serves 4

50 g (2 oz) butter

1.4 kg (3 lb) chicken, jointed

100 g (4 oz) streaky bacon, rinded and chopped

1.1 kg (2½ lb) floury potatoes such as King Edwards

2 large onions, skinned and sliced

salt and freshly ground pepper

10 ml (2 tsp) chopped fresh thyme or 2.5 ml (½ tsp) dried

600 ml (1 pint) chicken stock

snipped chives, to garnish

1 Melt 25 g (1 oz) of the butter in a frying pan and fry the chicken and bacon for 5 minutes until lightly browned.

2 Peel the potatoes and cut into 5 mm (¼ inch) slices. Place a thick layer of potato slices, then sliced onion, in the base of a casserole. Season well, add the thyme and dot with butter.

3 Add the chicken, season and dot with butter. Cover with the remaining onions and finally a layer of potatoes. Season and dot with butter. Pour over the stock.

4 Cover and cook in the oven at 150°C (300°F) mark 2 for about 2 hours until the chicken is tender and the potatoes are cooked, adding a little more hot stock if necessary.

5 Just before serving sprinkle snipped chives over the top of the dish.

Menu Suggestion

Chicken and potatoes are cooked together in this casserole recipe. A seasonal vegetable such as carrots, peas or green beans is all that is needed for a family meal.

STOVED CHICKEN

This hearty dish made with simple, everyday ingredients would originally have been made with a boiling fowl, but nowadays these are not so easy to obtain, so an oven-ready or roasting chicken is used instead. The recipe originated in Scotland, where it is also sometimes called 'stovies', from the French verb 'étouffer', meaning to cook in an enclosed pot. During the alliance between the Scottish and the French in the 17th century, there were many words such as this one with a French derivation. Stoved Chicken or Stovies used to be served at rural weddings in the Highlands, but this custom has died out now and the dish has become traditional family fare.

GOLDEN BAKED CHICKEN

1.15	324 cals

Serves 4

4 chicken portions

1 small onion, skinned and finely chopped

salt and freshly ground pepper

50 g (2 oz) fresh white breadcrumbs

15 ml (1 tbsp) chopped fresh parsley and thyme or 5 ml (1 tsp) dried mixed herbs

50 g (2 oz) butter or margarine, melted

1 Wipe the chicken portions and season well with salt and freshly ground pepper.

2 Mix the breadcrumbs with the onion and herbs.

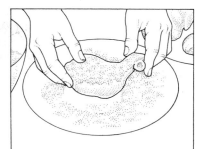

3 Brush the chicken joints all over with the butter or margarine; toss them in the herbed breadcrumbs and place in a buttered ovenproof dish.

4 Bake in the oven at 190°C (375°F) mark 5, for about 1 hour or until golden. Baste occasionally during cooking. Serve hot, straight from the dish.

Menu Suggestion
Serve with jacket-baked potatoes cooked in the oven at the same time, and a salad of tomato and raw onion with a lemony vinaigrette dressing.

FRENCH-STYLE ROAST CHICKEN

1.00	349–465 cals

Serves 3–4

1–1.4 kg (2¼–3 lb) oven ready chicken

5–6 sprigs fresh tarragon or parsley or 5 ml (1 tsp) dried tarragon or parsley

100 g (4 oz) butter, softened

salt and freshly ground pepper

150 ml (¼ pint) chicken stock

watercress, to garnish

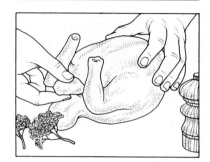

1 Wipe the inside of the chicken, then put the tarragon or parsley inside it, with 15 g (½ oz) of the butter and some pepper.

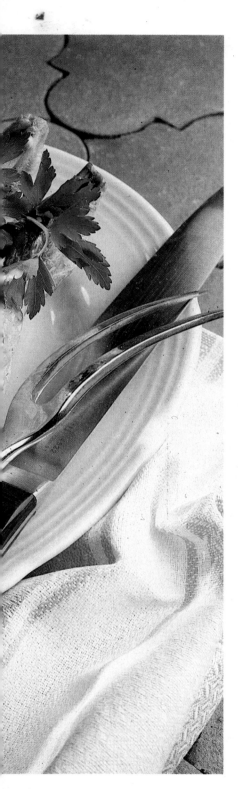

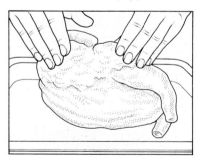

2 Place on one side in a roasting tin, smear all over with one third of the remaining butter and roast in the oven at 220°C (425°F) mark 7 for 15 minutes.

3 Turn the chicken onto the other side, smear with half the remaining butter and return to the oven. Roast for another 15 minutes.

4 Turn the chicken breast side up, smear with the rest of the butter, return to the oven and roast at 190°C (375°F) mark 5 for 20–30 minutes, or until tender.

5 Place the chicken on a serving dish and keep warm while making the gravy.

6 To make the gravy, place the roasting tin on top of the cooker and scrape any sediment sticking to the bottom. Add the stock and bring to the boil, then simmer for 2–3 minutes, stirring. Add seasoning to taste and pour into a warmed gravy boat. Garnish the chicken with watercress and serve immediately, with the gravy handed separately.

Menu Suggestion
Serve with the French potato dish *gratin dauphinois*—thinly sliced potatoes baked in a gratin dish with onion, cream and Gruyère cheese. Follow with a simple green salad tossed in vinaigrette dressing.

FRENCH-STYLE ROAST CHICKEN

The French have a unique way of cooking chicken which gives a wonderfully moist and succulent flesh. The secret lies in smearing the bird with plenty of butter and turning it over at regular intervals during roasting. Tarragon has a natural affinity with chicken, and is the most popular herb to cook with it in France, so try to use it if you want an authentic 'French' flavour—it grows very easily in the garden in summer.

HINDLE WAKES

3.15*	281–421 cals

* plus overnight soaking

Serves 4–6

1.6 kg (3½ lb) boiling chicken with
  giblets, trussed

600 ml (1 pint) water

salt and freshly ground pepper

50 g (2 oz) butter or margarine

450 g (1 lb) leeks, sliced and washed

6 carrots, peeled and thickly sliced

225 g (8 oz) prunes, soaked
  overnight and stoned

25 g (1 oz) plain flour

1 Place the giblets in a saucepan
with the water and 5 ml (1 tsp)
salt. Bring to the boil, then cover
and simmer for 30 minutes.

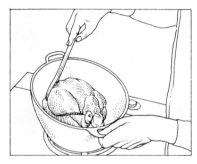

2 Meanwhile, melt 25 g (1 oz) of
the fat in a large flame-
proof casserole and fry the chicken
for about 8 minutes until browned
all over. Remove from casserole.

3 Fry the leeks and carrots for 3
minutes. Return the chicken
and add the drained prunes.
Strain in the giblet stock and
season with pepper.

4 Cover and cook in the oven at
170°C (325°F) mark 3 for
about 2–2½ hours or until tender.

5 Arrange the chicken, vegetables and prunes on a large
warmed platter. Keep hot.

6 Skim any fat off the sauce.
Blend together the remaining
fat and the flour to form a paste.
Add to the sauce, a little at a time,
and stir over a gentle heat until
thickened. Do not boil. Adjust the
seasoning to taste and serve the
sauce separately.

Menu Suggestion
Serve this old English dish with
jacket baked potatoes or creamed
potatoes and a green vegetable.

272

TURKEY PAPRIKA WITH PASTA

| 0.40 | 385 cals |

Serves 4

30 ml (2 tbsp) vegetable oil

75 g (3 oz) onion, skinned and sliced

450 g (1 lb) turkey breasts

10 ml (2 tsp) paprika

450 ml ($\frac{3}{4}$ pint) chicken stock

salt and freshly ground pepper

1 green pepper, cored, seeded and sliced

100 g (4 oz) small pasta shapes

142 ml (5 fl oz) soured cream

paprika, to garnish

1 Heat the oil in a large sauté pan and fry the onion for 5 minutes until golden brown.

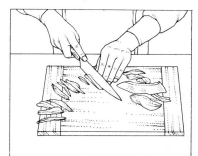

2 Skin the turkey breasts, discard any bone and cut flesh into small finger-sized pieces.

3 Add the turkey and paprika to the pan and toss over a moderate heat for 2 minutes.

4 Stir in the stock and seasoning and bring to the boil. Add the green pepper and pasta, cover and simmer gently for 15–20 minutes until turkey and pasta are tender.

5 Stir in the soured cream and adjust the seasoning. To serve, garnish with a little paprika.

Menu Suggestion

Quick and easy to make, this casserole needs no accompaniment other than a crisp green salad.

TRADITIONAL ROAST TURKEY

5.30–6.30	668–834 cals

Serves 8–10

50 g (2 oz) butter

3 medium onions, skinned and
    finely chopped

225 g (8 oz) lean veal, minced

175 g (6 oz) lean bacon, rinded and
    minced

175 g (6 oz) fresh white
    breadcrumbs

2 large mushrooms, chopped

15 ml (1 tbsp) chopped fresh
    parsley or 5 ml (1 tsp) dried

2.5 ml ($\frac{1}{2}$ tsp) mace

1.25 ml ($\frac{1}{4}$ tsp) cayenne

salt and freshly ground pepper

1 egg, beaten

100 g (4 oz) suet or 60 ml (4 tbsp)
    beef dripping

225 g (8 oz) medium oatmeal

4.5–5.5 kg (10–12 lb) turkey

melted dripping or butter, for
    brushing

1 Make the veal forcemeat stuffing. Melt the butter in a small frying pan, add 1 of the onions and fry gently for 5 minutes.

2 Meanwhile, put the veal and bacon in a bowl and beat well.

3 Stir in the fried onions, breadcrumbs, mushrooms, parsley, mace, cayenne and salt and pepper to taste. Bind with the beaten egg; if the mixture is too stiff, add a little milk. Cool for 20 minutes.

4 Make the oatmeal stuffing. Melt the suet or dripping in a frying pan, add the remaining onions and fry gently for 5 minutes until soft but not coloured. Stir in the oatmeal and cook over a gentle heat, stirring, until the mixture is thick and thoroughly cooked. Add plenty of salt and pepper to taste. Turn into a greased 600 ml (1 pint) pudding basin. Cover with greaseproof paper and foil.

5 Remove the giblets and wash the bird. Drain well and pat dry with absorbent kitchen paper.

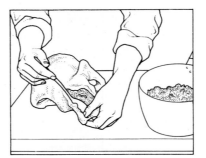

6 Stuff the neck end of the turkey with the veal stuffing, taking care not to pack it too tightly. Cover the stuffing smoothly with the neck skin.

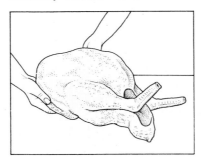

7 With the bird breast side up, fold the wing tips neatly under the body, catching in the neck skin.

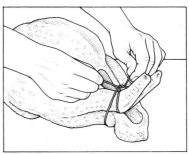

8 Truss the bird and tie the legs together. Make the body as plump and even in shape as possible.

9 Weigh the bird and calculate the cooking time, allowing 20 minutes per 450 g (1 lb) plus 20 minutes. Put the bird breast side up on a rack in a roasting tin. Brush with melted dripping and sprinkle with plenty of salt and pepper.

10 Cover the bird loosely with foil. Roast in the oven at 180°C (350°F) mark 4 for the calculated cooking time until tender, removing the foil and basting the turkey 30 minutes before the end of cooking time. Turn off the oven and leave the turkey to rest for up to 30 minutes before carving. One hour before the end of cooking the turkey; put the oatmeal stuffing to steam.

TRADITIONAL ROAST TURKEY

Turkey has been the traditional meat for Christmas in Britain since the 16th century. Turkeys were in fact brought to England from the New World by a Yorkshireman, William Strickland, and in his home town of Boynton-on-the-Wold, near Bridlington, there is a wooden turkey lectern in his honour in the local church.

In early days, the turkeys were walked to market at Christmastime, sometimes hundreds of miles. To protect their feet during the long journey, they wore leather 'boots', or their feet were painted with tar!

TURKEY IN SPICED YOGURT

1.30*	328 cals

* plus overnight marinating

Serves 6

turkey leg on the bone, about 1.1 kg
(2½ lb) in weight

7.5 ml (1½ tsp) ground cumin

7.5 ml (1½ tsp) ground coriander

2.5 ml (½ tsp) ground turmeric

2.5 ml (½ tsp) ground ginger

salt and freshly ground pepper

284 g (10 oz) natural yogurt

30 ml (2 tbsp) lemon juice

45 ml (3 tbsp) vegetable oil

225 g (8 oz) onions, skinned and
sliced

45 ml (3 tbsp) desiccated coconut

30 ml (2 tbsp) plain flour

150 ml (¼ pint) chicken stock or
water

chopped fresh parsley, to garnish

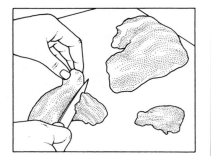

1 Cut the turkey meat off the
bone into large fork-sized
pieces, discarding the skin (there
should be about 900 g [2 lb] meat).

2 Make the marinade. In a large
bowl mix the spices with the
seasoning, yogurt and lemon juice.
Stir well until evenly blended.
Fold through the turkey meat until
coated with the yogurt mixture.
Cover tightly with cling film and
refrigerate overnight.

3 Heat the oil in a medium
flameproof casserole, add the
onion and fry for about 5 minutes
until lightly brown. Add the coconut and flour and fry gently, stirring for about 1 minute.

4 Off the heat stir in the turkey
with its marinade, and the
stock. Return to the heat and bring
slowly to the boil, stirring all the
time to prevent sticking.

5 Cover tightly and cook in the
oven at 170°C (325°F) mark 3
for 1–1¼ hours or until the turkey
is tender when tested with a fork.
To serve, adjust the seasoning and
serve garnished with parsley.

YOGURT

Plain unsweetened yogurt is used
extensively in Indian and Middle
Eastern cooking for many
reasons. It is often used as a
marinade as in this recipe, because it has the effect of ten-
derizing meat—it contains certain
live bacteria which help break
down tough fibres and sinews,
making the meat more succulent
and juicy when cooked.

Plain yogurt is also used to
offset the hotness of chillies and
the rawness of spices. For this
reason it can be combined with
the other ingredients as here, although it is often served as a side
dish for people to help themselves whenever they feel a dish
is too hot for their liking. It is
for this same reason that Indians
often drink yogurt when eating
curry—to counteract the heat of
the food, refresh the palate and
aid digestion. Called *lassi*, this
yogurt drink is made by diluting
yogurt with water then whisking
it until frothy.

BAKED TURKEY ESCALOPES WITH CRANBERRY AND COCONUT

| 0.50 | 🍳 | ✳* | 391 cals |

* freeze after step 2

Serves 4

| 450 g (1 lb) boneless turkey breast |
| salt and freshly ground pepper |
| 20 ml (4 tsp) Dijon mustard |
| 60 ml (4 tbsp) cranberry sauce |
| 15 g (½ oz) flour |
| 1 egg, beaten |
| 15 g (½ oz) desiccated coconut |
| 40 g (1½ oz) fresh breadcrumbs |
| 50 g (2 oz) butter or margarine |

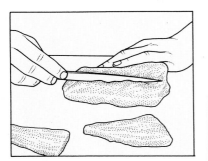

1 Thinly slice the turkey breast to give four portions.

2 Bat out the escalopes between two sheets of damp grease-proof paper or cling film. Season, then spread each portion with mustard and cranberry sauce.

3 Roll up, starting from the thin end, and secure with a cocktail stick or toothpick. Dust each portion with flour, then brush with egg. Combine the coconut and breadcrumbs then coat the turkey with the mixture.

4 Melt the fat in a frying pan, add the turkey portions, and fry until brown on both sides. Transfer to a baking tin just large enough to take the turkey in a single layer and baste with more fat. Bake in the oven at 180°C (350°F) mark 4 for about 40 minutes until tender.

Menu Suggestion

Serve these scrumptiously crisp escalopes with a salad of chopped and grated raw vegetables (e.g. celery, peppers, white cabbage, carrot and onion) tossed in a mayonnaise, soured cream or yogurt dressing. Alternatively, serve with a simple green salad.

BAKED TURKEY ESCALOPES WITH CRANBERRY AND COCONUT

Cranberries are a distinctively sharp-tasting fruit which make a delicious sauce, used here to add zest to turkey meat. The fresh fruit have a limited season, but they can also be bought frozen or canned throughout the year. Cultivated mainly in America, the ruby red berries grow on vines in flooded marshy soil. To harvest them, the water is whipped up by a machine. This dislodges the fruit which floats to the surface and is separated off from the leaves and other debris. The sorting process includes a special machine which bounces the berries over a barrier seven times—if the berries don't bounce they are rejected as unsound!

Cranberry sauce is good mixed with fresh orange juice and poured over vanilla ice-cream, sweet pancakes or waffles, and whole berries are good in beef and pork casseroles.

TURKEY GROUNDNUT STEW

1.15	465–698 cals

Serves 4–6

30 ml (2 tbsp) vegetable oil

2 onions, skinned and chopped

1 garlic clove, skinned and crushed

1 large green pepper, cored, seeded and chopped

900 g (2 lb) boneless turkey, cut into cubes

175 g (6 oz) shelled peanuts

600 ml (1 pint) chicken stock

salt and freshly ground pepper

60 ml (4 tbsp) crunchy peanut butter

10 ml (2 tsp) tomato purée

225 g (8 oz) tomatoes, skinned and roughly chopped

2.5–5 ml (½–1 tsp) cayenne pepper

few drops of Tabasco sauce

chopped green pepper, to garnish

1 Heat the oil in a flameproof casserole, add the onion, garlic and green pepper and fry gently for 5 minutes until they are soft but not coloured.

2 Add the turkey and fry for a few minutes more, turning constantly until well browned on all sides.

3 Add the peanuts, stock and salt and pepper to taste and bring slowly to boiling point. Lower the heat, cover and simmer for 45 minutes or until the turkey is tender.

4 Remove the turkey from the cooking liquid with a slotted spoon and set aside. Leave the cooking liquid to cool for about 5 minutes.

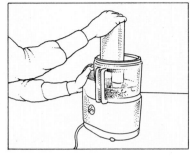

5 Work the cooking liquid and nuts in an electric blender or food processor, half at a time, until quite smooth. Return to the pan with the remaining ingredients, add the turkey and reheat. Taste and adjust seasoning before serving, adding more cayenne if a hot flavour is liked. Garnish with chopped green pepper.

Menu Suggestion

Groundnut stews are traditionally served in the Caribbean with plain boiled rice and a dish of root vegetables such as turnip, swede or parsnip. If liked, hot pepper sauce can also be offered as an additional accompaniment.

TURKEY GROUNDNUT STEW

Groundnut stews originated in West Africa, where groundnuts (or peanuts as we call them) grow in profusion. The cook would buy fresh peanut paste from the market to make groundnut stew, which was a popular Sunday lunch dish — served with ice-cold beer and garnished with fried bananas. Due to the slave trade, groundnut stews spread to the West Indies, becoming an integral part of the local cuisine.

Recipes for groundnut stew vary enormously, some using beef, others chicken, turkey or rabbit. Some recipes use only peanut butter, others like this one, a combination of whole peanuts and peanut butter, which is more authentic. If you like, you can toast or roast the peanuts after shelling, for a darker colour.

STUFFED TURKEY LEGS

2.00	459 cals

Serves 6

2 turkey legs (drumsticks), at least 900 g (2 lb) total weight

225 g (8 oz) pork sausagemeat

15 ml (1 tbsp) chopped fresh tarragon or 2.5 ml ($\frac{1}{2}$ tsp) dried tarragon

10 ml (2 tsp) chopped fresh parsley

salt and freshly ground pepper

50 g (2 oz) button mushrooms, sliced

25 g (1 oz) flour

1 egg white, beaten

175 g (6 oz) fresh white breadcrumbs

100 g (4 oz) butter or margarine, softened

15 ml (1 tbsp) French mustard

watercress, to garnish

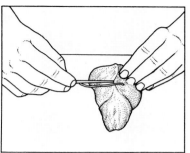

3 Reshape the stuffed turkey legs, then sew them up neatly, using fine string.

4 Dip the legs in flour, brush with beaten egg white and place seam side down in a greased roasting tin.

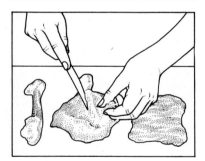

1 Skin the turkey legs, slit the flesh and carefully ease out the bone and large sinews.

2 Mix the sausagemeat, herbs and seasoning, and spread one quarter of the mixture over each boned leg. Cover with a layer of sliced mushrooms, then top with more sausagemeat stuffing.

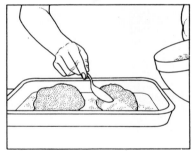

5 Beat together the breadcrumbs, butter and mustard. Spread over the tops and sides only of the legs.

6 Bake in the oven at 190°C • (375°F) mark 5 for about 1 hour 40 minutes, until tender with a crisp, golden crust. Remove the string, slice, and serve with gravy made from the pan juices. Garnish with a sprig of watercress.

Menu Suggestion
Serve these roasted turkey legs sliced, as an unusual alternative to the traditional Sunday roast, with vegetables, roast potatoes and gravy made from the turkey's cooking juices.

TURKEY SAUTÉ WITH LEMON AND WALNUTS

| 0.20 | 383 cals |

Serves 4

450 g (1 lb) turkey breast steaks
30 ml (2 tbsp) cornflour
1 green pepper
30 ml (2 tbsp) vegetable oil
40 g (1½ oz) walnut halves or pieces
25 g (1 oz) butter or margarine
60 ml (4 tbsp) chicken stock
30 ml (2 tbsp) lemon juice
45 ml (3 tbsp) lemon marmalade
5 ml (1 tsp) white wine vinegar
1.25 ml (¼ tsp) soy sauce
salt and freshly ground pepper

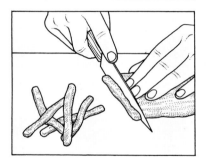

1 Cut up the turkey flesh into 5-cm (2-inch) pencil thin strips. Toss in the cornflour.

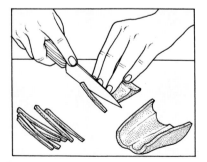

2 Slice the green pepper into fine strips, discarding the core and all the seeds.

3 Heat the oil in a large sauté or deep frying pan, add the walnuts and pepper strips and fry for 2–3 minutes. Remove from the pan with a slotted spoon.

4 Melt the fat in the residual oil and fry the turkey strips for 10 minutes until golden. Stir in the stock and lemon juice, stirring well to remove any sediment at the bottom of the pan. Add the lemon marmalade, vinegar, soy sauce and some salt and pepper.

5 Return the walnuts and green pepper to the pan. Cook gently for a further 5 minutes, until the turkey is tender. Taste and adjust seasoning and serve immediately.

Menu Suggestion
The subtle sweetness of this simple-to-make sauté dish gives it a most unusual flavour. Serve with a plain accompaniment such as boiled rice or Chinese egg noodles, so your guests can appreciate its flavour to the full.

TURKEY SAUTÉ
The French word sauté (literally 'to jump') has been adopted into the English language, and this method of quick cooking is now very popular.

Whatever food you choose to cook, the principles of sautéing are always the same — the meat is cut into fairly small pieces and tossed quickly in hot fat or oil. It is then cooked for the minimum amount of time with the other chosen ingredients and a dash of liquid to moisten the pan until the food is just tender. The whole process is easy, and it's a conveniently quick and tasty way of cooking.

TURKEY STROGANOFF

0.15	310 cals

Serves 4

450 g (1 lb) turkey fillet

15 ml (1 tbsp) vegetable oil

50 g (2 oz) butter

30 ml (2 tbsp) brandy

1 garlic clove, skinned and crushed

salt and freshly ground pepper

225 g (8 oz) button mushrooms, sliced

1 green pepper, cored, seeded and sliced

60 ml (4 tbsp) soured cream

1 Slice the piece of turkey fillet into pencil-thin strips, using a sharp knife.

2 Heat the oil and butter in a large sauté pan and brown the turkey strips. Remove from the heat. Heat the brandy in a small pan, ignite and pour over the turkey. Return to the heat then add the garlic and seasoning.

3 Cover the pan and simmer for about 4–5 minutes or until the turkey is just tender.

4 Increase the heat, add the mushrooms and pepper and cook for 3–4 minutes, turning occasionally, until just softened.

5 Reduce the heat, stir in the soured cream, taste and adjust seasoning. Serve immediately.

Menu Suggestion
Serve on a bed of boiled white rice or buttered noodles, with a crisp green salad to follow.

TURKEY AND BACON KEBABS

0.45* ✳* 551 cals

* plus at least 4 hours marinating;
freeze in the marinade

Serves 4

30 ml (2 tbsp) cranberry sauce

90 ml (6 tbsp) vegetable oil

45 ml (3 tbsp) freshly squeezed
orange juice

1 garlic clove, skinned and crushed

2.5 ml ($\frac{1}{2}$ tsp) ground allspice

salt and freshly ground pepper

700 g (1$\frac{1}{2}$ lb) boneless turkey
escalopes

1 small onion, skinned

1 large red pepper, cored, seeded
and cut into chunks

6 streaky bacon rashers, rinded and
halved

1 Put the cranberry sauce, oil
and orange juice in a shallow
dish with the garlic, allspice and
seasoning to taste. Whisk with a
fork until well combined.

2 Cut the turkey into bite-sized
pieces and place in the dish.
Stir to coat in the oil and orange
juice mixture, then cover and
leave to marinate for at least 4
hours. Stir the meat in the marinade occasionally during this time.

3 When ready to cook, cut the
onion into squares or even-
sized chunks.

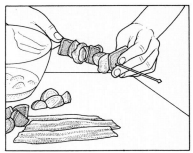

4 Thread the turkey, onion and
red pepper on to oiled skewers
with the bacon, dividing the ingredients as evenly as possible.

5 Grill under a preheated
moderate grill for about 20
minutes, turning the skewers frequently and basting with the remaining marinade. Serve hot.

Menu Suggestion
Make a quick, hot sauce to pour
over the kebabs by heating
together bottled cranberry sauce
with orange juice to taste. Serve
on a bed of saffron rice with a
chicory, orange and walnut salad
tossed in a sharp oil and vinegar
dressing.

**TURKEY AND BACON
KEBABS**
Turkey is lean and flavoursome,
but it has little natural fat, so it
can be dry if not prepared and
cooked in the correct way. The
marinade of oil and orange juice
in this recipe is an excellent way
of adding moisture to the flesh,
and the acid content of the
orange helps break down any
tough connective tissue. Don't
be tempted to omit the
marinating time if you are in a
hurry; the longer the turkey is
marinated the better. If it is
more convenient, the turkey can
be marinated in the refrigerator
overnight, but allow it to come to
room temperature before
grilling.

ROAST DUCK WITH APPLE STUFFING

2.30–3.00*	610 cals

* plus 15 minutes cooling

Serves 4

15 g (½ oz) butter

1 celery stick, trimmed and finely chopped

2 small onions, skinned and chopped

100 g (4 oz) fresh white breadcrumbs

1 small eating apple, peeled, cored and grated

15 ml (1 tbsp) chopped fresh sage or 5 ml (1 tsp) dried

salt and freshly ground pepper

1 egg, beaten

2 kg (4 lb) oven-ready duck (with giblets)

1 bay leaf

15 ml (1 tbsp) plain flour

watercress, to garnish

1 Melt the butter in a saucepan, add the celery and half of the chopped onions and fry gently until soft but not brown.

2 Put the breadcrumbs, apple and sage into a bowl and add the softened celery and onion. Mix very well together, add salt and pepper to taste, then bind with the beaten egg. Cool for 15 minutes.

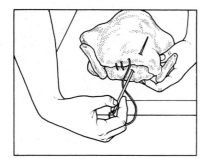

3 Stuff the neck cavity of the duck with this mixture, then sew or truss it together to keep in the stuffing. (If there is too much stuffing for the duck, make the rest into small balls.)

4 Weigh the stuffed duck and calculate the cooking time, allowing 30–35 minutes per 450 g (1 lb). Put the duck on a wire rack in a roasting tin —duck is very fatty and this stops it cooking in its own fat.

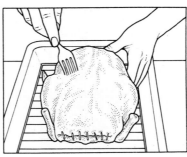

5 Prick the skin of the duck all over to let the fat escape and sprinkle the breast with salt and pepper. Roast in the oven at 180°C (350°F) mark 4 for the calculated cooking time. Cook the stuffing balls in a separate tin on the oven shelf below the duck for the last 30 minutes.

6 While the bird is cooking, make the gravy. Put the giblets in a saucepan with the remaining chopped onion, 600 ml (1 pint) water, the bay leaf and salt and pepper. Simmer for 1 hour; strain.

7 When the duck is cooked, remove from the tin and keep warm in a low oven. Pour off any excess fat from the tin, leaving behind the sediment and about 30 ml (2 tbsp) fat. Transfer to the top of the cooker and blend in the flour. Cook until browned, stirring continuously and scraping any sediment from the bottom of the tin. Slowly stir in the giblet stock and bring to the boil, stirring. Taste and adjust seasoning.

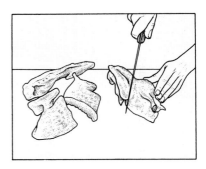

8 To serve, joint the duck into 4 portions, arrange on a warmed serving dish, with the stuffing balls if there are any. Pour the gravy round and garnish with sprigs of watercress. Serve immediately.

Menu Suggestion

Serve roast duck for the Christmas Day meal as an alternative to turkey. It is the traditional bird to serve for a small gathering. The usual trimmings for turkey can be served with duck —roast potatoes, bacon rolls and chipolatas, and Brussels sprouts with chestnuts.

ROAST DUCK WITH APPLE STUFFING

It was the Chinese who first discovered how delicious ducks were to eat, and who first bred the white, or Peking, duck for the table. Now ducks are farmed all over the world, and the duck breeding industry is enormous. Of all the duck breeds, it is the English Aylesbury duck which is the most famous. The Aylesbury duck is believed to be a strain of the original Peking duck, taking its name from the Vale of Aylesbury in Buckinghamshire, where it was originally bred. If you see Aylesbury duckling for sale, then you can be sure of buying a good-quality, meaty bird; the flesh will be tender, and the flavour superb.

PEKING DUCK WITH THIN PANCAKES

4.00* 🗋 🗋 768 cals

* plus chilling during the previous day and overnight

Serves 4

2.3 kg (5 lb) duck
4.5 litres (8 pints) boiling water
15 ml (1 tbsp) salt
15 ml (1 tbsp) dry sherry
thin pancakes (see below)
60 ml (4 tbsp) maple-flavoured syrup
100 ml (4 fl oz) hoisin sauce
4 spring onions, cut into 5-cm (2-inch) pieces

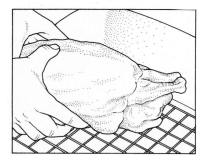

1 Early on the day before serving the duck, rinse the bird and drain on a rack in the sink. Pour the boiling water slowly over the duck until the skin whitens. Drain well.

2 Gently pat dry the skin and body cavity with absorbent kitchen paper. Rub the body cavity with the salt and sherry.

3 Put the duck, breast side down, on a rack in a roasting tin and refrigerate until the evening. Do not cover. Meanwhile, make the thin pancakes.

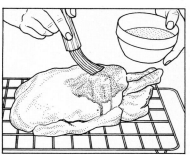

4 Early that evening, brush the duck all over with maple syrup. Leave on rack, breast side up, and refrigerate uncovered overnight.

5 About 3 hours before serving, put the duck breast down on its rack in the tin, and cook in the oven at 190°C (375°F) mark 5 for 1½ hours. Turn, and cook for 1–1½ hours more until the skin is crisp and golden.

6 To serve, slice the duck thinly into pieces about 5 × 2.5 cm (2 × 1 inch) and arrange on a warmed plate. Put the hoisin sauce in a small bowl and the spring onions on a small plate.

7 Each person assembles their own portion. Put one or two slices of duck in the centre of a pancake, add a dab of hoisin sauce and some spring onion. Roll up, and eat with your hands.

THIN PANCAKES

275 g (10 oz) flour
2.5 ml (½ tsp) salt
225 g (8 fl oz) boiling water
vegetable oil, for brushing

1 Sift the flour and salt into a large bowl. Gradually blend in the boiling water with a fork.

2 Press the dough into a ball, place on a floured surface and knead for about 5 minutes.

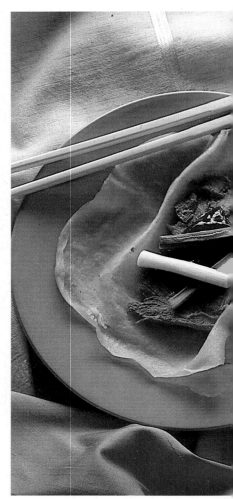

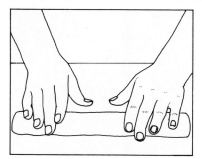

3 Shape the dough into a roll measuring about 40 cm (16 inches) long.

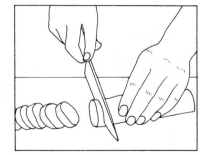

4 Slice crossways into sixteen pieces. Cover with a damp cloth. Take two pieces of dough at a time and put them on a lightly floured surface.

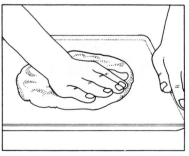

5 Flatten into 10 cm (4-inch) circles. Brush with oil. Place the circles one on top of another, oiled surfaces together. With a lightly floured rolling pin, roll from the centre to form a 20-cm (8-inch) circle.

6 Heat an ungreased frying pan. Add the circle of dough and cook each side for 2–3 minutes or until light brown. Remove to an ovenproof plate and separate the two layers. Stack the pancakes, browned side up, and cover with foil. Repeat to make 16 pancakes.

7 To reheat, put the plate of pancakes over a pan of boiling water and cover with foil. Reduce the heat and simmer until hot.

Menu Suggestion
Serve as part of a Chinese feast—after a first course of soup or pancake rolls and before a stir-fried main course.

293

CHRISTMAS ROAST GOOSE

2.35		744 cals

Serves 6

3.2–3.6 kg (7–8 lb) goose

½ lemon

salt and freshly ground pepper

350 g (12 oz) cooking apples, cored and roughly chopped

450 g (1 lb) prunes, soaked, stoned and chopped

25 g (1 oz) butter or margarine

40 g (1½ oz) flour

60 ml (4 tbsp) redcurrant jelly (optional)

For the garnish

175 g (6 oz) sugar

300 ml (½ pint) water

4 even-sized eating apples, peeled, cored and halved

225 g (8 oz) prunes

port, sherry or Madeira

whole blanched almonds (optional)

1 Remove the neck, giblets and fat from the body cavity and reserve the neck and giblets for making the gravy.

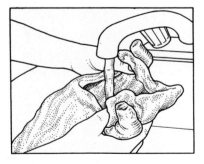

2 Rinse the goose under cold running water (letting the water run through the body cavity). Dry inside and out with absorbent kitchen paper.

3 Rub the cavity inside and out with the lemon and season with salt and pepper. Mix together the chopped apples and prunes and stuff the cavity.

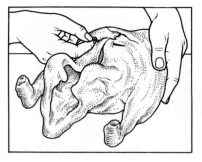

4 Sew or skewer the opening, to contain the stuffing, then weigh the bird.

5 Prick the bird all over with a sharp skewer or fork to let the fat run during cooking. Rub the skin with salt, and place the bird on a trivet or rack in a roasting tin containing 1 cm (½ inch) water. Place the neck and giblets (except the liver) in the water.

6 Roast in the oven at 220°C (425°F) mark 7 for 20 minutes. Cover the breast with greased paper and reduce the heat to 180°C (350°F) mark 4 and roast for 13–15 minutes per 450 g (1 lb). About 20 minutes before the end of the cooking time, uncover the breast and pour off the liquid from the tin. Reserve for gravy.

7 Meanwhile, prepare the garnish. In a shallow pan, dissolve 125 g (4 oz) of the sugar in the water. Boil for 3 minutes, then lower the heat to a gentle simmer. Add the apple halves and simmer for about 10–15 minutes until just tender. Lift out the apples with a slotted spoon and keep warm.

8 In a different saucepan, cover the prunes with water and bring to the boil. Drain, return the prunes to the pan and add the remaining 50 g (2 oz) sugar and enough port, sherry or madeira to cover the prunes. Simmer for 15–20 minutes. Cool for 15 minutes then drain, reserving the wine.

9 Remove the stones from the prunes carefully and, if liked, replace each stone with a blanched almond. Place a prune in each apple hollow and keep warm.

10 Skim the fat off the reserved roasting juices and strain the liquid to remove the neck and giblets. Add enough water to make up to 450 ml (¾ pint) and transfer to a saucepan. Bring to the boil. Cream together the fat and flour and gradually whisk into the liquid. As the butter melts, the gravy will thicken.

11 Simmer for 5 minutes and finally stir in the redcurrant jelly (if using) with the reserved wine. Simmer again for 5 minutes and check seasoning, adding more water if gravy is too thick.

12 Serve the goose surrounded by the stuffed apple halves and hand the gravy separately.

Menu Suggestion

Serve with roast potatoes and Brussels sprouts. A beetroot salad with horseradish dressing would offset the richness of the goose.

RABBIT CASSEROLE WITH CIDER AND MUSTARD

2.30	445 cals

Serves 4

50 g (2 oz) butter or margarine

100 g (4 oz) streaky bacon, rinded and diced

12–18 small button onions, skinned

1 rabbit, jointed

25 g (1 oz) plain flour

salt and freshly ground pepper

10 ml (2 tsp) French mustard

300 ml (½ pint) dry cider

450 ml (¾ pint) chicken stock

1 Melt the fat in a frying pan and fry the bacon and onions for 5 minutes until lightly browned. Remove to a casserole with a slotted spoon.

2 Coat the rabbit in a little flour seasoned with salt and pepper and fry in the pan for about 8 minutes until golden brown. Arrange in the casserole.

3 Stir the remaining flour and the French mustard into the pan. Gradually add the cider and stock. Season, bring to the boil and pour over the rabbit.

4 Cover and cook in the oven at 170°C (325°F) mark 3 for about 2 hours or until the rabbit is tender. Adjust the seasoning before serving.

Menu Suggestion

A delicious main course dish for a winter dinner party, Rabbit Casserole with Cider and Mustard tastes good with ribbon noodles tossed in butter and chopped fresh parsley. Finish with a crisp green salad in a vinaigrette dressing.

PIGEON AND CABBAGE CASSEROLE

| 2.00 | 547 cals |

Serves 4

1 green, white or red cabbage, quartered

salt and freshly ground pepper

25 g (1 oz) bacon fat or butter

2–4 pigeons, depending on size

8 chipolatas

2 onions, skinned and chopped

6 streaky bacon rashers, rinded and chopped

2.5 ml ($\frac{1}{2}$ tsp) ground cloves

300 ml ($\frac{1}{2}$ pint) red wine or wine and stock

1 Blanch the cabbage for 5 minutes in boiling salted water. Drain.

2 Melt the bacon fat or butter in a large frying pan and fry the pigeons and chipolatas for about 8 minutes until browned all over. Remove from the pan. Fry the onions in the fat remaining in the pan for 5 minutes until golden. Sprinkle the chopped bacon over the base of a casserole.

3 Shred the cabbage and mix with the onions and ground cloves. Spread half the cabbage mixture over the bacon, season with pepper and place the pigeons and chipolatas on top. Cover with the remaining cabbage, season with more pepper and pour over the wine.

4 Cover and cook in the oven at 170°C (325°F) mark 3 for about 1$\frac{1}{2}$ hours or until the birds are tender. Serve hot.

Menu Suggestion

Simple homely fare, this pigeon casserole is best served with mashed or creamed potatoes and a seasonal vegetable such as carrots or broccoli.

PIGEON AND CABBAGE CASSEROLE

For this recipe, an older pigeon can be used because of the long, slow cooking. Young pigeons and squabs (pigeons under 5 weeks old) are best reserved for roasting and grilling. Although classed as game birds, pigeons do not have a closed season and are therefore available all year round. Wood pigeons, which weigh around 700 g (1$\frac{1}{2}$ lb) each, are the ones to look for in your local poulterer or game dealer, especially in the spring and summer months, when they are said to be at their best. For those who find the flavour of game, rather strong, and their smell too 'high', pigeons are ideal. They are not hung like other game birds and are therefore quite mild in flavour, like poultry.

JUGGED HARE

| 3.30 | ✳ | 469 cals |

Serves 6

| 1.6 kg (3½ lb) hare, jointed, with its blood |
| 75 ml (5 tbsp) seasoned plain flour |
| 5 ml (1 tsp) red wine vinegar |
| 125 g (4 oz) streaky bacon, rinded and chopped |
| 50 g (2 oz) butter |
| 900 ml (1½ pints) beef stock |
| 150 ml (¼ pint) port |
| 5 ml (1 tsp) dried marjoram |
| 45 ml (3 tbsp) redcurrant jelly |
| 2 onions, skinned |
| 12 whole cloves |
| salt and freshly ground pepper |
| parsley sprigs, to garnish |

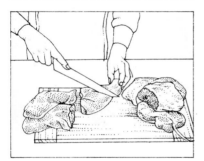

1 Wipe the hare and divide into smaller pieces if necessary. Toss in the seasoned flour.

2 Mix the blood with the vinegar (to keep it fresh), cover and refrigerate until required.

3 Meanwhile, fry the bacon in its own fat in a large flame-proof casserole for about 5 minutes until browned. Remove from the pan. Add the butter to the pan and fry the hare joints for 5 minutes until they are lightly browned.

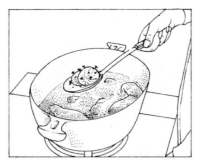

4 Add the stock, port, marjoram and redcurrant jelly with the onions studded with the cloves. Replace bacon and season well.

5 Bring to the boil, cover and cook in the oven at 170°C (325°F) mark 3 for 3 hours until tender. Remove hare to a serving dish and keep warm. Discard the onions.

6 Mix the blood with some cooking juices until smooth. Add to the pan and heat. Adjust seasoning and pour over hare. Garnish with parsley sprigs.

OLD ENGLISH GAME STEW

| 3.00 | ✳* | 542 cals |

* freeze after step 4

Serves 6

225 g (8 oz) chuck steak

700 g (1½ lb) stewing venison

75 g (3 oz) butter

4 large celery sticks, trimmed and roughly sliced

2 onions, skinned and finely sliced

45 ml (3 tbsp) plain flour

150 ml (¼ pint) port

450 ml (¾ pint) chicken stock

salt and freshly ground pepper

100 g (4 oz) streaky bacon

1 small onion, skinned and finely chopped

125 g (4 oz) fresh white breadcrumbs

1.25 ml (¼ tsp) dried thyme

1 egg, beaten

celery leaves, to garnish

1 Cut the steak and venison into cubes 2.5 cm (1 inch) square, discarding excess fat and sinew.

2 Melt 50 g (2 oz) of the butter in a large flameproof casserole and fry the steak pieces for about 5 minutes until browned. Remove from the pan and drain. Add the venison to the pan and fry for about 8 minutes until browned. Remove from the pan.

3 Add the celery and sliced onions to the pan and lightly brown for about 5 minutes. Stir in the flour, port, stock and seasoning and bring to the boil.

4 Return the steak and venison to the casserole. Cover tightly and cook in the oven at 180°C (350°F) mark 4 for 1½–2 hours or until the meats are almost tender.

5 Meanwhile make the force-meat balls. Grill the bacon until crisp and, removing rind, snip into small pieces.

6 Melt the remaining butter in a saucepan and fry the chopped onion for about 5 minutes until golden. Stir into the breadcrumbs together with the bacon, thyme and seasoning.

7 Bind the mixture with beaten egg and shape into 6 even-sized balls.

8 Place them between the meat in the casserole and cover. Increase the oven temperature to 190°C (375°F) mark 5 and return the casserole to the bottom of the oven for a further 30 minutes. Adjust the seasoning and garnish with celery leaves.

Menu Suggestion
Serve this rich stew for a winter dinner party with creamed or jacket baked potatoes and a selection of seasonal vegetables.

GAME PIE

| 2.45 | ⊔ | ✻* | 602–903 cals |

* freeze after stage 5

Serves 4–6

450 g (1 lb) boned game (e.g.
    pigeon, venison, partridge, hare
    or pheasant)

30 ml (2 tbsp) plain flour, for
    coating

10 ml (2 tsp) dried thyme

2.5 ml ($\frac{1}{2}$ tsp) ground cinnamon

salt and freshly ground pepper

45 ml (3 tbsp) vegetable oil

300 ml ($\frac{1}{2}$ pint) red wine

6 juniper berries, lightly crushed

350 g (12 oz) pork sausagemeat

225 g (8 oz) packet frozen puff
    pastry, thawed

1 beaten egg, to glaze

1 Cut the meat into even-sized cubes, then toss in the flour mixed with the thyme, cinnamon and seasoning.

2 Heat the oil in a flameproof casserole, add the meat and fry over moderate heat for 5 minutes until browned on all sides. Pour in the wine, add the juniper berries, then cover and simmer gently for 1–1$\frac{1}{2}$ hours until tender. Leave until cold, preferably overnight.

3 Put half the sausagemeat in the bottom of an ovenproof pie dish. Put the game mixture on top, then cover with the remaining sausagemeat and level the surface.

4 Roll out the dough on a floured surface and cut a thin strip long enough to go around the rim of the pie dish. Moisten the rim with water, then place the strip on the rim.

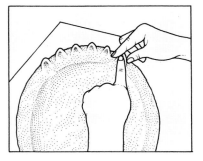

5 Roll out the remaining dough for a lid, moisten the strip of dough, then place the lid on top and press to seal. Knock up and flute the edge, and use pastry trimmings to make decorations for the top of the pie, sticking them on with water.

6 Brush the pastry with beaten egg, then bake in the oven at 200°C (400°F) mark 6 for 30 minutes until golden brown and crisp. Leave to stand for 15 minutes before serving, or serve cold.

GAME

When buying game for a casserole or pie such as this one, it is not necessary to buy young, small birds (these are best reserved for roasting). Ask your dealer for an older bird, which should be less expensive.

Fresh venison is excellent meat for casseroles and pies, since certain cuts such as shoulder benefit from long, slow cooking, and they are not too expensive. It is only in season for a short time, but some supermarkets sell frozen venison out of season which is ready cut up. This—and cubed hare and rabbit (which is not strictly speaking game)—is usually a good buy for pies and casseroles.

All game bought from a licensed dealer will have been hung for the appropriate length of time (to tenderize the flesh and intensify the 'gamey' flavour), so you will not have to worry about this—or plucking and drawing. Carefully remove the raw flesh from the carcass, then cut into bite-sized pieces. You will need approximately 4 pigeons, 2–3 partridges or 1–2 pheasants to obtain 450 g (1 lb) boneless meat for the game pie recipe on this page. Venison can be simply cut up like stewing steak; hare and rabbit joints should be boned and cut up as for chicken portions. If using frozen game, it should be defrosted before cooking—allow a full 24 hours in the refrigerator.

Fish and Shellfish

SCALLOPS IN CREAMY BASIL SAUCE

0.25		457 cals

Serves 4

900 g (2 lb) shelled scallops, defrosted if frozen

30 ml (2 tbsp) vegetable oil

15 g (½ oz) butter

1 small onion, skinned and finely chopped

2 garlic cloves, skinned and crushed

150 ml (¼ pint) dry white wine

20 ml (4 tsp) chopped fresh basil

salt and freshly ground pepper

150 ml (5 fl oz) double cream

few fresh basil sprigs, to garnish

5 Remove the scallops from the liquid with a slotted spoon and set aside on a plate. Boil the liquid until reduced by about half, then stir in the cream a little at a time and simmer until the sauce is thick.

6 Return the scallops to the pan and heat gently. To serve, taste and adjust the seasoning, and serve garnished with basil sprigs.

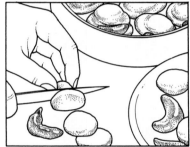

1 Cut the scallops (including the coral) into fairly thick slices. Pat dry with absorbent kitchen paper and set aside.

2 Heat the oil and butter in a large frying pan, add the onion and garlic and fry gently for 5 minutes until soft and lightly coloured.

3 Add the scallops to the pan and toss to coat in the oil and butter. Stir in the wine, basil and salt and pepper to taste.

4 Fry the scallops over moderate heat for 10 minutes until they are tender, turning them constantly so that they cook evenly on all sides. Do not overcook or they will become tough and rubbery.

SCALLOPS

One of the prettiest of shellfish, fresh scallops are sold in their delicately-coloured, fan-shaped shells. Frozen scallops, now available at high-class fish-mongers, are sold off the shell, but your fishmonger will let you have shells for serving if you ask him. Scald them in boiling water and scrub them before use.

Scallops are amongst the most expensive of shellfish, but their rich creaminess means a small amount goes a long way. The beautiful dark pink coral is considered a great delicacy. If you still feel they are extravagant, use half the quantity specified in this recipe and make up the weight with white button mushrooms.

HADDOCK AND CARAWAY CHEESE SOUFFLÉ

1.20	🍴	466 cals

Serves 4

450 g (1 lb) floury potatoes

450 g (1 lb) fresh haddock fillets

100 g (4 oz) button mushrooms, wiped and thinly sliced

300 ml (½ pint) milk

1 bay leaf

25 g (1 oz) butter

25 g (1 oz) plain flour

2.5 ml (½ tsp) caraway seeds

125 g (4 oz) mature Cheddar cheese, grated

2 eggs, separated

salt and freshly ground pepper

1 Scrub the potatoes, boil until tender. Drain and peel, then mash three-quarters of the potatoes. Grate the remaining quarter into a bowl and set aside.

2 Meanwhile, place the haddock, mushrooms, milk and bay leaf in a small saucepan. Cover and poach for 15–20 minutes until tender. Drain, reserving milk and mushrooms. Flake fish, discarding skin and bay leaf.

3 Make the sauce. Melt the butter in a pan, stir in the flour and cook gently for 1 minute, stirring. Remove from the heat, add the caraway seeds and gradually stir in the milk. Bring to the boil, stirring, and simmer for 2–3 minutes until thickened and smooth.

4 Stir the mashed potato into the sauce with 75 g (3 oz) cheese, the egg yolks, fish and mushrooms. Season well.

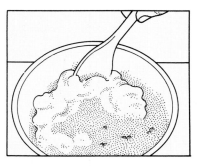

5 Stiffly whisk the egg whites. Fold into the fish mixture. Turn into a 1.6-litre (2¾-pint) buttered soufflé dish.

6 Sprinkle over the reserved grated potato and remaining grated cheese. Bake in the oven at 190°C (375°F) mark 5 for about 1 hour or until just set and golden brown.

TIPS FOR MAKING HOT SOUFFLÉS

● Always make sure to use the exact size of soufflé dish specified in the recipe.

● Check your oven temperature carefully and don't be tempted to bake a soufflé at a different temperature from the one specified.

● Preheat oven and baking sheet to required temperature well before baking.

● Fold egg whites in with a large metal spoon in a figure of eight motion so that the maximum amount of air is incorporated.

● Don't open the oven door during baking.

● Serve *immediately*—have your guests seated at the table well before the soufflé is due to come out of the oven.

HADDOCK AND MUSHROOM PUFFS

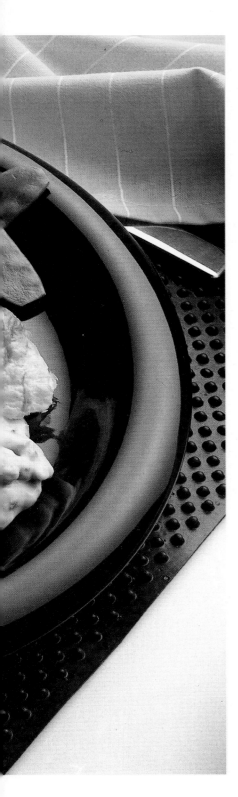

| 0.40* | ✳ | 791 cals |

* plus 30 minutes chilling

Serves 4

**397 g (14 oz) packet puff pastry,
  thawed if frozen**
450 g (1 lb) haddock fillet, skinned
**213 g (7½ oz) can creamed
  mushrooms**
5 ml (1 tsp) lemon juice
20 ml (4 tsp) capers, chopped
**15 ml (1 tbsp) snipped fresh chives
  or 5 ml (1 tsp) dried**
salt and freshly ground pepper
1 egg

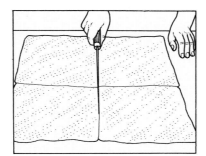

1 Roll out the pastry on a
floured surface into a 40.5 cm
(16 inch) square. Using a sharp
knife, cut into four squares, trim
the edges and reserve the
trimmings of pastry.

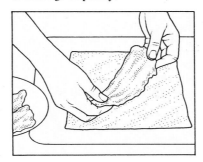

2 Place the squares on dampened
baking sheets. Divide the fish
into four and place diagonally
across the pastry squares.

3 Combine the creamed mushrooms with the lemon juice,
capers, chives and seasoning to
taste. Mix well, then spoon over
the pieces of haddock fillet.

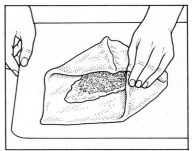

4 Brush the edges of each square
lightly with water. Bring the
four points of each square together
and seal the edges to form an
envelope-shaped parcel.

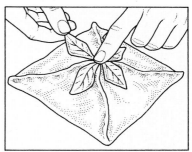

5 Decorate with pastry trimmings and make a small hole
in the centre of each parcel. Chill
in the refrigerator for 30 minutes.

6 Beat the egg with a pinch of
salt and use to glaze the pastry.
Bake in the oven at 220°C (425°F)
mark 7 for about 20 minutes or
until the pastry is golden brown
and well risen. Serve hot.

Menu Suggestion
Serve for a substantial supper dish
with a seasonal green vegetable
such as French beans.

STUFFED PLAICE WITH LEMON SAUCE

| 0.50 | 🍴🍴 | 232 cals |

Serves 4

4 small whole plaice, cleaned

65 g (2½ oz) butter

100 g (4 oz) button mushrooms, finely chopped

100 g (4 oz) white breadcrumbs

90 ml (6 tbsp) chopped parsley

45 ml (3 tbsp) green peppercorns, crushed

finely grated rind and juice of 2 lemons

1.25 ml (¼ tsp) mustard powder

salt and freshly ground pepper

1 egg, beaten

150 ml (¼ pint) dry white wine

25 g (1 oz) plain flour

150 ml (¼ pint) water

60 ml (4 tbsp) single cream

lemon slices and parsley sprigs, to garnish

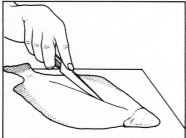

1 With the white skin uppermost, cut down the backbone of each of the four plaice.

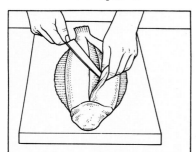

2 Carefully make a pocket on each side of the backbone by easing white flesh from bone.

3 Make the stuffing. Beat 15 g (½ oz) butter until softened then add the mushrooms, breadcrumbs, parsley, 30 ml (2 tbsp) peppercorns, lemon rind, mustard and salt and pepper to taste. Mix well and moisten with the egg and a little of the lemon juice.

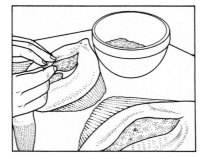

4 Spoon the stuffing carefully into the pockets in the fish. Then place the fish in a single layer in a buttered ovenproof dish. Pour the wine around the fish and cover loosely with foil. Cook in the oven at 190°C (375°F) mark 5 for 30 minutes.

5 Remove the fish from the dish and place on a warmed serving dish. Cover and keep warm in the oven turned to its lowest setting.

6 Make the sauce. Melt the remaining butter in a pan, add flour and stir over low heat for 1–2 minutes. Gradually stir in the fish cooking juices, the water and the remaining lemon juice. Bring to the boil, stirring, then lower the heat and stir in the remaining peppercorns and the cream.

7 To serve, taste and adjust the seasoning, then pour into a warmed sauceboat. Garnish the fish and serve at once, with the sauce handed separately.

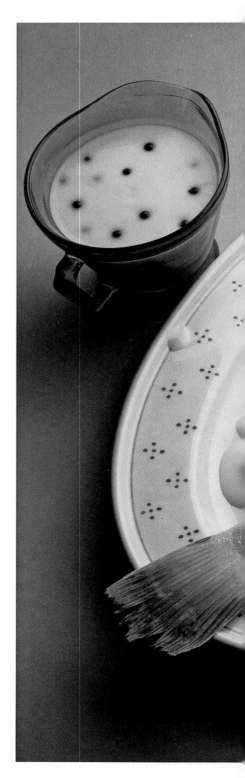

FRICASSÉE OF MONKFISH WITH CORIANDER

0.40	288 cals

Serves 6

700 g (1½ lb) monkfish fillets
450 g (1 lb) halibut cutlets
150 ml (¼ pint) dry vermouth
300 ml (½ pint) water
1 small onion, skinned and sliced
salt and freshly ground pepper
125 g (4 oz) small button
  mushrooms, wiped
40 g (1½ oz) butter
45 ml (3 tbsp) plain flour
30 ml (2 tbsp) chopped fresh
  coriander and sprigs to garnish
60 ml (4 tbsp) single cream

1 Cut the monkfish and halibut into large, fork-sized pieces, discarding skin and bone.

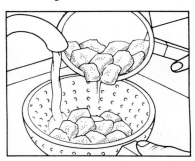

2 Place the fish in a medium saucepan, cover with cold water and bring slowly to the boil. Strain fish in a colander and then rinse off any scum.

3 Return the fish to the clean pan and pour over the vermouth with the 300 ml (½ pint) water. Add the onion with seasoning and bring to the boil. Cover the pan, reduce heat, and simmer gently for 8–10 minutes or until the fish is just tender and beginning to flake.

4 Add the mushrooms after 6 minutes of the cooking time. Strain off the cooking liquor and reserve for the sauce.

5 Melt the butter in a separate saucepan and stir in the flour followed by the cooking liquor. Bring slowly to the boil, stirring all the time, and bubble for 2 minutes until thickened and smooth.

6 Stir in the coriander, cream, mushrooms, onion and fish and adjust seasoning. Warm through gently, being careful not to break up the fish. Serve hot, garnished with sprigs of coriander.

MONKFISH

Most good fishmongers stock monkfish nowadays, although it hasn't always been a popular fish because of its ugly appearance when whole. For this reason it is almost always displayed without the head, which is its ugliest part, and many fishmongers also skin and fillet it before offering it for sale. Monkfish fillets and steaks taste very like lobster and scampi, however, at a fraction of the price.

Monkfish has always been popular in Mediterranean countries, particularly Spain where it is called *rape* and France where it is known as *lotte de mer* or *baudroie*. The Spanish like to serve it cold in the same way as lobster, or hot with potatoes and tomatoes; the French braise it in white wine or serve it *en brochette* (on skewers).

SEAFOOD SAFFRON RISOTTO

0.45		488–732 cals

Serves 4–6

good pinch of saffron strands

150 ml ($\frac{1}{4}$ pint) boiling water

45 ml (3 tbsp) olive oil

30 ml (2 tbsp) butter or margarine

1 onion, skinned and chopped

2 garlic cloves, skinned and crushed

$\frac{1}{2}$ green pepper, finely chopped

$\frac{1}{2}$ red pepper, finely chopped

400 g (14 oz) Italian risotto rice

about 600 ml (1 pint) hot fish or chicken stock

120 ml (8 tbsp) dry white wine

1 bay leaf

salt and freshly ground pepper

350–450 g ($\frac{3}{4}$–1 lb) frozen shelled scampi or jumbo prawns, thawed and thoroughly drained and dried

24 cooked mussels, shelled

a few mussels in shells, to garnish

freshly grated Parmesan cheese, to serve

1 Prepare the saffron water. Soak the saffron strands in the 150 ml ($\frac{1}{4}$ pint) boiling water for at least 30 minutes.

2 Meanwhile, heat the oil and half the butter in a heavy-based pan, add the onion, garlic and peppers and fry gently for 5 minutes until soft.

3 Add the rice and stir until coated in the oil and butter. Pour in a few spoonfuls of the stock and the wine, then add the saffron liquid.

4 Add the bay leaf and salt and pepper to taste and simmer gently, stirring frequently, until all the liquid is absorbed by the rice.

5 Add a few more spoonfuls of stock and simmer again until it is absorbed. Continue adding stock in this way for about 15 minutes, stirring frequently until the rice is *al dente* (tender but firm to the bite).

6 Melt the remaining butter in a separate pan, add the scampi and toss gently for about 5 minutes until they change colour.

7 Remove the bay leaf from the risotto, then stir in the scampi and juices and the mussels. Warm through, taste and adjust seasoning. Turn into a warmed serving dish. Top with whole mussels and serve at once with grated Parmesan cheese handed separately.

HOW TO MAKE AN AUTHENTIC RISOTTO

An Italian risotto is quite unlike any other rice dish in consistency —it is creamy and moist (the Italians call this *all'onda*) and the grains of rice tend to stick together unlike the fluffy individual grains of an Indian pilau, for example. The reasons for this are the type of rice used, and the method of incorporating the liquid, both of which are incredibly important if the risotto is to look and taste authentic.

Italian risotto rice has a rounded grain (but not so rounded as pudding rice); it is available in supermarkets in boxes labelled 'Italian risotto rice', but the best risotto rice to buy are *avorio* and *arborio*, both of which are available loose at Italian delicatessens.

When making a risotto, follow the instructions in the method carefully, adding the liquid a little at a time as in this recipe. The rice should absorb each amount of liquid before you add the next, therefore it is really a case of standing over it and stirring and adding liquid almost constantly until the correct consistency is obtained. Don't worry if you do not need to add all the liquid specified in a recipe—this will depend on the type of rice used, the quantity of other ingredients and the cooking temperature.

In Italy, risotto is always served on its own before the main course of fish or meat, but it can of course be served as a meal in itself, accompanied by fresh crusty bread, a salad and a bottle of chilled white wine—a dry Soave or Frascati would go well with the seafood in this risotto.

TARRAGON STUFFED TROUT

1.30 🗇	320 cals

Serves 6

25 g (1 oz) long-grain rice

100 g (4 oz) peeled prawns

225 g (8 oz) button mushrooms, wiped

100 g (4 oz) onion, skinned

50 g (2 oz) butter

5 ml (1 tsp) chopped fresh tarragon or 1.25 ml ($\frac{1}{4}$ tsp) dried

salt and freshly ground pepper

30 ml (2 tbsp) lemon juice

6 whole trout, about 225 g (8 oz) each, cleaned

tarragon sprigs, to garnish

1 Make the stuffing. Cut up each of the peeled prawns into two or three pieces. Boil the rice until tender; drain.

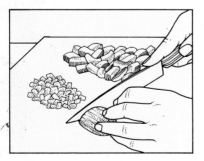

2 Roughly chop the mushrooms and finely chop the onion. Melt the butter in a large frying pan, add the onion and fry for 5 minutes until golden brown.

3 Add the mushrooms with the tarragon and seasoning and cook over high heat for 5–10 minutes until all excess moisture has evaporated. Cool for about 30 minutes.

4 Mix the prawns, rice, lemon juice and mushroom mixture together and season with salt and freshly ground pepper to taste.

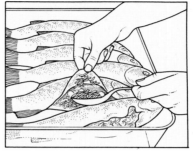

5 Place the fish side by side in a lightly buttered oven-proof dish and stuff with the mixture. Cover and cook in the oven at 180°C (350°F) mark 4 for about 30 minutes. To serve, garnish the fish with sprigs of tarragon.

TYPES OF TROUT

When buying the fish for this recipe, choose between salmon trout and rainbow trout—both are available in suitable sizes for stuffing, although salmon trout can be as large as true salmon, so check carefully with your fishmonger first. Both are members of the salmon family, although the salmon trout, also called the sea trout because it spends the major part of its life at sea, is the closest to the salmon or 'king of the river'.

Fresh salmon trout are in season from early to mid summer, but frozen fish can be bought at other times of year. The flesh of salmon trout is a pretty, delicate shade of pink when cooked—similar to that of true salmon. Because it is less expensive than salmon it is a popular substitute in recipes calling for salmon.

For this recipe, rainbow trout is ideal. A freshwater fish, rainbow trout is now reared in large quantities on trout farms, and so is available all year round—fresh at fishmongers, chilled or frozen from supermarkets.

It is easily recognisable by its attractive silver skin and the shimmer of pink running down the centre of the fish from head to tail. The flesh of rainbow trout is pale and creamy in colour when cooked, the texture is soft and smooth, and the flavour very delicate.

Other kinds of trout which can be used for this recipe include grilse (a salmon which has only spent one year at sea before returning to spawn in fresh water) or brown or red trout.

SEAFOOD CURRY

| 0.30 | 361 cals |

Serves 4

1 fresh green chilli
45 ml (3 tbsp) vegetable oil
2 onions, skinned and sliced into
    rings
25 g (1 oz) desiccated coconut
15 ml (1 tbsp) plain flour
5 ml (1 tsp) ground coriander
450 g (1 lb) fresh haddock fillet,
    skinned and cut into chunks
150 ml (¼ pint) white wine
25 g (1 oz) salted peanuts
125 g (4 oz) frozen prawns, thawed,
    drained and thoroughly dried
salt and freshly ground pepper
coriander sprigs and shredded
    coconut, toasted, to garnish

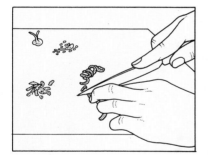

1 Halve the chilli, remove seeds and finely chop the flesh. Heat the oil in a large sauté pan, and brown the onion rings.

2 Mix coconut, flour and coriander and toss with the haddock and chopped chilli. Add to pan and fry gently for 5–10 minutes until golden, stirring.

3 Pour in wine, bring to boil and add peanuts, prawns and seasoning. Cover tightly and simmer for 5–10 minutes or until fish is tender. To serve, garnish with coriander and coconut.

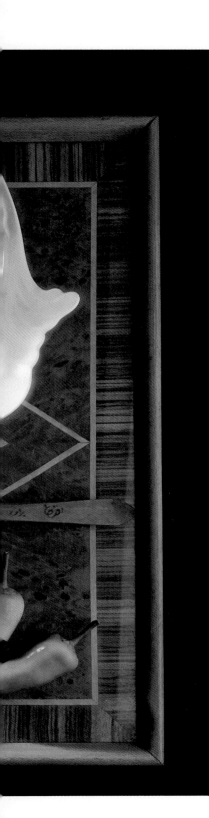

SKATE WITH CAPERS AND BLACK BUTTER

0.20	290 cals

Serves 4

700–900 g (1½–2 lb) wing of skate

salt

50 g (2 oz) butter

15 ml (1 tbsp) white wine vinegar

10 ml (2 tsp) capers

10 ml (2 tsp) chopped fresh parsley, to garnish

1 Simmer the fish in salted water for 10–15 minutes until tender, drain and keep warm.

2 Heat the butter in a pan until lightly browned. Add the vinegar and capers, cook for a further 2–3 minutes and pour it over the fish. Serve at once, garnished with the parsley.

SPECIAL PARSLEY FISH PIE

1.00	683 cals

Serves 4

450 g (1 lb) haddock fillets

300 ml ($\frac{1}{2}$ pint) milk, plus 90 ml (6 tbsp)

1 bay leaf

6 peppercorns

1 onion, skinned and sliced

salt

65 g ($2\frac{1}{2}$ oz) butter or margarine

45 ml (3 tbsp) plain flour

freshly ground pepper

2 eggs, hard-boiled and chopped

150 ml (5 fl oz) single cream

30 ml (2 tbsp) chopped fresh parsley

100 g (4 oz) cooked prawns

900 g (2 lb) potatoes, peeled

1 egg, beaten, to glaze

1 Rinse and drain the fish. Place in a pan and pour over 300 ml ($\frac{1}{2}$ pint) of milk; add the bay leaf, peppercorns, onion and a pinch of salt. Bring to the boil and simmer for 10 minutes until just tender.

2 Lift from the pan, flake the flesh and remove the skin and bones. Strain the cooking liquid and reserve.

3 Make the sauce. Melt 40 g ($1\frac{1}{2}$ oz) of the butter in a pan, stir in the flour and cook gently for 1 minute, stirring. Remove the pan from the heat and gradually stir in the reserved cooking liquid. Bring to the boil, stirring, until sauce thickens, then cook for a further 2–3 minutes. Season to taste.

4 Add the eggs to the sauce with the fresh cream, fish, parsley and prawns. Check the seasoning, and spoon the mixture into a 1.1-litre (2-pint) pie dish.

5 Meanwhile, boil the potatoes, drain and mash without any liquid. Heat the remaining 90 ml (6 tbsp) of milk and remaining 25 g (1 oz) butter and beat into the potatoes; season.

6 Spoon the potatoes into a piping bag and pipe across the fish mixture. Alternatively, spoon the potato over the fish and roughen the surface with a fork.

7 Bake in the oven at 200°C (400°F) mark 6 for 10–15 minutes, until the potato is set. Brush the beaten egg over the pie. Return to oven for a further 15 minutes, until golden brown.

ITALIAN FISH STEW

1.00	481 cals

Serves 4

good pinch of saffron strands

about 900 g (2 lb) mixed fish fillets
(e.g. red mullet, bream, bass,
brill, monkfish, plaice or cod)

10–12 whole prawns, cooked

60 ml (4 tbsp) olive oil

1 large onion, skinned and finely
chopped

3 garlic cloves, skinned and
crushed

2 slices of drained canned
pimiento, sliced

450 g (1 lb) tomatoes, skinned,
seeded and chopped

2 canned anchovy fillets, drained

150 ml ($\frac{1}{4}$ pint) dry white wine

150 ml ($\frac{1}{4}$ pint) water

2 bay leaves

45 ml (3 tbsp) chopped fresh basil

salt and freshly ground pepper

10–12 mussels, in their shells

4 slices of hot toast, to serve

1 Prepare the saffron water. Soak
the saffron strands in a little
boiling water for 30 minutes.

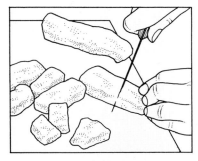

2 Meanwhile, skin the fish and
cut into chunky bite-sized
pieces. Shell the prawns.

3 Heat the oil in a large heavy-
based pan, add the onion, garlic
and pimiento and fry gently for 5
minutes until soft.

4 Add the tomatoes and anchovies and stir with a wooden
spoon to break them up. Pour in
the wine and the water and bring
to the boil, then lower the heat
and add the bay leaves and half
the basil. Simmer uncovered for
20 minutes, stirring occasionally.

5 Add the firm fish to the
tomato mixture, then strain in
the saffron water and add salt and
pepper to taste. Cook for 10 minutes, then add the delicate-
textured fish and cook for a further
5 minutes or until tender.

6 Add the prawns and mussels
and cook, covered, for 5 minutes or until the mussels open.
Remove the bay leaves and discard.

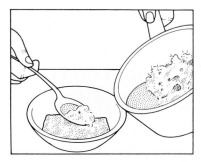

7 To serve, put one slice of toast
in each of four individual soup
bowls. Spoon over the soup,
sprinkle with the remaining basil
and serve at once.

ITALIAN FISH STEW

This type of fish stew is
popular in coastal regions, especially in the regions around the
Adriatic Sea and in the southern
part of Italy around Sicily.

There are numerous different
versions of fish stew or soup,
called *zuppa di pesce* in Italian,
with recipes varying from one
village and one cook to another—
there are no hard and fast rules.
Burrida is the famous fish and
tomato stew from Genoa; it contains many unusual fish which
are not available outside local
waters, but it can be made
successfully outside the region
with monkfish, octopus and
squid, together with clams,
mussels and shrimps.

Around the Adriatic Sea, fish
soup is called *brodetto*—the
ones from Venice, Rimini and
Ravenna being the most famous.
These fish soups use similar fish
to the Genoese *burrida*, but they
do not contain tomatoes and they
are traditionally served with
bread fried or baked in oil—
called *casada*. Another well-
known Italian fish soup is
caciuccio Livornese, a main course
dish flavoured strongly with
tomatoes and hot red peppers,
and served with *casada*.

Don't worry if you can't find
the authentic fish when making
an Italian fish stew or soup. The
recipe on this page suggests sub-
stitutes which are readily available outside Italy and which will
taste equally good—as long as
you use a good variety and make
sure they are as fresh as possible. Try to include at least some
red or grey mullet; monkfish is
also a good buy—it has a strong
flavour and dense texture, and
does not break up easily during
cooking.

SPANISH COD WITH PEPPERS, TOMATOES AND GARLIC

1.30	🍴	324 cals

Serves 4

700 g (1½ lb) cod fillets

1.1 litres (1¾ pints) mussels or about 450 g (1 lb) weight

30 ml (2 tbsp) vegetable oil

2 onions, skinned and sliced

1 red pepper, cored, seeded and sliced

1 green pepper, cored, seeded and sliced

1–2 garlic cloves, skinned and crushed

450 g (1 lb) tomatoes, skinned and chopped

300 ml (½ pint) white wine

2.5 ml (½ tsp) Tabasco sauce

1 bay leaf

salt and freshly ground pepper

1 Using a sharp knife, skin the cod and cut it into chunks.

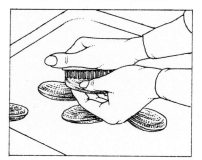

2 Scrub the mussels, discarding any which are open. Place in a pan, cover and cook over a high heat for about 8 minutes or until mussels have opened.

3 Shell all but four mussels. Heat the oil in a frying pan and cook the onions, peppers and garlic for about 5 minutes until starting to soften. Add the tomatoes and wine, bring to the boil and simmer for 5 minutes, then add the Tabasco.

4 Layer the fish and vegetables in a casserole and add the bay leaf and seasoning. Pour over the wine. Push the four mussels in shells into the top layer. Cover and cook in the oven at 180°C (350°F) mark 4 for 1 hour. Serve hot.

Menu Suggestion

Serve with hot French bread, followed by a crisp green salad tossed in an olive oil and lemon juice dressing.

SPANISH COD WITH PEPPERS, TOMATOES AND GARLIC

As soon as you get fresh mussels home from the fishmonger, immerse them in a bowl of cold water until you are ready to start dealing with them. If you add 15 ml (1 tbsp) oatmeal to the water, the live mussels will feed on it and this will help 'flush them out' so that you can be sure they are thoroughly clean inside. If the water becomes very murky during this time, replace it with fresh water and more oatmeal. Before preparation in step 2 of the recipe, tap any open mussels against the bowl or work surface—if they do not close they should be thrown away.

CREAMY FISH CASSEROLE

1.30	379–569 cals

Serves 4–6

700 g (1½ lb) cod steaks, skinned and cut into bite-sized pieces

30 ml (2 tbsp) plain flour

salt and freshly ground pepper

40 g (1½ oz) butter

15 ml (1 tbsp) vegetable oil

600 ml (1 pint) dry cider

2 bay leaves, crumbled

900 g (2 lb) old floury potatoes, scrubbed

150 ml (5 fl oz) single cream

30 ml (2 tbsp) chopped fresh parsley

1 Coat the pieces of cod in the flour seasoned with salt and pepper to taste.

2 Melt 25 g (1 oz) of the butter with the oil in a frying pan, add the pieces of cod and fry gently until golden on all sides. Remove from the pan with a slotted spoon and set aside.

3 Pour the cider into the frying pan and stir to dislodge the sediment from the bottom and sides of the pan. Add the bay leaves and salt and pepper to taste. Bring to the boil and simmer for a few minutes, then pour into a jug.

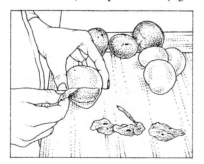

4 Blanch the potatoes in their skins in boiling salted water for 10 minutes. Drain, leave until cool enough to handle, then peel off the skins and slice.

5 Put half the fish in the bottom of a shallow casserole. Stir the cream into the cider mixture, then pour half over the fish.

6 Cover with half the potato slices, overlapping them so that they cover the fish completely. Sprinkle with half the parsley. Put the remaining fish on top of the potatoes, then pour over the remaining cider and cream.

7 Cover with the remaining potato slices as before, then dot with the remaining butter. Cook in the oven at 190°C (375°F) mark 5 for 45 minutes. Sprinkle the remaining parsley over the top before serving.

Menu Suggestion
Serve for a family supper accompanied by a seasonal green vegetable such as courgettes or French beans. Ice-cold dry cider is the ideal drink with this casserole.

SMOKED HADDOCK WITH CREAM AND PERNOD

0.40	382 cals

Serves 4

4 smoked haddock fillets, about 700 g (1½ lb) total weight

300 ml (½ pint) milk

few slices of onion

2 bay leaves

few black peppercorns

2.5 ml (½ tsp) crushed fennel seeds

150 ml (5 fl oz) double cream

15 g (½ oz) butter

60 ml (4 tbsp) Pernod

salt and freshly ground pepper

fennel sprigs, to garnish

1 Put the smoked haddock fillets in a large flameproof casserole. Pour in the milk and add the onion slices, bay leaves, peppercorns and fennel seeds. Pour in a little water if the liquid does not completely cover the smoked haddock.

2 Bring slowly to boiling point, then lower the heat, cover and simmer gently for 15 minutes or until the fish flakes easily when tested with a fork.

3 Remove the fish fillets from the cooking liquid and then flake into chunky pieces. Discard all skin and any bones.

4 Strain the cooking liquid and return to the rinsed-out pan. Boil to reduce slightly, then add the cream, butter and Pernod and boil again until the sauce thickens.

5 Return the fish to the liquid and heat through. Add salt and pepper to taste (taking care not to add too much salt as the fish is salty), then transfer to a warmed serving dish. Garnish with fennel sprigs and serve immediately.

Menu Suggestion

A rich and filling dinner party main course, best served with a plain accompaniment such as boiled rice or duchesse potatoes. If liked, the quantities may be halved and the dish served as a first course, with hot French bread.

SMOKED HADDOCK WITH CREAM AND PERNOD

As a starter this dish is most unusual, with its subtle flavouring of fennel and aniseed. Serve it for a special dinner party when you want to surprise your guests with something just that little bit different, but be sure to serve something quite plain as the main course.

The choice of smoked haddock at the fishmonger can sometimes be confusing. The bright yellow fish sold as 'golden cutlets' is in fact smoked cod. Thicker than smoked haddock, it is an excellent fish for dishes like this one where the fish needs to be flaked into chunky pieces.

INDONESIAN FISH CURRY

| 0.40 | 287 cals |

Serves 4

1 small onion, skinned and
    chopped

1 garlic clove, skinned and chopped

2.5 cm (1 inch) piece fresh root
    ginger, skinned and chopped

5 ml (1 tsp) ground turmeric

2.5 ml ($\frac{1}{2}$ tsp) laos powder (see box)

1.25 ml ($\frac{1}{4}$ tsp) chilli powder

30 ml (2 tbsp) vegetable oil

salt

700 g (1$\frac{1}{2}$ lb) haddock fillets, skinned
    and cut into bite-sized pieces

225 g (8 oz) peeled prawns

300 ml ($\frac{1}{2}$ pint) coconut milk (see
    box)

juice of 1 lime

shredded coconut and lime
    wedges, to garnish

1 Work the first seven ingredients in an electric blender or
processor with 2.5 ml ($\frac{1}{2}$ tsp) salt.

2 Transfer the mixture to a
flameproof casserole and fry
gently, stirring, for 5 minutes.
Add the haddock pieces and
prawns and fry for a few minutes
more, tossing fish to coat with the
spice mixture.

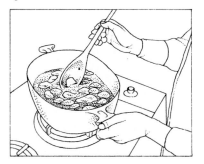

3 Pour in the coconut milk,
shake the pan and turn the fish
gently in the liquid. (Take care not
to break up the pieces of fish.)
Bring slowly to boiling point, then
lower the heat, cover and simmer
for 10 minutes until tender.

4 Add the lime juice, taste and
adjust seasoning, then transfer
to a warmed serving dish and
sprinkle with coconut. Serve hot,
garnished with lime wedges.

Menu Suggestion
Serve with plain boiled rice,
prawn crackers and lime pickle.

INDONESIAN FISH CURRY
Laos powder is used extensively
in the cooking of Southeast Asia;
it comes from a root rather like
ginger and has a peppery hot
taste. Look for it in specialist
delicatessens in small bottles,
sometimes labelled galangal or
galingale. To make 300 ml
($\frac{1}{2}$ pint) coconut milk, break
100 g (4 oz) block creamed
coconut into a measuring jug,
pour in boiling hot water up to
the 300 ml ($\frac{1}{2}$ pint) mark and stir
to dissolve. Strain before using.

MONKFISH WITH LIME AND PRAWNS

0.45	294 cals

Serves 4

550 g (1¼ lb) monkfish

salt and freshly ground pepper

15 ml (1 tbsp) plain flour

30 ml (2 tbsp) vegetable oil

1 small onion, skinned and chopped

1 garlic clove, skinned and chopped

225 g (8 oz) tomatoes, skinned and chopped

150 ml (¼ pint) dry white wine

finely grated rind and juice of 1 lime

pinch of sugar

100 g (4 oz) peeled prawns

lime slices, to garnish

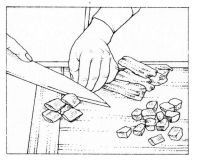

1 Using a sharp knife, skin the fish, if necessary, then cut fish into 5 cm (1 inch) chunks and toss in seasoned flour.

2 Heat the oil in a flameproof casserole and gently fry the onion and garlic for 5 minutes. Add fish and fry until golden.

3 Stir in the tomatoes, wine, rind and juice of the lime, sugar and seasoning. Bring to the boil.

4 Cover and cook in the oven at 180°C (350°F) mark 4 for 15 minutes. Add the prawns and continue to cook for a further 15 minutes until the monkfish is tender. Garnish with lime slices.

Menu Suggestion
Served in a ring of saffron rice, this Monkfish Casserole with Lime and Prawns makes an exceptionally pretty main course dish for a dinner party.

TROUT POACHED IN WINE

0.45	357 cals

Serves 4

4 small trout, with heads on

salt and freshly ground pepper

50 g (2 oz) butter

1 large onion, skinned and sliced

2 celery sticks, trimmed and sliced

2 carrots, peeled and very thinly sliced

300 ml (½ pint) dry white wine

bouquet garni

15 ml (1 tbsp) plain flour

lemon wedges and chopped fresh parsley, to garnish

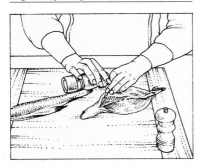

1 Wash the trout under cold running water and drain. Pat dry and season the insides.

2 Melt 25 g (1 oz) of the butter in a small saucepan, add the onion, celery and carrots and stir well to cover with butter. Cover and sweat for 5 minutes.

3 Lay the vegetables in a greased casserole and arrange the fish on top. Pour over the wine and add the bouquet garni.

4 Cover tightly and cook in the oven at 180°C (350°F) mark 4 for about 25 minutes until the trout are cooked.

5 Transfer the trout and vegetables to a warmed serving dish and keep hot.

6 Pour the cooking juices into a small pan, discarding the bouquet garni. Blend together the remaining butter and the flour. Whisk into the sauce and simmer gently, stirring, until thickened. Pour into a sauceboat or jug. Garnish the trout with lemon wedges and parsley.

Menu Suggestion
Serve with steamed or boiled new potatoes and a seasonal green vegetable or salad.

TROUT POACHED IN WINE

If you are unused to buying whole fresh fish at the fishmonger, you may find the different types of trout confusing. Sea trout are the larger of the species, so called because they have migrated to the sea from the rivers. Some fishmongers call them 'salmon trout', because their flesh is firm and salmony pink, and they can be used as an inexpensive alternative to fresh salmon.

For this recipe you will need to buy freshwater trout, i.e. river, rainbow or lake trout, which are now becoming increasingly widely available, both fresh and frozen, at supermarkets. Look for shiny, slippery skin and bright eyes—both good indications of freshness.

SWEDISH HERRINGS

1.00*	452 cals

* plus 2–3 hours cooling

Serves 4

4 fresh herrings, filleted
salt and freshly ground pepper
4 whole cloves
2 dried chillies
12 peppercorns
1 bay leaf
1 blade of mace
60 ml (4 tbsp) malt vinegar
75 ml (5 tbsp) tarragon vinegar
150 ml ($\frac{1}{4}$ pint) water
1 shallot, skinned and finely chopped
lemon slices, to garnish
142 ml (5 fl oz) soured cream, to serve

1 Sprinkle the herring fillets with salt and freshly ground pepper and roll up from the head end, skin side outermost.

2 Arrange in a casserole and add the cloves, chillies, peppercorns, bay leaf and mace. Cover with the vinegars and water and sprinkle the shallot on top.

3 Cover and cook in the oven at 170°C (325°F) mark 3 for about 45 minutes or until tender.

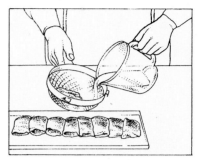

4 Transfer the fish carefully to a serving dish and strain or pour the liquor over. Leave to cool for about 2–3 hours.

5 Garnish the casserole with lemon slices and serve cold with soured cream.

Menu Suggestion

Swedish Herrings make an excellent cold dish for a summer luncheon served with fresh French bread and butter and a selection of salads. Alternatively, halve the quantities given in the recipe and serve for a starter.

SWEDISH HERRINGS

Herrings are inexpensive to buy, yet extremely nutritious. Being oily fish, they are rich in vitamins A and D as well as minerals, and contain almost as much protein as meat. Although they are eaten fresh just as any other oily fish, herrings are immensely popular pickled or soused, especially in northern European and Scandinavian countries where they are a favourite starter. Such herrings are easy to obtain from delicatessens and supermarkets, either loose or in jars (rollmops are a kind of soused herring), but it is so much nicer to make your own using fresh herring fillets as here. For a neat appearance to the finished dish, try to get fillets which are all of an even size and thickness.

SEAFOOD STIR FRY

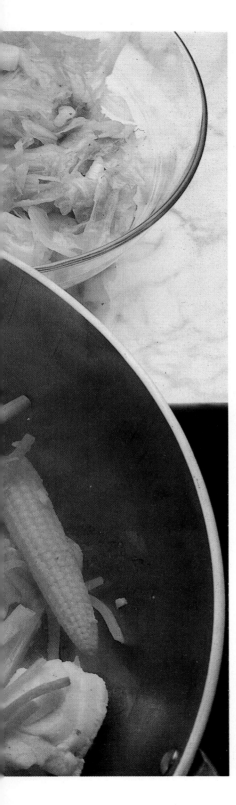

0.25	288 cals

Serves 4

2 celery sticks, washed and trimmed

1 medium carrot, peeled

350 g (12 oz) coley, haddock or cod fillet, skinned

350 g (12 oz) Iceberg or Cos lettuce

about 45 ml (3 tbsp) peanut oil

1 garlic clove, skinned and crushed

100 g (4 oz) peeled prawns

425 g (15 oz) can whole baby sweetcorn, drained

5 ml (1 tsp) anchovy essence

salt and freshly ground pepper

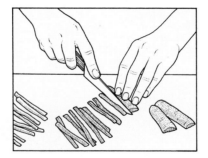

1 Slice the celery and carrot into thin matchsticks, 5 cm (2 inch) long. Cut the fish into 2.5 cm (1 inch) chunks.

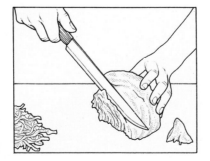

2 Shred the lettuce finely with a sharp knife, discarding the core and any thick stalks.

3 Heat 15 ml (1 tbsp) of the oil in a wok or large frying pan until smoking. Add the lettuce and fry for about 30 seconds until lightly cooked. Transfer to a serving dish with a slotted spoon and keep warm in a low oven.

4 Heat another 30 ml (2 tbsp) of oil in the pan until smoking. Add the celery, carrot, white fish and garlic and stir-fry over high heat for 2–3 minutes, adding more oil if necessary.

5 Lower the heat, add the prawns, baby sweetcorn and anchovy essence. Toss well together for 2–3 minutes to heat through and coat all the ingredients in the sauce (the fish will flake apart).

6 Add seasoning to taste, spoon on top of the lettuce and serve immediately.

Menu Suggestion
This stir-fried dish has its own vegetables and therefore needs no further accompaniment other than a dish of plain boiled rice.

SEAFOOD STIR FRY

It may seem unusual to stir fry lettuce, which is usually only served as a raw salad vegetable, but it is a method often used in Chinese cookery. As long as you use the crisp varieties suggested here—Iceberg or Cos—you will find it gives a fresh, crunchy texture to the dish which contrasts well with the softness of the fish. Avoid using round or cabbage lettuces, which would become limp on cooking, and make sure to time the cooking accurately.

ITALIAN MARINATED TROUT

0.15*	221 cals

* plus at least 8 hours marinating

Serves 4

30 ml (2 tbsp) olive oil

4 whole trout, about 225 g (8 oz) each, cleaned

30 ml (2 tbsp) flour

1 small bulb Florence fennel, trimmed and finely sliced

1 onion, skinned and finely sliced

300 ml (½ pint) dry white Italian wine

finely grated rind and juice of 1 orange

salt and freshly ground pepper

orange slices and chopped fennel tops, to garnish

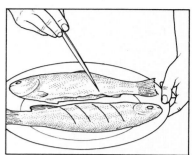

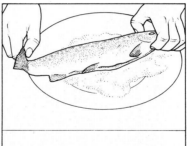

1 Heat the olive oil in a frying pan. Dip the trout in the flour and fry gently for 4 minutes on each side. With a fish slice, transfer the fish to a shallow dish.

2 With a sharp knife, score the skin diagonally, being careful not to cut too deeply into the flesh. Set aside.

3 Add the fennel and onion to the frying pan and fry for 5 minutes. Add the wine, orange rind and juice, and seasoning to taste. Bring to the boil. Boil rapidly for 1 minute, add the chopped fennel tops and pour immediately over the fish. Cool.

4 Marinate in the refrigerator for at least 8 hours, but no more than 3 days.

5 Serve at room temperature, garnished with orange slices and the chopped fennel tops.

Menu Suggestion
Serve for a cold summer supper party with hot garlic or herb bread and a mixed salad.

ITALIAN MARINATED TROUT

The bulb vegetable Florence fennel looks rather like a squat version of celery with feathery leaves. The flavour of fennel is like aniseed; for the most subtle taste of aniseed, buy white or pale green fennel, for a stronger flavour, choose vegetables which are dark green in colour. In this recipe, fennel is fried with onion and used in a marinade for fish, with which it has a particular affinity. Other more usual uses for fennel are sliced or chopped raw in salads (fennel and tomato are particularly good together), and braised in the oven with stock or a white or cheese sauce. As its name suggests, Florence fennel comes from Italy, where it is used extensively in cooking.

Vegetables

HOT POTATOES WITH DILL

0.35	174 cals

Serves 6

900 g (2 lb) potatoes

salt

4 spring onions, washed and finely chopped

15 ml (1 tbsp) chopped fresh dill and a sprig, to garnish

freshly ground pepper

142 ml (5 fl oz) soured cream

1 Place the potatoes in cold, salted water, bring to the boil and cook for 12–15 minutes until tender.

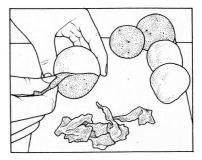

2 Drain the potatoes, leave until just cool enough to handle, then remove the skins.

3 Cut the potatoes into small dice and place in a bowl. Add the chopped onions to the potatoes with the dill and salt and pepper to taste.

4 Thin the soured cream, if necessary, with a little boiling water or milk, stir it into the potatoes and toss gently.

5 Leave to stand for a few minutes so that the flavours can blend. To serve, garnish with a sprig of dill.

HERBY COURGETTE FINGERS WITH CREAM

0.30*	147–196 cals

* plus 1 hour to dégorge

Serves 6–8

900 g (2 lb) small or medium
  courgettes

salt and freshly ground pepper

50 g (2 oz) butter

1–2 garlic cloves, skinned and
  crushed

150 ml (¼ pint) vegetable stock or
  water

20 ml (4 tsp) chopped fresh basil or
  10 ml (2 tsp) dried

150 ml (¼ pint) double cream

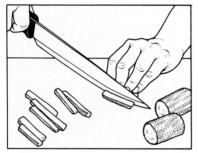

1 Trim the courgettes, then cut
them into neat strips about
5 cm (2 inches) long and 0.5 cm
(¼ inch) wide.

2 Put the courgette strips in a
colander, sprinkling each layer
with salt. Cover with a plate, place
heavy weights on top and leave to
dégorge for 1 hour.

3 Rinse the courgette strips
thoroughly under cold running
water, then pat dry in a clean tea
towel.

4 Melt half of the butter in a
heavy-based saucepan, add the
courgettes and garlic and toss over
moderate heat for a few minutes.

5 Pour in the stock, then add
half of the basil with salt and
pepper to taste. Cover the pan and
simmer gently for 5 minutes or
until the courgettes are tender but
still with some crunch. Transfer
the courgettes to a warmed serving
dish with a slotted spoon, cover
and keep hot.

6 Increase the heat and boil the
liquid to reduce slightly. Add
the cream and the remaining
butter and basil. Simmer until the
sauce is of a coating consistency.
Taste and adjust seasoning, then
pour over the courgettes. Serve
immediately.

Menu Suggestion
Serve this creamy vegetable dish
in summer when courgettes are
plentiful; it goes especially well
with lamb and chicken dishes.

HERBY COURGETTE FINGERS WITH CREAM

Courgettes are members of the
same cucurbit family as
pumpkins, gourds, marrows,
squashes and cucumbers. They
are believed to have been eaten
originally by the American
Indians, who ground down the
seeds of gourds rather than
eating the flesh. Marrows were
known in Roman times, and
courgettes were cultivated from
them.

It is a good idea to dégorge
courgettes before cooking, as in
this recipe. They are a watery
vegetable, and can dilute sauces
such as this creamy one if they
are not dégorged beforehand.
Older courgettes can also be
bitter, another reason for
extracting the juice before
cooking. Always rinse them
thoroughly after dégorging, or
the finished dish may be salty.

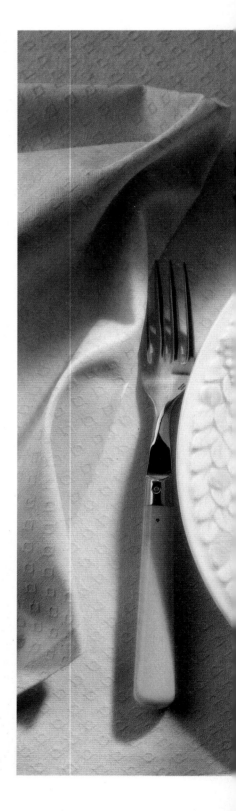

FRENCH BEANS IN SOURED CREAM WITH PAPRIKA

0.25	141 cals

Serves 4

700 g (1½ lb) French beans

25 g (1 oz) butter or margarine

1 small onion, skinned and chopped

5 ml (1 tsp) paprika

salt and freshly ground pepper

150 ml (¼ pint) chicken stock

142 ml (5 fl oz) soured cream

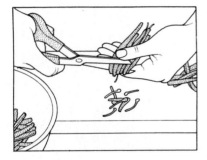

1 Using kitchen scissors, top and tail the French beans and cut them into 2.5-cm (1-inch) lengths. Melt the butter in a pan, add the onion and cook gently for 5 minutes until soft and golden, but do not brown.

2 Stir in 2.5 ml (½ tsp) paprika, beans, seasoning and stock. Bring to the boil, cover and simmer for 5–10 minutes until the French beans are tender.

3 Stir the cream into the pan and reheat without boiling. Turn into a heated serving dish and dust the top with the remaining paprika.

New Potatoes with Tarragon Cream

0.15	204 cals

Serves 4

15 g (½ oz) butter or margarine

**4 spring onions, washed, trimmed
  and chopped**

142 ml (5 fl oz) soured cream

salt and freshly ground pepper

3 sprigs of fresh tarragon

**700 g (1½ lb) cooked new potatoes,
  drained and kept hot**

1 Melt the butter in a pan, add
the onions and cook for 5
minutes until soft. Stir in the
cream, seasoning, and two tarragon
sprigs and heat without boiling.

2 Add the cooked potatoes to
the creamy onion and tarragon
mixture in the pan. Reheat gently,
do not boil.

3 Turn the potatoes and the
sauce into a warm serving dish
and serve garnished with a sprig of
fresh tarragon.

343

SPINACH TIMBALE

1.20	257 cals

Serves 6

25 g (1 oz) butter or margarine

1 onion, skinned and finely chopped

900 g (2 lb) fresh spinach, washed, trimmed and roughly chopped

150 ml ($\frac{1}{4}$ pint) milk

150 ml (5 fl oz) single cream

4 eggs

50 g (2 oz) Gruyère cheese, grated

50 g (2 oz) fresh white breadcrumbs

pinch of grated nutmeg

salt and freshly ground pepper

thin tomato strips and fresh coriander, to garnish

tomato sauce, (right)

1 Melt the butter in a saucepan, stir in the onion and cook gently for about 5 minutes until soft. Stir in the spinach and cook for a further 5 minutes until soft, stirring occasionally. Stir in the milk and cream and heat gently.

2 Beat the eggs in a bowl and stir in the spinach mixture, cheese, breadcrumbs, nutmeg and salt and pepper.

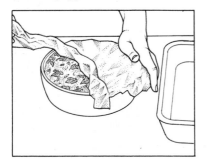

3 Turn the mixture into a greased 1.1-litre (2-pint) ring mould, cover with foil and place the dish in a roasting tin, half filled with hot water. Bake in the oven at 180°C (350°F) mark 4 for 1$\frac{1}{4}$ hours until firm to the touch and a knife, inserted in the centre, comes out clean. Meanwhile, prepare the tomato sauce.

4 Remove the dish from the water and leave for 5 minutes. Loosen the timbale from the sides of the dish with a knife.

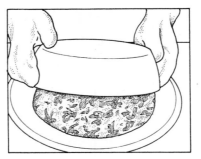

5 Turn the timbale out on to a warmed flat serving dish. Garnish with thin tomato strips and coriander. If liked, serve with a tomato sauce.

TIMBALES

The French word *timbale* is used to describe a container, usually silver or gold, which has a handle on either side and is designed for holding drinks. The word has also taken on a broader meaning in culinary terms, however, and is now generally used to describe a dish which is baked and then turned out of its cooking dish – as in this recipe.

TOMATO SAUCE

Makes about 300 ml ($\frac{1}{2}$ pint)

1 small onion, skinned and chopped

1 small carrot, peeled and chopped

25 g (1 oz) butter

25 ml (1$\frac{1}{2}$ tbsp) flour

450 g (1 lb) tomatoes, quartered, or a 397-g (14-oz) can tomatoes, drained

300 ml ($\frac{1}{2}$ pint) chicken stock

1 bay leaf

1 clove

2.5 ml ($\frac{1}{2}$ tsp) sugar

10 ml (2 tsp) tomato purée

15–60 ml (1–4 tbsp) dry white wine (optional)

salt and freshly ground pepper

1 Lightly fry the onion and carrot in the butter for 5 minutes. Stir in the flour and add the tomatoes, stock, bay leaf, clove, sugar, tomato purée, wine, if used, and salt and pepper.

2 Bring to the boil, cover and simmer for 30–45 minutes, or until the vegetables are cooked. Sieve, reheat and adjust seasoning, if necessary.

——— VARIATION ———

NEAPOLITAN TOMATO SAUCE

450 g (1 lb) tomatoes, skinned or a 397-g (14-oz) can tomatoes, drained

1 garlic clove, skinned and crushed

50 ml (2 fl oz) olive oil

2.5 ml ($\frac{1}{2}$ tsp) sugar

3 basil leaves, torn, or 10 ml (2 tsp) chopped fresh parsley, or 5 ml (1 tsp) oregano

salt and freshly ground pepper

Place all the ingredients in a saucepan and simmer, uncovered, stirring occasionally for about 10 minutes until the oil has separated from the tomatoes.

RATATOUILLE

| 2.05* | ✳ | 252 cals |

* includes 30 minutes standing time

Serves 6

450 g (1 lb) aubergines

salt

450 g (1 lb) courgettes

3 red or green peppers

120 ml (8 tbsp) olive oil

450 g (1 lb) onions, skinned and chopped

1 garlic clove, skinned and crushed

450 g (1 lb) tomatoes, skinned, seeded and chopped, or one 397-g (14-oz) can tomatoes, drained

30 ml (2 tbsp) tomato purée

bouquet garni

freshly ground pepper

1 Cut the aubergines into thin slices. Sprinkle liberally with salt and set aside to drain in a sieve or colander for 30 minutes. Rinse under cold running water and pat dry with absorbent kitchen paper.

2 Meanwhile, wash the courgettes and pat dry with absorbent kitchen paper. Top and tail them and then cut into thin slices.

3 Wash the peppers; pat dry with absorbent kitchen paper. Slice off the stems and remove the seeds. Cut into thin rings.

4 Heat the oil in a large saucepan. Add the onions and garlic and cook gently for about 10 minutes until soft and golden.

5 Add the tomatoes and purée and cook for a few more minutes, then add the aubergines, courgettes, peppers, bouquet garni and salt and pepper. Cover and simmer gently for 1 hour. The vegetables should be soft and well mixed but retain their shape and most of the cooking liquid should have evaporated.

6 To reduce the liquid, remove the lid and cook gently for another 20 minutes. Check the seasoning and serve hot or cold.

SUMMER VEGETABLE FRICASSÉE

0.30	114–171 cals

Serves 4–6

4 courgettes, washed and trimmed

225 g (8 oz) French beans, topped
   and tailed and cut into 5-cm
   (2-inch) lengths

salt and freshly ground pepper

45 ml (3 tbsp) olive oil

1 onion, skinned and sliced

2 garlic cloves, skinned and
   crushed

5 ml (1 tsp) crushed coriander
   seeds

3 peppers (red, yellow, green),
   cored, seeded and sliced

150 ml ($\frac{1}{4}$ pint) dry white wine

10 ml (2 tsp) tomato purée

2.5 ml ($\frac{1}{2}$ tsp) sugar

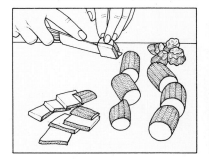

1 Cut the courgettes crossways
into thirds, then cut them
lengthways into slices about 0.5 cm
($\frac{1}{4}$ inch) thick.

2 Blanch the courgettes and
beans in boiling salted water
for 5 minutes only. Drain and set
aside until required.

3 Heat the oil in a flameproof
casserole, add the onion, garlic
and coriander seeds and fry gently
for 5 minutes until onion is soft.

4 Add the pepper slices and fry
gently for a further 5 minutes,
stirring constantly. Stir in the
wine, tomato purée and sugar,
with salt and pepper to taste. Bring
to the boil, then simmer for a few
minutes, stirring all the time until
the liquid begins to reduce.

5 Add the courgettes and beans
to the pan and stir gently to
combine with the sauce. Heat
through, taking care not to overcook the vegetables. Taste and adjust seasoning. Serve hot, straight
from the casserole.

CABBAGE WITH CARAWAY

0.15	110 cals

Serves 6

1.4 kg (3 lb) green cabbage
salt
50 g (2 oz) butter or margarine
5 ml (1 tsp) caraway seeds
freshly ground pepper

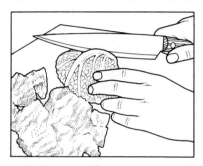

1 Shred the cabbage finely, discarding any core or tough outer leaves. Wash well under cold running water.

2 Cook in a large pan of boiling salted water for 2 minutes only—the cabbage should retain its crispness and texture. Drain well.

3 Melt the butter in the saucepan; add the drained cabbage with the caraway seeds and seasoning. Stir over a moderate heat for 2–3 minutes until the cabbage is really hot. Adjust seasoning and serve immediately.

Peppered Carrots

$\boxed{0.20}$	157 cals

Serves 4

50 g (2 oz) butter or margarine

5 ml (1 tsp) sugar

450 g (1 lb) carrots, peeled or scrubbed and thinly sliced

3 spring onions, washed and trimmed

1.25 ml ($\frac{1}{4}$ tsp) cayenne pepper or to taste

45 ml (3 tbsp) soured cream

salt and freshly ground pepper

1 Melt the butter with the sugar in a deep sauté pan which has a tightly fitting lid. Put the carrots into the pan, cover tightly and cook gently for 10–15 minutes until tender.

2 Remove the lid from the pan and snip in the spring onions with a pair of sharp kitchen scissors. Transfer carrots and onions with a slotted spoon to a serving dish and keep warm.

3 Stir the cayenne pepper and soured cream into the pan. Taste and adjust seasoning, and warm through for 1–2 minutes. Pour over the carrots and serve.

TURNIPS IN CURRY CREAM SAUCE

0.30	270 cals

Serves 4

700 g (1½ lb) small turnips

salt

50 g (2 oz) butter or margarine

1 onion, skinned and finely
    chopped

100 g (4 oz) cooking apple

50 g (2 oz) sultanas

5 ml (1 tsp) mild curry powder

5 ml (1 tsp) plain flour

150 ml (¼ pint) dry cider

150 ml (5 fl oz) single cream

10 ml (2 tsp) lemon juice

freshly ground pepper

1 Peel the turnips, boil in salted water for 10–15 minutes until just tender. Meanwhile, make the sauce. Melt the butter, add the onion, cover and cook gently for 10 minutes until soft and tinged with colour. Peel and finely chop the apple and add to the onion, together with the sultanas, curry powder and flour. Cook, stirring constantly, for 3–4 minutes.

2 Pour the cider into the pan, bring to the boil, bubble gently for 2 minutes, stirring. Off the heat stir in the cream, lemon juice and seasoning. Keep warm without boiling.

3 Drain the turnips in a colander. To serve, place in a heated dish and pour over the curry cream sauce. Serve immediately.

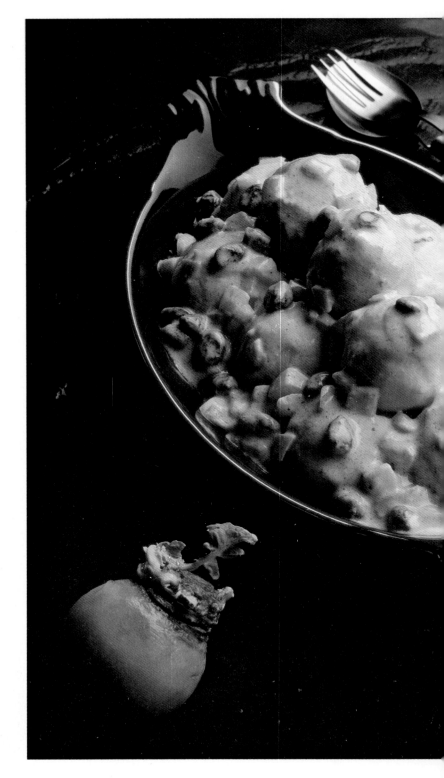

HOT BEETROOT WITH HORSERADISH

| 0.20 | 53–80 cals |

Serves 4–6

450 g (1 lb) cooked beetroot

15 ml (1 tbsp) caster sugar

60 ml (4 tbsp) red wine vinegar

30 ml (2 tbsp) freshly grated horseradish

salt and freshly ground pepper

15 ml (1 tbsp) cornflour

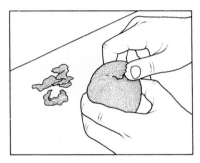

1 Rub the skin off the beet-root carefully, using your fingers. Slice the beetroot neatly into rounds.

2 Put the beetroot in a large heavy-based pan, then sprinkle with the sugar. Pour in the wine vinegar and add the horseradish with salt and pepper to taste.

3 Bring to the boil, without stir-ring, then lower the heat, cover and simmer gently for 10 minutes.

4 Transfer the beetroot slices carefully with a slotted spoon to a warmed serving dish. Mix the cornflour to a paste with a little cold water, then stir into the cook-ing liquid in the pan. Boil for 1–2 minutes, stirring vigorously until the liquid thickens. To serve, taste and adjust seasoning, then pour over the beetroot. Serve immediately.

CHINESE VEGETABLE STIR-FRY

0.15	157 cals

Serves 4

1 turnip, peeled

4 small carrots, peeled

4 celery sticks

2 young leeks, washed and trimmed

30 ml (2 tbsp) sesame oil

15 ml (1 tbsp) vegetable oil

100 g (4 oz) beansprouts, washed and drained

10 ml (2 tsp) soy sauce

5 ml (1 tsp) white wine vinegar

5 ml (1 tsp) soft brown sugar

5 ml (1 tsp) five-spice powder

salt

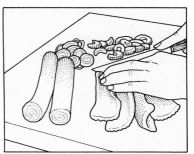

2 Slice the celery and leeks finely. Then heat the oils in a wok, and add the prepared vegetables with the beansprouts. Stir-fry over moderate heat for 3–4 minutes, then sprinkle in the soy sauce, wine vinegar, sugar, five-spice powder and salt to taste. Stir-fry for 1 further minute. Serve at once, while piping hot.

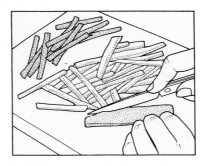

1 Using a sharp knife, cut the turnip and the peeled carrots into matchstick strips.

STIR-FRYING

The beauty of the Chinese stir-frying technique is that it is so quick and easy — perfect for entertaining when you want to be with your guests as much as possible. With stir-frying, everything can be prepared ahead of time so that all you have to do is quickly cook the ingredients at the last moment.

A Chinese wok is best for stir-frying, but not absolutely essential. The reason why a wok is so successful is that the bottom is round and cone-shaped so that the heat is concentrated in the centre — food cooks very fast when it is pushed to the base of the pan. A Chinese wok keeps an intense level of heat throughout cooking, but if you don't have one, a cast iron frying-pan can be used instead.

Traditionally, very long chopsticks are used to push the food around the wok during stir frying, but if you find it easier you can use a wooden spatula or fork.

BARBECUED BEANS

4.20*	213 cals

* plus overnight soaking

Serves 6

350 g (12 oz) red kidney beans,
  soaked overnight
1.1 litres (2 pints) tomato juice
1 large onion, skinned and sliced
30 ml (2 tbsp) soy sauce
60 ml (4 tbsp) cider vinegar
15 ml (1 tbsp) Worcestershire sauce
15 ml (1 tbsp) mustard powder
15 ml (1 tbsp) honey
2.5 ml ($\frac{1}{2}$ tsp) chilli powder
salt and freshly ground pepper

1 Drain the beans and place in a saucepan. Cover with cold water, bring to the boil and boil rapidly for 10 minutes then drain.

2 Put the tomato juice, onion, soy sauce, vinegar, Worcestershire sauce, mustard, honey and chilli powder in a flameproof casserole. Bring to the boil then add the beans.

3 Cover and cook in the oven at 140°C (275°F) mark 1 for about 4 hours until the beans are tender. Season well with salt and freshly ground pepper.

Menu Suggestion
Serve as a vegetable accompaniment to any roast or grilled meat or poultry.

RED CABBAGE AND APPLE CASSEROLE

3.30	121–182 cals

Serves 4–6

700 g (1½ lb) red cabbage

2 cooking apples

1 large Spanish onion

15 g (½ oz) butter or margarine

50 g (2 oz) raisins

salt and freshly ground pepper

30 ml (2 tbsp) granulated sugar

60 ml (4 tbsp) white wine or wine vinegar

30 ml (2 tbsp) port (optional)

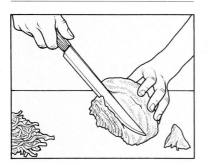

1 Shred the cabbage finely, discarding the thick central stalk. Peel and core the apples and slice them thinly. Skin the onion and slice thinly.

2 Brush the inside of a large ovenproof dish with the butter. Put a layer of shredded cabbage in the bottom and cover with a layer of sliced apple and onion. Sprinkle over a few of the raisins and season with salt and pepper to taste.

3 In a jug, mix the sugar with the wine, and the port if using. Sprinkle a little of this mixture over the ingredients in the dish.

4 Continue layering the ingredients in the dish until they are all used up. Cover the dish and bake in the oven at 150°C (300°F) mark 2 for 3 hours. Taste and adjust seasoning, then turn into a warmed serving dish. Serve the casserole hot.

Menu Suggestion

This vegetable casserole has a tangy fruit flavour, which makes it the ideal accompaniment for rich meats. It is especially good with roast pork, duck, pheasant and partridge, and would also go well with the festive turkey at Christmastime.

RED CABBAGE AND APPLE CASSEROLE

Casseroles of cabbage like this one are popular in northern France, particularly in Ardennes, which borders on Belgium. Both white and red cabbage are used, but with white cabbage dry white wine is usually preferred to the red used here. A spoonful or two of redcurrant jelly is sometimes added to red cabbage casseroles. Substitute this for the port if liked, plus a few crushed juniper berries, which are a favourite flavouring ingredient in northern Europe.

This quantity of cabbage makes enough for 4–6 good helpings; reheat any leftover casserole for another supper as it will have an excellent flavour. If there is any left over, refrigerate it in a covered bowl overnight, then the next day, toss it in a pan with a little butter until hot.

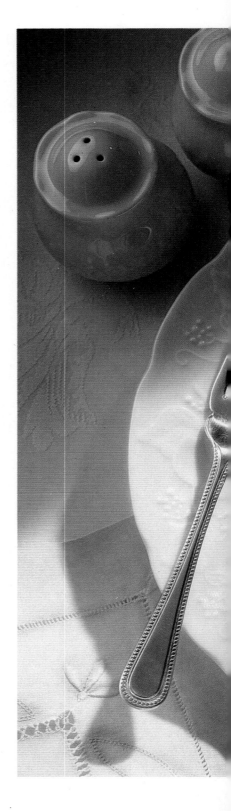

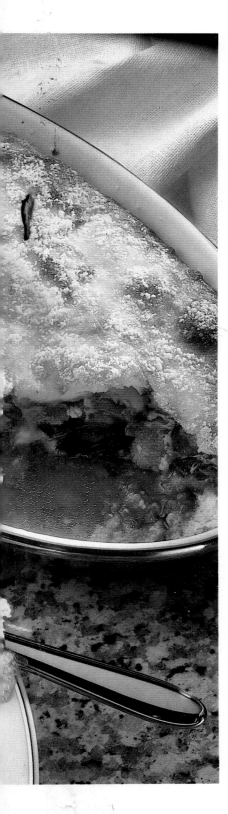

TIAN À LA PROVENÇALE
(AUBERGINE GRATIN)

1.15	🍳	✳*	428 cals

* freeze before baking at step 6

Serves 4

450 g (1 lb) aubergines

salt and freshly ground pepper

25 g (1 oz) butter or margarine

25 g (1 oz) plain flour

300 ml ($\frac{1}{2}$ pint) milk

60 ml (4 tbsp) Parmesan cheese, freshly grated

1.25 ml ($\frac{1}{4}$ tsp) freshly grated nutmeg

about 150 ml ($\frac{1}{4}$ pint) olive or vegetable oil

350 g (12 oz) tomatoes, skinned and sliced

2 garlic cloves, skinned and roughly chopped

2 eggs, beaten

1 Slice the aubergines thinly, then place in a colander, sprinkling each layer with salt. Cover with a plate, place heavy weights on top and leave to dégorge for 30 minutes.

2 Meanwhile, melt the butter in a saucepan, add the flour and cook gently, stirring, for 1–2 minutes. Remove from the heat and gradually blend in the milk. Bring to the boil, stirring constantly, then simmer for 3 minutes until thick and smooth. Add half of the cheese, the nutmeg and salt and pepper to taste, stir well to mix, then remove from the heat.

3 Rinse the aubergine slices under cold running water, then pat dry with absorbent kitchen paper.

4 Pour enough oil into a heavy-based frying pan to cover the base. Heat until very hot, then add a layer of aubergine slices. Fry over moderate heat until golden brown on both sides, turning once. Remove with a slotted spoon and drain on absorbent kitchen paper. Repeat with more oil and aubergines.

5 Arrange alternate layers of aubergines and tomatoes in an oiled gratin or baking dish. Sprinkle each layer with garlic, a little salt and plenty of pepper.

6 Beat the eggs into the sauce, then pour slowly into the dish. Sprinkle the remaining cheese evenly over the top. Bake in the oven at 200°C (400°F) mark 6 for 20 minutes or until golden brown and bubbling. Serve hot.

Menu Suggestion
This substantial, creamy vegetable dish is excellent served with roast lamb or grilled chops. It also makes a tasty vegetarian dinner with potatoes and a salad.

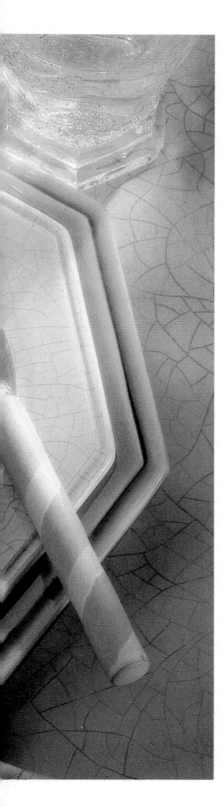

CELERIAC WITH TOMATO SAUCE

| 1.10 | ✳* | 295 cals |

* freeze before baking at end of step 6

Serves 4

60 ml (4 tbsp) olive oil

1 large onion, skinned and finely chopped

3 garlic cloves, skinned and crushed

350 g (12 oz) ripe tomatoes, skinned and finely chopped

15 ml (1 tbsp) tomato purée

30 ml (2 tbsp) red wine or red wine vinegar

60 ml (4 tbsp) chopped fresh parsley

5 ml (1 tsp) ground cinnamon

1 bay leaf

salt and freshly ground pepper

2 heads of celeriac, total weight about 900 g (2 lb)

5 ml (1 tsp) lemon juice

50 g (2 oz) dried brown or white breadcrumbs

50 g (2 oz) Parmesan cheese, freshly grated

1 Prepare the tomato sauce. Heat the oil in a heavy-based saucepan, add the onion and garlic and fry gently for about 10 minutes until very soft and lightly coloured.

2 Add the tomatoes, tomato purée, wine, parsley, cinnamon, bay leaf and salt and pepper to taste. Add 450 ml ($\frac{3}{4}$ pint) hot water and bring to the boil, stirring with a wooden spoon to break up the tomatoes.

3 Lower the heat, cover and simmer the tomato sauce for 30 minutes, stirring occasionally.

4 Meanwhile, peel the celeriac, then cut into chunky pieces. As you prepare the celeriac, place the pieces in a bowl of water to which the lemon juice has been added, to prevent discoloration.

5 Drain the celeriac, then plunge quickly into a large pan of boiling salted water. Return to the boil and blanch for 10 minutes.

6 Drain the celeriac well, then put in an ovenproof dish. Pour over the tomato sauce (discarding the bay leaf), then sprinkle the breadcrumbs and cheese evenly over the top.

7 Bake the celeriac in the oven at 190°C (375°F) mark 5 for 30 minutes, until the celeriac is tender when pierced with a skewer and the topping is golden brown. Serve hot, straight from the dish.

Menu Suggestion
With its strongly flavoured tomato sauce, this gratin of celeriac tastes good with plain roast or grilled meat and poultry.

COLCANNON
(IRISH MASHED POTATOES WITH KALE AND LEEKS)

0.35	211 cals

Serves 6

450 g (1 lb) potatoes, peeled and quartered

salt and freshly ground pepper

450 g (1 lb) kale or cabbage, cored and shredded

2 small leeks, sliced and washed

150 ml (¼ pint) milk or double cream

50 g (2 oz) butter or margarine

melted butter, to serve

1 Cook the potatoes in boiling salted water for 15–20 minutes until tender. Meanwhile, cook the kale in a separate saucepan of boiling salted water for 5–10 minutes until tender. Drain both potatoes and kale.

2 Put the leeks and milk or cream in a saucepan and simmer gently for 10–15 minutes until soft.

3 Put the leeks in a large bowl, add the potatoes, then the kale, butter and salt and pepper to taste. Beat together over gentle heat until the mixture is thoroughly blended.

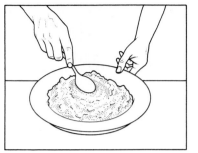

4 Mound the mixture on a warmed serving dish and make a hollow in the top. Pour a little melted butter into the hollow, to be mixed in at the last minute.

Menu Suggestion
Serve Colcannon for a mid-week family meal with chops or sausages.

COLCANNON

In Ireland, Colcannon is traditionally eaten on All Hallows' Day, which is Hallowe'en, 31 October. Older recipes were made with kale, which was cooked with bacon to make it really tasty, but nowadays cabbage is often used or a mixture of kale and cabbage. Minced onion can be substituted for the leeks, if leeks are not available. Although Colcannon is essentially a homely dish, the addition of cream and butter makes it quite rich and special. There is a superstition surrounding Colcannon in Ireland, much the same as the one associated with plum pudding in Britain. Years ago, Irish cooks are said to have hidden gold wedding rings in the mixture, and it was believed that the finder would be married within the year. If the cook hid a thimble, however, this would mean the finder would remain unmarried.

GREEK-STYLE NEW POTATOES

0.45	🍳	280 cals

Serves 4

1 kg (2 lb) small new potatoes, preferably Cyprus
250 ml (8 fl oz) vegetable oil
125 ml (4 fl oz) white or red wine (see box)
60 ml (4 tbsp) chopped fresh coriander, mint or parsley
salt and freshly ground pepper

1 Scrub the potatoes clean, leaving them whole. Pat the potatoes thoroughly dry with a clean tea towel.

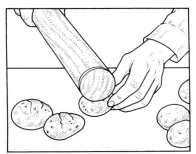

2 With a meat mallet, hit each potato once or twice so that the flesh breaks slightly. Heat the oil in a heavy-based deep frying pan, skillet or saucepan until a stale bread cube turns golden in 2–3 seconds.

3 Add the potatoes to the hot oil and fry over moderate heat, turning them frequently, until golden brown on all sides.

4 Pour off the oil, then pour the wine over the potatoes. Add half of the chopped coriander and a liberal sprinkling of salt and pepper. Shake the pan to combine the ingredients, then cover and simmer for about 15 minutes, until the potatoes are tender.

5 Turn the potatoes into a warmed serving dish and sprinkle with the remaining coriander. Serve immediately.

Menu Suggestion
These tasty potatoes are good with plain roast or grilled lamb; they are also excellent with barbecued meat, especially lamb kebabs.

GREEK-STYLE NEW POTATOES

For an authentic flavour to these potatoes, cook them in Greek retsina wine. Most retsina is white, but you can use either white or red, depending on which is easier to obtain. Retsina, or resinated wine, is something of an acquired taste. It has a strong bouquet and flavour of turpentine, which was discovered almost my mistake.

Originally, some hundreds of years ago, the wine jars or amphorae were sealed with a mixture of resin and plaster, and the flavour of the seal naturally made its way into the wine. The Greeks became so fond of the taste, that they began to add pine resin to the must during fermentation, which resulted in a heady wine with a distinctive flavour.

PETITS POIS WITH PARMA HAM

| 0.25 | 206 cals |

Serves 4

50 g (2 oz) Parma ham

50 g (2 oz) butter or margarine

900 g (2 lb) fresh young peas, shelled

12 spring onions, washed, trimmed and sliced

1 firm-hearted lettuce, washed and shredded

5 ml (1 tsp) sugar

salt and freshly ground pepper

150 ml (¼ pint) chicken stock

sprig of mint, to garnish

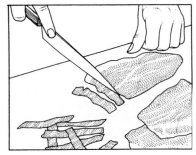

1 Using a sharp knife, cut the ham into small strips. Then melt the butter in a large pan, add the peas, ham and the next 6 ingredients.

2 Bring to the boil, cover and simmer gently for 15–20 minutes. Serve in a warm serving dish with the cooking liquid. Garnish with a sprig of mint.

PETITS POIS

These are small, sweet, tender young peas, much used in continental Europe. The term literally means 'little peas' in French. This recipe, with Parma ham, is claimed by the Italians. The ham can be omitted if liked, or other varieties of ham used. Without the addition of ham it is known as *petits pois à la française*, a traditional, well-known French dish.

This recipe can only be made in spring and summer, when all the vegetables are fresh and young. Fresh young peas should be eaten with their cooking liquid so that their full flavour is appreciated.

It is essential to cook peas as soon as possible after they are picked, as the sugar in them begins to 'die' and turn to starch the moment they leave the parent plant. When you are picking or buying fresh peas, the pods should be crisp, young and well-filled.

If fresh peas are unavailable, good quality frozen varieties are available, and make a good substitute. Ordinary frozen peas, however, cannot be substituted for *petits pois*.

SWISS CHALET POTATOES WITH CREAM AND CHEESE

1.20	529–793 cals

Serves 4–6

1.4 kg (3 lb) even-sized small potatoes, peeled

salt and freshly ground pepper

300 ml (½ pint) double cream

1–2 garlic cloves, skinned and crushed

good pinch of freshly grated nutmeg

75 g (3 oz) Gruyère or Emmental cheese, grated

75 g (3 oz) Parmesan cheese, freshly grated

1 Parboil the potatoes in a large saucepan of salted water for 10 minutes. Drain well.

2 Stand the potatoes upright in a buttered baking dish. Mix the cream with the garlic, nutmeg and salt and pepper to taste, then pour over the potatoes.

3 Mix the 2 cheeses together and sprinkle over the potatoes to cover them completely. Bake, uncovered, in the oven at 190°C (375°F) mark 5 for 1 hour, or until the potatoes feel tender when pierced with a skewer. Serve hot, straight from the dish.

Menu Suggestion
This luscious potato dish is very rich, and therefore best reserved for special occasions.

SWISS CHALET POTATOES WITH CREAM AND CHEESE

The Swiss cheeses Gruyère and Emmental are expensive, but their uniquely sweet and nutty flavour makes them well worth the extra cost for a potato dish such as this one—and you only need a small amount to appreciate their special flavour.

Genuine Gruyère cheese has the alpenhorn symbol and the red 'Switzerland' stamp on its rind; it is full in flavour, which comes from its long ripening period of up to 12 months. It is a moist cheese, with few holes when cut, and is excellent for melting, which is why it is the traditional cheese to use in fondue.

Emmental is a relation of Gruyère and also carries the red Switzerland stamp on its rind. It differs from Gruyère in that it is milder in flavour, with holes the size of cherries. Both Gruyère and Emmental are widely available.

Side Salads

THREE BEAN SALAD

1.15*	223–334 cals

* plus 30 minutes cooling; 2–3 hours chilling

Serves 4–6

75 g (3 oz) dried red kidney beans, soaked overnight

75 g (3 oz) dried black-eyed beans, soaked overnight

75 g (3 oz) dried pinto or borlotti beans, soaked overnight

100 ml (4 fl oz) basic sauce vinaigrette

15 ml (1 tbsp) chopped fresh coriander

1 small onion, skinned and sliced into rings

salt and freshly ground pepper

sprig of fresh coriander, to garnish

1 Drain the beans and place in a saucepan of water. Bring to the boil and boil rapidly for 10 minutes (this is important), then boil gently for 1½ hours until tender.

3 Combine the vinaigrette and coriander, and pour over the beans while they are still warm.

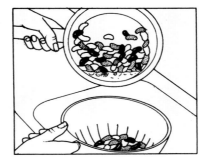

2 Using a colander or a metal sieve, drain the cooked beans thoroughly and place them in a large salad bowl.

4 Toss thoroughly and leave to cool for 30 minutes. Mix the onion into the beans, season well and chill for 2–3 hours before serving. To serve, garnish with fresh coriander.

COOKING BEANS

If you don't have time to soak the beans overnight and you want to cook them quickly, then there is a short cut: the hot-soak method. Put the beans in a pan, cover with cold water and bring to the boil. Boil rapidly for 2 minutes, then remove from the heat, cover with a tight-fitting lid and leave to soak for 1 hour. Drain, then continue with the recipe as when using beans which have been soaked in cold water overnight. *Always* boil red kidney beans for a full 10 minutes before you cook them – this is to destroy the poisonous enzyme they contain.

MOZZARELLA, AVOCADO AND TOMATO SALAD

0.20	283 cals

Serves 4

2 ripe avocados

120 ml (8 tbsp) vinaigrette

175 g (6 oz) Mozzarella cheese, thinly sliced

4 medium tomatoes, thinly sliced

chopped fresh parsley and mint, to garnish

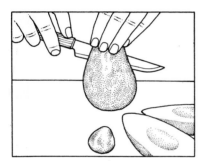

1 Halve the avocados lengthways and carefully remove the stones. Then peel and cut the avocados into slices.

2 Pour the vinaigrette over the avocado slices. Stir to coat the avocado slices thoroughly and prevent discoloration.

3 Arrange slices of Mozzarella, tomato and avocado on four individual serving plates. Spoon over the dressing and garnish with chopped parsley and a sprig of mint.

PREPARING AVOCADOS

To prepare avocados, use a stainless steel knife, cut the avocados in half lengthways, through to the stone. Hold the pear in both hands and gently twist. Open the halves and remove the stone. If necessary, the peel can either be removed with a potato peeler or lightly score the skin once or twice and peel back the skin. Always brush the exposed flesh immediately with lemon juice to prevent discoloration.

BEETROOT SALAD WITH MINT

| 0.15* | 43–64 cals |

* plus 2–3 hours or overnight chilling

Serves 4–6

120 ml (8 tbsp) chopped fresh mint

700 g (1½ lb) cooked beetroot

150 ml (¼ pint) malt vinegar

5 ml (1 tsp) granulated sugar

salt and freshly ground pepper

2 medium onions, skinned and finely sliced into rings

1 Put 90 ml (6 tbsp) of the mint in a bowl and pour over 150 ml (¼ pint) boiling water. Leave to stand for 2–3 minutes.

2 Peel the beetroot and slice thinly. Place in a large shallow dish. Add the vinegar and sugar to the mint and water with salt and pepper to taste. Pour over the beetroot. Cover and chill in the refrigerator for at least 2–3 hours or overnight.

3 To serve, place alternate layers of beetroot and onion in a serving dish. Pour over the mint dressing and garnish with the remaining chopped fresh mint. Serve chilled.

Menu Suggestion
Beetroot salads go especially well with roast lamb, turkey and duck, and cold meats such as ham and salami.

BEETROOT SALAD WITH MINT
Did you know that the Victorians were extremely fond of beetroots? They not only used them as a salad vegetable, but also dried and ground them with coffee to make the coffee go further, pickled them, made them into wine, candied them as sweets—and made them into a lotion for rinsing hair!

RICE SALAD

0.40*	577 cals

* plus 1 hour cooling

Serves 4

275 g (10 oz) long grain brown rice

salt and freshly ground pepper

1 head of fennel

1 red pepper

175 g (6 oz) beansprouts

75 g (3 oz) cashew nuts

90 ml (6 tbsp) corn or vegetable oil

finely grated rind and juice of
   1 large orange

few orange segments, to garnish

1 Cook the brown rice in plenty of boiling salted water for 30 minutes (or according to packet instructions), until tender but firm to the bite.

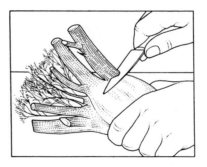

2 Meanwhile, prepare the remaining ingredients. Trim the fennel, reserving a few feathery tops for the garnish. Cut the top off the red pepper and remove the core and seeds. Wash the pepper and pat dry with absorbent kitchen paper.

3 Chop the fennel and red pepper finely. Wash the beansprouts and drain well. Chop the cashew nuts roughly.

4 In a jug, whisk the oil, orange rind and juice together, with salt and pepper to taste.

5 Drain the rice thoroughly, then turn into a bowl. Add the dressing while the rice is still hot and toss well to combine. Leave to stand for about 1 hour, or until the rice is cold.

6 Add the prepared vegetables and nuts to the rice and toss well to mix. Taste and adjust seasoning. Turn the salad into a serving bowl and garnish with the reserved fennel tops and the orange segments. Serve at room temperature.

Menu Suggestion

This nutty brown rice salad has a tangy orange dressing, which makes it the perfect accompaniment to rich meat dishes such as pork and duck. Alternatively, it can be served with other vegetable salads for a vegetarian meal—it goes particularly well with green salad ingredients such as chicory, endive, lettuce and watercress.

TOMATO, AVOCADO AND PASTA SALAD

| 0.20 | 626 cals |

Serves 4

175 g (6 oz) small wholemeal pasta
  shells
salt and freshly ground pepper
105 ml (7 tbsp) olive oil
45 ml (3 tbsp) lemon juice
5 ml (1 tsp) wholegrain mustard
30 ml (2 tbsp) chopped fresh basil
2 ripe avocados
2 red onions
16 black olives
225 g (8 oz) ripe cherry tomatoes,
  if available, or small salad
  tomatoes
fresh basil leaves, to garnish

1 Cook the pasta in plenty of
  boiling salted water for about 5
minutes until just tender. Drain in
a colander and rinse under cold
running water to stop the pasta
cooking further. Cool for 20
minutes.

2 Meanwhile, whisk the oil in a
  bowl with the lemon juice,
mustard, chopped basil and salt
and pepper to taste.

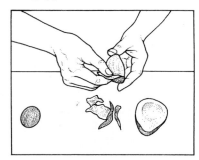

3 Halve and stone the avocados
  then peel off the skins. Chop
the avocado flesh into large pieces
and fold gently into the dressing.

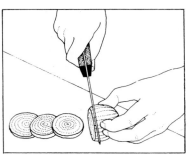

4 Slice the onions thinly into
  rings. Stone the olives. Halve
the tomatoes and mix them with
the onion rings, the olives and the
cold pasta shells.

5 Spoon the pasta and tomato on
  to 4 individual serving plates.
Spoon over the avocado and dressing and garnish with fresh basil
leaves. Serve immediately.

Menu Suggestion
This pretty salad makes a
delicious summer starter. Serve
with chunky slices of fresh
wholemeal bread and butter, with
a chilled dry white wine to drink.
Alternatively, serve the salad as an
accompaniment to barbecued or
grilled meat.

RAW SPINACH AND MUSHROOM SALAD

0.50	402–604 cals

Serves 2–3

225 g (8 oz) young spinach leaves
225 g (8 oz) button mushrooms
2 thick slices of white bread
90 ml (6 tbsp) olive oil
25 g (1 oz) butter or margarine
1 garlic clove, skinned and
    crushed
30 ml (2 tbsp) tarragon vinegar
5 ml (1 tsp) tarragon mustard
salt and freshly ground pepper

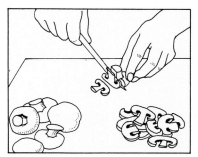

1 Wash the spinach well, discarding any damaged or yellowing leaves. Cut out and discard any thick ribs.

2 Tear the spinach leaves into a large salad bowl, discarding any thick stalks.

3 Wipe the mushrooms but do not peel them. Slice them thinly into neat 'T' shapes.

4 Add the mushrooms to the spinach. Using your hands, toss the 2 ingredients together. Set aside while making the croûtons and dressing.

5 Cut the crusts off the bread and cut the bread into 1 cm (½ inch) cubes. Heat the oil and butter in a frying pan, add the garlic and the cubes of bread and fry until crisp and golden. Remove the croûtons with a slotted spoon and drain well on absorbent kitchen paper.

6 Add the vinegar to the oil in the pan, with the mustard and salt and pepper to taste. Stir well to combine, then remove the pan from the heat and leave to cool for 5 minutes.

7 Add the croûtons to the salad, then the dressing. Toss well to combine and serve immediately.

Menu Suggestion

This nutritious salad of raw ingredients tossed in a warm oil and vinegar dressing makes an unusual light lunch or supper. Serve with hot crusty rolls.

CELERIAC AND BEAN SALAD

1.10*	226–339 cals

* plus overnight soaking, 20 minutes cooling and 1 hour chilling

Serves 4–6

225 g (8 oz) dried flageolet beans, soaked in cold water overnight

1 large green pepper

finely grated rind and juice of 1 lemon

60 ml (4 tbsp) olive or vegetable oil

15 ml (1 tbsp) whole grain mustard

1 garlic clove, skinned and crushed

45 ml (3 tbsp) chopped fresh parsley

salt and freshly ground pepper

225 g (8 oz) celeriac

1 Drain the soaked beans and rinse well under cold running water. Put the beans in a large saucepan and cover with plenty of fresh cold water. Bring slowly to the boil, then skim off any scum with a slotted spoon. Half cover the pan with a lid and simmer gently for about 1 hour, or until the beans are just tender.

2 Meanwhile, halve the pepper and remove the core and seeds. Cut the flesh into strips and then into cubes.

3 In a bowl, whisk together the grated lemon rind, about 30 ml (2 tbsp) lemon juice, the oil, mustard, garlic, parsley and salt and pepper to taste.

4 Just before the beans are ready, peel the celeriac and chop roughly into 2.5 cm (1 inch) cubes. Blanch in boiling salted water for 5 minutes. Drain well.

5 Drain the beans well and place in a bowl. Add the celeriac and toss all the salad ingredients together while the beans and celeriac are still hot. Leave to cool for 20 minutes, then cover and chill in the refrigerator for at least 1 hour before serving. Serve chilled.

Menu Suggestion
Serve this tangy, nutritious salad as a first course with hot garlic or herb bread. It would also make a good side salad to serve with meat and poultry dishes.

WINTER CABBAGE AND CAULIFLOWER SALAD

0.25*	480 cals

* plus about 1 hour chilling

Serves 4

225 g (8 oz) hard white cabbage

225 g (8 oz) cauliflower florets

2 large carrots, peeled

75 g (3 oz) mixed shelled nuts, roughly chopped

50 g (2 oz) raisins

60 ml (4 tbsp) chopped fresh parsley or coriander

90 ml (6 tbsp) mayonnaise

90 ml (6 tbsp) soured cream or natural yogurt

10 ml (2 tsp) French mustard

30 ml (2 tbsp) olive or vegetable oil

juice of $\frac{1}{2}$ lemon

salt and freshly ground pepper

3 red-skinned eating apples

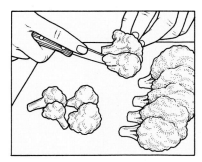

1 Shred the cabbage finely with a sharp knife and place in a large bowl. Divide the cauliflower florets into small sprigs and add to the cabbage. Mix the vegetables gently with your hands.

2 Grate the carrots into the bowl, then add the nuts, raisins and parsley. Mix the vegetables together again until evenly combined.

3 Put the remaining ingredients except the apples in a jug. Whisk well to combine, then pour over the vegetables in the bowl and toss well.

4 Core and chop the apples, but do not peel them. Add to the salad and toss again to combine with the other ingredients. Cover the bowl and chill the salad in the refrigerator for about 1 hour before serving.

Menu Suggestion

This crunchy, colourful salad can be served as an accompaniment to a selection of cold meats for a quick and nutritious lunch. With extra nuts, for vegetarians, it would make a meal in itself, served with cheese and wholemeal or granary bread.

INDONESIAN FRUIT AND VEGETABLE SALAD

| 0.55* | 260 cals |

* including 30 minutes standing time

Serves 4

1 small fresh pineapple

¼ cucumber

175 g (6 oz) young carrots, peeled

1 crisp green eating apple

100 g (4 oz) beansprouts

30 ml (2 tbsp) crunchy peanut butter

20 ml (4 tsp) soy sauce

60 ml (4 tbsp) olive oil

juice of ½ lemon

salt and freshly ground pepper

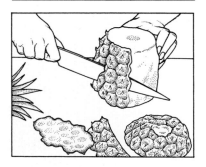

1 Cut the top and bottom off the pineapple. Stand the fruit upright on a board. Using a large, sharp knife, slice downwards in sections to remove the skin and 'eyes' of the fruit.

2 Slice off the pineapple flesh, leaving the core. Then discard the core.

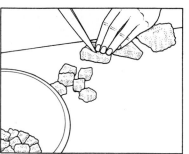

3 Cut the pineapple flesh into small cubes, then cut the cucumber and carrots lengthways into thin matchstick shapes. Quarter and core the apple (but do not peel), then chop roughly. Then combine all the fruit and vegetables together in a bowl with the beansprouts.

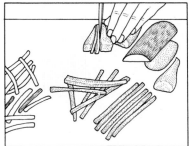

4 Make the dressing. Put the peanut butter in a bowl, then gradually whisk in the remaining ingredients with a fork. Season.

5 Pour the dressing over the salad and toss well to mix. Cover and leave to stand for 30 minutes before serving.

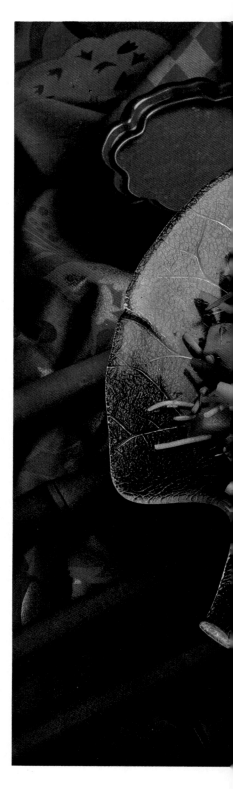

CAESAR SALAD

| 0.45 | 438 cals |

Serves 4

1 large garlic clove, skinned and crushed

150 ml (¼ pint) olive oil

75 g (3 oz) stale white bread

1 lettuce

salt and freshly ground pepper

1 egg

30 ml (2 tbsp) lemon juice

25 g (1 oz) grated Parmesan cheese

8 anchovy fillets, chopped and drained

croûtons, to serve

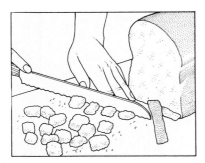

1 Add the garlic to the oil and leave to stand for 30 minutes. Cut the stale white bread into 0.5-cm (¼-inch) dice.

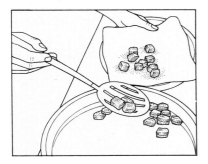

2 Heat a little of the garlic oil in a frying pan and fry the bread until golden brown on all sides. Lift from the pan and drain.

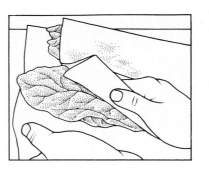

3 Carefully wash the lettuce under cold running water. Drain well and pat dry with absorbent kitchen paper.

4 Tear into bite-sized pieces and place in a salad bowl. Pour over the remaining garlic oil and toss until the leaves are completely coated. Season well.

5 Add the lemon juice, cheese, anchovies and croûtons and toss well. Boil the egg for 1 minute only, add to the salad and give the salad a final toss. Serve immediately.

TOMATO AND OKRA VINAIGRETTE

0.15	191 cals

Serves 8

450 g (1 lb) okra
150 ml (¼ pint) vegetable oil
30 ml (2 tbsp) lemon juice
5 ml (1 tsp) tomato purée
pinch of caster sugar
salt and freshly ground pepper
450 g (1 lb) tomatoes, skinned

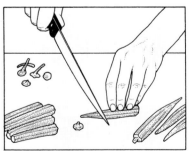

1 Trim off the tops and tails of the okra. Cook in boiling salted water for about 4 minutes or until just tender. Drain well and place in a bowl.

2 In a jug, whisk together the oil, lemon juice, tomato purée, sugar, and salt and pepper to taste. Pour over the warm okra and fold gently to mix.

3 Slice the tomatoes thinly. Arrange in a serving bowl with the okra and vinaigrette. Cover and chill in the refrigerator for at least 30 minutes before serving.

Menu Suggestion
Serve for an unusual and attractive first course, with hot garlic or herb bread. Or serve as a side salad—okra goes particularly well with lamb.

RADICCHIO AND ALFALFA SALAD

0.15	141–212 cals

Serves 4–6

2 heads of radicchio

50–75 g (2–3 oz) alfalfa sprouts

90 ml (6 tbsp) olive or vegetable oil

30 ml (2 tbsp) white wine vinegar

15 ml (1 tbsp) single cream (optional)

1 small garlic clove, skinned and crushed

1.25 ml ($\frac{1}{4}$ tsp) granulated sugar

salt and freshly ground pepper

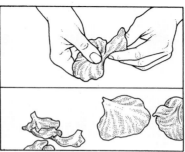

1 Tear the radicchio into bite-sized pieces. Wash, drain and pat dry on absorbent kitchen paper. Wash and dry the alfalfa sprouts.

2 Mix the alfalfa and radicchio together in a serving bowl. In a jug, whisk together the remaining ingredients, with salt and pepper to taste. Just before serving, pour over the radicchio and alfalfa and toss together.

Menu Suggestion
Serve as a side salad whenever a colourful and crunchy accompaniment is required, or serve with a selection of cheeses and wholemeal or granary bread for a nutritious lunch.

CHILLI, AUBERGINE AND RED PEPPER SALAD

| 1.15* | ✳ | 256 cals |

* 30 minutes cooling and 1 hour chilling

Serves 4

2 red peppers

3 medium aubergines, total weight about 700 g (1½ lb)

salt and freshly ground pepper

90 ml (6 tbsp) olive or vegetable oil

2 medium onions, skinned and roughly chopped

15 ml (1 tbsp) chilli seasoning

1.25 ml (¼ tsp) chilli powder

150 ml (¼ pint) dry white wine

30 ml (2 tbsp) tomato purée

15 ml (1 tbsp) lemon juice

15 ml (1 tbsp) wine vinegar

2.5 ml (½ tsp) granulated sugar

chopped fresh parsley, to garnish

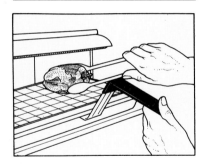

1 Put the red peppers whole under a preheated moderate grill and turn them constantly until their skins are charred all over. Put the peppers in a bowl.

2 Trim the aubergines and cut into 2.5 cm (1 inch) cubes. Place in a colander, sprinkling each layer with salt. Cover with a plate, put heavy weights on top and leave to dégorge for about 30 minutes.

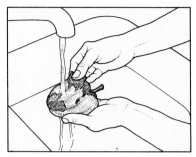

3 Meanwhile, hold the peppers under cold running water and rub the skins off with your fingers. Discard the skins, stems, cores and seeds. Cut the pepper flesh into long, thin shreds and add to the bowl.

4 Rinse the aubergines under cold running water, then pat dry with absorbent kitchen paper. Heat the oil in a heavy-based saucepan. Add the aubergines and onions and fry over moderate heat for 3–4 minutes. Stir in the chilli seasoning and powder. Fry for 1–2 minutes, then add the wine, tomato purée, lemon juice, vinegar, sugar and salt and pepper to taste.

5 Bring to the boil, cover and simmer for 10–12 minutes, or until the aubergine is cooked. Leave to cool for 30 minutes, then turn into a serving bowl.

6 Stir in the red pepper shreds. Cover and chill in the refrigerator for 1 hour. Sprinkle with plenty of chopped parsley before serving.

Menu Suggestion
Serve this smoky flavoured salad with plain roast, barbecued or grilled meat. Or serve for a tasty lunch dish, with hot pitta bread.

CRISP ENDIVE WITH ORANGE AND CROÛTONS

0.20	138 cals

Serves 8

1 large head of curly endive
½ bunch of watercress
2 large oranges
2 thick slices of white bread
vegetable oil, for shallow frying
60 ml (4 tbsp) olive oil
60 ml (4 tbsp) white wine vinegar
2.5 ml (½ tsp) caster sugar
salt and freshly ground pepper

1 Remove and discard any coarse or discoloured leaves from the endive. Tear the endive into pieces, wash and dry thoroughly with a clean tea towel. Wash, trim and dry the watercress.

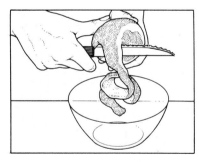

2 With a small serrated knife and working over a bowl to catch the juices, cut away all the skin and pith from the oranges. Reserve the juices.

3 Cut the orange flesh into segments, leaving the membrane behind. Remove any pips with the tip of the knife.

4 Arrange the endive, watercress and orange in a serving bowl. Cut the crusts off the bread and cut the bread into 1 cm (½ inch) cubes. Heat the vegetable oil in a frying pan, add the cubes of bread and fry until crisp and golden. Remove the croûtons with a slotted spoon and drain well on absorbent kitchen paper. Sprinkle with salt.

5 In a jug, whisk the reserved orange juice with the olive oil, vinegar, sugar and salt and pepper to taste. Pour over the salad and add the croûtons just before serving.

Menu Suggestion
This colourful winter salad is good with rich meat dishes, especially duck and game.

CRISP ENDIVE WITH ORANGE AND CROÛTONS

Although native to the Mediterranean, curly endive is now grown in other temperate countries throughout the world, and is available virtually all year round. At its best, curly endive is crisp, pale green and frondy, with a mildly bitter flavour. It does not keep well and quickly goes limp and yellow. Most heads of endive are very large, but some greengrocers will split them in halves or quarters. Take care not to confuse curly endive with the torpedo-shaped chicory. In France, chicory is called endive, whereas curly endive is called *chicorée frisée* or 'frizzy chicory'.

FENNEL À LA GRECQUE
(GREEK-STYLE MARINATED FENNEL)

| 1.10* | ✳ | 249 cals |

* plus 30 minutes cooling and 1 hour
chilling

Serves 4

---

90 ml (6 tbsp) olive or vegetable oil

1 large onion, skinned and finely
    chopped

1 garlic clove, skinned and finely
    chopped

150 ml ($\frac{1}{4}$ pint) dry white wine

4 ripe tomatoes, skinned and
    chopped

juice of $\frac{1}{2}$ lemon

10 ml (2 tsp) tomato purée

1 bay leaf

5 ml (1 tsp) coriander seeds,
    crushed

5 ml (1 tsp) granulated sugar

2.5 ml ($\frac{1}{2}$ tsp) chopped fresh basil

salt and freshly ground pepper

2 medium fennel heads

---

1 Heat the oil in a large saucepan, add the onion and garlic
and fry gently for about 10
minutes or until they are soft but
not coloured.

2 Add the wine, tomatoes,
lemon juice, tomato purée, bay
leaf, crushed coriander, sugar,
basil and salt and pepper to
taste. Bring to the boil, stirring,
then cover and simmer for 20
minutes.

3 Meanwhile, trim the fennel of
any green feathery tops and set
aside for the garnish.

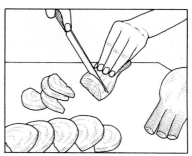

4 Remove and discard any
discoloured patches from the
fennel, halve the heads and slice
them thinly.

5 Bring a large saucepan of
salted water to the boil, add
the fennel and blanch for 5
minutes. Drain the fennel well,
add to the tomato sauce, cover and
simmer gently for about 30
minutes.

6 Leave to cool for 30 minutes,
then cover with cling film and
chill in the refrigerator for at least
1 hour.

7 Before serving, chop the
reserved fennel tops finely.
Taste and adjust the seasoning of
the tomato sauce, then turn into a
serving dish and garnish with the
chopped fennel. Serve chilled.

Menu Suggestion
The flavour of fennel goes particularly well with lamb and chicken,
and the tomato sauce makes this
dish most suitable for serving with
plain roast or grilled meat. The
salad also makes the most
delicious first course, served with
crusty French bread to mop up
the juices.

Barbecues

TURKEY AND HAM PARCELS

2.35*	242 cals

* includes 2 hours chilling time

Serves 8

700 g (1½ lb) turkey escalopes
8 thin slices of cooked ham
100 g (4 oz) Cotswold cheese
30 ml (2 tbsp) creamed horseradish
salt and freshly ground pepper
20 ml (4 tsp) plain flour
egg, beaten
90 ml (6 tbsp) dried breadcrumbs
vegetable oil
lime slices, to garnish

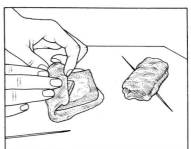

3 Enclose each ham roll in a slice of the turkey meat, securing firmly with wooden cocktail sticks pierced through the centre.

4 Coat the turkey parcels in flour, beaten egg and dried breadcrumbs. Then chill in the refrigerator for at least 2 hours.

5 Brush the turkey and ham parcels with plenty of oil and barbecue or grill them for about 8 minutes on each side. Serve hot, garnished with lime slices.

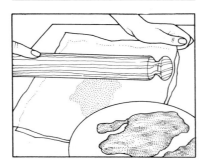

1 Cut the escalopes into sixteen even-sized pieces. Using a rolling pin or meat mallet, bat out thinly between sheets of greaseproof paper.

2 Halve each of the eight slices of ham and cut the cheese into sixteen pieces. Then wrap a piece of cheese, a little creamed horseradish and seasoning in each of the slices of ham.

COTSWOLD CHEESE

The Cotswold cheese specified for the filling of Turkey and Ham Parcels may sound unusual, but it is in fact a variety of Double Gloucester – an English semi-hard cheese which is now widely available in supermarkets and delicatessens. Cotswold is Double Gloucester flavoured with chopped onions and chives; it has a rich, golden colour, a velvety texture and a slightly sharp, tangy flavour. Like Cheddar, all Double Gloucester cheeses are excellent in cooking for their melting qualities.

CHICKEN AND BEEF SATAY WITH PEANUT SAUCE

0.35*	✳	594 cals

* plus 4 hours marinating

Serves 4

2 boneless chicken breast fillets, about 350 g (12 oz) total weight

350 g (12 oz) flash-fry steak

5 ml (1 tsp) coriander seeds

5 ml (1 tsp) cumin seeds

1 onion, skinned and chopped

60 ml (4 tbsp) tamarind liquid (see box, opposite)

30 ml (2 tbsp) soy sauce

2 garlic cloves, skinned and crushed

30 ml (2 tbsp) vegetable oil

5 ml (1 tsp) ground turmeric

5 ml (1 tsp) 5-spice powder

salt

100 g (4 oz) crunchy peanut butter

100 g (4 oz) creamed coconut, crumbled

300 ml (½ pint) boiling water

20 ml (4 tsp) lemon juice

15 ml (1 tbsp) soft brown sugar

2.5–5 ml (½–1 tsp) chilli powder

1 Prepare the satay. Using a sharp knife, cut the chicken and the flash-fry steak into small chunks. Set aside.

2 Heat a small frying pan, add the coriander and cumin and fry over dry heat for 1–2 minutes, stirring constantly. Remove from the heat and pound to a fine powder in a mortar and pestle.

3 Put the pounded spices in a blender or food processor with the onion, tamarind liquid, 15 ml (1 tbsp) soy sauce, garlic, vegetable oil, turmeric, 5-spice powder and a pinch of salt. Work for a few seconds, then pour over the meat. Cover and leave to marinate for 4 hours, turning the meat occasionally during this time.

4 Thread the meat on oiled wooden sticks, keeping the chicken and beef separate if liked. Place on the barbecue and grill for 10–15 minutes, turning frequently and basting with any remaining marinade.

5 Meanwhile, make the peanut sauce. Put the peanut butter, coconut, water, lemon juice, 15 ml (1 tbsp) soy sauce, sugar and chilli powder in a pan and bring slowly to the boil, stirring constantly. Lower the heat and simmer gently for about 5 minutes until the coconut has dissolved and the sauce thickens. Taste and adjust seasoning according to taste.

6 Serve the satay sticks hot on a platter, with a small bowl of peanut sauce for dipping.

SATAY

Satay is a Malaysian dish, which is usually served as a starter on wooden sticks, with the sauce for dipping. Although metal kebab skewers can be used, wooden ones are more authentic; they are available from oriental specialist shops. Remember to soak them in cold water for 2 hours before using – this helps prevent them setting alight on the barbecue!

Tamarind pulp and 5-spice powder are also available at oriental shops. Make tamarind liquid by soaking a 2.5-cm (1-inch) piece of tamarind pulp in about 100 ml (3 fl oz) hot water for a few minutes, then squeezing the pulp to extract as much liquid as possible. Discard the pulp.

In Malaysia, the traditional accompaniments to satay are wedges of unpeeled cucumber, spring onions and cubes of rice cake, which is made by boiling glutinous rice, then pressing it until it can be cut like a cake. Although not authentic, cubes of bean curd (available at health food shops as well as oriental stores) may be served instead of rice cake.

CHILLI CHICKEN

0.35*	✳*	70 cals

* plus at least 4 hours marinating;
freeze in marinade, before cooking

Serves 4

8 chicken drumsticks

150 ml ($\frac{1}{4}$ pint) vegetable oil

4 garlic cloves, skinned and roughly chopped

$\frac{1}{2}$ onion, skinned and chopped

45 ml (3 tbsp) natural yogurt

15 ml (1 tbsp) tomato purée

5 ml (1 tsp) ground turmeric

2.5 ml ($\frac{1}{2}$ tsp) chilli powder

2.5 ml ($\frac{1}{2}$ tsp) salt

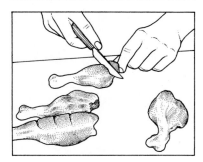

1 Skin the drumsticks, then slash the flesh with a sharp, pointed knife. Make the marinade. Blend the remaining ingredients in a blender or food processor to a smooth purée.

2 Put the drumsticks in a single layer in a shallow container, then pour over the marinade. Cover and leave for at least 4 hours, preferably overnight. Turn drumsticks occasionally and baste with the marinade.

3 Put the drumsticks on the barbecue and grill for 20 minutes, turning them frequently and basting them with the marinade until nicely charred on all sides. Serve hot or cold.

Barbecued Spare Ribs

1.35	309 cals

Serves 4

1.8 kg (4 lb) American pork spare ribs

1 onion, skinned and sliced

350 ml (12 fl oz) tomato juice

45 ml (3 tbsp) cider vinegar

30 ml (2 tbsp) clear honey

10 ml (2 tsp) salt

5 ml (1 tsp) paprika

3.75 ml (¾ tsp) chilli powder

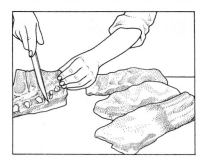

1 Divide the spare ribs into portions of two or three ribs each. Put them all in a large flameproof casserole or saucepan, add the onion and cover with cold water.

2 Bring to the boil, reduce the heat, cover and simmer for 1 hour or until almost tender. Drain and cover until required. Make the sauce. Mix all the remaining ingredients in a bowl together.

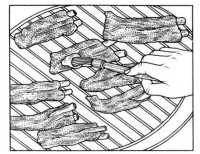

3 Put the spare ribs on the barbecue and brush with sauce. Cook for 20 minutes until tender; brush with sauce and turn occasionally. Heat remaining sauce to serve separately.

BARBECUED AUBERGINE DIP

| 0.40* | 199 cals |

* plus 2–3 hours chilling

Serves 4

2 large aubergines, wiped

3 garlic cloves, skinned

salt

about 150 ml (¼ pint) tahini (paste of finely ground sesame seeds)

juice of about 3 lemons

coriander leaves, black olives and lemon wedges, to garnish

hot pitta bread, to serve

1 Place the aubergines on the barbecue and grill for about 20 minutes until the skin blisters and chars and the flesh feels soft. Turn the aubergines constantly.

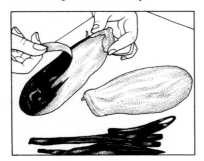

2 Remove from the heat and leave until cool enough to handle. Then carefully peel off the skins and discard them.

3 Put the aubergine flesh in a blender or food processor and blend to form smooth purée. Alternatively, push it through a sieve

4 Crush the garlic with salt, then add to the aubergine flesh. Add half the tahini paste and the juice of 1½ lemons and work again until evenly incorporated.

5 Taste the dip and add a little more tahini paste and lemon juice. Continue adding tahini and lemon gradually until the flavour is to your liking. Add more salt if liked.

6 Turn the dip into a shallow serving bowl and smooth the surface. Garnish with coriander and olives and refrigerate for 2–3 hours until serving time. Serve with hot pitta bread cooked on the barbecue.

AUBERGINE DIP

A recipe from the Middle East, where it is called *baba ghanoush* or *papa ghanooye*, this Barbecued Aubergine Dip has a wonderfully smoky flavour and creamy texture. In the Middle East it is served as part of the *mezze* at the beginning of a meal, but you can serve it on its own as a starter — with hot pitta bread.

Although cooking the aubergines on the barbecue gives the dip its smoky flavour, this is not absolutely essential – the tahini paste made from finely ground sesame seeds is fairly strong. If you find it more convenient, grill the aubergines until their skins char and blister, taking care to watch them all the time they are under the grill and turning them frequently so they do not burn.

SPICY LAMB KEBABS

0.45*	516 cals

* plus 2–3 hours marinating

Makes 8

700 g (1½ lb) boned leg of lamb

450 g (1 lb) courgettes

8 tomatoes, halved

1 large corn on the cob

8 shallots

salt

142 g (5 oz) natural yogurt

1 garlic clove, skinned and crushed

2 bay leaves, crumbled

15 ml (1 tbsp) lemon juice

15 ml (1 tbsp) vegetable oil

5 ml (1 tsp) ground allspice

15 ml (1 tbsp) coriander seeds

freshly ground pepper

lemon wedges, to garnish

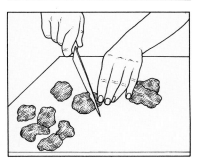

1 Using a sharp knife, cut the lamb into 2.5-cm (1-inch) cubes, making sure to trim off any excess fat from the meat.

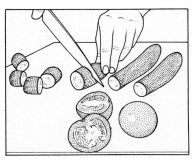

2 Cut the courgettes into 0.5-cm (¼-inch) slices, discarding the tops and tails. Halve the tomatoes.

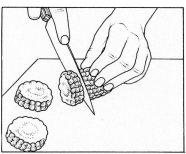

3 Cut the corn into eight slices. Blanch in boiling salted water, drain well and set aside.

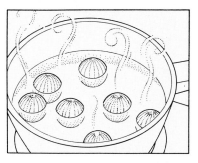

4 Blanch the shallots in boiling, salted water, skin and set aside. Make the marinade. Pour the yogurt into a shallow dish and stir in garlic, bay leaves, lemon juice, oil, allspice, coriander seeds and seasoning.

5 Thread the lamb cubes on to eight skewers with courgettes, tomatoes, corn and shallots. Place in dish, spoon over marinade, cover and leave for 2–3 hours, turning once to ensure even coating.

6 Cook the kebabs for about 15–20 minutes, turning and brushing with the marinade occasionally. To serve, spoon remaining marinade over the kebabs and garnish.

SHASHLIK
(CAUCASIAN LAMB KEBABS)

0.45*	✳*	723 cals

* plus at least 8 hours marinating;
freeze the lamb in the marinade

Serves 4

700–900 g (1½–2 lb) boneless lamb
(eg fillet or leg), trimmed of fat

75 ml (5 tbsp) red wine vinegar

90 ml (6 tbsp) olive oil

10 ml (2 tsp) grated nutmeg

10 ml (2 tsp) dried marjoram

salt and freshly ground pepper

8 thick rashers of unsmoked fatty
streaky bacon

4 small onions, skinned

16 bay leaves

extra olive oil, for brushing
(if necessary)

1 Cut the lamb into large cubes
(if you cut the cubes too small
the lamb will cook too quickly and
not be juicy).

2 Put the wine vinegar, oil,
nutmeg and marjoram in a
bowl with plenty of pepper. Whisk
with a fork until well combined,
then add the cubes of lamb and
stir to coat in the marinade.

3 Cover the bowl and marinate
the lamb in the refrigerator for
at least 8 hours, turning
occasionally during this time.

4 When ready to cook, cut each
bacon rasher into 4–6 pieces,
discarding the rind and any small
pieces of bone.

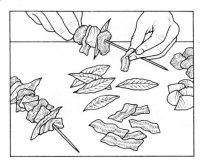

5 Cut the onions into eighths.
Thread the lamb, bacon,
onions and bay leaves on to 8 oiled
kebab skewers. Alternate the
ingredients as evenly as possible —
divide the meat equally between
the skewers, allow 4–6 pieces of
bacon per skewer, 4 onion pieces
and 2 bay leaves.

6 Cook over a charcoal barbecue
or under a preheated grill for
about 15 minutes until the lamb is
tender but still pink and juicy on
the inside. Turn the skewers
frequently during cooking and
baste with any remaining
marinade or olive oil. Sprinkle
with salt and pepper to taste
before serving.

Menu Suggestion
Serve Shashlik for a summer
barbecue meal in the garden.
Warm through pitta bread on the
barbecue grid for a few moments
and stuff the kebabs in the pockets
of bread. Accompany with lemon
wedges, a green salad and a tomato
and onion salad. Alternatively,
serve on a bed of rice.

BASS ON THE BARBECUE

1.00* ✳* 478 cals

* plus 2–3 hours chilling time; freeze before cooking

Serves 4

100 g (4 oz) unsalted butter
20 ml (4 tsp) dried dillweed
finely grated rind and juice of
    1 lemon
salt and freshly ground pepper
1.5-kg (3-lb) sea bass, cleaned
75 ml (3 fl oz) dry white wine
lemon slices and dill sprigs, to
    garnish

1 Work the butter with the dill-weed, lemon rind and salt and pepper to taste. Form into a roll, wrap in foil and chill in the refrigerator for 2–3 hours until firm.

2 Cut a sheet of foil large enough to enclose the fish. Place the fish in the centre of the foil.

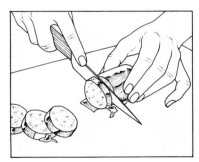

3 Using a sharp knife, cut the flavoured butter into slices. Peel off and discard foil after cutting.

4 Place the butter slices inside the belly of the fish. Sprinkle the outside of the fish with salt and pepper, then slowly pour over the wine and lemon juice.

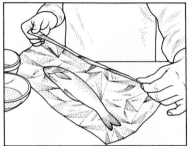

5 Fold the foil over the fish to form a loose package so that the wine and juices do not leak out. Place the foil package on the barbecue and grill for 45 minutes. Serve hot, straight from the foil, garnished with a few lemon slices and fresh dill sprigs.

SAUSAGE KEBABS

0.25* | 294 cals

* plus 1–2 hours marinating

Serves 8

8 rashers streaky bacon

24 cocktail sausages

24 cherry tomatoes or 6 small tomatoes, quartered

24 silverskin onions, well drained

90 ml (6 tbsp) vegetable oil

45 ml (3 tbsp) lemon juice

15 ml (1 tbsp) French mustard

10 ml (2 tsp) Worcestershire sauce

salt and freshly ground pepper

1 Remove the rind from the bacon and cut each rasher into 3 pieces with sharp kitchen scissors.

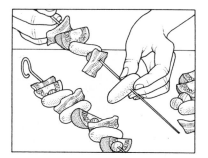

2 Thread 3 pieces of bacon on to each of 8 oiled kebab skewers, with 3 cocktail sausages, 3 tomatoes, or tomato quarters and 3 onions.

3 Make the marinade. Whisk together the oil, lemon juice, mustard and Worcestershire sauce. Add seasoning to taste. Brush over the kebabs.

4 Leave the kebabs to marinate in the refrigerator for 1–2 hours, brushing them with any marinade that collects under them.

5 Cook the kebabs on a pre-heated barbecue for about 10 minutes until the sausages and bacon are cooked. Turn the skewers often and brush with any remaining marinade. Serve hot.

RICE SALAD RING

0.30* | 160 cals

* plus at least 1 hour chilling

Serves 8

225 g (8 oz) long grain rice

salt and freshly ground pepper

1 green pepper, seeded and diced

3 caps canned pimento, diced

198 g (7 oz) canned sweetcorn, drained

75 ml (5 tbsp) chopped fresh parsley

50 g (2 oz) salted peanuts

45 ml (3 tbsp) lemon juice

celery salt

watercress, to garnish

1 Cook the rice in plenty of boiling salted water for 10–15 minutes until tender, then tip into a sieve and drain.

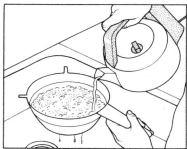

2 Rinse the rice through with hot water from the kettle, then rinse under cold running water and drain thoroughly. Leave to cool completely.

3 Blanch the green pepper in boiling water for 1 minute, drain, rinse under cold running water and drain again.

4 In a large bowl, mix the cold rice, pepper and pimento, sweetcorn, parsley, peanuts and lemon juice, and season well with celery salt and pepper.

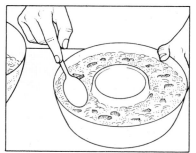

5 Press the salad into a lightly oiled 1.4 litre (2½ pint) ring mould and refrigerate for 1 hour.

6 Turn the rice salad ring out on to a flat serving plate and fill with watercress. Serve chilled.

SPARKLING FRUIT CUP

0.05	230 cals

Makes 3.4 litres (8 pints)

½ bottle (350 ml/12 fl oz) orange-
   flavoured liqueur

4 × 75 cl (1¼ pint) bottles
   sparkling cider

ice cubes

350 g (12 oz) fresh or frozen
   raspberries, defrosted

fresh mint sprigs

1 Make this drink up just as the
guests arrive. Pour half of the
liqueur into a cold glass bowl.
Pour in half the wine and cider
and stir quickly with a ladle.

2 Drop a few ice cubes into the
bowl, then float half of the
raspberries and mint sprigs on the
top. Ladle into glasses
immediately.

3 Make up more with the
remaining ingredients as soon
as the bowl needs replenishing.

BARBECUED BANANAS WITH TROPICAL SAUCE

0.20	195 cals

Serves 8

25 g (1 oz) unsalted butter

30 ml (2 tbsp) clear honey

150 ml (¼ pint) dark rum

150 ml (¼ pint) freshly squeezed
   orange juice

150 ml (¼ pint) pineapple juice

1.25 ml (¼ tsp) ground ginger

1.25 ml (¼ tsp) ground cinnamon

8 firm, ripe bananas

blanched orange shreds,
   to decorate

pouring cream or scoops of vanilla
   ice cream, to serve (optional)

1 Make the tropical sauce.
Melt the butter in a heavy-
based pan, add the honey and stir
until melted. Stir in the rum,
orange and pineapple juices, then
add the spices.

2 Bring to the boil, stirring, then
simmer for a few minutes to
allow the flavours to mingle. Pour
into a heatproof jug and stand on
the barbecue grid to keep warm.

3 When the barbecue coals are
just dying down, place the
bananas (in their skins) on the
barbecue grid. Cook for 7
minutes, turning once, until the
skins become quite black.

4 To serve, peel off the banana
skins and place the bananas in
a warmed serving dish. Pour over
the sauce and sprinkle with orange
shreds. Serve immediately, with
cream or vanilla ice cream handed
separately, if liked.

FRUIT KEBABS WITH YOGURT AND HONEY DIP

1.15*	298 cals

* includes 30 minutes marinating

Serves 4

1 small pineapple
3 large firm peaches
2 large firm bananas
3 crisp eating apples
1 small bunch large black grapes, seeded
finely grated rind and juice of 1 large orange
60 ml (4 tbsp) brandy, or orange-flavoured liqueur
50 g (2 oz) unsalted butter, melted
200 ml (7 fl oz) natural yogurt
45 ml (3 tbsp) clear honey
few fresh mint sprigs

YOGURT AND HONEY
The combination of natural yogurt and honey is popular all over Greece, Turkey and the Middle East. Served on its own or with fresh fruit as in this sweet kebab recipe, it is most refreshing in hot climates.

When choosing natural yogurt, check the label on the carton carefully: there are many different varieties now available. All are suitable for this dip, choose according to your own personal taste.

Yogurt labelled 'live' means that it contains live bacteria, and that a special culture (or starter) has been used. Bulgarian and Greek 'live' yogurts are noted for being thick and creamy, although they can be tangy in flavour. Yogurt labelled simply 'natural', is always unsweetened; sometimes it is made with whole milk, sometimes it is low-fat — check the small print carefully. Natural set yogurt is very thick, as its name suggests; it is also sometimes called 'thick set' or 'dairy yogurt'. All the thick-set yogurts are made with whole milk.

1 Prepare the fruit. Cut the top and bottom off the pineapple. Stand the fruit upright on a board. Using a large, sharp knife, slice downwards in sections to remove the skin and 'eyes'. Slice off the flesh, leaving the core. Then cut the flesh into small cubes.

2 Skin and halve the peaches and remove the stones. Cut the flesh into chunks.

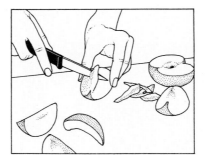

3 Peel the bananas and then slice them into thick chunks. Quarter and core the apples, but do not skin them.

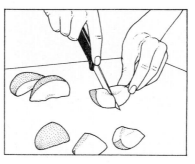

4 Cut each quarter in half cross-ways. Then put all the fruit together in a bowl. Mix together the orange rind and juice and the brandy or liqueur. Pour over the fruit, cover and leave for at least 30 minutes.

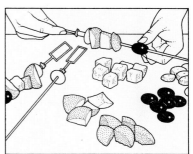

5 Thread the fruit on to kebab skewers, then brush with the melted butter. Place on the barbecue and grill for 10–15 minutes, turning and basting frequently during this time.

6 Meanwhile, make the dip. Whisk together the yogurt and 30 ml (2 tbsp) of the honey. Pour into a serving bowl and drizzle over the remaining 15 ml (1 tbsp) of honey. Garnish with a few fresh mint sprigs.

7 Serve the fruit kebabs as soon as possible after barbecuing, with the yogurt dip handed separately in a small bowl.

Puddings
and Desserts

TRADITIONAL TRIFLE

1.00*	497–663 cals

* plus 20 minutes infusing, 1 hour cooling and 4–6 hours chilling
Serves 6–8

8 trifle sponges
175 g (6 oz) strawberry jam
100 g (4 oz) macaroons
200 ml (7 fl oz) medium sherry
568 ml (1 pint) milk
1 vanilla pod
2 whole eggs
2 egg yolks
15 ml (1 tbsp) cornflour
30 ml (2 tbsp) caster sugar
450 ml ($\frac{3}{4}$ pint) whipping cream
glacé cherries and angelica, or
    toasted flaked almonds,
    to decorate

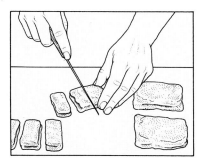

1 Split the trifle sponges in half and spread with the jam. Sandwich together and cut into fingers. Arrange in the bottom of a large, shallow glass serving dish.

2 Crush the macaroons lightly and sprinkle on top. Spoon over the sherry and leave for 30 minutes to soak.

3 Meanwhile, put the milk and vanilla pod in a saucepan, bring to the boil, then remove from the heat. Cover the pan and leave to infuse for 20 minutes.

4 Put the eggs, egg yolks, corn-flour and sugar in a heatproof bowl standing over a saucepan of gently simmering water (or in the top of a double boiler). Add the milk, removing the vanilla pod. Place over gentle heat and cook until the custard is thick enough to coat the back of a wooden spoon, stirring all the time.

5 Pour the custard over the sponges. Leave for 1 hour until cold, then chill in the refrigerator for 3–4 hours.

6 Whip the cream until stiff. Spread half on top of the custard. Pipe the remaining cream on top and decorate with the cherries and angelica, or scatter with almonds. Chill again for 1–2 hours before serving.

Menu Suggestion
Trifle is traditional in England at teatime on Christmas Day, but it can also be served as a dessert at any time during the festive season.

TRADITIONAL TRIFLE
It seems we have to thank the Victorians for giving us the trifle, although they would probably frown upon the elaborate fruit and cream concoctions that call themselves trifles these days. The original Victorian trifle was similar to this recipe, a bottom layer of plain cake sandwiched together with jam, a light sprinkling of crushed macaroons, and a heavy soaking of sherry! This was then topped with a vanilla-flavoured egg custard and then a final layer of whipped cream. Cherries, angelica and almonds were the traditional trifle decoration.

ZUCCOTTO
(FLORENTINE TIPSY CAKE)

0.45*	✳	902 cals

* plus 12 hours chilling

Serves 6

50 g (2 oz) blanched almonds

50 g (2 oz) hazelnuts

45 ml (3 tbsp) brandy

30 ml (2 tbsp) orange-flavoured liqueur

30 ml (2 tbsp) cherry- or almond-flavoured liqueur

350 g (12 oz) trifle sponges or Madeira cake

150 g (5 oz) plain chocolate

450 ml (15 fl oz) double cream

150 g (5 oz) icing sugar

25 g (1 oz) cocoa powder, to decorate

1 Spread the almonds and hazelnuts out separately on a baking tray and toast in the oven at 200°C (400°F) mark 6 for 5 minutes until golden.

2 Transfer the hazelnuts to a clean tea towel and rub off the skins while still warm. Spread all the nuts out to cool for 5 minutes and then roughly chop.

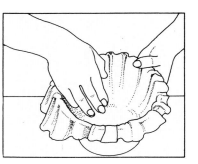

3 Line a 1.4-litre (2½-pint) pudding basin or round-bottomed bowl with damp muslin.

4 In a separate bowl, mix together the brandy and the liqueurs and set aside.

5 Split the trifle sponges in half through the middle (if using Madeira cake, cut into 1 cm (½ inch) slices). Sprinkle with the brandy and liqueurs.

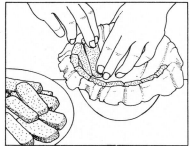

6 Line the basin with the moistened split sponges, reserving enough to cover the top.

7 Using a sharp knife, chop 75 g (3 oz) of the plain chocolate into small pieces, and set aside.

8 In a separate bowl, whip the cream with 125 g (4 oz) icing sugar until stiff and fold in the chopped chocolate and nuts.

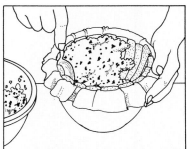

9 Divide this mixture in two and use one half to spread over the sponge lining in an even layer.

10 Melt the remaining chocolate, cool slightly, then fold into the remaining cream mixture. Use this to fill the centre of the pudding.

11 Level the top of the zuccotto and cover with the remaining moistened sponge. Trim edges. Cover and refrigerate for at least 12 hours.

12 To serve. Uncover, invert a flat serving plate over basin and turn upside down. Lift off the bowl, and carefully remove the muslin. Serve cold, dusted with the remaining icing sugar and cocoa powder.

RHUBARB AND ORANGE FOOL

1.35*	✳	201 cals

* plus 1–2 hours chilling

Serves 6

450 g (1 lb) rhubarb
grated rind and juice of 1 orange
pinch of cinnamon
25–50 g (1–2 oz) sugar
300 ml (10 fl oz) whipping cream
5 ml (1 tsp) orange flower water
shredded orange rind, to decorate
sponge fingers, to serve

1 Wipe the rhubarb and chop into 2.5-cm (1-inch) pieces, discarding the leaves and the white ends of the stalks.

2 Put the rhubarb, orange rind, juice, cinnamon, and sugar into a pan and cook gently, covered, for about 15 minutes.

3 Remove the lid and boil rapidly for 10 minutes, stirring frequently, until the mixture becomes a thick purée. Cool for 1 hour.

4 When cool, whip the cream until stiff. Fold into the mixture with the orange flower water to taste. Spoon into glasses and chill for 1–2 hours until required. Decorate with orange rind and serve with sponge fingers.

STRAWBERRY AND ORANGE MOUSSE

0.45*	🔲 🔲	440 cals

* plus 2–3 hours chilling

Serves 6

700 g (1½ lb) fresh strawberries, hulled

finely grated rind and juice of 1 large orange

45 ml (3 tbsp) icing sugar

3 egg yolks and 2 egg whites

100 g (4 oz) caster sugar

45 ml (3 tbsp) water

15 ml (3 tsp) gelatine

300 ml (10 fl oz) double cream

150 ml (5 fl oz) single cream

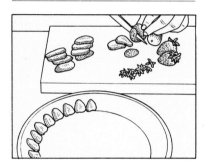

1 Thinly slice enough strawberries to line the sides of a 2.3-litre (4-pint) shallow glass dish.

2 Purée half the remainder in a blender or food processor with the finely grated orange rind, 75 ml (5 tbsp) juice and the icing sugar. Pass through a nylon sieve to give a very smooth texture. Reserve rest of strawberries for decoration.

3 Using electric beaters, whisk the egg yolks and caster sugar until thick and light. Then gradually whisk in the strawberry purée.

4 Place the water in a bowl and sprinkle in the gelatine. Stand the bowl over a saucepan of hot water and heat gently until dissolved. Leave to cool, then stir it into the mousse mixture.

5 Lightly whip the creams together. Fold one-third through mousse and keep the rest covered in refrigerator. Lastly, whisk the two egg whites and fold through the mixture. Turn carefully into the strawberry-lined glass dish, and refrigerate for 2–3 hours, until the mousse is set.

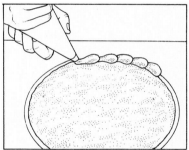

6 To serve, pipe the reserved cream on top of the strawberry and orange mousse and top with the remaining strawberries.

STRAWBERRIES
Strawberries and cream spell summer magic – and this beautifully decorated mousse literally makes your mouth water to look at it! The flavour of fresh orange complements strawberries perfectly, and the delicate texture of the mousse itself is irresistible.

COEURS À LA CRÈME

0.20*		325–487 cals

* plus overnight draining

Serves 4–6

225 g (8 oz) cottage cheese

25 g (1 oz) caster sugar

300 ml (10 fl oz) double cream

5 ml (1 tsp) lemon juice

2 egg whites, stiffly whisked

150 ml (5 fl oz) single cream, and fresh raspberries or strawberries, to serve

1 Press the cottage cheese through a nylon sieve into a bowl. Add sugar and mix well.

2 Whip the cream until stiff then add the lemon juice. Mix into the cheese and sugar mixture.

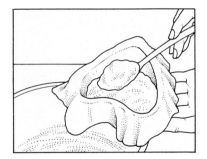

3 Line 4 or 6 small heart-shaped moulds with muslin (this is unnecessary if serving in the moulds). Fold stiffly whisked egg whites into cheese mixture. Spoon mixture into moulds. Drain overnight in refrigerator. Serve with cream and fruit.

DANISH 'PEASANT GIRL IN A VEIL'

0.30*	601 cals

* plus cooling and 2–3 hours chilling

Serves 4

50 g (2 oz) butter or margarine
175 g (6 oz) fresh breadcrumbs
75 g (3 oz) soft brown sugar
700 g (1½ lb) cooking apples
30 ml (2 tbsp) water
juice of ½ a lemon
sugar to taste
150 ml (5 fl oz) double or whipping cream
50 g (2 oz) grated chocolate, to decorate

1 Melt the fat in a frying pan. Mix the crumbs and sugar together and fry in the hot fat until crisp, stirring frequently with a wooden spoon to prevent the crumbs from catching and burning.

2 Peel, core and slice the apples. Put them in a saucepan with the water, lemon juice and some sugar to taste. Cover and cook gently for 10–15 minutes until they form a pulp. Leave to cool, then taste for sweetness.

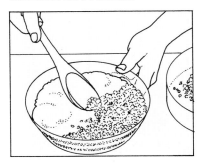

3 Put alternate layers of the fried crumb mixture and the apple pulp into a glass dish, finishing with a layer of crumbs. Refrigerate for 2–3 hours.

4 Whip the cream until stiff. Pipe over the top of the crumb mixture and decorate with grated chocolate. Serve chilled.

DANISH 'PEASANT GIRL IN A VEIL'

This simple but delicious pudding of stewed apples layered with fried breadcrumbs and sugar is very similar to an apple charlotte. In Denmark, where it is called *bondepige med slør*, it takes its name from the fact that the apple and crumbs are 'veiled' or covered with cream. Like apple charlotte, it is a country-style pudding, yet it tastes so good that it would be perfect for any type of special occasion, especially if made in a glass bowl so that the layers can be seen.

You can ring the changes by using different breadcrumbs. White breadcrumbs can of course be used, but wholemeal or granary bread give a more nutty texture. In Denmark, rye bread would be used to make the crumbs, so if you can find a bakery or Jewish delicatessen that sells rye bread, it is well worth trying.

R∅DGR∅D

0.35*	✳	339–452 cals

* plus 10 minutes cooling and 30
minutes chilling
Serves 6–8

450 g (1 lb) fresh redcurrants or
    425-g (15-oz) can, drained
450 g (1 lb) fresh raspberries or
    425-g (15-oz) can, drained
45 ml (3 tbsp) arrowroot
225–350 g (8–12 oz) caster sugar, if
    using fresh fruit
25 g (1 oz) blanched almonds and
    whipped cream, to decorate

1 Place the fresh fruits in a
saucepan with 60 ml (4 tbsp)
water. Simmer gently for about 20
minutes or until really soft.

2 Purée in a blender or food processor until smooth, then push
through a nylon sieve. If using
canned fruit, push through a sieve.

3 Blend a little of the purée with
the arrowroot, put the rest
into a saucepan and bring slowly
to boiling point. Stir into the
blended mixture, then return it all
to the pan. Bring to the boil again,
cook for 2–3 minutes and sweeten
to taste if using fresh fruit. Leave
to cool for 10 minutes.

4 Shred the almonds into thin
strips with a sharp knife. Toast
them lightly under the grill. Cool
for 5 minutes.

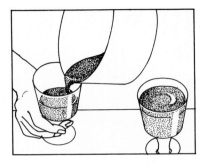

5 Pour the rødgrød into individual tall or shallow glasses and
refrigerate for 30 minutes. Top
with whipped cream and the
shredded almonds just before
serving.

RØDGRØD

Rødgrød is a Danish dessert which
is best described as a fruit soup.
It is always made with fresh soft
summer fruit: redcurrants and
raspberries are used in our
version, although blackcurrants,
blackberries, strawberries,
cherries and even rhubarb can be
used, depending on what is available. The important thing is to
mix at least two of these fruits
together to provide good flavour
and colour.

    Such fruit soups are popular all
over Scandinavia, and are sometimes even eaten as a starter,
either hot or cold. In Finland,
they are called *kiisseli*, and are
often made with more unusual
soft red fruits such as bilberries,
cloudberries and cranberries.

    This recipe for rødgrød is re-
freshingly simple, whereas some
recipes use spices such as cinnamon and the thinly pared zest
of citrus fruit—you can add
these too if you wish. Fresh
whipped cream to serve is traditional, or you can use soured
cream or natural yogurt, in
which case the soup will look
most attractive if the cream or
yogurt is swirled over the top
just before serving.

TEA CREAM

0.45* 🥛	293 cals

* plus 2–3 hours setting

Serves 4

300 ml (½ pint) milk

15 g (½ oz) Earl Grey tea

2 eggs, separated

30 ml (2 tbsp) caster sugar

45 ml (3 tbsp) water

15 ml (3 tsp) gelatine

150 ml (5 fl oz) double cream

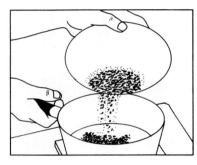

1 Put the milk into a saucepan, add the tea and bring to the boil. Remove from the heat and leave to infuse for 10–15 minutes, or until the milk is well coloured with the tea.

2 Beat the egg yolks with the sugar, then strain on the milk and mix well. Return to the pan and cook gently for 10 minutes, stirring all the time, until the custard thickens slightly and just coats the back of the spoon.

3 Put the water in a small heat-proof bowl and sprinkle in the gelatine. Stand the bowl over a saucepan of hot water and heat gently until dissolved. Mix into the tea mixture, then leave for about 2 hours until beginning to set. Stir the mixture occasionally.

4 Whip the cream until thick but not stiff, then fold into the custard. Finally, whisk the egg whites until stiff and fold into the mixture.

5 Pour the cream mixture into a dampened 600-ml (1-pint) mould and refrigerate for about 2–3 hours until set. Turn out on to a chilled dish to serve.

TEA CREAM

Earl Grey tea, a blended black tea flavoured with bergamot oil, gives this unusual tea cream a subtle, perfumed flavour.

It isn't essential to use Earl Grey, however, you can use any of your favourite Ceylon or China teas, although aromatic teas are more flavoursome in cooking. Why not try jasmine tea, lapsang souchong or orange pekoe?

MANDARIN AND LYCHEE MOUSSE

| 0.45* | ✳ | 292 cals |

* plus 30 minutes cooling and at least
2 hours setting

Serves 6

3 eggs, separated

2 egg yolks

75 g (3 oz) caster sugar

298-g (10½-oz) can mandarin
   oranges in natural juice

310-g (11-oz) can lychees in syrup

15 ml (3 tsp) gelatine

150 ml (5 fl oz) double cream

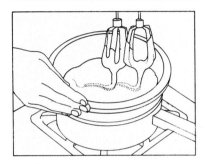

1 Put the 5 egg yolks and sugar in a large heatproof bowl and stand over a saucepan of gently simmering water. Whisk until the mixture is thick and holds a ribbon trail, then remove the bowl from the pan. Leave for 30 minutes, whisking occasionally.

2 Reserve 60 ml (4 tbsp) of the mandarin juice. Purée half the oranges and the remaining juice in a blender or food processor with the lychees and half the syrup.

3 Put the reserved mandarin syrup in a heatproof bowl and sprinkle in the gelatine. Stand the bowl over a saucepan of hot water and heat gently until dissolved. Remove the bowl from the pan and leave to cool slightly.

4 Stir the mandarin purée into the cooled egg yolk mixture, then stir in the gelatine liquid until evenly mixed.

5 Whip the cream until standing in soft peaks. Whisk the egg whites until stiff. Fold first the cream and then the egg whites into the mousse until evenly blended. Turn into a glass serving bowl and chill for at least 2 hours until set.

6 When the mousse is set serve decorated with the reserved mandarin oranges and extra whipped cream, if liked.

LYCHEES

The tree fruit lychee (lichee or litchi as it is also known) originated in China, but it is now grown in tropical countries elsewhere in the world. Canned peeled lychees, with their translucent white flesh, are readily available. The skin of a lychee is a most attractive reddish brown with a rough almost brittle texture, but the fresh fruit is rarely seen outside specialist markets. The unique perfumed flavour of lychees, and their beautifully smooth texture, makes them an interesting ingredient to include in a mousse such as the one on this page.

TANGERINE SYLLABUB

1.00* 🄴		335 cals

* plus 2 hours macerating and 2 hours chilling

Serves 6

700 g (1½ lb) tangerines—about 6
30 ml (2 tbsp) lemon juice
30 ml (2 tbsp) orange-flavoured liqueur
50 g (2 oz) dark soft brown sugar
300 ml (½ pint) double cream
sponge fingers, to serve

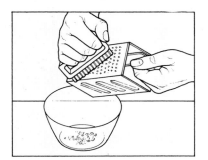

1 Finely grate the rind from 3 tangerines into a small bowl; use a stiff brush to remove all the rind from the teeth of the grater.

2 Peel these 3 tangerines and pull the segments apart. Remove the membranes from around each segment if tough.

3 Halve and squeeze the remaining tangerines, or liquidise the flesh and strain it.

4 Measure out 120 ml (8 tbsp) juice. Strain over the tangerine rinds. Add the lemon juice and liqueur, then cover and leave to soak for at least 2 hours.

5 Put the sugar in a bowl and strain in the liquid. Mix well until the sugar has dissolved.

6 Whip the cream until stiff, then gradually whisk in the juices, keeping the cream thick.

7 Put the tangerine segments in the base of 6 stemmed glasses, reserving 6 segments for decoration. Divide the cream mixture between the glasses, cover with cling film and chill in the refrigerator for 2 hours.

8 Decorate with tangerine segments and serve with sponge fingers.

TANGERINE SYLLABUB

The syllabub is one of the oldest of English desserts. Originally it was made with very fresh milk—wine was poured into a bowl, then the cow milked straight into it! The idea behind this was that the acid in the wine curdled the warm milk. Early 19th century recipes for syllabub suggested that the milk should be poured from a height onto the alcohol, in the absence of a cow ready for milking. These days, fresh double cream is used, with equal success!

GRAPE SORBET

0.30* 🄴	❋	221 cals

* plus 6–7 hours freezing

Serves 6

900 g (2 lb) black grapes
125 g (4 oz) granulated sugar
10 ml (2 tsp) lemon juice
1 egg white
45 ml (3 tbsp) kirsch
brandy snaps, to serve

1 Pluck the grapes off the stalks but do not bother to peel or seed them.

2 Put the sugar in a heavy-based saucepan with 450 ml (¾ pint) water and heat gently until the sugar has dissolved. Bring to the boil and bubble for 5 minutes. Remove from the heat, stir in the lemon juice, then cool slightly.

3 Put the grapes and sugar syrup together in a blender or food processor and work to a purée. Sieve to remove the seeds and skin.

4 Pour into a shallow freezer container and freeze for 4–5 hours or until the mixture is beginning to set. Remove the sorbet from the freezer and mash with a fork to break down the ice crystals.

5 Whisk the egg white lightly, then fold the kirsch and egg white into the sorbet. Return to the freezer and freeze for at least a further 2 hours until firm.

6 Serve the grape sorbet straight from the freezer, with brandy snaps handed separately.

ÉCLAIRS

| 1.45* | 🗂 | ❋* | 213 cals* |

* includes 20–30 minutes cooling;
freeze after stage 3; 201 cals with
plain chocolate

Makes 12

100 g (4 oz) choux pastry

300 ml (10 fl oz) double cream

275 g (10 oz) chocolate glacé icing
or 50 g (2 oz) plain chocolate

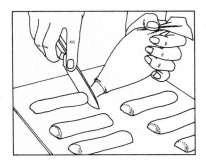

1 Dampen a baking sheet with
water. Put the choux pastry
into a piping bag fitted with a
medium plain nozzle and pipe
fingers, 9 cm (3½ inches) long, on
to the baking sheet, keeping the
lengths even and cutting the pastry
off with a wet knife.

2 Bake in the oven at 200°C
(400°F) mark 6 for about 35
minutes until crisp and golden.

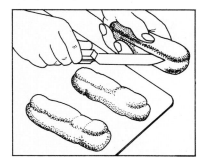

3 Make a slit down the side of
each bun with a sharp, pointed
knife to release the steam then
transfer to a wire rack and leave for
20–30 minutes to cool completely.

4 Just before serving, whip the
double cream until stiff and
use it to fill the éclairs.

5 Ice with chocolate glacé icing
or break the chocolate into a
heatproof bowl and place over
simmering water. Stir until the
chocolate is melted.

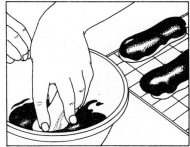

6 Pour into a shallow bowl and
dip in the filled éclairs, drawing each one across the surface of
the chocolate.

——————— VARIATIONS ———————

For less rich éclairs, replace the
double cream with 300 ml (½ pint)
crème pàtissière.
Although chocolate is the
favourite flavour for éclairs,, ring
the changes with coffee glacé icing.
  To make savoury éclairs for a
cocktail party, shape the choux
pastry into very small éclairs and
bake for 15–20 minutes. When
cold, fill them with a mixture of
100 g (4 oz) full fat soft cheese
creamed with 50 g (2 oz) butter
and seasoned with 5 ml (1 tsp)
lemon juice and salt and pepper to
taste. Or cream 100 g (4 oz) full fat
soft cheese with 50 g (2 oz) butter,
10 ml (2 tsp) tomato purée, a few
drops of Worcestershire sauce and
salt and pepper to taste. For anchovy éclairs, cream 175–225 g
(6–8 oz) butter with 10 ml (2 tsp)
anchovy essence and pepper to
taste; pipe into the éclairs when
cold.

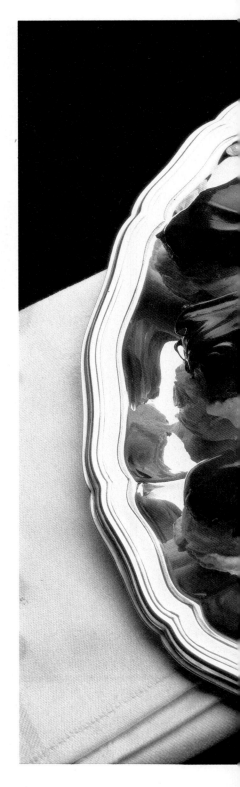

GLAZED FRUIT TARTS

Illustrated on front cover

2.00	🍴	✳*	377 cals

* after stage 2

Makes 8

225 g (8 oz) pâte sucrée
150 ml (5 fl oz) double cream
50 ml (2 fl oz) single cream
225 g (8 oz) fresh strawberries
60 ml (4 tbsp) redcurrant jelly, to
  glaze

1 Roll out the pâte sucrée on a lightly floured working surface and use to line eight 9-cm (3½-inch) shallow patty tins.

2 Bake 'blind' in the oven at 190°C (375°F) mark 5 for 15–20 minutes until pale golden. Turn out on to a wire rack and leave for 30 minutes to cool.

3 Whip the double and single creams together until stiff. Spread a layer of cream over the tart bases.

4 Using a sharp knife, slice the strawberries. Arrange on top of the cream in an overlapping circle on each tart.

5 Melt the redcurrant jelly over a very low heat, adding a little water if necessary. Brush over the strawberries to glaze.

431

GOOSEBERRY MACAROON CRUNCH

0.25*	321 cals

* plus several hours chilling

Serves 6

450 g (1 lb) gooseberries, topped
   and tailed

30 ml (2 tbsp) water

100 g (4 oz) caster sugar

30 ml (2 tbsp) kirsch

100 g (4 oz) French almond
   macaroons (ratafias), crumbled

150 ml ($\frac{1}{4}$ pint) whipping cream

3 macaroons or 6 ratafias,
   to decorate

1 Cook the gooseberries with the water and sugar for 10–15 minutes until the fruit is soft and well reduced, then sieve it. Stir in the kirsch. Chill for 30 minutes.

3 Whip the cream until it barely holds its shape. Spoon some of the soft cream over each glass and top each with a halved macaroon or whole ratafias. Serve immediately.

2 Arrange the macaroon crumbs and gooseberry purée in alternate layers in 6 tall glasses. Chill in the refrigerator for several hours for the flavours to mellow.

GOOSEBERRY MACAROON CRUNCH

There are many variations of this pretty dessert. According to seasonal availability, you can use different fruit from the gooseberries and an alternative liqueur to the kirsch. For example, cherries and kirsch would go well together; strawberries or raspberries and an orange-flavoured liqueur (in which case you can use the fruit raw); stewed apples and calvados or brandy; banana with rum; peaches or apricots go well with the Italian almond-flavoured liqueur Amaretto, which would also complement the flavour of the almond macaroons. For a less rich (and less fattening) dessert, natural yogurt can be used instead of the whipping cream or, for those who are not so keen on yogurt, a combination of half cream, half yogurt, which is less sharp in flavour.

SPICED DRIED FRUIT COMPOTE

| 0.50* | 218 cals |

* plus 1–2 hours cooling and at least 2 hours chilling

Serves 4

15 ml (1 tbsp) jasmine tea

2.5 ml ($\frac{1}{2}$ tsp) ground cinnamon

1.25 ml ($\frac{1}{4}$ tsp) ground cloves

300 ml ($\frac{1}{2}$ pint) boiling water

100 g (4 oz) dried apricots, soaked overnight, drained

100 g (4 oz) dried prunes, soaked overnight, drained and stoned

100 g (4 oz) dried apple rings

150 ml ($\frac{1}{4}$ pint) dry white wine

50 g (2 oz) sugar

toasted flaked almonds, to decorate

1 Put tea, cinnamon and cloves in a bowl; pour in boiling water. Leave for 20 minutes.

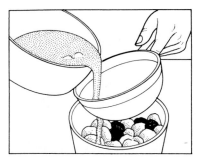

2 Put dried fruit in a saucepan, then strain in tea and spice liquid. Add wine and sugar; heat gently until sugar has dissolved.

3 Simmer for 20 minutes until tender, then cover and leave for 1–2 hours until cold.

4 Turn the compote into a serving bowl and chill for at least 2 hours. Sprinkle with almonds just before serving.

COFFEENUT ICE CREAM

| 0.40* | 🥛 | ❄ | 669 cals |

* plus at least 6 hours freezing and 30 minutes softening

Serves 4

| 100 g (4 oz) shelled hazelnuts |
| 50 ml (2 tbsp plus 4 tsp) coffee-flavoured liqueur |
| 15 ml (1 tbsp) coffee and chicory essence |
| 300 ml (10 fl oz) double cream |
| 300 ml (10 fl oz) single cream |
| 75 g (3 oz) icing sugar, sifted |

1 Toast the hazelnuts under the grill for a few minutes, shaking the grill pan constantly so that the nuts brown evenly.

2 Tip the nuts into a clean tea-towel and rub to remove the skins. Chop finely.

3 Mix 30 ml (2 tbsp) coffee liqueur and the essence together in a bowl. Stir in the chopped nuts, reserving a few for decoration.

4 In a separate bowl, whip the creams and icing sugar together until thick. Fold in the nut mixture, then turn into a shallow freezerproof container. Freeze for 2 hours until ice crystals form around the edge of the ice cream.

5 Turn the ice cream into a bowl and beat thoroughly for a few minutes to break up the ice crystals. Return to the freezer container, cover and freeze for at least 4 hours, preferably overnight (to allow enough time for the flavours to develop).

6 To serve, transfer the ice cream to the refrigerator for 30 minutes to soften slightly, then scoop into individual glasses. Spoon 5 ml (1 tsp) coffee liqueur over each serving and sprinkle with the remaining nuts. Serve immediately.

ICE CREAM MAKERS

It is always satisfying to make your own ice cream, but sometimes the texture is disappointing because large ice crystals have formed in the mixture due to insufficient beating. Electric ice cream makers help enormously with this problem: they are not very expensive and are well worth buying if you like to make ice cream for occasions such as dinner parties when everything needs to be as near perfect as possible. The mixture is placed in the machine, which is then put into the freezer and switched on (the cable is flat so that the freezer door can close safely on it). Paddles churn the mixture continuously until the mixture is thick, creamy and velvety smooth—a consistency that is almost impossible to obtain when beating by hand.

ICED TUTTI FRUTTI PUDDING

| 0.30* | 🍽 | ❄ | 624 cals |

* plus 2–3 hours soaking fruit, 6–7 hours freezing and 20 minutes standing before serving

Serves 8

100 g (4 oz) glacé cherries

40 g (1½ oz) angelica

50 g (2 oz) blanched almonds

4 canned pineapple rings, drained

120 ml (8 tbsp) orange-flavoured liqueur

900 ml (1½ pints) whipping cream

130 g (4½ oz) caster sugar

6 eggs, beaten

1 Cut the cherries in half, finely chop the angelica, almonds and roughly chop the pineapple.

2 Pour over the liqueur, cover and leave to macerate for 2–3 hours, stirring occasionally.

3 Meanwhile, put the cream, sugar and eggs in a heatproof bowl standing over a saucepan of gently simmering water (or in the top of a double boiler). Place over gentle heat and cook until the custard is thick enough to coat the back of a wooden spoon, stirring all the time. Do not boil.

4 Pour the custard into a large bowl, cover and leave to cool for about 1 hour. When cold, freeze the custard for about 2 hours until mushy in texture.

5 Mash the frozen mixture with a fork, then freeze again for about 2 hours until slushy.

6 Mash the frozen mixture again and stir in the fruit mixture. Mix well and pack into a 1.4 litre (2½ pint) pudding basin, base-lined with non-stick paper. Return to freezer for 2–3 hours until firm.

7 About 1 hour before serving, remove from the freezer and leave to soften slightly at room temperature. Turn out and serve immediately.

Menu Suggestion

This dessert is like an ice cream version of Christmas pudding. Serve it instead of Christmas pudding for a change—children usually prefer it to the rich and heavy traditional plum pudding.

ICED TUTTI FRUTTI PUDDING

Tutti frutti, which literally translated means 'all fruit' in Italian, was originally an American invention. Assorted fruits such as cherries, currants, raspberries, strawberries, apricots, peaches and pineapple were steeped in brandy in a stone crock for at least 3 months.

RASPBERRY REDCURRANT FREEZE

| 0.30* | ✳ | 284–392 cals |

* plus 1 hour chilling, 4 hours freezing
and 1 hour standing before serving

Serves 4–6

**350 g (12 oz) fresh or frozen
  raspberries**

225 g (8 oz) jar redcurrant jelly

300 ml (½ pint) soured cream

small crisp biscuits, to serve

1 Put the raspberries and jelly in
a saucepan and heat gently,
stirring frequently, until the fruit
is soft. Transfer to a blender or
food processor and work to a
purée. Sieve to remove the seeds.
Chill in the refrigerator for about
1 hour until cold.

2 Whisk in the soured cream,
then pour into a freezer container (not metal) at least 5 cm
(2 inches) deep. Freeze for about 2
hours until firm but not hard.

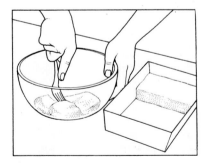

3 Turn the frozen mixture into a
bowl and break into pieces.
Beat until smooth, creamy and
lighter in colour. Return to the
freezer container and freeze for a
further 2 hours until firm.

4 Allow to soften slightly in the
refrigerator for about 1 hour
before serving with biscuits.

Menu Suggestion
Serve for a cool and refreshing
dessert after a rich main course.

STRAWBERRIES WITH RASPBERRY SAUCE

0.20*	91 cals

* plus at least 30 minutes chilling

Serves 6

900 g (2 lb) small strawberries

450 g (1 lb) raspberries

50 g (2 oz) icing sugar

1 Hull the strawberries and place them in individual serving dishes.

2 Purée the raspberries in a blender or food processor until just smooth, then work through a nylon sieve into a bowl to remove the pips.

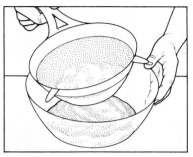

3 Sift the icing sugar over the bowl of raspberry purée, then whisk in until evenly incorporated. Pour over the strawberries. Chill in the refrigerator for at least 30 minutes before serving.

STRAWBERRIES WITH RASPBERRY SAUCE

Freshly picked raspberries freeze successfully (unlike strawberries which tend to lose texture and shape due to their high water content). If you have raspberries which are slightly overripe or misshapen, the best way to freeze them is as a purée; this takes up less space in the freezer and is immensely useful for making quick desserts and sauces at the last minute. For this recipe, for example, you can freeze the purée up to 12 months in advance, then it will only take a few minutes to put the dessert together after the purée has thawed. The purée can be frozen with or without the icing sugar.

ORANGE SHERBET

0.10* | 268 cals

* plus 4–5 hours freezing

Serves 8

178 ml (6¼ oz) carton frozen orange juice

175 g (6 oz) caster sugar

45 ml (3 tbsp) golden syrup

45 ml (3 tbsp) lemon juice

568 ml (1 pint) milk

300 ml (½ pint) single cream

shreds of orange rind and sprigs of mint, to decorate

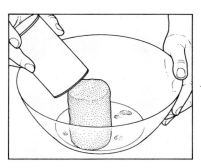

1 Tip the frozen, undiluted orange juice into a deep bowl. Leave until beginning to soften, then add the sugar, golden syrup and lemon juice. Whisk until smooth.

2 Combine the orange mixture with the milk and cream and pour into a deep, rigid container. Cover and freeze for 4–5 hours. There is no need to whisk the mixture during freezing.

3 Transfer to the refrigerator to soften 45 minutes–1 hour before serving. Serve scooped into individual glasses or orange shells, decorated with orange shreds and sprigs of mint.

Menu Suggestion
Make up a batch or two and keep in the freezer for dinner parties. It makes a tangy and refreshing end to a rich meal.

ORANGE SHERBET
There is always some confusion over the term 'sherbet' when used to describe a dessert. The word 'sherbet' is in fact the American term for a sorbet, although it is often mistakenly used to describe a water ice. Water ices are simple concoctions of sugar syrup and fruit purée or fruit juice, sometimes with liqueur or other alcohol added. Sorbets are a smoother version of water ices. They are made in the same way, with sugar syrup and fruit, but at the half-frozen stage they have whisked egg whites or other ingredients folded into them.

ICED STRAWBERRY MERINGUES

0.20*	✳ 344 cals

* plus 1 hour cooling, 6–8 hours open
freezing and 20–30 minutes standing
before serving

Serves 6

225 g (8 oz) strawberries, hulled

25 g (1 oz) caster sugar

30 ml (2 tbsp) water

300 ml (10 fl oz) double cream

18 medium meringue shells, about
    150 g (5 oz) total weight

30 ml (2 tbsp) brandy

double cream, to decorate
    (optional)

1 Place the strawberries (reserving 3 to decorate) in a small
saucepan with the caster sugar and
water. Cover the pan and heat
gently for about 5 minutes until
mushy, cool slightly.

2 Purée the pan ingredients in a
blender or food processor and
rub through a nylon sieve to remove any pips; allow the purée to
cool for about 1 hour.

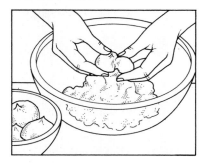

3 Lightly whip the cream in a
large mixing bowl. Break each
meringue shell up into three or
four pieces.

4 Fold the pieces of meringue
shell through the double cream
together with the brandy and the
cold fruit purée.

5 Spoon the mixture into six
individual soufflé or ramekin
dishes. Open freeze for 6–8 hours
or overnight until firm, then wrap
with foil and return to the freezer
until required.

6 20–30 minutes before serving,
transfer to the refrigerator. If
wished, serve decorated with a
whirl of cream and reserved strawberries, halved.

STRAWBERRIES

If you have frozen strawberries
or frozen strawberry purée in the
freezer, this is the ideal dessert to
use them for. You could even
freeze some summer strawberries
away specifically for making this
dessert in wintertime. Whole
strawberries do not retain their
shape in the freezer because they
have too high a water content,
but as this recipe involves
working the fruit to a purée before combining it with the
meringues and cream, this will
not matter – save your perfect
whole strawberries for eating as
they are.

BANANA CHEESECAKE

0.40* ⬚ ❄*

428–570 cals

* plus 3–4 hours chilling; freeze after
step 5. Defrost in refrigerator
overnight, then continue with step 6.

Serves 6–8

225 g (8 oz) ginger biscuits
100 g (4 oz) unsalted butter, melted
    and cooled
225 g (8 oz) full fat soft cheese
142-ml (5-fl oz) carton soured
    cream
3 bananas
30 ml (2 tbsp) clear honey
15 ml (1 tbsp) chopped preserved
    ginger (with syrup)
15 ml (3 tsp) gelatine
60 ml (4 tbsp) lemon juice
banana slices and preserved ginger
    slices, to decorate

1 Make the biscuit crust. Crush
the biscuits finely in a bowl
with the end of a rolling pin. Stir
in the melted butter.

2 Press the mixture over the
base of a 20.5-cm (8-inch)
springform tin or deep cake tin
with a removable base. Chill in
the refrigerator for about 30
minutes.

3 Meanwhile, make the filling.
Beat the cheese and cream together until well mixed. Peel and
mash the bananas, then beat into
the cheese mixture with the honey
and ginger.

4 Sprinkle the gelatine over the
lemon juice in a small heatproof bowl. Stand the bowl over a
saucepan of hot water and heat
gently until dissolved.

5 Stir the dissolved gelatine
slowly into the cheesecake
mixture, then spoon into the
biscuit-lined tin. Chill in the
refrigerator for about 3–4 hours
until the mixture is set.

6 To serve, remove the cheesecake carefully from the tin and
place on a serving plate. Decorate
around the edge with banana and
ginger slices. Serve as soon as possible or the banana will discolour.

——— VARIATION ———

The flavours of banana and ginger
go very well together, but you can
ring the changes by using
chocolate digestive biscuits for the
base of this cheesecake instead of
ginger biscuits, and omitting the
preserved ginger from the filling.
Decorate the top with banana
slices arranged alternately with
chocolate buttons.

GOOSEBERRY CHEESECAKE

| 2.30* | 🔲 | ✳* | 664 cals |

* plus 30 minutes cooling and 1–2
hours chilling; freeze after stage 8

Serves 6

450 g (1 lb) gooseberries, topped
and tailed

75 ml (5 tbsp) water

125 g (4 oz) caster sugar

75 g (3 oz) shelled hazel nuts

75 g (3 oz) butter

175 g (6 oz) digestive biscuits, finely
crushed

125 g (4 oz) cottage cheese

225 g (8 oz) full fat soft cheese

150 ml (5 fl oz) double cream

2 eggs, separated

15 ml (1 tbsp) lemon juice

7.5 ml (1½ tsp) gelatine

1 Put the gooseberries into a pan
with 60 ml (4 tbsp) water and
75 g (3 oz) caster sugar. Cover and
cook slowly for 20 minutes until
the fruit becomes mushy.

2 To remove the pips, push the
fruit through a nylon sieve into
a clean bowl and let the purée cool
for 30 minutes.

3 Roughly chop 50 g (2 oz) hazel
nuts and fry gently in the
butter until golden, stir in the
finely crushed digestive biscuits.

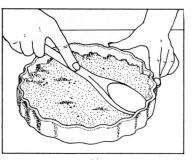

4 Press the digestive biscuit mixture into the base of a 24-cm
(9½-inch) deep fluted flan dish.
Refrigerate for 30 minutes to 1
hour to set.

5 Sieve the cottage cheese into a
large bowl and gradually beat
in the soft cheese followed by the
cream to give a smooth consistency.

6 Whisk the egg yolks and remaining caster sugar until
thick enough to leave a trail on the
surface when the whisk is lifted.
Stir into the cheese mixture.

7 Spoon the lemon juice into a
small bowl with the remaining
water and sprinkle in the gelatine.
Leave to soak for 10 minutes.
Stand the bowl over a pan of gently
simmering water until the gelatine
dissolves then stir into the cheese
mixture with half the fruit purée.

8 Whisk one egg white until stiff
and fold into the mixture then
spoon into the lined flan dish. Refrigerate for 1–2 hours.

9 Meanwhile, brown the remaining nuts: spread them out on a
baking sheet and brown in the
oven at 200°C (400°F) mark 6 for
5–10 minutes. Put into a soft tea
towel and rub off the skins. Chop
and use to decorate. Serve remaining purée separately.

MINI GRAPE CHEESECAKES

1.30* ✳* 247 cals

* plus 30 minutes cooling and 1 hour chilling; freeze after stage 5

Makes 24

275 g (10 oz) plain flour plus 10 ml (2 tsp)

pinch of salt

175 g (6 oz) butter or block margarine, cut into pieces

75 g (3 oz) caster sugar

about 60 ml (4 tbsp) water

225 g (8 oz) full fat soft cheese

2 eggs, beaten

finely grated rind and juice of ½ lemon

175 g (6 oz) black grapes, halved and seeded

150 ml (5 fl oz) whipping cream, whipped

1 Put 275 g (10 oz) flour and the salt into a bowl. Rub in the butter with the fingertips until the mixture resembles breadcrumbs. Stir in 50 g (2 oz) sugar, and water to mix to a smooth dough.

2 Roll out the dough on a lightly floured surface and cut out twelve 7.5-cm (3-inch) circles using a fluted pastry cutter. Use to line twenty-four deep patty tins.

3 Cook the pastry cases 'blind' (see page 147) in the oven at 200°C (400°F) mark 6 for 10 minutes, remove the foil and beans, then return to the oven for a further 5 minutes.

4 Meanwhile, make the filling. In a bowl, beat the soft cheese, eggs, the remaining sugar and flour and the lemon rind and juice until evenly mixed.

5 Pour the filling into the pastry cases. Lower the oven temperature to 150°C (300°F) mark 2 and bake the cheesecakes for 15 minutes until the fillings are set. Cool on a wire rack for 30 minutes then refrigerate for at least 1 hour.

6 Just before serving, decorate the top of each cheesecake with the grapes and piped whipped cream.

LEMON CHEESECAKE

1.00* 🔲 ✳* 375–500 cals

* plus 2–3 hours chilling; freeze after stage 7

Serves 6

1½ packets of lemon jelly

60 ml (4 tbsp) water

2 eggs, separated

300 ml (½ pint) milk

grated rind of 2 lemons

90 ml (6 tbsp) lemon juice

450 g (1 lb) cottage cheese

65 g (2½ oz) caster sugar

150 ml (5 fl oz) double cream

100 g (4 oz) digestive biscuits, finely crushed

50 g (2 oz) butter, melted

fresh lemon slices, to decorate

1 Lightly oil a 20-cm (8-inch) spring-release cake tin fitted with a tubular base.

2 Put the jelly and water into a small pan and warm gently over a low heat, stirring until dissolved. Remove from the heat.

3 Beat together the egg yolks and milk, pour on to the jelly, stir and return to the heat for a few minutes without boiling. Remove from the heat and add the lemon rind and juice.

4 Sieve the cottage cheese and stir into the jelly or put jelly and cottage cheese into an electric blender or food processor and blend to form a smooth purée. Turn the mixture into a bowl and leave to cool for 10 minutes.

5 Whisk the egg whites until stiff, add 15 g (½ oz) sugar and whisk again until stiff. Fold into the cooled cheese mixture.

6 Whip the cream until stiff and fold into the mixture. Turn into the cake tin.

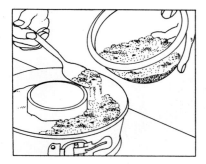

7 Mix together the biscuit crumbs and remaining sugar and stir in the melted butter. Use to cover the cheesecake mixture, pressing it on lightly. Refrigerate for 2–3 hours or overnight. To serve, turn cheesecake out and decorate with slices of lemon.

HOT CHOCOLATE CHEESECAKE

2.45	🎩 🎩	377–471 cals

Serves 8–10

100 g (4 oz) unsalted butter, melted

225 g (8 oz) chocolate digestive
    biscuits, crushed

2 eggs, separated

75 g (3 oz) caster sugar

225 g (8 oz) curd cheese

40 g (1½ oz) ground or very finely
    chopped hazel nuts

150 ml (5 fl oz) double cream

25 g (1 oz) cocoa powder

10 ml (2 tsp) dark rum

icing sugar, to finish

1 Stir the melted butter into the
    crushed biscuits and mix well,
then press into the base and 4 cm
(1½ inches) up the sides of a 20–cm
(8–inch) loose-bottomed cake tin.
Refrigerate for 30 minutes.

2 Whisk the egg yolks and sugar
    together until thick enough to
leave a trail on the surface when
the whisk is lifted.

3 Whisk in the cheese, nuts,
    cream, cocoa powder and rum
until evenly blended.

4 Whisk the egg whites until
    stiff, then fold into the cheese
mixture. Pour into the biscuit base,
then bake in the oven at 170°C
(325°F) mark 3 for 1½–1¾ hours
until risen.

5 Remove carefully from the tin,
    sift the icing sugar over the
top to coat lightly and serve
immediately while still hot.

451

MINCEMEAT TART

| 1.30* | 🔲 | ✳* | 662–993 cals |

* plus chilling and cooling; freeze
before baking at step 7

Serves 4–6

225 g (8 oz) plain flour

pinch of salt

100 g (4 oz) ground almonds

100 g (4 oz) caster sugar

100 g (4 oz) butter

1 egg, beaten

225 g (8 oz) mincemeat

50 g (2 oz) slivered or flaked
almonds, chopped

30 ml (2 tbsp) almond-flavoured
liqueur, rum or brandy

1 medium cooking apple

45–60 ml (3–4 tbsp) apricot jam,
to glaze

single cream or vanilla ice
cream, to serve

1 Make the almond pastry. Sift
the flour and salt onto a
marble slab or other cold surface
and stir in the almonds and sugar.
Make a well in the centre.

2 Cut the butter into small dice
and place in the centre of the
flour. Work with the fingertips,
gradually drawing the flour
mixture into the centre and
rubbing it into the butter. Stir in
the beaten egg.

3 Gather the dough together and
form into a rough ball. (The
dough is rich and quite sticky, so
work as quickly and lightly as
possible, with cold hands.) Wrap
the ball of dough in foil and chill
in the refrigerator for 30 minutes.

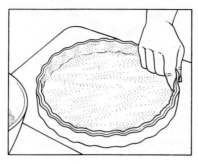

4 Reserve a little dough for the
lattice. With your fingertips,
press the remaining dough into a
20.5 cm (8 inch) loose-bottomed
flan tin standing on a baking sheet.
Chill in the refrigerator for a
further 15 minutes.

5 Meanwhile, prepare the filling.
Put the mincemeat in a bowl
with the chopped almonds and
liqueur. Peel and core the apple,
then grate into the bowl. Stir well
to mix, then spoon into the chilled
flan case. Level the surface.

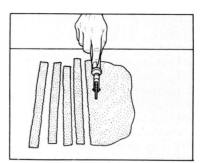

6 Roll out the reserved dough
and cut into strips for the
lattice, using a pastry wheel to give
a pretty edge.

7 Place the strips over the filling
in a lattice pattern, then seal
the edges with water. Bake in the
oven at 190°C (375°F) mark 5 for
35 minutes until the pastry is a
light golden brown.

8 Leave the filling to settle for
10–15 minutes. Heat the
apricot jam gently in a saucepan,
then sieve and brush over the top
of the tart to glaze. Leave for a
further 10–15 minutes and serve
warm or cold, with single cream
or scoops of vanilla ice cream.

Menu Suggestion
Mincemeat Tart makes the most
delicious dessert with cream or ice
cream, but it is just as good served
plain as a teatime cake.

MINCEMEAT TART

As its name suggests, mincemeat
was originally made with minced
meat. The combination of fruit,
spices and a large amount of
alcohol had a preservative effect
on the meat, which was stored in
stone crocks, and always left to
mature from at least the
beginning of December. Beef,
tongue and venison were the
usual meats included in mincemeat, but nowadays only fruit is
used, and shredded beef suet is
added to make up for the lack of
meat. If you can spare the time,
it is much better to make your
own mincemeat for Christmas,
to be sure of knowing exactly
what goes into it. Many
commercial brands have far too
much suet and a watery flavour
and texture, although some of
the more expensive varieties do
contain plump fruit and a fair
amount of alcohol. Read the
label carefully before buying,
and inspect the contents through
the glass jar if possible.

ALMOND AND CHERRY FLAN

1.25	676 cals

Serves 6

225 g (8 oz) plain flour

225 g (8 oz) butter or margarine

2 eggs, separated

30–45 ml (2–3 tbsp) water

350 g (12 oz) fresh ripe black
cherries, stoned

50 g (2 oz) caster sugar

125 g (4 oz) ground almonds

5 ml (1 tsp) almond flavouring

15 ml (1 tbsp) almond-flavoured
liqueur (optional)

50 g (2 oz) self-raising flour

2.5 ml (½ tsp) baking powder

30 ml (2 tbsp) milk

25 g (1 oz) flaked almonds

thick pouring cream, to serve

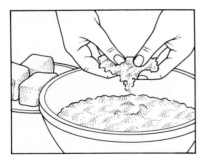

1 Place the plain flour in a large
mixing bowl. Cut up and rub
in 175 g (6 oz) butter until mixture
resembles fine breadcrumbs. Bind
to a firm dough with 1 egg yolk
mixed with water.

2 Roll out the pastry, and use to
line a 24-cm (9½-inch) flan
dish. Bake blind in the oven at
200°C (400°F) mark 6 for 15–20
minutes until set but not browned;
cool slightly.

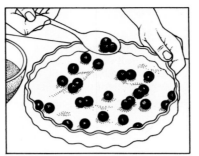

3 Scatter the cherries over the
pastry. Then cream the remaining butter and sugar well together and beat in ground almonds
with the almond flavouring, liqueur, if using, and the remaining
egg yolk. Fold in the self-raising
flour and baking powder, sifted
together, and lightly stir in the
milk.

4 Whisk the two egg whites until
they are stiff, and fold them
into the creamed ingredients.

5 Spread over the cherries in the
flan case and scatter the flaked
almonds on top. Bake in the oven
at 180°C (350°F) mark 4 for about
30 minutes. Serve warm with
cream.

AMARETTO

Almond-flavoured liqueur—
amaretto—a famous Italian
liqueur, which comes from the
town of Saronno near Milan in
northern Italy, is said to be the
best. Look for it in specialist off
licences or Italian delicatessens
with wine counters, and don't be
confused between it and the little
almond-flavoured macaroons
called *amaretti*. The Italians are
so fond of almonds that they
even eat *amaretti* with *amaretto*
after the coffee at the end of a
meal!

BUTTERSCOTCH CREAM PIE

1.15*	❄ 574 cals

* plus 30 minutes chilling and 1 hour cooling

Serves 6

150 g (6 oz) plain flour
1.25 ml ($\frac{1}{4}$ tsp) salt
165 g (5$\frac{1}{2}$ oz) butter or block margarine
10 ml (2 tsp) caster sugar
5 egg yolks and 1 egg white
150 ml ($\frac{1}{4}$ pint) milk
170 g (6 oz) evaporated milk
50 g (2 oz) dark soft brown sugar
15 ml (1 tbsp) cornflour
300 ml (10 fl oz) double cream

1 Put the flour into a bowl with half the salt. Add the 100 g (4 oz) fat in pieces and rub in with the fingertips until the mixture resembles fine breadcrumbs.

2 Stir in the sugar and 1 egg yolk and draw the dough together to form a ball. Add a few drops of cold water if the dough is too dry.

3 Press the dough gently into a 20.5-cm (8-inch) loose-bottomed fluted flan tin or ring placed on a baking sheet. Refrigerate for 30 minutes.

4 Prick the base of the pastry case and bake blind in the oven at 200°C (400°F) mark 6 for 10 minutes. Remove the foil and beans, brush the pastry with the egg white, then return to the oven and bake for a further 10 minutes until crisp and lightly coloured. Leave to cool.

5 Meanwhile, make the filling. Put the milk and evaporated milk in a saucepan and scald by bringing up to boiling point. Put the brown sugar, cornflour, remaining butter, egg yolks and salt in a heavy-based saucepan. Heat gently until the butter has melted and sugar dissolved, then gradually stir in the scalded milks. Stir well until heated through.

6 Cook over gentle heat, whisking constantly until the custard is thick. (Don't worry if the mixture is lumpy at first—keep whisking vigorously with a balloon whisk and it will become smooth.)

7 Remove from the heat and cool slightly, then pour into the baked pastry case. Cover the surface of the butterscotch cream closely with cling film (to prevent a skin forming) and leave for about 1 hour until completely cold.

8 To serve, whip the cream until stiff, then pipe on top of pie. Chill until serving time.

APPLE AND BANANA FRITTERS

1.00	218–328 cals

Serves 4–6

100 g (4 oz) plain flour

pinch of salt

90 ml (6 tbsp) lukewarm water

20 ml (4 tsp) vegetable oil

2 egg whites

1 large cooking apple

2 bananas

juice of $\frac{1}{2}$ a lemon

vegetable oil, for deep frying

caster sugar, to serve

1 Place the flour and salt into a bowl. Make a well in the centre. Add the water and oil and beat to form a smooth batter.

2 Beat the egg whites in a clean dry bowl until they are stiff; then set aside.

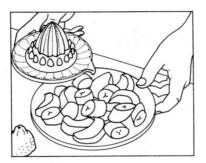

3 Peel, quarter and core the apple. Peel the bananas. Slice the fruit thickly and sprinkle at once with the lemon juice to prevent discoloration.

4 Fold the beaten egg whites into the batter, then immediately dip in the slices of fruit.

5 Deep-fry the fritters a few at a time in hot oil until puffed and light golden. Remove with a slotted spoon and pile on to a serving dish lined with absorbent kitchen paper. Serve immediately, sprinkled with caster sugar.

RUM AND COFFEE JUNKET

0.15*	283 cals

* plus 4 hours setting and 1 hour chilling

Serves 4

568 ml (1 pint) plus 60 ml (4 tbsp) milk—not UHT, long-life or sterilised

30 ml (2 tbsp) caster sugar

10 ml (2 tsp) essence of rennet

10 ml (2 tsp) rum

142 ml (5 fl oz) soured cream

10 ml (2 tsp) coffee and chicory essence

plain and white chocolate, to decorate

1 Put the 568 ml (1 pint) milk in a saucepan and heat until just warm to the finger.

2 Add the sugar, rennet and rum and stir until the sugar has dissolved.

3 Pour the mixture at once into four individual dishes or a 900-ml (1½-pint) shallow, edged serving dish. Put in a warm place, undisturbed, for 4 hours to set.

4 Lightly whisk the soured cream. Gradually add the 60 ml (4 tbsp) milk and the coffee essence, whisking until smooth.

5 Carefully flood the top of the junket with the coffee cream, taking care not to disturb the junket. Decorate with pared or coarsely grated chocolate. Refrigerate for 1 hour.

SPICED APPLE AND PLUM CRUMBLE

1.10*	✳	402 cals

*plus 30 minutes cooling

Serves 6

450 g (1 lb) plums

700 g (1½ lb) cooking apples

100 g (4 oz) butter or margarine

100 g (4 oz) sugar

7.5 ml (1½ tsp) ground mixed spice

175 g (6 oz) plain wholewheat flour

50 g (2 oz) blanched hazelnuts, toasted and chopped

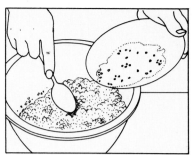

4 Stir the flour and remaining mixed spice well together, then rub in the remaining fat until the mixture resembles fine bread-crumbs. Stir in the rest of the sugar with the chopped hazelnuts.

5 Spoon the crumble mixture over the fruit and bake in the oven at 180°C (350°F) mark 4 for about 40 minutes or until the top is golden, crisp and crumbly.

1 Using a sharp knife, cut the plums in half and then carefully remove the stones.

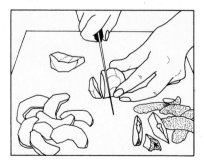

2 Peel, quarter, core and slice the apples. Place in a medium saucepan with 25 g (1 oz) fat, half the sugar and about 5 ml (1 tsp) mixed spice.

3 Cover the pan and cook gently for 15 minutes until the apples begin to soften. Stir in the plums and turn into a 1.1-litre (2-pint) shallow ovenproof dish. Leave to cool for about 30 minutes.

PLUMS FOR COOKING

All plums can be cooked, but dessert varieties tend to be more expensive, therefore it makes good sense to look for cooking plums. Unfortunately, green-grocers and supermarkets do not always specify the variety of plums on sale, but it is always worth asking. Whether you cook with red or yellow plums is entirely a matter of personal choice, but cooking plums worth looking for are Czars, small red cherry plums, Pershore Yellow Egg, Purple Pershore and Belle de Loutain. The famous Victoria plum is a dual purpose fruit: sweet and juicy, it is equally suitable for cooking and eating. Greengages and damsons come from the same family as the plum, and can be used in any recipe calling for plums, although extra sugar may be required.

BLACKBERRY AND PEAR COBBLER

| 0.45 | ✳ | 424 cals |

Serves 4

450 g (1 lb) blackberries

450 g (1 lb) ripe cooking pears (e.g. Conference)

finely grated rind and juice of 1 lemon

2.5 ml (½ tsp) ground cinnamon

225 g (8 oz) self raising flour

pinch of salt

50 g (2 oz) butter or block margarine

25 g (1 oz) caster sugar

about 150 ml (¼ pint) milk plus extra to glaze

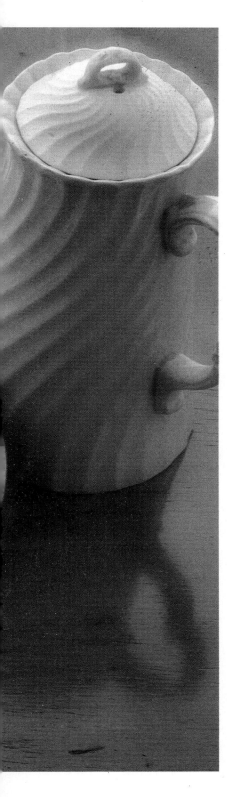

1 Pick over the blackberries and wash them. Peel and core the pears, then slice them thickly.

2 Put the blackberries and pears into a saucepan with the lemon rind and juice and the cinnamon. Poach gently for 15 or 20 minutes until the fruit is juicy and tender.

3 Meanwhile, place the flour and salt into the bowl. Rub in the fat, then stir in the sugar. Gradually add the milk to mix to a fairly soft dough.

4 Roll out the dough on a floured work surface until 1.5 cm (½ inch) thick. Cut out rounds using a fluted 5-cm (2-inch) pastry cutter.

5 Put the fruit in a pie dish and top with overlapping pastry rounds, leaving a gap in the centre. Brush the top of the pastry rounds with milk. Bake in the oven at 220°C (425°F) mark 7 for 10–15 minutes until pastry is golden brown. Serve hot.

COBBLER

Recipes with the strange-sounding title of 'cobbler' are invariably American in origin, although very little is known for certain about the meaning behind the word in culinary terms. Cobblers can be sweet or savoury; they always have a scone dough topping which is stamped into small rounds — sometimes the whole surface of the dish is covered with these rounds of dough, although often they are simply placed around the outside to reveal the filling in the centre. One theory is that the word cobbler originates from the fact that the rounds of dough look like 'cobbles' or stones.

SUSSEX POND PUDDING

4.30	🥄	649 cals

Serves 6

350 g (12 oz) self raising flour
2.5 ml (½ tsp) salt
175 g (6 oz) shredded suet
about 175 ml (6 fl oz) water
100 g (4 oz) butter, cut into pieces
100 g (4 oz) demerara sugar
1 large lemon

1 Place the flour and salt into a bowl, then stir in the suet and enough cold water to make a light, elastic dough. Knead lightly until it is smooth.

2 Roll out two thirds of the pastry on a floured work surface to a circle, 2.5 cm (1 inch) larger all round than the top of a 1.5-litre (2½-pint) pudding basin.

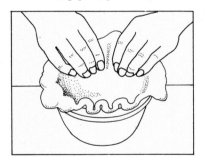

3 Use the rolled-out pastry to line the pudding basin. Put half the butter into the centre with half the sugar.

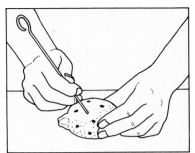

4 Prick the lemon all over with a skewer. Put the whole lemon on top of the butter and sugar. Add the remaining butter and sugar.

5 Roll out the remaining pastry to a circle to fit the top of the pudding. Dampen the edges and seal the lid. Cover with grease-proof paper and foil.

6 Place over a pan of boiling water and steam for about 4 hours, topping up the water as necessary. Remove paper and turn out on to a warm serving dish. During cooking the lemon inside the pudding bursts and produces a delicious lemon sauce. Each serving should have a piece of the lemon, which will be much softened by the cooking.

SUSSEX POND PUDDING

An old-fashioned recipe from the south of England, Sussex Pond Pudding takes its name from the fact that during cooking the whole lemon inside bursts, and the resulting juice combines with the other ingredients of butter and sugar to produce a delicious pool or 'pond' of lemon sauce.

Be sure to prick the fruit thoroughly all over with a skewer before placing it inside the suet pastry case—if you do not do this the lemon will remain whole and spoil the finished effect. This pudding is rich enough to be served on its own, but pouring cream can be handed separately for those who like to indulge themselves!

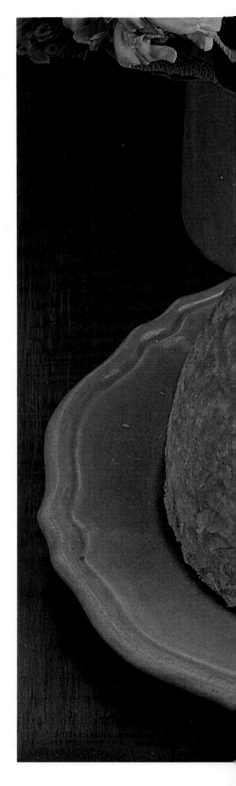

ALMOND EVE'S PUDDING

1.30	784 cals

Serves 4

700 g (1½ lb) cooking apples
5 ml (1 tsp) ground cinnamon
175 g (6 oz) demerara sugar
125 g (4 oz) butter, softened
2 eggs, beaten
125 g (4 oz) self raising flour
25 g (1 oz) ground almonds
2.5 ml (½ tsp) almond flavouring
30 ml (2 tbsp) milk
25 g (1 oz) flaked almonds
icing sugar, to dredge
single cream, to serve

1 Peel, quarter and core the cooking apples, then slice them thickly into a 1.4-litre (2½-pint) ovenproof dish. Combine the cinnamon with 50 g (2 oz) of the demerara sugar and scatter over the apples. Cover tightly with cling film while preparing the topping.

2 Beat the butter and remaining sugar, creaming them together until fluffy. Gradually beat in eggs.

3 Fold in the flour, ground almonds, flavouring and milk. Spread the mixture over the cooking apples.

4 Place the flaked almonds on top in six squares to form a chequerboard effect. Bake in the oven at 180°C (350°F) mark 4 for 50–60 minutes until the apples are tender and the sponge risen and golden brown.

5 Dredge icing sugar between the flaked nut squares. Serve with cream.

— VARIATION —

If liked, you can add 50 g (2 oz) sultanas, currants or raisins to the apple mixture in the base of this delicious family pudding. Grated orange or lemon zest added to the sponge topping also adds extra flavour—and goes particularly well with the cinnamon-flavoured apples.

LOCKSHEN PUDDING

1.00	356 cals

Serves 4

100 g (4 oz) vermicelli (lockshen)
pinch of salt
1 egg
50 g (2 oz) sugar
1.25 ml ($\frac{1}{4}$ tsp) ground cinnamon
finely grated rind of $\frac{1}{2}$ a lemon
50 g (2 oz) currants
50 g (2 oz) chopped almonds (optional)
25 g (1 oz) margarine

1 Drop the vermicelli into rapidly boiling salted water and cook for about 10 minutes until tender.

2 Drain into a sieve and rinse with plenty of hot water to remove excess starch. Drain well.

3 Whisk the egg and sugar together and stir in the cinnamon, rind, currants and nuts, if using. Then stir in the vermicelli.

4 Melt the margarine in a 5-cm (2-inch) deep, flameproof baking dish until hot but not smoking. Swirl around the dish to coat the sides and pour the excess into the noodle mixture.

5 Stir well and pour the mixture into the baking dish. Bake in the oven at 190°C (375°F) mark 5 for 45 minutes until set, crisp and brown on top. Serve hot.

ROLY-POLY WITH HOT JAM SAUCE

2.30	499 cals

Serves 4

175 g (6 oz) self raising flour
1.25 ml ($\frac{1}{4}$ tsp) salt
75 g (3 oz) shredded suet
finely grated rind of 1 orange
45–60 ml (3–4 tbsp) hot water
90 ml (6 tbsp) red jam plus 45 ml (3 tbsp)
a little milk
finely grated rind of 1 orange
10 ml (2 tsp) arrowroot
150 ml ($\frac{1}{4}$ pint) fresh orange juice

1 Place the flour and salt into a bowl, then stir in the suet and orange rind. Gradually stir in the hot water until the dough binds together. Form into a ball, turn out on to a floured surface and knead lightly until smooth.

2 Roll out the dough on a floured work surface to a 25 × 20 cm (10 × 8 inch) oblong. Spread the first quantity of jam over the dough to 0.5 cm ($\frac{1}{4}$ inch) of the edges. Brush the edges with milk.

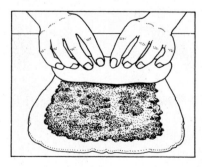

3 Roll up the pastry evenly like a Swiss roll, starting from one short side.

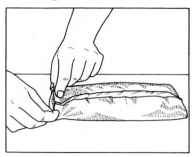

4 Place the roll, seam side down, on a sheet of greased foil measuring at least 35 × 23 cm (12 × 9 inches). Wrap the foil loosely around the roll to allow room for expansion during cooking. Seal well.

5 Place the roly-poly in the top of a steamer over a pan of boiling water and steam for 1$\frac{1}{2}$–2 hours, topping up the water as necessary.

6 Just before serving, make the sauce. Put the remaining jam and orange rind in a heavy-based saucepan. Mix the arrowroot to a paste with a little of the orange juice, then stir the remaining orange juice into the pan. Heat gently until the jam has melted, then stir in the arrowroot paste and bring to the boil. Simmer until thickened, stirring constantly.

7 Unwrap the roly-poly and place on a warmed serving plate. Pour over the hot jam sauce and serve immediately.

SPOTTED DICK

2.30	604 cals

Serves 4

100 g (4 oz) fresh white breadcrumbs
75 g (3 oz) self raising flour
pinch of salt
75 g (3 oz) shredded suet
50 g (2 oz) caster sugar
175 g (6 oz) currants
finely grated rind of ½ a lemon
75–90 ml (5–6 tbsp) milk
custard, to serve

1 Place the breadcrumbs, flour, salt, suet, sugar, currants and lemon rind in a bowl. Stir well until thoroughly mixed.

2 Add enough milk to the dry ingredients to bind together, cutting it through with a palette knife until well mixed. Using one hand only, bring the ingredients together to form a soft, slightly sticky dough.

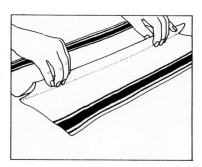

4 Make a 5-cm (2-inch) pleat across a fine-textured, colourfast teatowel or pudding cloth. Alternatively pleat together sheets of greased, greaseproof paper and strong kitchen foil. Encase the roll in the cloth or foil, pleating the open edges tightly together. Tie the ends securely with string to form a cracker shape. Make a string handle across the top.

5 Lower the suet roll into a large saucepan, two-thirds full of boiling water, curling it if necessary to fit the pan. Cover the pan, lower the heat to a gentle boil and cook for 2 hours. Top up with boiling water at intervals.

6 Lift the spotted dick out of the water. Snip the string and gently roll the pudding on to a serving plate. Decorate with lemon slices if liked and serve immediately, with custard.

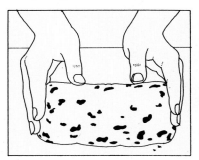

3 Turn the dough out on to a floured work surface. Dust lightly with flour, then knead gently until just smooth. Shape the dough into a neat roll about 15 cm (6 inches) in length.

QUEEN OF PUDDINGS

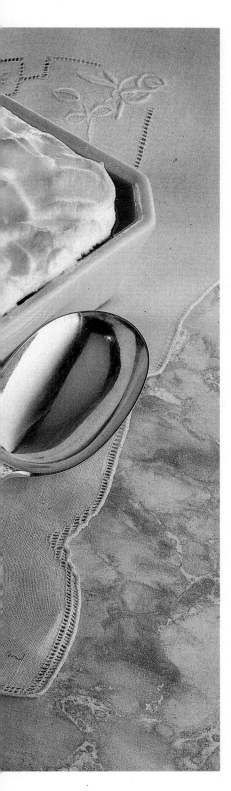

1.30	306 cals

Serves 4

450 ml (¾ pint) milk

25 g (1 oz) butter or margarine

finely grated rind of ½ a lemon

2 eggs, separated

50 g (2 oz) caster sugar

75 g (3 oz) fresh white breadcrumbs

30 ml (2 tbsp) red jam

1 Put the milk, fat and lemon rind in a saucepan and heat gently. Whisk the egg yolks and half of the sugar lightly and pour on the milk, stirring well.

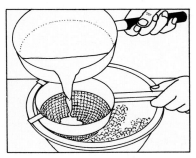

2 Strain the milk over the breadcrumbs. Pour into a greased 1.1-litre (2-pint) ovenproof dish and leave to stand for 15 minutes.

3 Bake in the oven at 180°C (350°F) mark 4 for 25–30 minutes, until lightly set; remove from the oven.

4 Put the jam in a small saucepan. Warm it over low heat, then spread it over the pudding.

5 Whisk the egg whites until stiff and add half the remaining sugar; whisk again and fold in the remaining sugar.

6 Pile the meringue on top of the jam and bake for a further 15–20 minutes, until the meringue is lightly browned.

QUEEN OF PUDDINGS

Queen of Puddings is a traditional English pudding from the nineteenth century. Original recipes for this homely dish (which can be made entirely from store-cupboard ingredients) used red jam and flavoured the pudding with lemon rind, but you can make your own version according to what ingredients you have to hand. Any kind of jam can be used of course, or orange marmalade or ginger marmalade can be used instead of the jam, and grated orange rind or a little finely chopped stem ginger instead of the lemon. Lemon curd makes a delicious Queen of Puddings, with 25 g (1 oz) desiccated coconut added to the breadcrumb and sugar mixture.

When finishing the pudding with the meringue topping, make absolutely sure that it covers the surface completely and that there are no gaps around the edges for the jam to seep through during baking. After piling the meringue on top, draw it up into peaks with the back of a metal spoon for an attractive effect. Better still, for a neater finish, pipe the meringue on top with a large star nozzle.

CREMA FRITTA

1.25*	🍴	314–471 cals

* plus 2–3 hours cooling

Serves 4–6

3 eggs

50 g (2 oz) caster sugar

50 g (2 oz) plain flour

225 ml (8 fl oz) milk

300 ml (10 fl oz) single cream

finely grated rind of ½ a lemon

100 g (4 oz) dry white breadcrumbs

vegetable oil, for frying

caster sugar, to serve

1 In a large bowl, beat 2 eggs and the sugar together until the mixture is pale.

2 Add the flour, beating all the time, and then, very slowly, beat in the milk and cream. Add the lemon rind.

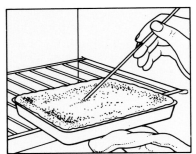

3 Pour the mixture into a buttered shallow 18-cm (7-inch) square cake tin. Bake in the oven at 180°C (350°F) mark 4 for about 1 hour, until a skewer inserted in the middle comes out clean. Leave to cool for 2–3 hours, preferably overnight.

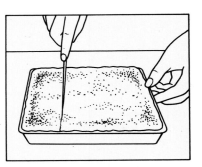

4 When completely cold, cut into sixteen cubes and remove from the cake tin.

5 Beat the remaining egg in a bowl. Dip the cubes in the egg and then in the breadcrumbs until well coated.

6 Heat the oil in a frying pan and when hot, slide in the cubes. Fry for 2–3 minutes until golden brown and a crust is formed. Turn and fry the second side. Drain well on absorbent kitchen paper. Serve immediately, sprinkled with caster sugar.

CREMA FRITTA

Literally translated, this simple Italian dessert means 'fried cream', which is in fact exactly what it is—a thick creamy sauce which is baked, chilled and cut into squares, then fried in oil until crisp and golden.

In Italy, it is traditional to celebrate *Carnevale*—the day be-fore Lent—by eating *crema fritta*. Children and young people invite friends home and everyone eats *crema fritta* in the way that people in other countries eat pancakes. Sprinkled liberally with white sugar, they are always eaten in-formally—with the fingers.

FLOATING ISLANDS

0.50*	🍳	412 cals

* plus 1 hour chilling

Serves 4

5 egg yolks, beaten

450 ml (¾ pint) milk

50 g (2 oz) caster sugar plus 75 ml (5 tbsp)

2.5 ml (½ tsp) vanilla flavouring

1 egg white

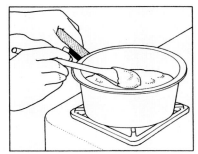

1 Make custard. Put egg yolks, milk and 50 g (2 oz) sugar in the top of a double boiler, or in a heavy-based saucepan over low heat. Cook gently for about 15 minutes, stirring constantly, until the mixture thickens and coats the back of the spoon. Stir in the vanilla flavouring.

2 Divide the custard between four stemmed glasses or dessert dishes. Cover and refrigerate for 1 hour.

3 Meanwhile, whisk the egg white until it will stand in stiff peaks. Add 30 ml (2 tbsp) sugar and whisk again until the sugar is dissolved.

4 Put some cold water into a shallow tin. Bring to a gentle simmer and spoon on the meringue in four even mounds. Poach for about 5 minutes until set, turning once.

5 Remove the meringues with a slotted spoon, drain for a minute on absorbent kitchen paper and spoon on to the custard in the glasses.

6 Put the remaining sugar into a heavy-based saucepan and cook, stirring constantly, for about 3 minutes or until it forms a golden syrup.

7 Remove from the heat and leave for 2 minutes to cool slightly, then drizzle a little of the warm syrup over the top of each meringue. Serve immediately.

Baking

DARK GINGER CAKE

1.45*	✳*	332–442 cals

* plus 2 hours cooling, freeze after
   stage 3

Serves 6–8

75 g (3 oz) black treacle

75 g (3 oz) golden syrup

50 g (2 oz) dark soft brown sugar

75 g (3 oz) butter or block
  margarine

225 g (8 oz) flour

10 ml (2 tsp) ground ginger

5 ml (1 tsp) mixed spice

5 ml (1 tsp) bicarbonate of soda

1 egg, beaten

100 ml (4 fl oz) milk

100 g (4 oz) icing sugar

15 ml (1 tbsp) warm water

50 g (2 oz) stem ginger, drained and
  sliced

1 Base-line and grease an 18-cm
(7-inch) round deep cake tin.
In a saucepan, gently heat the
treacle, syrup, sugar and butter
for 5 minutes until blended.

2 Sift the flour, spices and bicarbonate of soda together into
a bowl. Make a well in the centre
and pour in the treacle mixture
with egg and milk. Beat well with
a wooden spoon until smooth.

3 Pour into the prepared tin and
bake in the oven at 150°C
(300°F) mark 2 for about 1 hour
30 minutes. Turn out on to a wire
rack to cool for at least 2 hours.

4 To make the glacé icing, sift
the icing sugar into a bowl and
gradually add the water. The icing
should be thick enough to coat the
back of a spoon. If necessary add
more water or sugar to adjust the
consistency. Use at once to decorate the cake. Leave for 30 minutes
to set slightly then decorate with
the ginger.

GINGER

This spicy, iced version of old-
fashioned gingerbread contains
two different forms of ginger—
ground ginger in the cake, stem
ginger in the icing. Both come
from the ginger root, a spice
which has origins long before
recorded history, when it was
used as a medicine rather than a
flavouring. Most of the ginger
we buy comes from the Far East,
where it first originated.

  Ground ginger is made by
grinding the dried root very
finely. Jamaica ginger is said to
be the finest and most delicate
in flavour, but it is rare that
the type of ginger is specified.

  Stem ginger is also called preserved or Chinese ginger. It is
the young tender roots which are
cleaned and peeled then simmered in a heavy syrup. Look for
it in the prettily patterned
Chinese jars, especially around
Christmas time.

GUERNSEY APPLE CAKE

2.00*	✳	337 cals

* plus 1–2 hours cooling

Serves 8

225 g (8 oz) wholewheat flour

10 ml (2 tsp) freshly ground
    nutmeg

5 ml (1 tsp) ground cinnamon

10 ml (2 tsp) baking powder

225 g (8 oz) cooking apples, peeled,
    cored and chopped

125 g (4 oz) butter

225 g (8 oz) soft dark brown sugar

2 eggs, beaten

a little milk (optional)

15 ml (1 tbsp) clear honey

15 ml (1 tbsp) demerara sugar

1 Grease an 18-cm (7-inch) deep
round cake tin. Line with
greaseproof paper and grease the
paper.

2 Add the wholewheat flour,
nutmeg, cinnamon and baking
powder into a bowl. Mix in the
chopped cooking apples.

3 Put the butter and sugar into a
bowl and beat until pale and
fluffy. Add the eggs, a little at a
time, and continue to beat.

4 Fold the flour mixture into the
creamed mixture with a little
milk, if necessary, to give a dropping consistency.

5 Turn the mixture into the prepared tin. Bake in the oven at
170°C (325°F) mark 3 for about
1½ hours. Turn out on to a wire
rack to cool for 1–2 hours. Brush
with honey and sprinkle with the
demerara sugar to decorate. Eat
within 1–2 days.

HALF-POUND CAKE

| 3.00* | ✳ | 658 cals |

* plus 2 hours cooling

Serves 8

225 g (8 oz) butter or margarine

225 g (8 oz) caster sugar

4 eggs, beaten

225 g (8 oz) plain flour

2.5 ml ($\frac{1}{2}$ tsp) salt

2.5 ml ($\frac{1}{2}$ tsp) mixed spice

225 g (8 oz) seedless raisins

225 g (8 oz) mixed currants and sultanas

100 g (4 oz) glacé cherries, halved

15 ml (1 tbsp) brandy

a few walnut halves

1 Grease a 20-cm (8-inch) round cake tin. Line with greaseproof paper and grease the paper.

2 Put the fat and sugar into a bowl and beat together until pale and fluffy. Add the egg a little at a time, beating well after each addition.

3 Sift the flour, salt and spice together into a bowl and stir in the raisins, mixed fruit and cherries. Fold the flour and fruit into the creamed mixture with a metal spoon.

4 Add the brandy and mix to a soft dropping consistency. Turn the mixture into the prepared tin, level the surface and arrange the nuts on top.

5 Bake in the oven at 150°C (300°F) mark 2 for about 2½ hours. Leave the cake for 15 minutes to cool slightly in the tin, then turn out on to a wire rack to cool completely for 2 hours.

ORANGE-GLAZED GINGER CAKE

1.45*	✳*	451 cals

* plus 1 hour setting and 2 hours cooling; freeze after stage 4

Serves 8

125 g (4 oz) lard

125 g (4 oz) caster sugar

1 egg, beaten

275 g (10 oz) plain flour

7.5 ml (1½ tsp) bicarbonate of soda

2.5 ml (½ tsp) salt

5 ml (1 tsp) ground cinnamon

5 ml (1 tsp) ground ginger

100 g (4 oz) golden syrup

100 g (4 oz) black treacle

225 ml (8 fl oz) water

pared rind and juice of 1 orange

1 Grease a 23-cm (9-inch) round cake tin. Line with greaseproof paper and grease the paper.

2 Put the lard and sugar into a bowl and beat together until pale and fluffy. Beat in the egg, then the flour, bicarbonate of soda, salt and spices.

3 Warm together the golden syrup and black treacle in a pan with the water and bring to the boil. Stir into the lard mixture, beating all the time until completely incorporated.

4 Turn the mixture into the prepared tin. Bake in the oven at 180°C (350°F) mark 4 for about 50 minutes or until a fine warmed skewer inserted in the centre comes out clean. Cool in the tin for about 10 minutes before turning out on to a wire rack to cool completely for 2 hours.

5 Cut the orange rind into strips; put into a pan and cover with water. Boil until tender, about 10 minutes and drain well. Make up 100 g (4 oz) glacé icing (see page 154), using 30 ml (2 tbsp) orange juice.

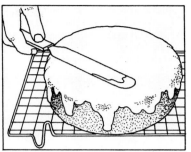

6 Evenly coat the top of the cake and leave to set for 1 hour. Sprinkle the orange strips around the top.

THE GILT ON THE GINGERBREAD

Medieval gingerbread would have been made with honey, not treacle or syrup, but it would have been spiced much the same as this cake. For sale in the markets and fairgrounds it was made in large slabs. Decorative patterns were traditionally made on the bread, sometimes with real gold leaf, and spices such as cloves, of which the heads might be gilded. Our strips of orange rind may seem a poor substitute, but they go well with the spices.

LEMON SWISS ROLL

| 1.00* | 🇪 | ✱* | 376–502 cals |

* plus 1 hour setting and 30 minutes
cooling; freeze after stage 4

Serves 6–8

3 eggs, size 2

100 g (4 oz) caster sugar

100 g (4 oz) plain flour

150 ml (5 fl oz) double cream

about 275 g (10 oz) lemon curd

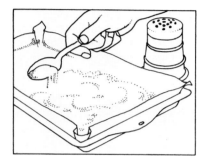

1 Grease a 33 × 23 × 1.5 cm
(13 × 9 × ½ inch) Swiss roll tin.
Line the base with greaseproof
paper and grease the paper. Dust
with caster sugar and flour.

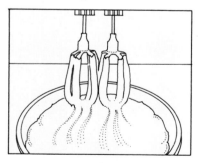

2 Whisk the eggs and sugar in a
bowl until thick enough to leave
a trail on the surface when the
whisk is lifted. Sift in flour and
fold gently through the mixture.

3 Turn the mixture into the prepared tin and level the surface.
Bake in the oven at 200°C (400°F)
mark 6 for 10–12 minutes or until
the cake springs back when pressed
lightly with a finger and has shrunk
away a little from the tin.

4 Sugar a sheet of greaseproof
paper and turn the cake out on
to it. Roll up with the paper inside.
Transfer to a wire rack and leave
to cool for 30 minutes.

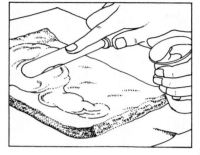

5 Whip the cream until it just
holds its shape. Unroll the
Swiss roll and spread with three
quarters of the lemon curd. Top
with cream then roll up again and
place on a serving plate.

6 Make 100 g (4 oz) glacé icing
(see page 154), using 20 ml (4
tsp) water and spoon on to the
Swiss roll. Immediately, using the
point of a teaspoon, draw rough
lines of lemon curd across the
icing and pull a skewer through to
form a feather pattern. Leave to
set, about 1 hour.

RASPBERRY ROULADE

1.00* ✳* 448 cals

* plus 30 minutes cooling; freeze after
rolling the roulade

Serves 6

450 g (1 lb) raspberries, hulled

5 eggs, separated

125 g (4 oz) caster sugar

50 g (2 oz) plain flour

30 ml (2 tbsp) orange-flavoured
liqueur

300 ml (10 fl oz) double cream

45 ml (3 tbsp) icing sugar

1 Cut out two sheets of greaseproof paper and one of foil,
38 × 40 cm (15 × 16 inches) each.

2 Place the papers on top of each
other with the foil underneath.
Fold up 4 cm (1½ inches) on all
four sides and secure the corners
with paperclips to form a case.

3 Brush the case out with melted
lard, and when set, dust with
caster sugar. Put the case on a
baking sheet.

4 Put half the raspberries into a
blender and work until just
smooth, then press through a nylon
sieve to remove the pips.

5 Whisk the egg yolks in a deep
bowl with the caster sugar
until really thick. Gradually whisk
in the raspberry purée, keeping
the mixture stiff.

6 Sift the flour over the surface
and fold lightly into the egg
and raspberry mixture.

7 Whisk the egg whites until
stiff, and fold them gently
through the raspberry mixture.

8 Turn into the prepared paper
case and smooth the surface.
Bake in the oven at 200°C (400°F)
mark 6 for about 12 minutes or
until the mixture springs back
when pressed lightly with a finger.

9 Cover immediately with a sheet
of greaseproof paper which has
been wrung out under the cold
tap. Lay a clean tea towel over the
top and leave for about 30 minutes
to cool.

10 Meanwhile, reserving six
raspberries for decoration,
sprinkle the rest with the liqueur
and sift over the icing sugar. Whip
the cream until it is just stiff
enough to hold its shape.

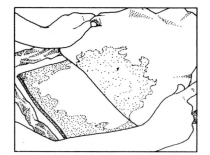

11 Remove the cloth from the
roulade and carefully ease
off the top greaseproof paper. Remove the paperclips. Trim the
edges of the roulade, spread three
quarters of the cream over the top
and scatter with raspberries.

12 Carefully roll up the
roulade, gradually easing off
the paper. Roll on to a large flat
serving plate and decorate with
whirls of cream. Just before
serving, dust with sieved icing
sugar and decorate with the reserved raspberries.

APRICOT CRUNCH

1.15*	✳	195 cals

* plus 1½ hours cooling

Makes 16 wedges

75 g (3 oz) dried apricots

200 ml (⅓ pint) water

100 g (4 oz) butter

100 g (4 oz) demerara sugar

75 ml (5 tbsp) golden syrup

200 g (7 oz) crunchy toasted
muesli cereal

140 g (5 oz) rolled oats

2.5 ml (½ tsp) mixed spice

10 ml (2 tsp) lemon juice

1 Base-line two 18-cm (7-inch) round sandwich tins with non-stick paper.

2 Simmer the apricots gently in the water for about 10 minutes, or until softened. Blend contents of pan to form a smooth purée. Cool for about 1 hour.

3 Slowly melt the butter, sugar and syrup. Stir in the cereal and oats and continue stirring until thoroughly combined. Add the puréed apricots, mixed spice and lemon juice. Mix well.

4 Divide the mixture between the prepared tins and spread evenly over the base. Press down well to level the surface.

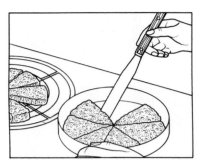

5 Bake in the oven at 180°C (350°F) mark 4 for about 35 minutes. Cut each round into eight wedges. Cool in the tin for 30 minutes until firm. Carefully ease the wedges out of the tin and store in an airtight container when completely cold.

LEMON SEED CAKE

1.35*	✳*	604–806 cals

*plus 1 hour cooling; freeze after stage 3

Serves 6–8

325 g (11 oz) butter

175 g (6 oz) soft brown sugar

finely grated rind and juice of 2 large lemons

3 eggs, separated

250 g (9 oz) self-raising flour

10 ml (2 tsp) caraway seeds

175 g (6 oz) icing sugar, plus a little extra to decorate

1 Grease and base-line an 18-cm (7-inch) round cake tin. In a bowl, cream together 175 g (6 oz) butter, the brown sugar and the rind from one lemon, until fluffy.

2 Beat in the egg yolks, then stir in flour, caraway seeds and 45 ml (3 tbsp) lemon juice.

3 Fold in the stiffly whisked egg whites; turn into tin. Bake in the oven at 180°C (350°F) mark 4 for 1 hour. Turn out onto a wire rack and leave to cool for 1 hour.

4 To make the butter icing, cream remaining butter until fluffy. Gradually sift in icing sugar until smooth. Beat in 15 ml (1 tbsp) lemon juice and the remaining grated lemon rind.

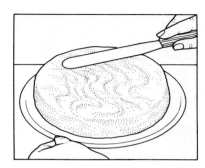

5 Use the lemon butter icing to completely coat the cake and then swirl using a small palette knife. Dust lightly with sifted icing sugar. Best eaten the next day.

CARAMEL BANANA TORTE

1.45*	🍳 🍳	✳*	403 cals

* plus 2 hours cooling; freeze after stage 4

Serves 8

175 g (6 oz) self-raising flour
1.25 ml (¼ tsp) baking powder
1.25 ml (¼ tsp) bicarbonate of soda
50 g (2 oz) butter, cut into pieces
150 g (5 oz) caster sugar
350 g (12 oz) ripe bananas
2.5 ml (½ tsp) freshly grated nutmeg
45 ml (3 tbsp) milk
1 egg, beaten
75 g (3 oz) sugar
175 g (6 oz) full fat soft cheese
30 ml (2 tbsp) lemon juice
30 ml (2 tbsp) icing sugar
50 g (2 oz) flaked almonds, browned

1 Grease a 20-cm (8-inch) round cake tin. Base-line with grease-proof paper and grease the paper.

2 Sift the flour, baking powder and bicarbonate of soda into a bowl. Rub in the butter until the mixture resembles fine bread-crumbs then stir in the caster sugar.

3 Peel half the bananas and mash them in a bowl then beat in the grated nutmeg, milk and egg and stir into the dry ingredients. Turn the mixture into the pre-pared tin and level the surface.

4 Bake in the oven at 180°C (350°F) mark 4 for about 40 minutes or until a warmed fine skewer inserted in the centre comes out clean. Cool in tin for 5 minutes before turning out on to wire rack to cool completely (about 2 hours). Slice the cake in half horizontally.

5 Make the caramel. Put rest of sugar into a small pan. Dissolve, without stirring, over gentle heat, then boil until a rich brown colour.

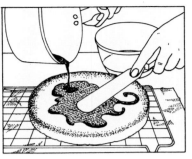

6 When the caramel is ready, immediately pour it over the top surface of the cake. Use an oiled knife to spread the caramel over the cake.

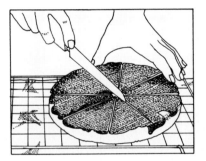

7 Mark the caramel topped cake into eight portions with the point of a knife.

8 Put the soft cheese, lemon juice and icing sugar into a bowl and beat together. Peel and chop the remaining bananas and add to half of the cheese mixture. Use to sandwich the cakes together.

9 Spread a little cheese mixture around the sides and cover with most of the almonds. Decorate top with the remaining cheese mixture and almonds.

BLACK FOREST GÂTEAU

1.45* 🍳 ✻✻

516–645 cals

* plus 30 minutes cooling; freeze after stage 5 after cooling

Serves 8–10

100 g (4 oz) butter

6 eggs

225 g (8 oz) caster sugar

75 g (3 oz) plain flour

50 g (2 oz) cocoa powder

2.5 ml (½ tsp) vanilla flavouring

two 425-g (15-oz) cans stoned black cherries

60 ml (4 tbsp) kirsch

600 ml (20 fl oz) whipping cream

100 g (4 oz) chocolate curls, to decorate (see page 153)

5 ml (1 tsp) arrowroot

1 Grease a 23-cm (9-inch) round cake tin. Line with greaseproof paper and grease the paper. Put the butter into a bowl, stand this over a pan of warm water and beat it until really soft but not melted.

2 Put the eggs and sugar into a large bowl and whisk until thick enough to leave a trail on the surface when the whisk is lifted.

3 Sift the flour and cocoa into the mixture and lightly fold in with a metal spoon. Fold in vanilla flavouring and softened butter.

4 Turn the mixture into the prepared tin, tilt the tin to spread the mixture evenly, and bake in the oven at 180°C (350°F) mark 4 for about 40 minutes until risen and firm to the touch.

5 Turn out of the tin on to a wire rack, covered with greaseproof paper, to cool for 30 minutes. Strain the syrup from the cans of cherries, reserving the cherries, 45 ml (3 tbsp) syrup for the glaze and 75 ml (5 tbsp) syrup for the filling. Add the kirsch to latter syrup.

6 Cut the cake into three horizontally. Place a layer on a flat plate and spoon over 45 ml (3 tbsp) of the kirsch-flavoured syrup.

7 Whip the cream until it holds its shape and spread a little thinly over the soaked sponge. Reserve a quarter of the cherries for decoration and scatter half the remainder over the cream.

8 Repeat the layers of sponge, syrup, cream and cherries. Top with the third cake round and spoon over the remaining kirsch-flavoured syrup.

9 Spread a thin layer of cream around the sides of the cake, reserving a third to decorate. Press on the chocolate curls, reserving a few to decorate the top.

10 Fill a piping bag, fitted with a large star nozzle, with the remaining whipped cream and pipe whirls of cream around the edge of the cake. Top each whirl with a chocolate curl.

11 Fill the centre with the reserved cherries. Blend the arrowroot with the reserved 45 ml (3 tbsp) syrup and boil, stirring. Brush the glaze over the cherries.

DEVIL'S FOOD CAKE

| 2.00* | ⏢ | ❋* | 696 cals |

* plus 30 minutes cooling and 1 hour standing time; freeze after stage 8

Serves 8

| 75 g (3 oz) plain chocolate plus 25 g (1 oz) (optional) |
| 250 g (9 oz) soft light brown sugar |
| 200 ml (⅓ pint) milk |
| 75 g (3 oz) butter or block margarine |
| 2 eggs |
| 175 g (6 oz) plain flour |
| 3.75 ml (¾ tsp) bicarbonate of soda |
| 450 g (1 lb) caster sugar |
| 120 ml (8 tbsp) water |
| 2 egg whites |

1 Lightly brush two 19-cm (7½-inch) sandwich tins with melted lard. Base-line with grease-proof paper and grease the paper. Leave for 5 minutes to set, then dust with sugar and flour.

2 Break 75 g (3 oz) of the chocolate in small pieces into a saucepan. Add 75 g (3 oz) of the brown sugar and the milk. Heat very gently, stirring to dissolve the sugar and blend the ingredients, then remove from the heat and leave to cool for 10 minutes.

3 Put the butter into a bowl and beat until pale and soft. Gradually add the remaining brown sugar and beat until pale and fluffy.

4 Lightly whisk the eggs and gradually beat into the creamed mixture. Slowly add the cooled chocolate mixture beating until combined.

5 Sift the flour and bicarbonate of soda into the creamed mixture and gently fold in using a metal spoon. Turn the mixture into prepared tins, then tap gently to level it.

6 Bake in the oven at 180°C (350°F) mark 4 for about 35 minutes. The cakes are cooked when they spring back when pressed lightly with a finger and have shrunk away a little from the sandwich tins.

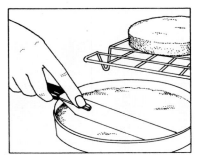

7 Cool in the tins for a couple of minutes before turning out on to a wire rack to cool completely. Ease them away from the tins using a palette knife, taking care not to break the crust.

8 Tap the tins on the work surface to loosen the cakes. Gently pull off the paper and leave to cool.

9 Put the sugar for the frosting in a pan with the water, dissolve over a low heat, then boil rapidly to 115°C (240°F) on a sugar thermometer, or until the mixture reaches the soft ball stage. Check by plunging a teaspoonful into a bowl of iced water. It should form a ball in your fingers.

10 Meanwhile, whisk the egg whites in a large bowl until stiff. Allow the bubbles in the syrup to settle, then slowly pour the hot syrup on to the egg whites, beating constantly. Once all the sugar syrup is added, continue beating until the mixture stands in peaks and just starts to become matt round the edges. (The icing sets quickly, so work rapidly.)

11 Sandwich the cakes together with a little of the frosting. Spread the remaining frosting over the cake with a palette knife. Pull the icing up into peaks all over, then leave the cake for about 30 minutes, to allow the icing to set slightly.

12 Break up the chocolate, if using, and put it in a small bowl over a pan of hot water. Heat gently, stirring, until the chocolate has melted. Dribble the chocolate over the top of the cake with a teaspoon to make a swirl pattern. Leave for 30 minutes before serving.

AMERICAN CAKES

Two classic cakes from America are Angel Food Cake and Devil's Food Cake. The first is an airy vanilla-flavoured sponge. It is very white in colour and light in texture because it is made with flour and egg whites, with no egg yolks. Its opposite number is the rich, moist chocolate cake recipe given here. Generously filled and coated with frosting, Devil's Food Cake is a favourite for serving as a dinnertime dessert, or at coffee parties.

MARBLED CHOCOLATE RING CAKE

| 2.00* | 🗋 🗋 | ✳* | 775 cals |

* plus 1¼ hours cooling and 1 hour
setting; freeze after stage 6

Serves 8

| 250 g (9 oz) plain chocolate |
| 5 ml (1 tsp) vanilla flavouring |
| 45 ml (3 tbsp) water |
| 350 g (12 oz) butter |
| 225 g (8 oz) caster sugar |
| 4 eggs, size 2, beaten |
| 225 g (8 oz) plain flour |
| 10 ml (2 tsp) baking powder |
| 2.5 ml (½ tsp) salt |
| 50 g (2 oz) ground almonds |
| 30 ml (2 tbsp) milk |

1 Grease a 1.7-litre (3-pint) ring
mould. Break 50 g (2 oz) chocolate into a heatproof bowl. Add the
vanilla flavouring and 15 ml
(1 tbsp) water and place over simmering water. Stir until the chocolate is melted, then remove from
heat and leave to cool for 10
minutes.

2 Put 225 g (8 oz) butter and the
caster sugar into a bowl and
beat together until pale and fluffy.
Beat in the eggs one at a time.

3 Fold the flour, baking powder
and salt into the creamed mixture with the ground almonds. Stir
in the milk. Spoon half the mixture into base of ring mould.

4 Stir the cooled but still soft
chocolate into the remaining
mixture. Spoon into the tin.

5 Draw a knife through the cake
mixture in a spiral. Level the
surface of the mixture again.

6 Bake in the oven at 180°C
(350°F) mark 4 for about 55
minutes or until a fine warmed
skewer inserted in the centre
comes out clean. Turn out on to a
wire rack to cool for 1 hour.

7 Make the chocolate frosting.
Break 150 g (5 oz) chocolate
into a heatproof bowl with 30 ml
(2 tbsp) water and the remaining
butter. Place over simmering water
and stir until the chocolate is
melted, then pour over the cooled
cake, working quickly to coat top
and sides. Leave to set for 1 hour.

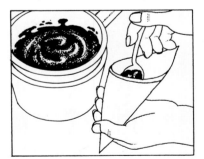

8 Melt the remaining chocolate
over simmering water as before. Spoon into a greaseproof
paper piping bag, snip off the tip
and drizzle chocolate over the cake.

CHOCOLATE COFFEE REFRIGERATOR SLICE

| 1.00* | 🍳 | ✳* |

752–1129 cals

* plus 3–4 hours chilling; freeze after stage 7

Serves 4–6

30 ml (2 tbsp) instant coffee granules

250 ml (7 fl oz) boiling water

45 ml (3 tbsp) brandy

125 g (4 oz) plain chocolate

125 g (4 oz) unsalted butter, softened

50 g (2 oz) icing sugar

2 egg yolks

300 ml (10 fl oz) whipping cream

50 g (2 oz) chopped almonds, toasted

about 30 sponge fingers

coffee beans, to decorate

1 Grease a 22 × 11.5 cm ($8\frac{1}{2} \times 4\frac{1}{2}$ inch) top measurement loaf tin and base-line with greaseproof paper. Grease the paper.

2 Make up the coffee granules with the boiling water and stir in the brandy. Set aside to cool for 15 minutes.

3 Break the chocolate into a small heatproof bowl with 15 ml (1 tbsp) water and place over simmering water. Stir until the chocolate is melted then remove from the heat and allow to cool for about 5 minutes.

4 Sift the icing sugar into a bowl. Add the butter and beat them together until pale and fluffy. Add the egg yolks, beating well.

5 Lightly whip the cream and refrigerate half of it. Stir the remaining cream, the cooled chocolate and the nuts into the butter and egg yolk mixture.

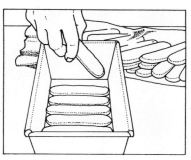

6 Line the bottom of the prepared loaf tin with sponge fingers, cutting to fit if necessary. Spoon over one quarter of the coffee and brandy mixture. Spoon over one third of the chocolate mixture.

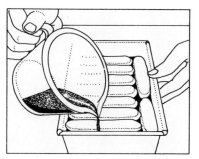

7 Continue layering the chocolate mixture and sponge fingers into the tin, soaking each layer with coffee and ending with soaked sponge fingers. Weight down lightly and refrigerate for 3–4 hours until set.

8 Turn out, remove the paper and decorate with the reserved whipped cream and the coffee beans.

CHOCOLATE MACAROON LOG

2.00*	🍴	477 cals

* plus overnight chilling

Serves 10

3 egg whites, size 6

175 g (6 oz) ground almonds

275 g (10 oz) caster sugar

7.5 ml (1½ tsp) almond flavouring

100 g (4 oz) shelled hazel nuts

100 g (4 oz) plain chocolate

300 ml (10 fl oz) double cream

45 ml (3 tbsp) almond liqueur

icing sugar, cocoa, chocolate leaves, to decorate

1 Line two baking sheets with non-stick paper. Whisk the egg whites until stiff then fold in the ground almonds, caster sugar and almond flavouring.

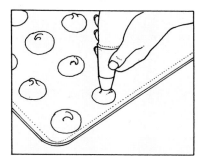

2 Spoon into a piping bag fitted with a 1-cm (½-inch) plain nozzle and pipe 30 small rounds on to the prepared baking sheets, allowing room between each for the mixture to spread.

3 Bake in the oven at 180°C (350°F) mark 4 for about 20 minutes. Transfer to a wire rack for 20 minutes to cool.

4 Spread the nuts out on a baking sheet and brown in the oven at 200°C (400°F) mark 6 for 5–10 minutes. Put into a soft tea towel and rub off the skins. Chop finely, reserving two whole nuts.

5 Break the chocolate in small pieces into a heatproof bowl and place over simmering water until the chocolate is melted, then remove from heat and cool for 5 minutes.

6 Whip the cream until it holds its shape and gradually beat in the cooled chocolate, nuts and liqueur.

7 Use some of the chocolate cream to sandwich the macaroons together.

8 Place side by side on a serving plate to form a double log. Spread chocolate cream on top and add a further layer of macaroons. Spread remaining chocolate cream over the top and sides, refrigerate overnight.

9 Dust with icing sugar and cocoa then decorate with chocolate leaves and the reserved whole hazel nuts. Serve with more whipped cream, if liked.

—— VARIATION ——

To make the hazel nut flavour more pronounced in this recipe, substitute ground, unblanched hazel nuts for the almonds when making the macaroons and omit the almond flavouring.

COFFEE PRALINE GATEAU

| 1.30* ⬠ | ✳* | 350 cals |

* plus 2–4 hours cooling; freeze after stage 4

Serves 6

2 eggs, size 2

100 g (4 oz) caster sugar

50 g (2 oz) plain flour

15 ml (1 tbsp) coffee essence

25 g (1 oz) blanched almonds

150 ml (5 fl oz) double cream

30 ml (2 tbsp) coffee-flavoured liqueur

icing sugar, for dusting

25 ml (5 tsp) instant coffee powder

7.5 ml (1½ tsp) arrowroot

170-g (6-oz) can evaporated milk

30 ml (2 tbsp) soft light brown sugar

1 Grease a 20-cm (8-inch) round cake tin. Base-line with grease-proof paper and grease the paper. Dust with caster sugar and flour.

2 Put eggs into a deep bowl with 75 g (3 oz) caster sugar and whisk vigorously until the mixture is very thick and light and leaves a trail. If hand mixing, whisk the mixture over a saucepan of simmering water.

3 Sift the flour evenly over surface of the egg mixture and fold in lightly until no traces of flour remain. Lightly fold in the coffee essence.

4 Turn into the prepared tin and bake at once in the oven at 180°C (350°F) mark 4 for about 30 minutes or until the sponge springs back when pressed lightly with a finger and has shrunk away a little from the tin. Turn out on to a wire rack and leave for 1–2 hours.

5 Meanwhile, make the praline. Oil a baking sheet. Put the remaining caster sugar into a small frying pan with the blanched almonds and heat gently until the sugar dissolves and caramelises.

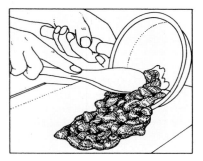

6 Pour the praline on to the prepared baking sheet and leave for 10–15 minutes to cool and harden.

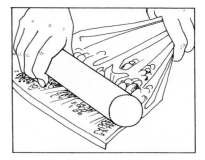

7 When cold, grind or crush with end of a rolling pin in a strong bowl. Whip the cream until it holds its shape then whisk in the liqueur and fold in three-quarters of praline (ground nut mixture).

8 Split the sponge in half and sandwich with the cream. Dust the top with icing sugar and decorate with praline. Refrigerate for 1–2 hours.

9 Make the coffee sauce. In a small pan, mix the coffee powder and arrowroot to a smooth paste with a little water then make up to 150 ml (¼ pint) with more water. Add the evaporated milk and brown sugar and bring slowly to the boil, stirring. Bubble for 1 minute. Serve warm.

HARVEST CAKE

3.45* 🍽 ✳* 605 cals

* plus 2–3 hours cooling; freeze after
stage 7

Serves 10

175 g (6 oz) butter or block
 margarine
175 g (6 oz) dark soft brown sugar
3 eggs, beaten
225 g (8 oz) plain flour
5 ml (1 tsp) baking powder
5 ml (1 tsp) ground cinnamon
5 ml (1 tsp) freshly grated nutmeg
pinch of salt
225 g (8 oz) sultanas
100 g (4 oz) seedless raisins
100 g (4 oz) dried apricots, chopped
175 g (6 oz) Brazil nuts, chopped
60 ml (4 tbsp) black treacle
finely grated rind and juice of 1
 lemon
about 30 ml (2 tbsp) brandy
300 g (11 oz) marzipan
icing sugar
15–30 ml (1–2 tbsp) apricot jam
marzipan fruits (see below)

1 Grease a 20-cm (8-inch) round
cake tin. Line with greaseproof
paper and grease the paper.

2 Put the butter and sugar into a
bowl and beat together until
pale and fluffy. Beat in the eggs a
little at a time.

3 Sift the flour with the baking
powder, spices and salt and
fold into the creamed mixture.
Stir in the dried fruit and nuts,
black treacle, lemon rind and juice
until evenly mixed.

4 Add enough brandy to give a
soft, dropping consistency.
(Add more brandy or a little milk
if the mixture is too stiff.)

5 Turn the mixture into the prepared tin and make a slight
hollow in the centre with the back
of a metal spoon. Bake at 170°C
(325°F) mark 3 for 1 hour.

6 Cover with foil and lower the
oven to 150°C (300°F) mark 2.
Cook for a further 2 hours or until
a fine warmed skewer inserted in
the centre comes out clean.

7 Leave the cake to cool in the
tin for 2–3 hours, then turn
out and peel off the lining paper.

8 Knead the marzipan on a
surface lightly dusted with
icing sugar. Roll out to a circle
slightly larger than the diameter of
the cake.

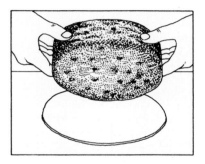

9 Brush the top of the cake with
the apricot jam, then press the
cake gently on to the marzipan,
jam-side down.

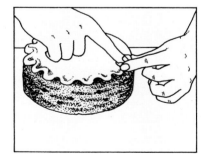

10 Turn the cake the right way
up, trim off the excess
marzipan with a sharp knife, then
crimp the edge and decorate with
marzipan fruits.

MARZIPAN FRUITS
Mould marzipan into fruit
shapes. Paint with diluted food
colouring; use cloves for stalks.

BÛCHE DE NOËL
(FRENCH CHRISTMAS LOG)

2.00* 🔲	✳*

759–1012 cals

* plus 35 minutes cooling; freeze after step 8

Serves 6–8

1 egg white

175 g (6 oz) caster sugar, plus a little extra for dredging

3 eggs, size 2

75 g (3 oz) plain flour, plus a little extra for dredging

30 ml (2 tbsp) cocoa powder

225 g (8 oz) unsalted butter

50 g (2 oz) plain chocolate

500 g (1 lb) icing sugar, plus a little extra for decorating

440 g (15½ oz) can sweetened chestnut purée

holly sprigs, to decorate

1 Line a baking sheet with non-stick paper. Make meringue mushrooms. Whisk the egg white until stiff, add 25 g (1 oz) of the sugar and whisk again until stiff. Fold in another 25 g (1 oz) sugar.

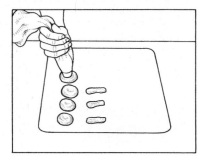

2 Spoon the meringue into a piping bag fitted with a plain nozzle. Pipe the meringue on to the prepared baking sheet to resemble small mushroom caps and stalks. Bake in the oven at 110°C (225°F) mark ¼ for about 1½ hours until dry. Leave to cool for at least 15 minutes.

3 Grease a 33 × 23 cm (13 × 9 inch) Swiss roll tin. Line with greaseproof paper and grease the paper. Dredge with the extra caster sugar then flour, knocking out any excess.

4 Put the eggs and measured caster sugar in a deep bowl which fits snugly inside the rim of a saucepan of simmering water.

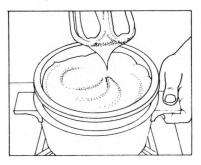

5 Whisk the eggs and sugar until thick enough to leave a trail on the surface when the beaters are lifted. Do not overheat the bowl by letting it come into contact with the simmering water or by having the heat under the saucepan too high.

6 Take the bowl off the saucepan and whisk the mixture for 5 minutes until cool. Sift in the measured flour and cocoa and gently fold through the mixture. Fold in 15 ml (1 tbsp) water.

7 Pour the mixture gently into the prepared tin and lightly level off the surface. Bake in the oven at 200°C (400°F) mark 6 for about 12 minutes until slightly shrunk away from the tin.

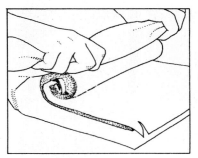

8 Meanwhile, place a sheet of greaseproof paper over a tea towel. Dredge the paper with caster sugar and turn the cake out on to it. Trim off the crusty edges with a sharp knife. Roll up with the paper inside. Transfer to a wire rack, seam side down. Leave to cool for 20 minutes.

9 Put the butter in a bowl and beat until soft. Put the chocolate and 15 ml (1 tbsp) water in a bowl over a pan of hot water. Melt, then leave to cool slightly. Gradually sift and beat the icing sugar into the softened butter, then add the cool chocolate.

10 Unroll the cold Swiss roll and spread the chestnut purée over the surface. Roll up again without the paper inside. Place on a cake board or plate.

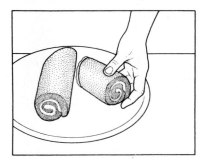

11 Cut a thick diagonal slice off one end of the Swiss roll and attach with butter cream to the side of the roll.

12 Using a piping bag and a large star nozzle, pipe thin lines of butter cream over the log. Pipe 1 or 2 swirls of butter cream to represent knots in the wood. Sandwich the meringues together with a little butter cream to form mushrooms. Decorate the log with the mushrooms and sprigs of holly. Dust lightly with sifted icing sugar. Store in an airtight container for up to 2–3 days.

Menu Suggestion
In France, Bûche de Noël is served on Christmas Eve as a dessert, after the traditional main course of Roast Turkey.

BÛCHE DE NOËL
Bûche de Noël is the traditional cake eaten in France at Christmas time. The tradition of serving this and the English Yule log dates back to the days when a huge log used to be burnt on Christmas Eve.

ALMOND SPONGE CHRISTMAS CAKE WITH GLACÉ FRUIT

2.30* 🥄 🥄	477–597 cals

* plus cooling

Serves 8–10

225 g (8 oz) butter or margarine
225 g (8 oz) caster sugar
4 eggs, beaten
125 g (4 oz) self-raising flour, sifted with a pinch of salt
100 g (4 oz) ground almonds
225 g (8 oz) can pineapple slices
about 30 ml (2 tbsp) warm water
30 ml (2 tbsp) apricot jam
50 g (2 oz) glacé cherries
50 g (2 oz) blanched almonds
25–40 g (1–1½ oz) candied angelica
red and green ribbon, to decorate

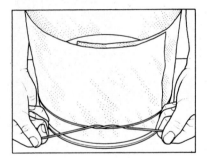

1 Prepare the cake tin. Grease and base line a deep 20.5 cm (8 inch) loose-bottomed round cake tin. Tie a double thickness of brown paper around the outside of the tin, to come about 5 cm (2 inches) above the rim.

2 Put the butter and sugar in a large bowl and beat until light and fluffy. Add the eggs a little at a time and beat until thoroughly combined. Add a little of the flour with the last addition of the egg, to prevent curdling, then beat in the ground almonds and the remaining flour.

3 Drain the pineapple slices and chop roughly. Dry thoroughly with absorbent kitchen paper. Fold into the cake mixture, then add enough warm water to give a soft dropping consistency. Spoon the mixture into the prepared cake tin and level the surface.

4 Bake the cake in the oven at 170°C (325°F) mark 3 for 1½ hours or until cooked through, covering the top with a double thickness of greaseproof paper after 1 hour's cooking time, if necessary, to prevent over-browning. To test if the cake is cooked, insert a warmed fine skewer in the centre—it should come out clean.

5 Leave the cake to settle in the tin for 5–10 minutes, then remove and stand on a wire rack.

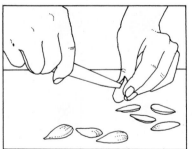

6 Make the decoration for the top of the cake while the cake is still warm. Cut the glacé cherries in half. Split the blanched almonds in half lengthways. Cut the angelica into diamond shapes.

7 Warm half of the jam until melted, then sieve and brush over the top of the warm cake. Press the cherries, nuts and angelica on top of the cake in a decorative design (as in the photograph or use your own design). Melt and sieve the remaining jam, then brush over the design.

8 To serve, tie red and green ribbon around the cake to give it a festive look. Store the cake in an airtight tin for up to 2 weeks.

Menu Suggestion
This cake is equally good served at teatime or with morning coffee.

ALMOND SPONGE CHRISTMAS CAKE WITH GLACÉ FRUIT

For those who do not like the traditional rich fruit cake at Christmas, this cake is the perfect alternative. The cake itself is light and moist, and the decoration looks as festive as a traditional snowscene, or any other design using marzipan and royal icing.

The decoration of glacé cherries, almonds and candied angelica gives a Christmassy look, but you can vary this according to taste; at Christmas-time, many stores and delicatessens stock other glacé fruit such as apricots and pineapples.

Fruit Crusted Cider Cake

1.15* 🍴	268–334 cals

* plus 1 hour cooling

Serves 8–10

45 ml (3 tbsp) golden syrup

150 g (5 oz) butter or block
  margarine

350 g (12 oz) cooking apples, peeled,
  cored and finely chopped

45 ml (3 tbsp) mincemeat

50 g (2 oz) cornflakes, crushed

125 g (4 oz) caster sugar

2 eggs, beaten

125 g (4 oz) self-raising flour

45 ml (3 tbsp) dry cider

1 Line a 35.5 × 11.5 cm (14 × 4½ inch) shallow rectangular tart frame with foil. Grease the foil. Put the syrup into a pan with 25 g (1 oz) butter and melt. Add apples, mincemeat, cornflakes. Set aside.

2 Put the remaining butter and the sugar into a bowl and beat together until pale and fluffy. Gradually beat in the eggs.

3 Fold the flour into the mixture. Pour in the cider and mix it in. Turn the mixture into the prepared frame and level the surface. Spread the apple mixture evenly over it.

4 Bake in the oven at 170°C (325°F) mark 3 for 45–50 minutes or until firm to the touch. Cool in the metal frame for 1 hour, then cut into bars for serving.

GINGERBREAD SLAB

| 1.40* | ❋ | 121–145 cals |

* plus 1 hour cooling; store for at least
2 days before eating

Makes 20–24 slices

125 g (4 oz) black treacle

125 g (4 oz) golden syrup

50 g (2 oz) butter or block
  margarine

50 g (2 oz) lard

225 g (8 oz) plain flour

1.25 ml ($\frac{1}{4}$ tsp) bicarbonate of soda

5 ml (1 tsp) mixed spice

5 ml (1 tsp) ground ginger

100 g (4 oz) dark soft brown sugar

150 ml ($\frac{1}{4}$ pint) milk

1 Grease an 18-cm (7-inch) square cake tin. Base-line with greaseproof paper and then grease the paper.

2 Put the black treacle, golden syrup, butter or margarine and lard into a saucepan and heat gently to melt the mixture.

3 Sift the flour, bicarbonate of soda and spices into a bowl and stir in the sugar.

4 Make a well in the centre of the dry ingredients and pour in the milk and the treacle mixture. Beat well until smooth and of a thick pouring consistency.

5 Turn into the prepared tin and bake in the oven at 170°C (325°F) mark 3 for 1–1$\frac{1}{4}$ hours or until a fine warmed skewer inserted in the centre of the cake comes out clean.

6 Cool in the tin for 1 hour. Remove from tin, wrap and store for at least 2 days in an airtight tin before eating. Serve sliced, plain or buttered.

CHERRY AND COCONUT CAKE

| 2.00* | ✳ | 336–420 cals |

* plus 1 hour cooling

Serves 8–10

250 g (9 oz) self-raising flour

1.25 ml ($\frac{1}{4}$ tsp) salt

125 g (4 oz) butter or block
    margarine, cut into pieces

75 g (3 oz) desiccated coconut

125 g (4 oz) caster sugar

125 g (4 oz) glacé cherries, finely
    chopped

2 eggs, size 6, beaten

225 ml (8 fl oz) milk

25 g (1 oz) shredded coconut

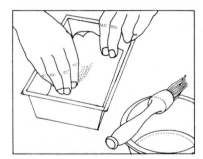

1 Grease a 1.3-litre (2$\frac{1}{4}$-pint)
loaf tin. Base-line with greaseproof paper, grease the paper and
dust with flour.

2 Put the flour and salt into a
bowl and rub in the fat until
the mixture resembles fine breadcrumbs. Stir in the coconut, sugar
and cherries.

3 Whisk together the eggs and
milk and beat into the dry ingredients. Turn the mixture into
the tin, level the surface and scatter
over the shredded coconut.

4 Bake in the oven at 180°C
(350°F) mark 4 for 1$\frac{1}{2}$ hours
until a fine warmed skewer inserted in the centre comes out
clean. Check after 40 minutes and
cover with greaseproof paper if
overbrowning. Turn out on to a
wire rack to cool for 1 hour.

PRUNE AND NUT TEABREAD

1.30* ⬚ ✳ 261–326 cals

* plus 1 hour cooling; wrap and store
for 1–2 days before slicing

Serves 8–10

275 g (10 oz) self-raising flour

pinch of salt

7.5 ml (1½ tsp) ground cinnamon

75 g (3 oz) butter or block
   margarine, cut into pieces

75 g (3 oz) demerara sugar

1 egg, beaten

100 ml (4 fl oz) milk

50 g (2 oz) shelled walnuts, chopped

100 g (4 oz) pitted tenderised prunes

15 ml (1 tbsp) clear honey

1 Grease a 2-litre (3½-pint) loaf tin. Base-line the loaf tin with greaseproof paper and grease the paper.

2 Sift the flour and salt into a bowl and add the cinnamon. Rub in the fat until the mixture resembles fine breadcrumbs.

3 Stir in the sugar, and make a well in the centre. Add the egg and milk and gradually draw in the dry ingredients to form a smooth dough.

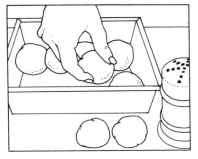

4 Using floured hands shape the mixture into sixteen even-sized rounds. Place eight in the base of the tin. Sprinkle over half the nuts.

5 Snip the prunes and sprinkle on top of the nuts. Place the remaining dough rounds on top and sprinkle over the remaining chopped walnuts.

6 Bake in the oven at 190°C (375°F) mark 5 for about 50 minutes or until firm to the touch. Check near the end of cooking time and cover with greaseproof paper if it is overbrowning.

7 Turn out on to a wire rack to cool for 1 hour. When cold brush with the honey to glaze. Wrap and store for 1–2 days in an airtight tin before slicing and buttering.

TEABREADS

A teabread mixture is usually less rich than cake, but no less delicious for that. Serve it sliced and thickly buttered, like good fresh bread. It is excellent served with afternoon tea or mid-morning coffee, or try it occasionally as a lunchtime pudding. A fruity teabread like this one improves as it matures, the flavour and moisture from the fruit penetrating the cake and mellowing it over a number of days.

In continental Europe it is traditional to serve sweet breads for breakfast, with either butter or cheese. Try thin slices of Edam or Gouda cheese, or spread with curd cheese instead of butter and omit the cheese.

GINGER MARMALADE TEABREAD

1.30*	✳	167–208 cals

* plus 1 hour cooling

Serves 8–10

200 g (7 oz) plain flour

5 ml (1 tsp) ground ginger

5 ml (1 tsp) baking powder

40 g (1½ oz) block margarine

65 g (2½ oz) soft light brown sugar

60 ml (4 tbsp) ginger marmalade

1 egg, beaten

60 ml (4 tbsp) milk

40 g (1½ oz) stem ginger, chopped

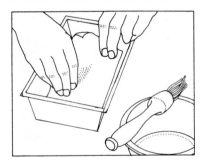

1 Grease a 900-ml (1½-pint) loaf tin with melted lard. Base-line with greaseproof paper and grease the paper.

2 Put the flour, ginger and baking powder into a bowl and rub in fat until mixture resembles fine breadcrumbs. Stir in sugar.

3 Mix together the marmalade, egg and most of the milk. Stir into the dry ingredients and add the rest of the milk, if necessary, to mix to a soft dough.

4 Turn the mixture into the prepared tin, level the surface and press pieces of ginger on top. Bake in the oven at 170°C (325°F) mark 3 for about 1 hour or until golden. Turn out on to a wire rack for 1 hour to cool.

MIXED FRUIT TEABREAD

1.35*	✳	229–287 cals

* plus overnight soaking, 1 hour cooling and 1–2 days maturing

Serves 8–10

175 g (6 oz) raisins

125 g (4 oz) sultanas

50 g (2 oz) currants

175 g (6 oz) soft brown sugar

300 ml ($\frac{1}{2}$ pint) strained cold tea

1 egg, beaten

225 g (8 oz) plain wholemeal flour

7.5 ml (1$\frac{1}{2}$ tsp) baking powder

2.5 ml ($\frac{1}{2}$ tsp) ground mixed spice

1 Place the dried fruit and the sugar in a large bowl. Pour over the tea, stir well to mix and leave to soak overnight.

2 The next day, add the egg, flour, baking powder and mixed spice to the fruit and tea mixture. Beat thoroughly with a wooden spoon until all the ingredients are evenly combined.

3 Spoon the cake mixture into a greased and base-lined 900 g (2 lb) loaf tin. Level the surface.

4 Bake in the oven at 180°C (350°F) mark 4 for about 1$\frac{1}{4}$ hours until the cake is well risen and a skewer inserted in the centre comes out clean.

5 Turn the cake out of the tin and leave on a wire rack until completely cold. Wrap in cling film and store in an airtight container for 1–2 days before slicing and eating.

Menu Suggestion

Serve this moist, fruity teabread sliced and buttered at teatime. Or serve with thin wedges of sharp Cheddar cheese for a snack at any time of day.

517

POPPY SEED GRANARY ROUND

1.15* 🍳 ✳ 280 cals

* plus 1½ hours rising and proving

Makes 8 rolls

15 g (½ oz) fresh yeast or 7.5 g (¼ oz)
   dried yeast and 2.5 ml (½ tsp)
   sugar

300 ml (½ pint) warm water

450 g (1 lb) granary bread flour

5 ml (1 tsp) salt

50 g (2 oz) butter

50 g (2 oz) Cheddar cheese, grated

25 g (1 oz) poppy seeds

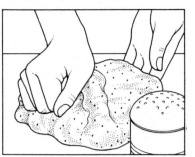

1 Grease a 20.5-cm (8-inch)
   sandwich tin. In a bowl,
crumble the fresh yeast into the
water and stir until dissolved. (If
using dried yeast, sprinkle it into
water mixed with the sugar. Leave
in a warm place for 15 minutes
until frothy.)

2 Make the dough. Place the
   flour and salt in a large bowl
and rub in the butter. Add the
cheese and the poppy seeds, reserving 5 ml (1 tsp) to garnish. Stir
in the yeast liquid and mix to a
stiff dough.

3 Turn on to a lightly floured
   surface and knead for 10 minutes until smooth. Place in a bowl,
cover with a cloth and leave to rise
in a warm place for about 1 hour
until doubled in size.

4 Turn on to a lightly floured
   surface and knead for 2–3
minutes until smooth.

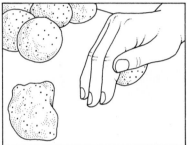

5 Using a sharp knife, divide the
   dough into eight equal pieces
and shape into neat, even-sized
rolls with your hands.

6 Arrange in the tin, cover with
   a clean cloth and leave to prove
in a warm place for about 30
minutes until doubled in size.

7 Sprinkle with the reserved
   poppy seeds. Bake in the oven
at 200°C (400°F) mark 6 for about
25 minutes until golden brown and
sounds hollow when the bottom of
the bread is tapped.

HERBY CHEESE LOAF

1.00*	1458 cals

* plus 1 hour cooling

Makes one 450-g (1-lb loaf)

225 g (8 oz) self-raising flour

7.5 ml (1½ tsp) salt

5 ml (1 tsp) mustard powder

5 ml (1 tsp) snipped fresh chives

15 ml (1 tbsp) chopped fresh parsley

75 g (3 oz) mature Cheddar cheese, grated

1 egg, beaten

150 ml (¼ pint) water

25 g (1 oz) butter or block margarine, melted

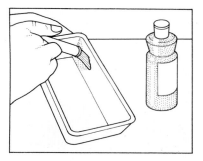

1 Grease a 450-g (1-lb) loaf tin. Sift the flour, salt and mustard into a bowl and stir in the herbs and cheese. Add the egg, water and melted fat and stir until well blended with a wooden spoon.

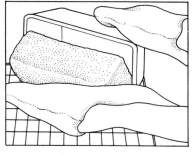

2 Spoon into the loaf tin and bake in the oven at 190°C (375°F) mark 5 for about 45 minutes. Turn out and cool on a wire rack for about 1 hour. Serve sliced and buttered while warm.

BROWN SODA BREAD

0.20*	3650 cals

* plus 30 minutes cooling

Serves 6

600 g (1¼ lb) plain wholewheat flour
350 g (12 oz) plain white flour
10 ml (2 tsp) bicarbonate of soda
20 ml (4 tsp) cream of tartar
10 ml (2 tsp) salt
10 ml (2 tsp) sugar (optional)
900 ml (1½ pints) milk and water,
  mixed

1 Sift the flours, bicarbonate of soda, cream of tartar and salt into a bowl. Stir in the bran (from the wholewheat flour) left in the bottom of the sieve, then the sugar. Add enough milk and water to mix to a soft dough.

2 Turn the dough onto a floured surface and knead lightly until smooth and soft.

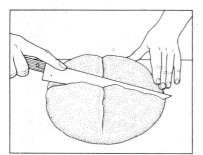

3 Shape the dough into a round. Score into quarters with a sharp knife and place on a greased baking sheet or tray.

4 Bake in the oven at 220°C (425°F) mark 7 for 25–30 minutes until the bottom of the bread sounds hollow when tapped with the knuckles of your hand. Cool on a wire rack before serving.

Menu Suggestion
Soda bread is best eaten really fresh—on the day of baking. Serve with a mature Farmhouse Cheddar, tomatoes and spring onions for a homemade 'ploughman's lunch'.

BROWN SODA BREAD

Soda bread is the ideal bread to make when you are short of time for baking. The raising agent in soda bread is bicarbonate of soda mixed with an acid, which releases the carbon dioxide necessary to make the bread light. In this recipe, fresh milk is made sour (acid) with cream of tartar, but you can use bicarbonate of soda on its own with sour milk or buttermilk, which will provide enough acid without the cream of tartar. The end result is much the same whichever ingredients you use, although bread made with buttermilk does tend to have a softer texture.

CINNAMON CHERRY BARS

2.15* | 170 cals

* plus 1 hour cooling

Makes 24

125 g (4 oz) ground almonds
1 egg, beaten
225 g (8 oz) plain flour
225 g (8 oz) caster sugar
175 g (6 oz) soft tub margarine
5 ml (1 tsp) ground cinnamon
grated rind of 1 lemon
125 g (4 oz) black cherry jam
icing sugar, to dredge

1 Lightly grease a 28 × 18 cm (11 × 7 inch) shallow tin. Put the first seven ingredients into a large bowl and beat well.

2 Knead lightly. Cover and refrigerate for at least 30 minutes. Press half the dough evenly into the prepared tin. Spread the jam over the surface.

3 On a lightly floured work surface, lightly knead the remaining dough. With well floured hands, roll into pencil-thin strips. Arrange over the jam to form a close lattice pattern. Refrigerate for 30 minutes.

LAMINGTONS

| 1.30* | 🥄🥄 | ✳* | 340 cals |

* plus 30 minutes cooling and 30 minutes setting; freeze after stage 6

Makes 12

| 50 g (2 oz) butter |
| 65 g (2½ oz) plain flour |
| 15 ml (1 tbsp) cornflour |
| 3 eggs, size 2 |
| 75 g (3 oz) caster sugar |
| 450 g (1 lb) icing sugar |
| 75 g (3 oz) cocoa |
| 100 ml (4 fl oz) milk |
| 75 g (3 oz) desiccated coconut |

1 Grease a 28 × 18 cm (11 × 7 inch) cake tin. Line the tin with greaseproof paper and grease the paper.

2 Melt 40 g (1½ oz) butter and let it stand for a few minutes for the salt and any sediment to settle. Sift the flour and cornflour.

3 Put the eggs and sugar into a large bowl and whisk until light and creamy—the mixture should be thick enough to leave a trail on the surface for a few seconds when the whisk is lifted. If whisking by hand, place the bowl over simmering water, then remove from the heat and whisk for 5–10 minutes until cool.

4 Re-sift the flours and fold half into the egg mixture with a metal spoon.

4 Bake at 180°C (350°F) mark 4 for 40 minutes. Cool for 1 hour; dredge with icing sugar. Cut into 24 bars and ease out of the tin. Wrap and store in an airtight tin for up to 1 week.

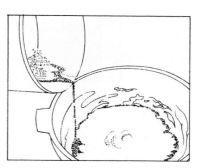

5 Pour the cooled but still flowing butter round the edge of the mixture, taking care not to let the salt and sediment run in.

6 Fold the butter very lightly into the mixture, alternating with the rest of the flour.

7 Turn the mixture into the tin. Bake in the oven at 190°C (375°F) mark 5 until firm to the touch, 20–25 minutes. Turn out on to a wire rack and leave to cool.

8 Meanwhile, for the icing: sift the icing sugar and cocoa into the top part of a double boiler or into a heatproof bowl placed over simmering water.

9 Add the remaining butter and the milk and stir over a gentle heat to a coating consistency.

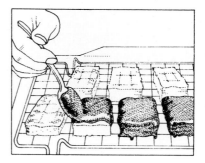

10 Cut the cake into twelve even-sized pieces. Place on a wire cooling rack. Spoon the icing over each cake to cover. Sprinkle the tops of each with coconut. Leave for 30 minutes until set.

ENGLISH MADELEINES

| 1.20 | 🍴 | ✳* | 239 cals |

* freeze after stage 3

Makes 10

100 g (4 oz) butter or block margarine

100 g (4 oz) caster sugar

2 eggs, beaten

100 g (4 oz) self-raising flour

30 ml (2 tbsp) red jam, sieved and melted

50 g (2 oz) desiccated coconut

5 glacé cherries, halved, and angelica pieces, to decorate

1 Grease ten dariole moulds. Put the butter and sugar into a bowl and beat together until pale and fluffy. Add the eggs a little at a time, beating well after each addition. Fold in half the flour, using a tablespoon. Fold in rest.

2 Turn the mixture into the moulds, filling them three-quarters full. Bake in the oven at 180°C (350°F) mark 4 for about 20 minutes until well risen and firm to the touch. Turn out on to a wire rack to cool for 20 minutes.

3 When the cakes are almost cold, trim the bases so they stand firmly and are about the same height.

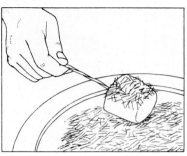

4 Spread the coconut out on a large plate. Spear each cake on a skewer, brush with melted jam, then roll in the coconut to coat.

5 Top each madeleine with half a glacé cherry and small pieces of angelica.

FRENCH MADELEINES

The continental cousin of the English madeleine is confusingly different. Made either from pastry or a firm, butter-rich cake mixture such as Genoese sponge, French madeleines are baked in shallow, shell-shaped moulds. They are served undecorated or lightly dusted with icing sugar.

French madeleines are a speciality of the town of Commercy, in Lorraine. Their history is said to go back to the early 18th century and the days of Stanislas Leszinski, a king of Poland who became Duke of Lorraine when ousted from his homeland.

STRAWBERRY SHORTCAKES

| 1.30 | ✳* | 611 cals |

* after stage 6

Serves 6

275 g (10 oz) self-raising flour

7.5 ml (1½ tsp) baking powder

good pinch of salt

75 g (3 oz) butter, cut into nut-size pieces

50 g (2 oz) caster sugar

1 egg, beaten

few drops vanilla flavouring

75–90 ml (5–6 tbsp) milk

450 g (1 lb) fresh strawberries, 6 set aside, the remainder hulled

30 ml (2 tbsp) orange-flavoured liqueur

30 ml (2 tbsp) icing sugar

300 ml (10 fl oz) double or whipping cream

45 ml (3 tbsp) redcurrant jelly

1 Brush a little melted lard over a large flat baking sheet; leave to cool for about 5 minutes. Dust the surface lightly with flour.

2 Sift the flour, baking powder and salt into a bowl. Rub in the butter until the mixture resembles breadcrumbs. Stir in the caster sugar.

3 Make a well in the centre of the dry ingredients and add the egg, vanilla flavouring and milk. Using a palette knife, cut through the dry ingredients until evenly blended, then quickly and lightly bring the mixture together using the fingertips of one hand.

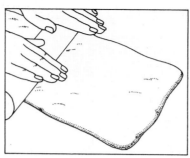

4 Turn the dough out on to a lightly floured surface and knead gently until just smooth. Roll out to a thickness of 1 cm (½ inch) and cut out six 9-cm (3½-inch) fluted rounds.

5 Gather up the scraps, knead lightly and roll out again. Place on the prepared baking sheet.

6 Brush the tops of the rounds with milk—don't let it trickle down the sides. Bake in the oven at 230°C (450°F) mark 8 for about 11 minutes or until the shortcakes are well risen and golden brown. Remove from the oven and keep warm.

7 Thickly slice half the strawberries. Put into a bowl and add the liqueur. Sieve in half the icing sugar.

8 With a fork, lightly crush the remaining strawberries and sieve in the rest of the icing sugar. Whip the cream until it just holds its shape and stir in the crushed strawberries.

9 Cut the shortcakes in half while they are still warm. Carefully run the point of a sharp knife from the side of the shortcake into the centre.

10 Rotate the shortcake and saw with the sharp knife until the cake is cut in two.

11 Spoon half the cream on to the shortcake bases and cover with the sliced strawberries. Spoon over the remaining cream and replace the shortcake tops.

12 Put the redcurrant jelly into a small pan and heat gently until liquid. Cool for 5–10 minutes, then brush over the shortcakes. Decorate with whole strawberries.

——————— VARIATION ———————

Any other soft fruits such as raspberries, loganberries, blackberries, bilberries or redcurrants can be used as an alternative filling for these delicious shortcakes. Skinned and roughly chopped peaches and nectarines would also be delicious. The tart flavour of berries or currants can be counteracted by adding a little more sugar.

ECCLES CAKES

| 1.00* | 🗋 | ✳ | 167–209 cals |

* plus 30 minutes cooling

Makes 8–10

212-g (7½-oz) packet frozen puff
    pastry, thawed

25 g (1 oz) butter, softened

25 g (1 oz) soft dark brown sugar

25 g (1 oz) finely chopped mixed
    peel

50 g (2 oz) currants

caster sugar

1 Roll out the pastry on a lightly
floured working surface and
cut into eight to ten 9-cm (3½-
inch) rounds.

2 For the filling: mix the butter,
sugar, mixed peel and currants
in a bowl.

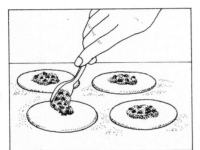

3 Place 5 ml (1 tsp) of the fruit
and butter mixture in the
centre of each pastry round. Draw
up the edges of each pastry round
to enclose the filling and then reshape.

4 Turn each round over and roll
lightly until the currants just
show through.

5 Prick the top of each with a
fork. Allow the pastry rounds
to 'rest' for about 10 minutes in a
cool place.

6 Dampen a baking sheet and
transfer the rounds to it. Bake
in the oven at 230°C (450°F)
mark 8 for about 15 minutes until
golden. Transfer to a wire rack to
cool for 30 minutes. Sprinkle with
caster sugar while still warm.

ECCLES CAKES

Dripping with butter and loaded
with currants, Eccles cakes are
among the nation's favourite re-
gional pastries. It is not just in
Lancashire that village bakeries
are obliged to produce them in
large quantities every morning.
Some versions are made with
shortcrust pastry, others favour
the richer puff or flaky pastries
suggested here, either way the
pastry must be rolled really
thinly, so that the dark fruit
shows through. Take care that it
does not burst though.

    Eccles cakes are at their best
very fresh, preferably still slightly
warm from the oven. If you want
to make them for eating next day
do not sprinkle with caster sugar;
store them in an airtight tin when
cold then reheat the next day and
sprinkle with sugar after they
come out of the oven.

SPICED WALNUT SCONES

| 0.25 | 123 cals |

Makes 16

125 g (4 oz) plain wholemeal flour
125 g (4 oz) plain white flour
15 ml (3 tsp) baking powder
2.5 ml ($\frac{1}{2}$ tsp) ground mixed spice
pinch of salt
50 g (2 oz) butter or block
  margarine
15 ml (1 tbsp) caster sugar
75 g (3 oz) walnut pieces, roughly
  chopped
10 ml (2 tsp) lemon juice
200 ml (7 fl oz) milk
honey and chopped walnuts,
  to decorate

1 Sift the flours into a bowl with the baking powder, mixed spice and salt. Stir in the bran (from the wholemeal flour) left in the bottom of the sieve. Rub in the fat. Stir in the sugar and two-thirds of the walnuts.

2 Mix the lemon juice with 170 ml (6 fl oz) of the milk and stir into the dry ingredients until evenly mixed.

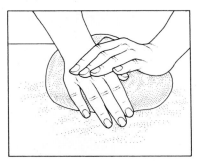

3 Turn the dough onto a floured surface and knead lightly until smooth and soft.

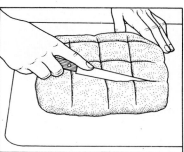

4 Roll out the dough to a 20.5 cm (8 inch) square and place on a baking sheet. Mark the surface into 16 squares, cutting the dough through to a depth of 3 mm ($\frac{1}{8}$ inch).

5 Lightly brush the dough with the remaining milk, then sprinkle over the remaining chopped walnut pieces.

6 Bake in the oven at 220°C (425°F) mark 7 for about 18 minutes or until well risen, golden brown and firm to the touch. Cut into squares. Serve warm, brushed with honey.

Menu Suggestion
Quick to make from store-cupboard ingredients, these Spiced Walnut Scones can be served plain or buttered, which-ever you prefer.

——— VARIATION ———

For a savoury scone mixture, use **2.5 ml ($\frac{1}{2}$ tsp) chilli powder** instead of the sugar and omit the mixed spice.

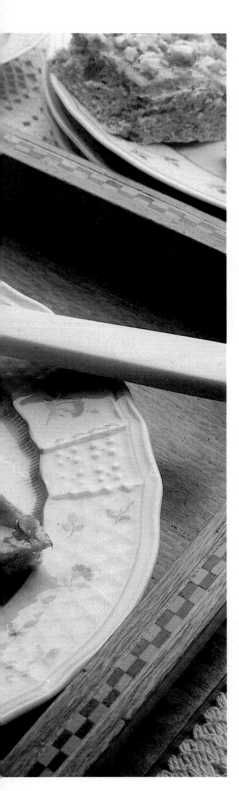

CHEWY CHOCOLATE BROWNIES

0.15*	156 cals

* plus cooling time

Makes 16

75 g (3 oz) plain flour

175 g (6 oz) dark soft brown sugar

25 g (1 oz) cocoa powder

1.25 ml (¼ tsp) salt

100 g (4 oz) butter or margarine

2 eggs, beaten

5 ml (1 tsp) vanilla flavouring

75 g (3 oz) chopped mixed nuts

1 Put all the ingredients in a bowl and beat thoroughly (preferably with an electric whisk) until evenly combined.

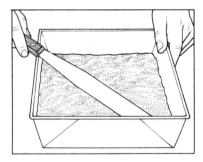

2 Turn the mixture into a greased 20.5 cm (8 inch) square cake tin and level the surface with a palette knife.

3 Bake in the oven at 180°C (350°F) mark 4 for 25 minutes until only just set (the mixture should still wobble slightly in the centre). Stand the cake tin on a wire rack and leave until the cake is completely cold. Cut into 16 squares and put in an airtight tin.

Menu Suggestion

Moist and munchy Chocolate Brownies are a favourite at any time of day. Try them as a fun dessert for children with scoops of vanilla ice cream and chocolate sauce or chopped nuts.

CHOCOLATE CHEQUERBOARDS

2.00 🍳	92 cals

Makes 32

200 g (7 oz) soft tub margarine

90 g (3½ oz) caster sugar

290 g (10½ oz) plain flour

15 ml (1 tbsp) cocoa powder

vanilla flavouring

beaten white egg

1 Beat together the margarine, sugar and flour to give a workable dough.

2 Remove two-thirds of the dough to another bowl. Into this, work the cocoa powder mixed to a paste with 15 ml (1 tbsp) water. Knead to an even coloured ball. Halve.

3 Work a few drops of vanilla into the remaining plain dough. On a floured surface, roll the vanilla dough into six 1 × 15 cm (½ × 6 inch) strips. Repeat with one piece of the chocolate dough.

4 Assemble the strips into 2 logs. Lay 3 strips, alternating vanilla and chocolate, side by side. Place another 3 strips on top to make a chequerboard pattern. Brush with a little beaten egg.

5 Halve the remaining chocolate dough. Roll out each piece into a sheet large enough to encase a log. Roll round each log and brush with beaten egg white.

6 Straighten up the logs and chill for about 1 hour until very firm. Cut each log into 1-cm (½-inch) slices. Place on lightly greased baking sheets and bake in the oven at 190°C (375°F) mark 5 for about 15–20 minutes. Turn out and cool on a wire rack for 30 minutes. Store in an airtight container for 2–3 weeks.

CHOCOLATE NUT SNAPS

1.20*	✳	109 cals

*plus 1 hour cooling and setting;
freeze after stage 5

Makes 24

1 egg, separated
100 g (4 oz) caster sugar
125 g (5 oz) plain chocolate
125 g (4 oz) hazel nuts, finely chopped
40 g (1½ oz) plain flour
200 g (7 oz) icing sugar
about 30 ml (2 tbsp) water

1 Grease two baking sheets. Whisk the egg white until stiff. Fold in the caster sugar.

2 Coarsely grate 75 g (3 oz) plain chocolate into the mixture and stir in with the hazel nuts, flour and egg yolk.

3 Turn out on a well floured surface and knead lightly. Cover and refrigerate for about 30 minutes.

4 Roll the dough out to 5 mm (¾ inch) thickness. Using a 5-cm (2-inch) plain cutter, cut out 24 shapes. Knead lightly and place on the prepared baking sheets. Cover and refrigerate the biscuits again for 30 minutes.

5 Bake in the oven at 190°C (375°F) mark 5 for about 20 minutes until crisp. Immediately ease off the baking sheet on to a wire rack to cool for 30 minutes.

6 Break the remaining chocolate into a heatproof bowl and place over simmering water. Stir until the chocolate is melted, then remove from heat.

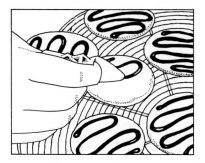

7 Cut the tip off a paper icing bag and spoon in the melted chocolate. Pipe lines of chocolate across the biscuits. Leave to set for 30 minutes. The biscuits can be stored, un-iced, in airtight containers for 2–3 weeks.

ROLLED BISCUITS

Short biscuit doughs are often difficult to roll without breaking. Chilling helps, but you could also try rolling the dough between sheets of cling film. This not only holds the dough together, but eliminates the need for extra flour on the board, which can harden the surface of the baked biscuits.

After rolling, remove the top sheet of film to cut the biscuits, then lift each one on the bottom piece of cling film to transfer it to the baking sheet.